T0375104

PETER BUTLER

BEYOND DECADENCE: EXPOSING THE NARRATIVE IRONY IN JAN OPOLSKÝ'S PROSE

CHARLES UNIVERSITY IN PRAGUE
KAROLINUM PRESS 2015

Reviewed by: Luboš Merhaut (Charles University Prague)
Robert B. Pynsent (University College London, SSEES)

CATALOGUING-IN-PUBLICATION – NATIONAL LIBRARY OF THE CZECH REPUBLIC

Butler, Peter
  Beyond decadence : exposing the narrative irony in Jan Opolský's prose / Peter Butler. –
First English edition. – Prague : Charles University in Prague, Karolinum Press, 2015
ISBN 978-80-246-2571-3

821.162.3-3 * 82.02"1866/1918" * 82.02"1890/1918" * 808.543-027.21 * 177.3 * 82.07 * (437.3)
– Opolský, Jan, 1875–1942
– Czech prose literature – 20th century
– symbolism (literary movement) – Czechia
– decadence (literary movement) – Czechia
– narratology
– irony
– interpretation and reception of literature
– monographs

891.8609 – Czech literature (on) [11]

ISBN 978-80-246-2571-3
ISBN 978-80-246-2711-3 (pdf)

In memory of

Karel Brušák
(1913–2004)

and

Helen Kay
(1951–2012)

CONTENTS

ACKNOWLEDGEMENTS

I owe my greatest debt of gratitude to the late Karel Brušák, the former doyen of Czech and Slovak Studies in the United Kingdom, who encouraged and supported me throughout the larger part of a task that proved to be vastly more challenging than either of us ever imagined. Sadly he did not live to see this book completed. I can only hope that he would have approved of the way it has turned out.

My search for, and quest for access to, Opolský's papers was aided by the Hřbitovní správa in Nová Paka, who kindly supplied me with the address of Opolský's daughter, Marta Kubenková, and by the staff of the Akviziční oddělení of the Památník národního písemnictví in Prague, who willingly agreed to purchase Opolský's papers from her, and went well beyond the call of duty in granting me early access to them.

I am obliged to the former director of the Podkrkonošské muzeum in Nová Paka for letting me have supernumerary copies of photographs of Jan Opolský and contemporary Nová Paka and for acquainting me with invaluable snippets of local gossip surviving from Opolský's time.

I am also grateful to the late Ivan Slavík, the late Bedřich Slavík and the late Zdeněk Kalista for receiving me so warmly and for readily sharing their knowledge of Opolský's life and work with me.

Finally, I am indebted to the British Department of Education and Science for providing two years of research funding, and to the British Council for providing two exchange scholarships to the Charles University in Prague, each for one academic year.

Drafts of this book were read by Andreas Guski (Basel), Luboš Merhaut (Prague), Robert Pynsent (London) and Ulrich Schmid (St. Gallen). Their comments have been invaluable and the manuscript is much improved as a result. However, responsibility for any errors and infelicities that remain is solely my own.

This book is dedicated to Karel Brušák and to my lifelong friend Helen Kay (born Vladimíra Plecháčová), who died at her home in Tokyo while this book was in the final stages of completion. Helen was the first person I ever heard speak Czech and it was my early exposure to this language that prompted me to learn it. This book would not have been written without either of them.

LIST OF ILLUSTRATIONS

INTRODUCTION

In 1968, the poet, translator and literary historian Ivan Slavík published an anthology of prose and verse by Jan Opolský (1875-1942), a writer then known largely only to a select circle of scholars of Czech literature and second-hand booksellers. The anthology, which borrowed its title *Představení v soumraku* from one of the prose pieces in the collection, appeared in the popular paperback *Světová četba* series of major publisher Odeon. It was a courageous and prescient attempt to rehabilitate a writer who had seldom been thought of as anything more than an epigon of the Czech Decadence.

Slavík, whose faible for *poetae minores* and especially for neglected and forgotten authors of Romantism, Decadence and Catholic Moderna, later led him to popularize writers like Vítězslav Hálek, Irma Geisslová, Hermor Lilia and Bohuslav Reynek,[1] was especially attracted to Opolský's prose, which he admired for its carefully crafted language and its ability to create atmospherically dense and sensually evocative images. He likened Opolský to a medieval illuminator of manuscripts ('dávný iluminator', 'malíř iniciál') and to a grinder of precious stones ('brusič drahokamů').[2] Believing that Opolský's later poetry had deteriorated into pedestrian dullness, Slavík saw his prose as the natural continuation of those early collections of verse – *Svět smutných* (1899), *Klékání* (1900), *Jedy a léky* (1901) – that had made such a favourable impression on major Decadent writer Jiří Karásek ze Lvovic and leading turn-of-the-century literary critic F. X. Šalda.[3]

Like Slavík, I too was drawn to Opolský's prose, in much the same way as I had, years earlier, been drawn to the prose of the nineteenth-century Austrian writer Adalbert Stifter. As with Stifter, there was strangely captivating elegance to his narrative, a rhythmic beauty even, but with apparent

---

1   See Vítěslav Hálek, *Srdce písněmi dotýkané* (Prague, 1974); Irma Geisslová, *Zraněný pták* (Prague, 1978); Hermor Lilia [František Bíbl], *Verše tajného básníka* (Prague, 1982); Bohuslav Reynek, *Rybí šupiny. Rty a zuby. Had na sněhu* (Prague, 1990) – all edited with an afterword by Ivan Slavík.

2   See Ivan Slavík, 'Básník miniatur a devadesátá léta', in Jan Opolský, *Představení v soumraku* (Prague, 1968), pp. 7-23; reprinted in Ivan Slavík, *Viděno jinak* (Prague, 1995), pp. 112-126. Neither image was original. Both had become part of the standard critical jargon on Opolský by the mid--1940s (see Chapter 3).

3   See Jiří Karásek, *Impresionisté a ironikové* (Prague, 1926), pp. 101-2; F. X. Šalda, 'Jan Opolský: Svět smutných', *Lumír* 27 (1899), pp. 299-300; reprinted in *Kritické projevy* 4, (Prague, 1951), pp. 256-258.

lapses into clumsiness and verbosity. A quick off-the-cuff calculation with Lubomír Doležel's kinetic coefficient of style produced a value so low that in terms of linguistic dynamism this prose seemed remarkably close to some sort of 'degré zéro de l'écriture', to misuse Roland Barthes's phrase.[4] The value was significantly lower than those I obtained for other Czech Decadent writers. This lack of dynamism may have been what Otakar Theer had in mind when he claimed that Opolský's style produced a narrative surface from which the spark of life had been extinguished ('povrch, z kterého vyprchla jiskra života')[5]. As I continued my reading of Opolský's prose *in extenso*, I began to notice that the heavily descriptive language was sometimes characterized by an ethereal lightness and sometimes by a dense weightiness that seemed to correlate with some sort of spiritual and physical states. Karel Sezima seems to have noticed something of the kind when he wrote: 'Opolský dovede [...] vyjadřovat představy matožné a lehce smyté [...] a hned opět jediným úderem štětce vzbudit dojem zcela syrové konkretnosti'.[6] Initially, I thought that these states might symbolize something like a basic opposition of principles. If this were true, I thought, it might be a sign of unexpected originality in a writer considered a mere epigon.

However, it was only when I began to concentrate on individual texts, examining their narrative perspective and paying attention to their precise wording that it gradually became clear to me that the texts could not be other than ironic. What is more, they seemed to be ironic through and through, as if the irony were not just one element in the narrative but its principal *raison d'être*. What I found myself confronting was a consistently sustained but subtle conventional narrative irony deploying an exceptional range of sophisticated linguistic and conceptual devices with resourcefulness and ingenuity. Within the framework of this irony, the narrator was gradually revealed as a morbid individual divorced from reality and alienated from healthy vitality. The measurable lack of linguistic dynamism in the texts and the impressions of rarefied lightness alternating with dead-weight heaviness were then easily explained as corollaries of this ironic stylization of the narrator.

This book tries to describe Opolský's irony in all its facets but it deliberately makes no attempt to retrace the tortuous process which led to its recognition. Every reader approaches irony differently and in ways that are impossible to predict. My exposition will be strictly linear and take the form of close readings of five selected texts. This mode of exposition present challenges of its own, as I shall explain.

---

4   The kinetic coefficient of style is obtained by dividing the verb-adjective ratio by the word-sentence ratio; see Lubomír Doležel and Richard Bailey (eds), *Statistics of style* (New York, 1969).
5   Otakar Theer, (Review of *Kresby uhlem*) *Lumír* 35 (1906–7), Nos 10–11, p. 451.
6   Karel Sezima, (Review of *Demaskování*) *Podobizny a reliefy* (Prague, 1919), pp. 131–138 (p. 132).

Quotations from Czech are given in the original and are not translated. The textual interpretations at the core of this book are so sensitive to the exact wording of the narrative that they can only be carried out on the original texts. To supply a continuous translation as an aid to comprehension would be constantly to beg the question of how the texts are meant to be understood, which is precisely what needs to be established. What is more, the resulting necessity for continual reference to an inevitably inadequate translation would greatly confuse the already complex issue of interpretation. A reading knowledge of Czech must therefore be assumed, and this will, by and large, limit the readership of this book to Slavists. However, it is hoped that with the detailed explanations and frequent glosses provided, even a Slavist who does not have Czech as a main language should be able to manage reasonably well. Quotations from French, German and Russian have also been left untranslated because a working knowledge of these languages is normally part of a Slavist's linguistic repertoire. For the time being, at least, the non-Slavist is largely excluded, which I regret but do not apologize for. I think it does no harm for us to be reminded occasionally that in the study of literature a knowledge of languages is not an optional extra.

I believe that once Opolský's irony is recognized, it will no longer possible to regard him as a Decadent epigon nor even as a minor writer. His consummate mastery of the genre sets him aside, not only from the many writers in Czech literature who have used irony at some point in their work, but also from many other writers in world literature. I venture to suggest that Opolský at his best will prove to be one finest practitioners of conventional narrative irony that literature has to offer, though the language in which he wrote and the challenge his texts present to translation may mean that his literary merit will never be broadly recognized.

1. BIOGRAPHY

Jan Opolský was born on 15 July 1875, in the small north-eastern Bohemian town of Nová Paka, as the son of Josef Opolský, a solicitor's clerk, and his wife Kateřina née Menčíková. Both parents came from working-class families. Josef Opolský was the son of a saddler from the nearby town of Nový Bydžov, and Kateřina was the daughter of a local confectioner and gingerbread-maker. The couple had three sons, of whom Jan was the second-born.

The family seems to have been harmonious, at least initially. Kateřina was an attentive mother who took the upbringing and education of her children seriously. It is to her credit that they were all taught to read and write before going to school. As a result of this early learning Jan was able to skip the first year at primary school after only three weeks. The rest of his school career, as far as it went, was remarkably successful and his standard of achievement consistently high.[7] After completing the basic nine-year course, he was ready to leave school on his thirteenth birthday. By this time he had developed a strong interest in art and handicraft and decided to become an engraver. He applied for an apprenticeship but was rejected because he was too young. Granted permission to stay on at school for another year, he hoped to succeed in his application second time round. But this was not to be. A year later, Opolský's father was already considerably less sympathetic to the idea of an apprenticeship, especially in a field in which there was no family tradition, and decided that it was time for his son to start earning a living. It is quite possible that his attitude was influenced by the critical situation which had developed at home. When Jan was ten years old, Kateřina died in her late thirties, leaving her husband to rear three children single-handed. This was in addition to the problems he already had trying to salvage the business of his negligent boss.

The search for employment led Jan Opolský to the commercial art studio of Václav Kretschmer, where he found a job that did not require formal training but nonetheless allowed him to use his natural artistic skills. It is hardly likely that Opolský found this work profoundly satisfying, even though he was to remain with Václav Kretschmer for a full twenty-five years. Kretschmer's

---

7   This is borne out by his school reports which from part of his papers held by the Památník ná-
     rodního písemnictví in Prague.

Plate 1: Nová Paka. Postcard. Main square with plague column and church of St. Nicholas (mentioned in 'Poledne').

studio was run on a strictly mercantile basis, churning out standard items of religious art, such as icons and gilded statuettes, but also, mainly to order, secular works such as landscapes, portraits, still-lifes and genre paintings. Many years later, Opolský reminisces sardonically:

Všech dílen, co jich na světě je, ta dílna byla vzorem,
neb co se dalo malovat, to mastili jsme skorem.
My robili jsme landšafty a portréty,
jež měly to vlastnost, že jsme obětí svých nikdy neviděli.
My malovali ikony, i žánry, jež jsou k tomu,
by krášlily svým humorem zdi měšťanského domu.
My tenkrát všecko uměli a mám na to dost svědků,
že překrásná už madona tak stála u nás pětku.
My malovali amóry. A zátiší. A báby,
a fortel měli na plátně tak jako na hedvábí.
No universum hotové, se dalo prostě říci,
a dřeli jsme to od kusu tak jako soustružníci.[8]

The eight employees were paid by the piece and worked from eight to twelve and from one to six every day.[9] There was no room for creative inspiration; all that was required was routine, technically proficient craftsmanship. As the literary historian Bedřich Slavík, later a close friend of Opolský's, comments euphemistically:

---

8   Jan Opolský, 'Sám o sobě', *Lumír*, 60 (1934), pp. 217–19, (p. 218).
9   See Arne Novák, 'Malířské počátky Jana Opolského', *Lidové noviny*, 20 December 1935, p. 2.

Plate 2: Jan Opolský's birthplace in Nová Paka

Při malbě nešlo o individuální vlohy a umělecký vývoj, ale časem se u malířů vyvinula zručnost mnohem podobná dovednosti středověkých řemeslníků.[10]

The painters worked in a team, each one specializing in certain aspects of the task: one would mix the paint, another would draw the outlines, another would paint hands and faces, another clothing, another background and so on, according to a system originally evolved by early Flemish painters. However, for all its dull routine, the workshop produced several artists of note, such as Bohumír Číla and Karel Havlata.[11]

At the age of nineteen, after five years with Václav Kretschmer, Opolský lost his father, who died suddenly in his late forties. Now orphaned, he not only was left to his own resources but also carried the responsibility of looking after his younger brother. There followed a period of hardship and loneliness. However, Opolský soon succeeded in overcoming this isolation and forming a circle of friends. Many of them were older than Opolský, and were

---

10   Bedřich Slavík, *U Suchardů* (Hradec Králové, 1973), p. 46.
11   Both painted mainly landscapes, still lifes and portraits. Bohumír Číla (1885–1957) is best known for creating a new copy of Josef Mánes's calendar plate on the famous astronomical clock that adorns Prague Town Hall. Karel Havlata (1885–1957) is best known for the frescos he painted in Suchardův dům in Nová Paka and for his landscape painting 'Permská krajina' (1935). Havlata was also an avid collector of fossils and precious stones. See Prokop Toman, *Nový slovník československých výtvarných umělců* (Ostrava, 1993).

probably as much fatherly mentors as friends. Among them were several of Opolský's former teachers: Vilém Polák, for example, headmaster of the local primary school and a musician of sorts; and Josef Nováček, languages and history master at the secondary school, whose English wife lent the studious youngster books from her private library and acquainted him with the works of Dickens and Meredith, as well as other works of English and European literature. Then there was Břetislav Jampílek, also a schoolmaster, something of a philosopher, but with theosophist leanings. Last but not least, there was Opolský's former classmate, the ironmonger Josef Anton, who had the largest library in the district and who ran a family table-top puppet theatre ('stolní rodinné divadlo'). Later on, Opolský was to make friends with two well-known writers resident locally, Karel Sezima and Josef Karel Šlejhar. He also became acquainted with the painter Josef Tulka and the sculptor Stanislav Sucharda.[12]

It was largely through the influence of these friends that Opolský began to evolve an extensive audodidactic activity. He eagerly consumed large quantities of literature both domestic and foreign. He regularly read the literary periodicals *Rozhledy*, *Lumír* and *Moderní revue*, to which he also began to contribute poetry, and acquainted himself with the work of Jiří Karásek, Karel Hlaváček, Antonín Sova, Otokar Březina and Julius Zeyer. His favourite writers, however, were Garborg, Hamsun, Flaubert, Rilke and Dehmel, especially Gautier, Dostoevsky and Gogol. In addition, he read numerous works on art history, above all on Renaissance and Baroque art and developed an interest in the Dutch, German and Italian masters.[13]

Opolský became something of a local character. Sezima has given us a charming vignette of Opolský, habitually clad in a long sleeveless hooded coat and a wide-brimmed hat, striding along the arcade around the main square of Nová Paka on his daily walk to his favourite watering-place, the 'Snake's Grotto', where he enjoyed the regard of local malcontents:

Básník denně, za každého počasí prošel ve svém věčném haveloku a karbonářském širáku podloubím, po jedné straně vroubícím náměstí mířil do své demokratické hospůdky, obecně nazývané 'Hadí Sluji'. Bylo tam dostaveníčko mistrů ševců novopackých a vůbec doupě místních nespokojených živlů, Opolský požíval mezi nimi značné autority.[14]

---

12   See Karel Sezima, *Z mého života*, 4 vols (Prague, 1946–9), I, pp. 160–72. On Josef Tulka, see Marie Freimannová, *Josef Tulka, malíř generace Národního divadla* (Prague, 1965) and the entry on Josef Tulka in Emanuel Poche et al. (ed.), *Encyklopedie českého výtvarného umění* (Prague, 1975). On Stanislav Sucharda, see Jiří Kotalík, Česká secese (Prague, 1966).

13   Bedřich Slavík, *Počátky básnické činnosti Jana Opolského* (Prague, 1935), p. 2.

14   Karel Sezima, *Paměti*, 4 vols, Prague, 1945, vol. 2, p. 160; quoted in Jan Stejskal, *Novopacko: portét paměti a srdce* (Nová Paka and Harrachov, 2009).

The Snake's Grotto was so named after a room at the rear that was hewn into the local sandstone like a cave. One wonders how many readers of his poem 'Hadí král' in *Svět smutných* saw the joke when he wrote:

Zde bylo k smrti úzko za noci!
Ta černá sluj, v níž kapraď vyhnívala,
kam vlét-li pták, už zhynul bez moci,
kde voda zelená se zabublati bála!

Opolský's daily quota of beer in the 'Snake's Grotto' was a pleasure he could hardly afford on his meagre wages, which meant he had to save on clothes and shoes. As his niece Jiřina Brabcová recalls:

[...] měl zlatku denně. To bylo málo, byl pivapitel, tedy vypil řadu pullitrů, a i když stál půllitr piva šest krejcarů, bylo to denně dost a nezbylo často ani na opravu bot, tím méně na doplnění prádla[15]

adding that her grandmother often had to go to the pub and pay for the drinks Opolský had put on tick.

Besides material hardship, the young Opolský was also afflicted by recurrent ill health. The basic complaint seems to have been a weak heart, although there may have been other contributory factors. He spent frequent periods in hospital in Jičín, the provincial capital, between the spring of 1895 and the summer of 1897. Often he was bed-ridden for several months at a time. However, by physical exercise and particularly by participating in the activities of the nationalist gymnastic association Sokol, he improved his state of health to such an extent that, in early 1899, he was found fit for military service.

At the beginning of April 1899 he was called up to serve with the 74th infantery regiment at Jičín. The experience of army life seems to have had a disconcerting effect on the young recruit. In a letter to his girlfriend, Františka Endová, he describes his impression of his first weeks' military service:

Minulé dny ztratily se pro mne jako plachý dým, a není ničeho než hrubého a bezduchého dření.[16]

---

15   Testimony of Jiřina Brabcová from the 1920s. Quoted from the menu of 'Novopacké sklepy' (as the 'Hadí sluj' is now known) in *Staré lesy* (Prague, 2010), edited by Václav Cílek and Pavel Kostiuk, pp. 121–122.

16   Letter from Jan Opolský to Františka Endová (16 April 1899), Prague, Památník národního písemnictví (PNP), Literární archiv (LA), Pozůstalost Jana Opolského (PJO).

Plate 3: Self-portrait with spouse by Jan Opolský. Photograph of painting (oil on canvas). Impishly, Opolský made himself look half a head taller than his wife although, in reality, it was the other way round.

But it was less the stultifying grind of army routine or the physical strain of military drill that distressed Opolský than the coarse atmosphere:

Jsem otráven více surovým ovzduším, nežli velikým tělesným dřením.[17]

In June 1901, Opolský was transferred from Jičín to Liberec, but the regiment and barracks in Liberec were, if anything, worse than those at Jičín.

Throughout his military service Opolský maintained a regular correspondence with Františka Endová, whom he had met originally at a dancing lesson in Nová Paka, and to whom he later became engaged. His relationship with Františka, the daughter of a well-to-do clothier, was the source of much hostility and resentment locally. Malicious gossipmongers had soon spread the conjecture that the indigent young suitor was only after his fiancée's money and social position. Opolský took these accusations very much to heart, and, at one point, even considered leaving Nová Paka for good, hoping that this

---

17   Letter from Jan Opolský to Františka Endová (undated), Prague, PNP, LA, PJO.

sacrifice would bring people to reason. Nonetheless, the courtship was successful and the couple were married in late 1902. A year later, a daughter, Marta, was born, their only child.

In 1914, with the outbreak of the First World War, Václav Kretschmer was forced to close his painters' workshop, having lost vital export markets in Germany, Serbia and Russia. Opolský subsequently transferred to the textile company of his local namesake Otto Kretschmer, where he was given a clerical position.[18] In 1921, Otto Kretschmer, a barytone of European standing, moved his entire business to Prague in order to accommodate his frequent concert commitments. Otto Kretschmer went on to become a highly successful entrepreneur and patron of the arts, living in a palace in Malá Strana and befrieding members of the cultural elite, such as the painter lithographer Max Švabinský, and the composers Leo Janáček and Josef Suk.[19] Opolský, who followed Otto Kretschmer to Prague, was given a managerial position in Kretschmer's new textile factory in Nusle.

Opolský's life in Prague is less well documented than his life in the provincial obscurity of Nová Paka. Nonetheless, we do know that he and his wife first lived on Vratislavova Street in the district of Vyšehrad, later moving to Boleslavova Street in adjacent Nusle, presumably in order to be closer to his workplace in Kretschmer's factory on Vlastislavova, now only a stone's throw away. Of the flat at the second of these addresses we have a rudimentary description.[20] It consisted of a small double-bedroom and a kitchen that also served as living-room. In the kitchen there was a large table on which Opolský was able to write after meals, and a sofa. The walls were decorated with a number of paintings, most of which were the work of Opolský himself, and there were a few bookshelves with volumes mainly on art history. The couple's circumstances, evidently, remained modest, even though Opolský eventually reached managerial level in Kretschmer's textile firm, and in spite of income from his publications, especially in periodicals and newspapers.

If moving to Prague did not bring about much of a material upswing, there can scarcely be any doubt that it did provide Opolský with more intellectual and cultural stimulation. It was in Prague that he first became acquainted with poet and novelist Viktor Dyk, who was later to be a very close friend, with the Decadent writers Jiří Karásek and Arnošt Procházka, with the graphic artist and painter František Kobliha and the sculptor Bohumil Kafka . His circle of friends was soon to include the doctor and minor novelist František Skácelík,

---

18   It is often claimed that Otto Kretschmer was Václav Kretschmer's nephew. Bedřich Slavík always insisted to me that they were unrelated. His assertion is borne out by Yvona Benčová, *Osobnosti Novopacka* (Nová Paka, 2011), which provides detailed genealogies of the two Kretschmer families.

19   See Yvona Benčová, *Osobnosti Novopacka*, p. 148.

20   See František Hampl, 'Básník života a smrti', *Nový večerník*, 13 March 1937, p. 3.

Plate 4: Jan Opolský around 1935.
Photograph.

the literary and art critic Štěpán Jež and the Decadent writer Jarmil Krecar. He also became acquainted with the poet and essayist Rudolf Medek, the cultural historian Zdeněk Kalista, the francophile literary historian Hanuš Jelínek and the short story-writers Karel Mašek and František Khol. Along with Fráňa Šrámek, Jiří Mahen and František Gellner, he was a frequent visitor at the then influential poet and essayist Stanislav Kostka Neumann's villa in Olšany, where his group of anarcho-socialist revolutionaries met. But besides finding many literary and personal friends, Opolský also made his mark publicly. On 20 November 1928, he was elected an honorary member of the Royal Bohemian Academy; in the course of 1929, he was admitted to the literary section ('literární odbor') of the Umělecká beseda,[21] and, on 11 October 1932, was made a member of the writers' association 'Kruh českých spisovatelů' there. He was an editor of the leading literary journal *Lumír* from 1928 to 1937, and received several awards for his work, including a State Prize in 1926.

---

21 The Umělecká beseda, one of the oldest Czech societies, was founded in 1862 to promote Czech music, literature and art, by organizing concerts, theatre performances, readings and exhibitions. From 1925 onwards it was housed in its own building in Besední ulice in Malá strana. Its founders included the composer Bedřich Smetana, and the painters Josef Mánes and Mikuláš Aleš. It was dissolved in 1972.

Opolský's life in Prague was also marked by a deteriorating state of health. In a letter to the novelist Emil Vachek in his capacity as editor of *Pramen*, undated, but probably from the period 1921–4, Opolský writes, excusing himself for not having sent a contribution to the journal:

> Jsem už delší dobu churav těžkou nervósou žaludku, přestálým diétním léčením a mor-fiovými injekcemi velmi zeslabený a stísněný, takže nyní nemohu vůbec pracovat.[22]

In Opolský's correspondence dating from the 1920s references to ill health are frequent, even when they are sometimes no more than passing remarks, such as the following in a letter to František Skácelík, where Opolský, referring to a previous meeting, observes apologetically:

> Tentokrát mne kromě nervósy seškubaly průdušky a trochu ledvinky.[23]

During the late 1920s and early 1930s, Opolský's heart condition also seems to have deteriorated, as his repeated and increasingly frequent visits to the thermal spa and health resort Poděbrady would seem to indicate. In March 1932, during a critical phase of his illness, he even had go to the sanatorium in Podolí.[24]

Finally, in 1935, just as he was about to retire, Opolský suffered a severe stroke which left the left side of his body paralysed. For the first two months after the stroke he was bedridden, lying completely immobile, first in the exclusive sanatorium in Smíchov, Sanopz, then in Prague General Hospital, to which he transferred for financial reasons. The hemiplegia proved chronic, and although Opolský learned to walk again he could never do without his stick and the supporting arm of his patient wife. His balance was permanently impaired, since the aural nerves had been affected. As he laments to Zdenka Dyková-Hásková, Viktor Dyk's widow:

> [...] chromota a ochrnutí těch ušních nervů, to mne mnohem skličuje, tím více když uvažuji o své někdejší hbitosti, ploužu se dnes o holi po ulicích jako vetchý prapor.[25]

Visiting him at home one afternoon in 1937, his friend František Hampl was shocked to see a crumpled, languishing figure:

---

22   Letter from Jan Opolský to Emil Vachek (undated), Prague, PNP, LA, Pozůstalost Emila Vachka.
23   Letter from Jan Opolský to František Skácelík (23 April 1928), Prague, PNP, LA, Pozůstalost Fran-tiška Skácelíka.
24   See 'Jan Opolský přijat do léčení', *Polední list*, 11 March 1932, p. 6.
25   Letter from Jan Opolský to Zdenka Dyková (undated), Prague, PNP, LA, Pozůstalost Zdenky Dy-kové.

Plate 5: Jan Opolský in his declining years. Signed photograph

Přišel jsem tam brzy po poledni a spatřil básníka v kuchyňce: ležel na pohovce, drobný jako chroustek, šedivý plnovous jako by mu neusále prochvíval vítr, ale jeho oči byly důtklivé, chvílemi z nich zablesklo až výhruzně, a vzápětí se z nich linulo pokorné světlo. Básník, tehdy dvaašedesátiletý, opravdu už dožíval svůj pozemský život – zemřel až pět let potom – a připadalo mi, že už nepatří do tohoto světa.[26]

During the year 1941, Opolský's state of health took a turn for the worse, possibly due to an aggravating arteriosclerosis. However, on top of this, Opolský seems to have been suffering from athetosis, a nervous disease resulting in involuntary writhing movements of the extremities, mostly the consequence of a hereditary illness like cerebral palsy or Huntington's chorea but

---

26   František Hampl, 'Basník z nejskromnějších', *Lidová demokracie*, 5 June 1970.

sometimes caused by lesion to the basal ganglia following a stroke. František Skácelík, himself a medical man, explains the diagnosis of Opolský's doctor:

> Říká vždy totéž, že je to athetósa, nervová choroba [...][27]
>
> Myslí, že to všechno vychází z jizvy, která zůstala v mozkové tkáni po záchvatu mrtvice [...][28]

Then, as now, there was no effective treatment for this insidious disease.

At the beginning of May 1942, Opolský's condition became critical and he was taken to the outpatients department of the General Hospital in Vinohrady, only to be transferred immediately and inauspiciously to the Sisters of Mercy Hospital (U milosrdných sester) in Malá Strana, a hospital for terminally ill run by Catholic nuns, where he died three weeks later on 22 May 1942. He was laid to rest in the municipal cemetry in Nová Paka.

---

27   Letter from František Skácelík to Jan Opolský (20 January 1942), Prague, PNP, LA, PJO.
28   Letter from František Skácelík to Jan Opolský (3 April 1942), Prague, PNP, LA, PJO.

2. INTRODUCTION TO THE OEUVRE

This chapter outlines Opolský's putative literary context, provides a short history of his publications, and charts the reception of his works up to the present. A more detailed account of how his prose oeuvre was interpreted will be provided in the next chapter.

2.1 A QUESTION OF CONTEXT

Opolský is commonly considered to be a belated Decadent. Although I shall try to show that Opolsky's creative project is of an entirely different order, it may be useful at this stage to take a cursory look at the Czech Decadence.[29] Doing so should help us to understand more fully the critical opinion I shall be presenting in the next chapter and may offer some insight into the way it came about.

Like its Western counterparts, the Czech Decadence set out to *épater le bourgeois* by indulging in extremes that marked a wholehearted rejection of social norms. Where society valued sobriety and realism, the Decadents expressed a preference for imagination over reality, for artificiality over nature, and for dandyism and aristocratic refinement over middle-class normality; where society valued bodily and mental well-being, the Decadents celebrated morbidity and neurosis; where society valued striving for material betterment, the Decadents were given to erethism and abulia; where society prized committed professionalism based on narrow specialisation, the Decadents inclined to insouciant dilettantism;[30] where society saw art as a limited cultural and material asset, the Decadents cultivated an overweening aestheti-

---

29 A comprehensive study of the Czech Decadence is still outstanding. For an introductory account, the reader may turn to Robert Pynsent, 'Czech Decadence', in Marcel Cornis-Pope and John Neubauer (eds), *History of the Literary Cultures of East-Central Europe*, 4 vols (Amsterdam and Philadelphia, 2004–2010), vol. 1, pp. 348–363; or to Jaroslav Med, 'Česká symbolistně-dekadentní literatura', in Petr Čornej et al. (eds), *Česká literatura na předělu století* (Prague, 2001), pp. 43–92. A more specialized account is available in Hana Bednaříková, *Česká dekadence* (Brno, 2000).

30 As set out in Charles Baudelaire, 'Dandysme', *Journaux intimes* (Paris, 2001) and Paul Bourget, *Ernest Renan* (Paris, 1883). With regard to the Czech Decadence, see Jan Staněk, 'Spor o diletantismus a jeho podoba v literatuře české dekadence', *Estetika*, 44 (2007), pp. 85–106.

cism and radical *l'art pour l'art* ideology; where society favoured conventional piousness, the Decadents expressed a fascination for ornament, mysticism and the occult; where society valued stable heterosexual relationships, the Decadents prized homosexuality, sexual excess and deviance, viewing women as a mixture of madonna and *femme fatale* (sometimes even *femme fragile*[31]); where society looked forward optimistically to a brighter and wealthier future, the Decadents indulged in pessimism and melancholy, sometimes thinking of themselves as the last scion of a dying dynasty.

The Czech Decadence, confusingly often also referred to as the Symbolist movement,[32] arose in the early 1890s and reached an early climax around the turn of the century. After this, it gradually lost impetus although some writers perservered in the Decadent mode until well into the 1930s.

The movement had both domestic and foreign roots. It derived inspiration from the French (Charles Baudelaire, Karel Huysmans), English (Edgar Allen Poe, Oscar Wilde, Algernon Swinburne, Julian Symons), Italian (Gabriele D'Annunzio) and Polish (Stanisław Przybyszewski) Decadence. Its philosophical outlook was informed by German philosophers like Friedrich Nietzsche, Oswald Spengler and Max Stirner.[33] Inside Bohemia, the Decadence can be traced back to Irma Geisslová, whose *Imortelly* (1879) is now often considered to mark its starting-point, and to the publications of the pre-Decadent writers Otakar Auředníček, Jaromír Borecký, and Jaroslav Kvapil in the late 1880s and early 1990s. It was also heavily influenced by the late Romanticism of Julius Zeyer and the Parnassianism of Jaroslav Vrchlický.[34]

The Czech Decadent movement produced two leading writers, Jiří Karásek (1871–1951) and Karel Hlaváček (1874–1998), both poets of European stature on a par with, and arguably often superior to, the likes of Algernon Swinburne or Arthur Symons. Two other Czech Decadents of note, Arnošt Procházka (1869–1925), the founding theorist of the movement, and Miloš Martén (1883–1917), both made their mark mainly as literary and art critics. In addition to these major figures, we find a host of minor Decadent writers whose many

---

31   See Ariane Thomalla, *Die femme fragile: Ein literarischer Frauentypus der Jahrhundertwende* (Düsseldorf, 1972).

32   The conflation of the two labels in the Czech critical tradition is often supported by the claim that the writers of the movement are Decadent in content but Symbolist in method. This is disconcerting to those of us who are accustomed to keeping the categories clearly distinct and who are no more likely to consider Mallarmé a Decadent because of his Symbolist method than we would be willing to consider Catulle Mendés or Jean Lorrain Symbolists because of their Decadent content. Even for Czech literature, the conceptual fit is by no means perfect. We can refer to Antonín Sova and Otokar Březina as Symbolists without having to think of them as Decadents and to Arthur Breiský and Miloš Martén as Decadents without having to call them Symbolists.

33   Especially the later Nietzsche of *Jenseits von Gut und Böse* (1886), *Zur Genealogie der Moral* (1887), *Götzendämmerung* (1889) and *Der Antichrist* (1895). On the role of Stirner in the Czech Decadence, see Robert Pynsent, 'Stirner und die tschechische Dekadenz', *Aeropag* 6 (1971), no. 1, pp. 63–71.

34   On Zeyer's influence, see Robert Pynsent, *Julius Zeyer: The Path to Decadence* (The Hague, 1973).

names even specialists struggle to keep in mind: Arthur Breiský, Vladimír Houdek, Bohdan Kaminský, Edvard Klas, Petr Kles, Bohuslav Knösl, Jarmil Krecar, Louis Křikava, Emanuel z Lešehradu, Hermor Lilia, Karel Nejč, Miroslav Rutte, Růžena Svobodová, Karel Šarlih, Jan z Wojkowicz, Louisa Ziková, etc. Many of these minor writers displayed a measure of originality – Breiský stood out as the Czech dandy;[35] others are little more than epigons. It is to the ranks of the latter that Opolský is mostly consigned.

Like its Western European counterparts, the Czech Decadence was not limited to works of literature. Just as the English Decadence extended to the graphic art of Aubrey Beardsley and James Whistler, and the French Decadence encompassed the paintings of James Ensor, Gustave Moreau, Félicien Rops and Odilon Redon, so the Czech Decadence included works by the sculptors Bohumil Kafka and Quido Kocian, the photographer František Drtikol, and the graphic artists Felix Jenewein, František Kobliha, Jaroslav Panuška, Jan Preisler and Josef Váchal. Hlaváček himself was a graphic artist of no mean talent, as we can see from his illustrations to Arnošt Procházka's *Prostibolo duše* (1897).[36]

However, in spite of broad similarities in motivation, content and expression, the Czech Decadence differs from other European Decadences in a number of crucial ways.

The Czech Decadence, unlike the French, resists any meaningful division into *hauts décadents* and *bas décadents*. The *hauts décadents* included major original poets like Verlaine and Baudelaire, who lent their creativity to the movement but were not constrained by it. The *bas décadents*, on the other hand, were dubious literati of the ilk of Josephin Péladan, Catulle Mendès or Pierre Louÿs, epigons (allegedly) interested mainly in exploiting the movement's sexual and erotic licence. Whatever their talents – and some were perhaps less talented than a Catulle Mendès or Pierre Louÿs – the Czech Decadents always strove to produce literature of merit. Many of them succeeded, but some only after having abandoned the Decadence to find their literary identity elsewhere. It is a feature of the Czech Decadence that it served as a

---

35   The importance of Breiský was first brought out by Robert Pynsent, 'A Czech Dandy: An Introduction to Arthur Breiský', *Slavonic and East European Review* 51 (1973), No. 4 (October), pp. 517-523. More recent contributions are: Jiří Pelan, 'Dandyovská estetika Arthura Breiského', Česká literatura 49 (2001), No. 3, pp. 243-253; and Peter Bugge, 'Naked Masks: Arthur Breiský or How To Be a Czech Decadent', *Slovo a smysl* 2 (2005), No. 3, pp. 135-148.

36   This aspect of the Czech Decadence was long neglected. Interest has recently been rekindled by Petr Wittlich, *Česká secese* (Prague, 1982) and *Umění a život – doba secese* (Prague, 1987); and by Tomáš Vlček, 'Počátky dějin moderního umění', *Kapitoly z českého dějepisu umění*, 2 vols (Prague, 1986-87), vol. 2, and 'České moderní umění', *Sen o říši krásy/Dream of the Empire of Beauty* (Prague, 2001), Sbírka Jiřího Karáska ze Lvovic. This resurgence of interest led to the exhibition *V barvách chorobných: Idea dekadence a umění v českých zemích 1880-1914* held in Prague in 2006 and the accompanying book of the same name edited by Otto Urban.

literary springboard for writers as diverse as the political ironist and satirist Viktor Dyk, the proletarian poets Jiří Wolker and Stanislav Kostka Neumann, and the vitalist Fraňa Šrámek.

The Czech Decadents, unlike their English counterparts, did not find that the aristocratic refinement they valued so much came naturally. The aristocratic manner that sat easily with an Oscar Wilde was for the largely working-class to lower middle-class writers of the Czech Decadence little more than a ridiculous and provocative pose. Jiří Karásek (the aristocratic title *ze Lvovic* is a conceit) was a post-office employee who sorted mail on the Prague-Brno express, Arnošt Procházka was bank clerk, and Arthur Breiský worked as a lift boy in New York. But the very artificiality of its aristocratic pose makes the Czech Decadence in this respect more truly Decadent than its Western counterparts. At the same time, the loathing for bourgeois reality expressed through this pose was, as Robert Pynsent has pointed out, more genuine and keenly felt than in any other Decadent tradition.[37]

More than the French or English Decadence, the Czech Decadence was marked linguistically. The movement showed an openness for Western European literature unprecedented in Bohemia since the Middle Ages and the Baroque, and with the foreign literature and its Czech translations came a spate of foreign loanwords, especially from Romance. These loanwords by their very novelty and unfamiliarity satisfied the Decadent penchant for the distinguished and artificial. The use of words like *phosphorekující*, often with characteristically un-Czech elements of original French spelling, became an inseparable part of Decadent style. But this was not only the stylistic idiosyncracy. To an unusual extent, the Czech Decadence made use of certain native terms, many hitherto more typical of Romanticism, such as *sen, vůně, opojení*, and words expressing spectral or penumbral vagueness, such as *mlha, soumrak, stín*, often adorned for good measure with a non-committal *jakýsi*, and words conveying a sense of lifelessness, such as *kovový, bledý*. It is no exaggeration to say that these terms form part of a Decadent linguistic code.

More than the English Decadence around Henry Harland's short-lived *Yellow Book* (1894–1897), or the French Decadence around Anatole Baju's equally ephemeral *Le Décadent* (1886–1889), or the Italian Decadence around Adolfo de Bosis' *Il Convito* (1895–1907) and Enrico Corradini's *Il Marzocco* (1896–1932), the Czech Decadence was centred on a single periodical: Arnošt Procházka's *Moderní revue* (1894–1925). While *Moderní revue* was characterized more by its 'utter cosmopolitanism' (to use Neil Stewart's phrase) than by a single-minded commitment to Decadence, any budding Czech writer who published there on a regular basis could hardly avoid the Decadent label.[38]

---

37   For example, in Robert Pynsent, *Julius Zeyer: The Path to Decadence*.
38   See Neil Stewart, 'The Cosmopolitanism of *Moderní revue* (1894–1925)', in Marcel Cornis-Pope

2.2 A PROFILE OF PUBLICATION

Opolský's first extant poems date from January 1895. They are preserved, along with several hundred other early poems, most of which were never published, in three albums, written in calligraphic script and illustrated with charcoal drawings, that form part of Opolský's papers.[39] It was not until May 1986 that Opolský made his debut in Josef Pelcl's periodical *Rozhledy* with a set of five poems. This publication was followed by the contribution of a single poem to Svatopluk Čech's periodical *Květy* in July 1896, which is often erroneously taken as marking the poet's debut.[40] Opolský's first contributions to *Rozhledy* already helped to establish a modest reputation that was soon to give him access to several other important periodicals. In March 1897, he began to write for the literary section of the art journal *Volné směry*, and in 1898 he started publishing in Jaroslav Kvapil's *Zlatá Praha* and the Decadent flagship journal *Moderní revue*. Only a little later did he begin to contribute to the major literary periodical *Lumír*, to S.K. Neumann's new radical left-wing journal *Nový kult* and to the popular literary review *Srdce*. It is mainly from publications in these journals that Opolský's first collections of verse, *Svět smutných* (1899), *Klekání* (1900), *Jedy a léky* (1901) and *Pod tíhou života* (1907), are drawn. *Jedy a léky* sports a frontispiece by Jan Preisler displaying a young man who has been described as effeminately hedonistic, even narcissistic. This Decadent image seemed to pledge a correspondingly Decadent content.[41]

After *Pod tíhou života*, Opolský continued to contribute poetry to a variety of journals. In 1916, a contribution to the socialist anarchist journal *Omladina*

---

and John Neubauer (eds), *History of the Literary Cultures of East-Central Europe*, 4 vols (Amsterdam and Philadelphia, 2004), vol. 3, pp. 63–70.

39   Prague, Památník národního písemnictví (PNP), Literární archiv (LA), Pozůstalost Jana Opolského (PJO).

40   This misconception was fostered by Jiří Karásek, 'První báseň Jana Opolského', *Lumír*, 61 (1934–5), pp. 445–7.

41   Petr Wittlich describes it as the 'drawing of an airy youth in buffoon's clothing with a sprig of vine in his hair, reverently but vainly admired by two females' ('kresba ležerního jinocha v paňácovském oděvu s révou ve vlasech, k němuž zbožně, ale marně vzhlížejí dvě ženské postavy'). Leading art historian Antonín Matějček felt that the figure of the young man was 'surprisingly sensuous for its time, with an effeminately hedonistic facial expression' ('tentokrát ku podivu smyslného, až zženstile rozkošnickým výrazem v tváři'). Wittlich calls him 'a Narcissus, self--enamoured and self-absorbed' ('Narcis, zamilovaný a zahleděný do sebe'), in accordance with the book's ostensibly Decadent content ('Odpovídá ovšem dobře dekadentnímu světu Opolského básní'). For Ladislav Zikmund-Lender, the man's narcissism is confirmed by the swooning gazes of his two female admirers. In Matějček's opinion, the frontispiece bears no relation to the content of Opolský's poems but is a reflection of Preisler's own obsessions. See Antonín Matějček, *Jan Preisler* (Prague, 1950), p. 50; Petr Wittlich, *Horizonty umění* (Prague, 2010), pp. 199, 200; and Ladislav Zikmund-Lender, 'Nakřivo rostlý výhonek. Obrazy homosexuality v umění české dekadence', in Martin Putna et al., *Homosexualita v dějinách české kultury* (Prague, 2013), pp. 321–337 (p. 327).

Jan Preisler, frontispiece to Opolský's *Jedy a léky*, 1901, original in the National Gallery in Prague, under the title *Titulní kresba k básním Jana Opolského*.

created a major political incident. His poem about the Hungarian national opposition leader and campaigner for an independent Hungary, Ferenc Kossuth, written as a parody of the Austro-Hungarian national anthem and published alongside an article by Count Kropotkin on the Paris Commune, led to the arrest of editors-in-chief Fráňa Šrámek and Michael Kácha and to the immediate cessation of the journal after only a handful of issues.[42]

Opolský continued to write and publish poetry for the rest of his life. The most prominent among his later collections are *Verše o životě a smrti* (1918), *Dědictví* (1923), *Hory doly a lesy* (1931), and *Čtení z hvězd a obelisků* (1936). Often overlooked, and consistently omitted from any general appraisal of Opolský's poetry, are two volumes of overtly satirical verse: *Hrst ironie a satiry* (1911), put together from material submitted to the satirical weekly *Kopřivy* in the period 1901–1911; and *Galerie zvířat* (1922), which drew on humorous poems originally published in *Zvířena* in the years 1919–1921. Two further volumes were compiled in manuscript form but never published: another volume of overtly satirical verse entitled *Satira válečná a popřevratová*, compiled in 1920, containing thirty-eight poems selected from over eighty originally submitted to the satirical weeklies *Nebojsa* and *Šibeničky* in 1918–20; and a collection called *Hlubina bezpečnosti*, containing poems published in the twenties and thirties.[43] Opolský also published four volumes of poetry in small bibliophile editions: *Hvězda mořská* (1925), *Pohádka o pěvci* (1929), *Dětský hymnus* (1929), and *Kameje* (1935).

Opolský's first attempts at prose are preserved in his private notebooks.[44] In a small coverless jotter, we find the four earliest drafts: 'Žije, žije...', dated October 1894, then 'Ve svaté chvíli', 'Legenda o Gotliebovi [sic]' and 'Srdce z vojny', probably written in the course of 1895. In a later hand-illustrated album, we find further prose pieces, dating from late 1898. The first three, 'Barevné západy', 'Medium' and 'Háj', remained manuscripts, but the last three were published: 'A pietoso' appeared in *Rozhledy* in September 1898, and the following two, 'Noc' and 'Konec', were published in *Srdce* under the heading 'Dvě básně v prose'.

Opolský's prose output now soon increased. From 1902–1906, he published eight prose pieces in *Rozhledy* and three in *Lumír*. Two more appeared in the radical yearbook *Kalendář revolucionářů* and another in *Moderní život*. Most of these later were brought together in his first book of prose *Kresby uhlem* (1907). This was followed by the semi-bibliophile *Demaskování* (1916), with illuminations by the expressionist artist Pravoslav Kotík, which con-

---

42   Jan Mukařovský et al. (ed.) *Dějiny české literatury* (Prague 1959–1995), 4 vols, vol. 4 (*Literatura od konce 19. století do roku 1945*), p. 144.
43   Both unpublished collections in Prague, PNP, LA, PJO.
44   Prague, PNP, LA, PJO.

tained prose from 1906–1910. Noticeably, not one of the pieces was less than six years old at the time of publication. In fact, from autumn 1910 to spring 1916, Opolský evidently wrote no prose at all, for even his private notebooks contain no prose entries in this period. The next works are two children's adventure stories: *Nová země*, written in late 1916 and published in Pasov in 1918, and the unpublished *U tůně*, written in early 1917. For this lapse in prose production and the subsequent recourse to children's stories there is no obvious explanation. Since Opolský's prose output is otherwise unbroken, it seems as if the writer experienced some form of creative crisis. About the nature of this crisis we can only speculate. Could it be that he realised that this prose writing was set in a mould and that he felt the need to break out of it?

Be that as it may, Opolský's prose writing now rapidly regained momentum. In autumn 1917, Opolský began to contribute regularly to *Národní listy*, which, by spring 1919, had published eight prose pieces and had to refuse many more for lack of space.[45] Another three pieces were published in *Moderní revue* between November 1917 and February 1920, and we find several contributions to *Zlatá Praha*, *Lumír* and *Venkov* in the same period.

However, it was not until the nineteen-twenties that his prose production began to outweigh his poetry. After *Muka a zdání* (1921), he went on to publish *Z těžkého srdce* (1925, expanded edition 1926), *Malé prosy* (1926) and *Upír a jiné prosy* (1926), featuring a total of almost one hundred prose pieces written in the period 1918–1926. For *Upir a jiné prosy*, Opolsky was awarded the State Prize (Státní cena) in 1926.

These volumes were followed by a spate of bibliophilia. *Ze tmy do tmy* (1926) released in an edition only one hundred copies, was an excerpt of four stories from *Malé prosy* embellished with illustrations by František Kobliha. Kobliha was also responsible for the portraits and vignettes in *Medailony* (1927), a collection of three prose pieces supplemented by three poems, released in a small complimentary edition intended exclusively for the poet's personal friends. Of the sixty-six copies printed, one third contained the original lithographs and woodcuts. The miniature edition *Vitrina* (1927), illustrated with a frontispiece by Arno Neumann, had a slightly larger edition, as did *Stradivari* (1928), a short story illustrated, once again, by František Kobliha. Also bibliophile or semi-bibliophile in character were *Víry i tůně* (1928), *Melusina* (1929), *Miniatury* (1930) and *O studně krásy* (1932).

Commercial-scale publication was resumed with *Visuté zahrady* (1935) and *Pod patinou věků* (1937), bringing together prose contributions to newspapers and journals in the years 1925–1937.

---

45   Letter from Karel Čapek-Chod to Jan Opolský (6 February 1919), Prague, PNP, LA, PJO.

Published posthumously in 1944 and strikingly illustrated by Alois Fišárek, a graphic artist famous for his monumental style, *Hranolem křišťálu* achieved such a wide circulation that copies of it are still regularly available in second-hand book shops today. Probably compiled as early as 1940, it was submitted to the publishing-house Novina in spring 1941. However, hampered by the slow machinery of German censorship, Novina, like many other Czech publishing-houses of the period, was unwilling to publish any but the most commercially viable of manuscripts.[46] Opolský subsequently approached his good friend Josef Vilímek, owner of one of the country's largest publishing houses, who accepted the book as a personal favour to the author.[47] *Hranolem křišťálu* drew together twenty-three prose pieces written over the space of two decades, and published in a broad range of magazines and newspapers such as *Československá republika* (1921), *Národní listy* (1927–38), *Sever a východ* (1928), *Salon* (1938), *Národní politika*, *Ženský list*, *Polední list* and *Národná politika* (1940).

Two further collections of prose remained unpublished. *V záři a v temnu* included prose pieces written during 1927–1935, while *Výtvarnické evokace* (originally to be called *Malířské evokace*) brought together contributions to the glossy weekly *Salon* and the specialist art journal *Sborník grafické práce Hollar* from 1933–1939.

Opolský's association with *Sborník grafické práce Hollar* also enabled him to publish a series of essays as independent supplements, namely *Belveder* (1931), *Pražský hrad* (1934), *Gustave Courbet* (1936) and *Nové město pražské* (1940).

Published posthumously, like *Hranolem křišťálu*, was the literary monograph and obituary *Růžena Jesenská* (1944).

Both prose and verse are included in an anthology of Opolský's work commissioned by Vilímek in the late thirties. It was compiled and edited by Bedřich Slavík in cooperation with the author himself and contained thirty-six items of prose and sixty-seven of verse. However, owing to the wartime publishing restrictions, this extensive selection, that in typescript bears the title *Studna krásy*, never appeared in print.[48]

2.3 RECEPTION

Opolský's first three collections of verse, published at the turn of the century, were widely acclaimed. Prominent Decadent writer Jiří Karásek celebrated the young Opolský as a 'talent formální a stylisační par excellence' and compared him to fellow Decadent, Karel Hlaváček:

---

46   Letters from František Křelina to Jan Opolský (7 March 1941, 27 May 1941), PNP, LA, PJO.
47   Bedřich Slavík, oral communication, May 1979.
48   Typescript in possession of Bedřich Slavík.

Své první básně stylisoval Opolský stejně jako Karel Hlaváček do jakéhosi archaismu, aby působily dojmem starého dřevorytu, aby byly hranaté, strnule drsné, ponuré. Rachot okovu na dně mrtvé studny, černý obraz svaté panny, sesmutněný štkajícími divokými doupňáky, kamenité, nahé mrtviny, bez pohybu a vzruchu, samé ruiny, kláštery, vězenské cely, černé revíry, hospitaly – to byla frazeologie knihy.[49]

In an idiom resonant with Decadent overtones, F.X. Šalda enthused:

Hle, jeden z rodu melancholiků, plachý, teskný a intuitivní snivec, který zná život mrtvých věcí, řeč němoty, smyl podvědomého a temného, narážky a signály predestinace a celý strašný úžas z toho snu, jiný je život. A přitom kouzelný malíř barvou i mlhou slova [...]. Jak cítíte a dýcháte v těch parnatých lehce jako oblaka nad propast tmy zavěšených hudebně dechnutých slovech prchavou hrůzu a nenávratnou věčnost okamžiku.[50]

After this successful debut, Opolský's popularity fell into gradual decline, as did the popularity of the Decadence generally. His poetry continued to have its admirers – for Jakub Deml, Opolský was a poet second only to František Halas[51], and Josef Palivec is said to have been able to recite entire passages of Opolský's early poetry more than fifty years later[52] – but like the prose he began to publish from 1907 onwards, it remained outside the literary mainstream.

When Opolský received the State Prize for Literature for his prose collection *Upír a jiné prósy* in 1926, it must have seemed as if he was poised to make a comeback. However, rather than enhance his reputation, this prize-winning volume, whose title echoed Hlaváček's programmatic poem 'Upír' in *Pozdě k ránu* (1896), probably only served to reinforce the view of Opolský as a Decadent epigon. In 'Upír', Hlaváček had hailed the vampire as the symbol of the Decadence, inspiring artist František Kobliha to a series of well-known woodcuts.[53]

---

49 Jiří Karásek, 'Jan Opolský', *Impresionisté a ironikové* (Prague, 1903).

50 F.X.Šalda, 'Jan Opolský: Svět smutných', *Lumír* 27 (1899), pp. 299-300; reprinted in *Kritické projevy* 4, (Prague, 1951), pp. 256-258.

51 Jakub Deml, *Šlépěje XXII* (Tasov, 1937), pp. 79, 80. In a letter to Opolský dated 20 October 1936 and published twice in the same book (pp. 84 and 122), Deml writes 'vidím, že máte se mnou něco příbuzného. [...] tato příbuznost je mi velmi milá'. See also Jakub Deml, *Zakázané světlo: Výbor z korespodence 1930-1939* (Prague and Litomyšl, 1999), edited by Jiří Olič, pp. 58-60, where Deml admits to following Opolský's work for over thirty years, adding 'je velmi blízké mému srdci' and 'zpívá jazykem tak čistým, že připomíná jiskřivé, bezoblačné noci prosincové'.

52 On the occasion of Josef Palivec's eighty-fifth birthday, Ivan Slavík writes in his diary: '[Palivec] četl první verše Opolského jako avantgardnou novinku a uměl z nich dosud pasáže zpaměti'. See Ivan Slavík, *Hory roků* (Prague, 1999), p. 95 (entry for 7 October 1971).

53 Otto Urban (ed.), *V barvách chorobných: idea dekadence a umění v českých zemích 1880-1914* (Prague, 2006), pp. 302-303.

After his death in 1942, Opolský was largely forgotten, both in academia and by the public at large. In 1946, art historian and essayist Jindřich Chalupecký published a small selection of Opolský's verse in *Listy pro umění i filosofii* but it met with little resonance.[54] Poet and essayist Jan Čarek's slim monograph on Opolský, published in 1949, did little to reverse the trend.[55] The Second World War had shifted intellectual and cultural priorities, and the Communist ideology that pervaded Czechoslovakia from 1948 onwards had little time for Decadents, even major ones (though Hlaváček continued to be published).

It was not until the political liberalization of mid- to late sixties that there was a brief resurgence of interest in Opolský. The Academy of Sciences dictionary of Czech writers published in 1964 includes a short article on Opolský. Far more influential was Ivan Slavík's anthology of Opolský's poetry and prose published in 1968 in the *Světová četba* series.[56] In his critical introduction, Slavík makes a case for Opolský's importance as a writer, emphasizing the significance of his prose over his poetry (the anthology contains twenty-nine prose pieces and only twelve poems). It may be due in part to Slavík's advocacy that Opolský was accorded a generous, if anonymous, mention in *Čeští spisovatelé z přelomu 19. a 20. století*, published in 1972.[57] However, as re-Stalinization (perversely dubbed 'normalizace') tightened its steely grip, Slavik's intercession ceased to bear fruit. Indeed Slavík himself became *persona non grata*, exiled from his post at Prague University to a provincial secondary school in Hořovice, a small town half-way between Prague and Pilsen.

During Slavík's enforced silence, the task of popularizing Opolský's prose fell mainly to famous linguist, translator and literary theorist Pavel Eisner, who writing under the pseudonym Jan Ort, included several pieces by Opolský in two collections of Czech prose published in 1977 and 1980.[58] In his postscript to the second of these, Eisner praises Opolský as an writer 'mistrně ovladájící miniaturní slovesné tvary'. Eisner does not see Opolský as a Decadent but as a detached observer of reality expressing himself succinctly and in a polished style ('úsporně a vytříbeným stylem').[59] Nine years later, literary historian Jiří Kudrnáč included a piece by Opolský in his anthology of short Decadent prose, published in the *Světová četba* series[60] Kudrnáč hails Opolský as 'nejpilnější prozaik českého symbolismu' and compares him to French symbolist writer Marcel Schwob.

54   Jindřich Chalupecký, 'Jan Opolský', *Listy pro umění a filosofii* 1(1947), vol. 4.
55   Jan Čarek, *Jan Opolský* (Prague, 1949).
56   Jan Opolský, *Představení v soumraku*, edited by Ivan Slavík (Prague, 1968).
57   *Slovník českých spisovatelů* (Prag, 1968); Čeští spisovatelé z přelomu 19. a 20. století (Prague, 1972).
58   Jan Ort [Pavel Eisner] (ed.), *Příběhy uplynulého času* (Hradec Králové, 1977) and Jan Ort (ed.), *Příběhy o lidech a zvířatech* (Hradec Králové, 1980). Eisner is best known for his monumental tribute to the Czech language *Chrám i tvrz* (Prague, 1946).
59   Jan Ort, [postscript], *Příběhy o lidech a zvířatech*, p. 481.
60   Jiří Kudrnáč (ed.), 'Drobná próza české secese', *Vteřiny duše* (Prague, 1989), p. 21.

In 1995, Opolský is accorded two pages in the Czech Academy's four-volume dictionary of Czech writers. However, in the Czechoslovak Academy's four-volume history of Czech literature, the last volume of which was completed in 1969 but published belatedly in 1995, he is mentioned largely only as a contributor to the journals *Lumír*, *Nový kult* and *Šibeničky*.[61] Also in 1995, Slavík resumed his efforts to rehabilitate Opolský by including his introduction to *Představení v soumraku* in a new volume called *Viděno jak*, a collection of studies of neglected and otherwise marginalized writers.[62] In two other essays in this collection, he argued for the influence of Opolský on poets like František Halas and Bohuslav Reynek. In a long article on the Czech Decadence, Jaroslav Med called Opolský one of the most talented poets in the group around *Moderní revue*.[63] In 2000, Hana Bednaříková, in her book-length study of the Czech Decadence, used Opolský's prose to demonstrate a quality she calls 'fragmentisation' (*fragmentizace*) that she considers to be a central and defining characteristic of Decadent narrative.[64]

These expressions of scholarly interest were amplified by further attempts at popularization. In 1999, Slavík included Opolský in an anthology of Czech mystery stories called *Příběhy temnot*.[65] In 2004, an anthology of Opolský's verse entitled *Sám všechen život býti* was made available in Petr Fabian's internet edition *Zapomenuté světlo*, accompanied by a small numbered paper edition.[66] In late 2010, an anthology of Opolský's prose and poetry was published under the title *Staré lesy*, with an introduction by Václav Cílek and a postscript by Pavel Kostiuk.[67] With forty-three poems and only seven prose pieces, the ratio of poetry to prose that we had in Slavik's anthology is reversed. However, far from reflecting a disregard for Opolský's prose, the preference for his poetry in this edition is intended to redress the imbalance allegedly created by Slavík's anthology.[68] Another anthology of Opolský's verse is planned by Host publishing house as part of its *Česká knižnice* series but is unlikely to be published before 2018.

Recognition of Opolský outside Bohemia has been even patchier. In his invaluable, and otherwise remarkably thorough, *Tschechische Erzählkunst im 20. Jahrhundert*, Heinrich Kunstmann does not give Opolský so much as

---

61   Jan Mukařovský et al. (ed.) *Dějiny české literatury* (Prague 1959–1995), 4 vols, vol. 4 (*Literatura od konce 19. století do roku 1945*), pp. 31, 39, 355.
62   Ivan Slavík, *Viděno jinak* (Brno, 1995).
63   Jaroslav Med, 'Česká symbolistně-dekadentní literatura'.
64   Hana Bednaříková, *Česká dekadence*.
65   Ivan Slavík (ed.), *Příběhy temnot* (Brno, 1999).
66   Jan Opolský, *Sám všechen život býti*, edited by Petr Fabian, available online at: *www.petr-fabian.cz/ zapomenute/opolsky*
67   Jan Opolský, *Staré lesy*, edited by Václav Cílek and Pavel Kostiuk (Prague, 2011).
68   Václav Cílek, introduction, in Jan Opolský, *Staré lesy*, p. 11.

a passing mention.[69] Robert Pynsent mentions Opolský's early verse in his study of Julius Zeyer and the Czech Decadence, but does not return to him in any of his subsequent publications.[70] Walther Schamschula mentions Opolský only in the second volume of his three-volume history of Czech literature, thereby effectively eclipsing after Opolsky's work after 1918.[71] Andreas Leben provides a rare account of Opolský as a prose writer.[72] In her history of Czech literature, Hana Voisine-Jechová deals with Opolský alongside the major Decadent writers and accords equal weight to his poetry and his prose.[73] Other literary historians mention Opolský only in passing or fail to mention him at all.[74]

Of late, Václav Cílek has been eager to promote Opolský as a subject for a student dissertations and seems to have persuaded the Czech literature department at Prague University to include him in a list of recommended topics for bachelor's theses.[75] In Prague no bachelor's thesis has been forthcoming but in 2010 Lucie Horčíková submitted a master's thesis on Opolský's prose. Unfortunately, despite its encouraging focus, this thesis fails to question the conventional view of Opolský as a Decadent epigon.[76] The same is true of Kateřina Dutšuková's bachelor's thesis devoted to the poetics of *art nouveau* in the works of Jan Opolský and Růžena Svobodová, submitted to Brno University in 2013. This thesis makes special reference to 'Čínská povídka', the text I analyse in Chapter 9, but offers only a superficial interpretation along established lines.[77]

Opolský's prose and verse has occasionally been translated. Early translations of poetry into French (1928/1930) and Portuguese (1958) were followed

---

69 Heinrich Kunstmann, *Tschechische Erzählkunst im 20. Jahrhundert* (Cologne, 1974).

70 Robert Pynsent, *Julius Zeyer: The Path to Decadence* (The Hague, 1971).

71 Walter Schamschula, *Geschichte der tschechischen Literatur*, 3 vols (Köln, 1990–2004), vol. 2 (*Von der Romantik bis zum zweiten Weltkrieg*) and vol. 3 (*Von der Gründung der Republik bis zur Gegenwart*).

72 Andreas Leben, *Aesthetizismus und Engagement: die Kurzprosa der tschechischen und slovakischen Moderne* (Vienna, 1997), p. 109.

73 Hana Voisine-Jechová, *Histoire de la littérature tchèque* (Paris, 2001).

74 Zofia Tarajło-Lipowska, *Historia literatury czeskiej* (Wrocław, 2010), p. 220, mentions Opolský as a symbolist poet, listing him rather oddly alongside Antonín Klášterský and Emanuel z Lešehradu. Antonín Měšťan, *Geschichte der tschechischen Literatur im 19. und 20. Jahrhundert* (Cologne, 1984), fails to mention Opolský at all.

75 Václav Cílek, introduction, in Jan Opolský, *Staré lesy*, p. 11; the list (available online at *www.cl.ff.cuni.cz/menu/soubory/bak_temata.doc*) specifies: 'Jan Opolský – monografická studie zaměřené zejména na inspirace a paralely výtvarné, na malířskost slohu, na situování do rámce expresionismu a symbolismu.'

76 Lucie Horčíková, ,Jan Opolský a jeho prozaické dílo v dobovém kontextu', M.A. thesis, Charles University Prague, January 2011, available online at https://is.cuni.cz/webapps/zzp/detail/93895

77 Kateřina Dutšuková, ,Poetika secese v díle Jana Opolského a Růženy Svobodové', B.A. thesis, Masaryk University Brno, May 2013, available online at https://is.muni.cz/th/261748/ff_m

by translations into Polish (1983). His prose has fared less well, but the title piece of Slavík's anthology, 'Představení v soumraku', is now available in Polish, German and Dutch versions.[78]

---

78   A number of poems were published in French in Jitka Utlerová (ed.), *Recueil de poèmes tchèques* (Pilsen, 1928) and Hanuš Jelínek (ed.), *Anthologie de la poésie tchèque* (Paris, 1930); and in Portuguese in *Vértice*, 18 (1958). Several poems have appeared in Polish in Jacek Baluch (ed.), *Czescy symboliści, dekadenci, anarchiści przełomu XIX i XX wieku* (Wrocław, 1983). 'Představení v soumraku', has been translated as 'Predstawenie o zmierzchu', in Andrzej Sławomir Jagodziński (ed.), *Czas i śmierć: Antologia czeskich opowiadań grozy z XIX i początków XX wieku* (Łódź, 1989); 'Vorstellung in der Dämmerung' in Ivan Slavík (ed.), *Zum roten Drachen: Geheimnisvolle Geschichten* (Berlin, 1989, and Frankfurt, 1990); and 'Voorstelling in het schemerdonker' in Wil Hansen and Kees Merckes (eds), *Praag en het fin-de-siècle* (Amsterdam, 1999), pp. 166–173.

3. CRITICAL OPINION ON THE PROSE OEUVRE

Opolský's prose production consists of some two hundred and seventy short pieces that are difficult to categorize in terms of genre, mainly because of their length. With only a few exceptions (some early prose poems and the fifteen-page *Stradivari*), they run to between 500 and 2000 words or between one and a half and six printed pages. As Jiří Kudrnáč has pointed out, many writers of the day wrote short prose pieces.[79] However, compared to the other pieces Kudrnáč has collected in his *Vteřiny duše*, Opolský's prose pieces are conspicuous for their shortness. They are also conspicuous for their heavily descriptive style and lack of dialogue, which sets them apart from the work of writers like Marcel Schwob, to which they are sometimes compared.

Opolský himself seems to have used, or tacitly endorsed, a variety of terms to describe his prose pieces. 'Pohár', 'Sudba' and 'Pavla', for example, are referred to as *povídky*; 'Snář', 'Zastřený hlas' and 'Mimo život' as črty; and 'Zázračná oslava' and 'Před pohřbem' as *novely*. 'Prostory světa', 'Básníci', 'Felicien Rops' and 'Biedermeier' are labelled as *eseje*; 'Řecké idyly' and 'Pracovníci různých národů' as *články*; and 'Vývoj poslanectví', 'Volná kapitola' and 'Tartufferie' as úvaha, *polemika* and *sloupek*, respectively. In addition to these conventional labels, Opolský also borrows terms from the field of art. 'Poledne' and 'Vnitřek chrámu' are called *žánrové obrázky*, while 'Na pranýři' is termed a *barevná skizza*. By identification with the title of the collection in which they occur, numerous pieces are referred to as *medailony, kresby uhlem, miniatury*.

Since recognition of Opolský's prose has been patchy, the survey of critical opinion offered here has had to avail itself not only of histories of literature, literary lexicons and academic monographs, but also of contemporary book reviews in periodicals and newspapers. Some of the passages quoted refer only to Opolský's prose, while others deal with both his prose and his verse, often equating the one to the other.

I have given priority to texts that make a serious and substantial attempt to characterize Opolsky's prose as a whole. This has meant neglecting early reviews because of their tendency to focus heavily on the specific content of an individual collection or even individual prose pieces.

---

79   Jiří Kudrnáč, ,Drobná próza české secese', in Václav Cílek (ed.), *Vteřiny duše* (Prague, 1989).

Tento básník od svého vystoupení stojí v romantickém zápolení s mocnostmi života a se zjevy skutečnosti. Jeho oči, přetvářející životní děje v grotesky, a všecky jeho smysly vnímají ze skutečnosti jen jakési stínové reflexy zjevu; jeho myšlení stejně zkresluje materiál smyslový. Ilusionista, šálený smysly i mozkem, zoufale bije do začarovaného kruhu a podezírá. Ulpívá proto na postřehu a analysuje jej s maniakální tvrdošíjností. Píše-li prózu, tož jí schází všecka epičnost.[80]
Antonín Hartl (1922)

[Jeho prózy jsou] v sobě ukončené, výpravně jen slabě zhodnocené kusy minuciosního malíře iniciál a iluminací. Umělec v nich dává vyžehovat nepředvídaným sdružením barev a třpytů, drahokamovým duhám a kovovým akordům; zavěšuje do vzduchu hudebné figury, kříší symboly pro symboly. S vážností a svrchovanou úctou k slovu subtilnímu a vypočtenému vytváří tak kusy ryzí nečasové krásy a absolutní samo-účelnosti.[81]
Josef B. Čapek (1926)

Jeho prózy jsou povídky, či spíše jen epické náznaky zasazené do širokého deskriptiv-ního a lyrického rámce. Jsou to intensivní a intuitivní evokace zapadlých světů podané s bohatým vylíčením kulturního prostředí i s jemnou pointou nejčastěji tragickou.[82]
Karel Hikl (1926)

Na dně těchto próz vždy virtuosně propracovaných šklebí se hořká resignace života, vykoupená jistě těžkými obětmi, poněvadž její výraz má přesvědčující opravdovost a osudovost, nevývratné poznání nicoty všeho pozemského a trpné vědomí marnosti i bláhovosti lidské touhy.[83]
Jan O. Novotný 1 (1926)

[...] projevuje se všudy vzácným umělcem slova a věty až do nejrafinovanějších od-stínů, [...] rozvíje tu [v jeho prózách] s virtuositou svrchovaného umělce svoje umné periody, zkrášlené obrazy, které mnohdy jsou samy sobě účelem.[84]
Jan O. Novotný 2 (1926)

Citovou zkušeností Jana Opolského stala se samota a melancholie. Měl ruce příliš cho-ré, než aby rozhoupal zvony světa. A srdce se mu stahovalo trpkostí, jež jej předurčila k výjimečnosti a věčnému smutku. Zamiloval si slovo, s jeho těžkou, volné tekoucí krá-sou rytmované melodie a zapomínal v jeho uspávající moci, že pro něho nikdy dnešek

---

80   Antonín Hartl, (Review of *Muka a zdání*) *Nové Čechy*, 5 (1922), p. 231.
81   Josef B. Čapek, 'Nové prosy Jana Opolského', *Národní osvobození*, 3 (1926), p. 4.
82   Karel Hikl, (Review of *Z těžkého srdce*) *Naše doba*, 34 (1926–7), p. 57.
83   Jan O. Novotný, (Review of *Malé prosy* and *Z těžkého srdce*) *Cesta*, 9 (1926–7), pp. 208–9 (p. 208).
84   Jan O. Novotný, pp. 208–9 (p. 209).

nebude dneškem [...]. Pečuje o slovo básnické, stával se jeho ciselérem. Koval je zvolna, s pečlivostí člověka, jenž je toliko jím sdružen s dalekým světem.

Nemoha nalézti dosti živných látek v přítomnosti, tvořil si mythus, fresku a baladické básně v prose. Umdlený a citlivý bojoval o tělo a smyslnost.

Základem všeho tvoření zůstala mu stylisace přísná, nečasová a barokně vzepřená. Dospíval jí k látkám historickým, jež si přetvořoval dle obrazu duše, ponořen v onen věčný, lethargický sen, který vypíjel jeho umělecké zdraví a dával zmrzati jeho rozběhu. [85]
Pavel Fraenkl 1 (1927)

Je zapředen do své nirvany, světa přísné odloučeného, nehybného a zapomenutého. Věčné mlčení smrti, z něhož vyzařuje časem pouze blesk orientální smyslnosti, či renessanční smyslové pohody dusí se v jeho prostředí. [86]
Pavel Fraenkl 2 (1927)

Všechno, co zařadilo Jana Opolského jako samostatného umělce vedle dekadence, jejímž je posledním věrným synem, je jeho výraz [...]. Slovo zvolna odvažované a těžce, ba pracně vyhledávané. Rytmus, který je krví. Melodie, která zpívá s oblou vláčností a hýřivou radostí, ze sebe samé. [87]
Pavel Fraenkl 3 (1927)

Vyšed z dekadentního aristokratismu, dekorativního symbolismu a estétského l'art--pour-l'artismu, [...] nepozměňuje nic na své podobizně, představující zaníceného obnovovatele zašlých obrazů, milovníka asketických linií a renesančně rozkošnických barev, pietního klenotníka slova a trpělivého ciseléra metafory a rytmu. [88]
Antonín M. Píša (1927)

[Jeho prózy jsou] pečlivé a zálibné drobnomalby na historickém podkladu, jsou to krajinné evokace, erotické výbuchy, místa vzdutého athosu, střídajícího se s líčením mdlobných stavů. Zatvrzelý ilusionism Opolského leckdy má znak skutečného poustevnictví, jež nesmlouvá se skutečností, jindy však se blíží rozmlsanému kochání, jež obšírně a vychutnávačsky se probírá svými motivy. [89]
Jaromír Borecký (1928)

[Jeho prózy jsou] pořád příběhy, jež jaksi symbolisují [...] stanovisko odvratu od bezprostředních realit a zahledění do světa umění [...]. Jsou to historie životního odvratu a bolestné klausury; je to estétství, jež více cení umění než život.[90]
František Götz (1928)

85 Pavel Fraenkl, 'Opolského malé prosy', *Sever a východ*, 3 (1927), pp. 107–8 (p. 107).
86 Pavel Fraenkl, pp. 107–8 (p. 108).
87 Pavel Fraenkl, pp. 107–8 (p. 108).
88 Antonín M. Píša, (Review of *Malé prosy*) *Pramen*, 7 (1927–8), p. 61.
89 Jaromír Borecký, (Review of *Víry i tůně*) *Zvon*, 29 (1928–9), p. 166.
90 František Götz, (Review of *Víry a tůně*) *Národní osvobození*, 5 (1928), p. 4.

Il y a une indéniable parenté intime entre Karel Hlaváček et M. Jan Opolský. La même incurable tristesse, la même nostalgie amère dort au fond de ces deux poètes [...]. Depuis quelques années, M. Opolský aime à composer, en prose d'un rythme parfait, de petits contes decoratifs, écrits de préference comme en marge de l'histoire d'art. [...] Avec un amour et une pitié qui rappellent les vieux moines enlumineurs, la main du poète dessine, avec un art suprême, des arabesques et des miniatures historiques; certaines de ces pièces sont comme de rares bibelots taillés dans l'ivorie; elles compteront parmi les pages les plus parfaits de la prose tchèque. [91]
Hanuš Jelínek (1935)

Opolský [...] od přítomna a reálné skutečnosti utíkal k minulosti, ať dějepravné nebo legendární. Arci nezřídka tak nevyjadřoval než sváteční vteřiny a stavy duše, ne-li půlnoční, podsvětné její vidiny a halucinace. Psychologicky to značí odvrácení od denního střízlivého světa a hlubší ponor v temnoty vnitřní. Koncepčně a skladebně definitivní odklon od epiky k lyrisující básni prózou, hledání a volbu námětu spíš jen jako záminky k poetické reflexi, bizarní dušemalbě nebo složitému deskriptivnímu ornamentu. [92]
Karel Sezima 1 (1935)

V próze vyšed od dřevorytových evokací minulosti a kreseb lidí osamocených a odvrácených od života, od nedůtklivých bdělých básnických vidin, pokusil se vyrovnati i se skutečností popřevratovou, kterou odmítl, nemoha se v poměru k ní dobrati stanoviska jasného a postihujícího kořenu dění. Zůstal subjektivistou, zavěšujícím v zřídlém vzduchu odtažité hudební figury. [93]
Bedřich Václavek (1935)

Opolský je vskutku slovní zlatotepec. Dovede užívat slov jak v jejich zvuku tak významu, že jsou tolik, co věci samy. Dovede je však uvádět v proud významných vět tu klidně ubíhajících, tu toužících, ale vždy dopravujících čtenáře do krajů zvláštní krásy ať vysněné, bájné nebo historicky věrné, oživené lidmi podivuhodnými, znící myšlenkami hlubokými a hýřícími obrazy jímavé krásy.[94]
František Skácelík (1938)

Meditativní fantastik a hořký melancholik samotářských sklonů vyšel ze vzrušeného dění let devadesátých a podle toho plnil obrazy, skládané ze skutečných v osobité celky, dusnou soumračnou náladou, v jejíž těžké atmosféře je zaklet celý jeho životní pesimismus. [95]
Jaroslav Kunc 1 (1945)

91   Hanuš Jelínek, *Histoire de la littérature tchèque*, 3 vols, (Paris, 1930–5), III, pp. 106–7.
92   Karel Sezima, (Review of *Visuté zahrady*) *Lumír*, 62 (1935–6), pp. 75–84.
93   Bedřich Václavek, *Česká literatura XX. století*, (Prague, 1935), p. 51.
94   František Skácelík, (Review of *Pod patinou věků*) *Samostatnost*, 14 July 1938, p. 3.
95   Jaroslav Kunc, 'Jan Opolský', in *Slovník soudobých českých spisovatelů*, edited by Jaroslav Kunc, 2 vols (Prague, 1945–6), I, pp. 61–20 p. 616).

Odstíněný impresionista pečoval hlavně o formu a styl, při čemž základním akordem je mu smutek duše, který je mu i východiskem k hlubokým pohledům do tajů života a stvoření. K smutku jako k inspiračnímu zdroji se pojí ještě stesk a resignace bez schopnosti vzdoru a výbojnosti. [96]
Jaroslav Kunc 2 (1945)

Samou starostí o krásu věty a stavbu verše nechal však svět jít kolem, vše viděl jako obraz, jeho fantasie malovala dávný svět vysněných postav. Podvědomá hořkost byla navozena do barokní nádhery dekadentními souvislostmi. [97]
Jaroslav Kunc 3 (1945)

Jako prozaik jevil Opolský zvláštní zálibu v krátké povídce, jejímiž hrdiny bývají lidé vnitřně uzavřené, zakletí do svého snu, jejichž život je sice tichý, ale vášnivý, svět představ vzrušeny, smrt zlá. Střídá báchorky a legendy, vise a evokace, fresky a miniatury, pohledy do oblasti snu a imaginace, soustředěnou kontemplaci i kouzlo zešeřelých nálad. [98]
Jaroslav Kunc 4 (1945)

Barokní, bohatá a tíživá moc pěstěného výrazu i krása zjemnělých smyšlených invencí ukazují jasně k dekadentní konstelaci Opolského inspiraci i v próze: zetlívající síla, do minulosti ponořený pohled, morbidní únava z konce století, samota, nehybnost a divý žal. Těžce rytá slova mu nahrazují skutečný život, pathos mystických abstrakcí nedovoluje črtám dějového rozvinutí.[99]
Jaroslav Kunc 5 (1945)

Rytmické básně prózou, psychologické miniatury a legendárními náměty i symbolickým jinotajem jsou psány pro rozkoš výtvarného dojmu, smyslového vnímání, ozřejmení významu umění. Problematika umělcova růstu je často až do krajnosti domyšlena a obrazy seskupovány s mnišskou askesí a schopností průkaznou logikou rozvésti náladový šerosvit i skvělou kombinaci barev. Opolský je v uctívaní krásy a v úctě ke slovu podoben starým mistrům, malířům iniciál i alchymistům, tolik neúmorného úsilí věnuje poznání osobitého života tvaru a jeho obrazné krystalizaci. [100]
Karel Sezima 2 (1945)

Unaven světskou marností vítá poselství smrti, ale jeho nihilismus má opravdový básnický ethos, který teprve budoucnost docení. Obrazný stavitel a hudební melodik

---

96   Jaroslav Kunc, pp. 616–20 (pp. 616–7).
97   Jaroslav Kunc, pp. 616–20 (p. 617).
98   Jaroslav Kunc, pp. 616–29 (p. 618).
99   Jaroslav Kunc, pp. 616–20 (p. 619).
100   Karel Sezima, *Z mého života*, 4 vols (Prague, 1946–9), vol. 2, p. 170.

nachází však i kouzlo teskné gracie, jež proudí ze života věcí, byť často až marnotratně hýřila skvělými vidmy a přece je ve výsledném dojmu upravovala do střídmé harmonie a meditace. V hrdém osamocení se uchýlil po mnohém vystřízlivění do samoty svého umění, příliš raněn v illusionismu a krasocitu. [101]

Karel Sezima 3 (1945)

[Jeho prózy jsou] v sobě ukončené, výpravně jen slabě zhodnocené kusy minuciosního malíře iniciál a iluminací. Umělec v nich dává vyžehovat nepředvídaným sdružením barev a třpytů, drahokamovým duhám a kovovým akordům; zavěšuje do vzduchu hudebné figury, křísí symboly pro symboly. S vážností a svrchovanou úctou k slovu subtilnímu a vypočtenému vytváří tak kusy ryzí nečasové krásy a absolutní samoúčelnosti. [102]

Karel Sezima 4 (1946)

[Jeho prózy jsou] dějově omezené portréty, reprodukce legend i stránek dějinných, jež básník odívá ve skvělé roucho slovní, lesknoucí se vybranými epithety a příměry, prohlubuje psychologicky a zintensivňuje v náladové sdílnosti. Některé z próz jako by nebyly více než básněmi v próze, které rozechvívají vnitřní rytmikou, znějící ve hlubokých polohách stlumenými tóny, jiné mají stupňování až k vyznívající pointě, která je zdůvodňuje. [103]

Karel Sezima 5 (1946)

Poezie J. Karáska a K. Hlaváčka byla vzorem Opolského hudebně naladěným veršům i lyrickým prózám, které prostřednictvím symbolů a metaphor vyjadřovaly pesimistický a krajně subjektivistický vztah k životu. Když zbavil svou tvorbu počáteční stylizovanosti a dekorativnosti, zůstal stále tlumočníkem prchavých nálad a bezútěšného životního pocitu. [104]

Dalibor Holub (1964)

Opolský byl možná špatný malíř štětcem, ale malíř slova byl takový, jako je málo. [...] Volil malý prostor miniatury, protože právě malý rozměr dovoloval zpracování dokonalé a absolutní, a filigránská drobnost umožňovala prokázat umělecké mistrovství. [105]

Ivan Slavík 1 (1968)

---

101   Karel Sezima, 'Brusič slovesných drahokamů'.
102   Karel Sezima, *Z mého života*, 4 vols (Prague, 1946–9), II, p. 170.
103   Karel Sezima, *Z mého života*, 4 vols (Prague, 1946–9), II, p. 170.
104   Dalibor Holub, 'Jan Opolský', in *Slovník českých spisovatelů*, edited by the Ústav pro českou literaturu ČSAV (Prague, 1964), p. 371.
105   Ivan Slavík, 'Básník miniatur a devadesátá léta', in Ivan Slavík (ed.) *Představení v soumraku* (Prague, 1968), p. 18–19; reprinted in Ivan Slavík, *Viděno jinak* (Brno, 1995), p. 121–122.

Jeho přístup k materiálu jazyka je vysloveně malířský. Vybírá pečlivě výraz, váží spojení tak, aby stín jednoho slova podtrhl blyštící hranu jiného [...]; některé jeho drobné prózy jsou ve pravém slova smyslu obrazové kompozice, ne děj a příběh, nýbrž scéna a výjev, nebo dokonce se zálibou a rozkoší zaranžované 'zátiší'.[106]
Ivan Slavík 2 (1968)

Některé miniatury jsou cosi jako 'obnovené obrazy', řečeno po zeyerovsku. Jsou z nejrůznějších dob a zemí [...]. Ale srovnáme-li je se Zeyerem, vynikne odlišnost. Na rozdíl od něho je jejich epická složka skrovná, příběhy jsou rozvinutý jen náznakově a výsledek je statický obraz, uzavřený do jedné scény. A ty doby a místa jsou celkem vedlejší. Je to vždy tátež snaha koncentrovat atmosféru, zastavit gesto a vnímat [...] barvy, tóny, vůně. Mám za to, že některý Opolského miniatury jsou nejčistší projev symbolismu v naší próze. Připomíná mi to Marcela Schwoba a ze starších Aloysia Bertranda s jeho *Kašparem noci*.[107]
Ivan Slavík 3 (1968)

Je jenom přírozené, že hlavními postavami miniatur tohoto slovního malíře jsou tak často dávní iluminatoři, cizeléři, řezbáři, sochaři, kteří úzkostlivě, pečlivě a v mlčení vypracovávají své dílo, v němž se pojí dokonalost ovládání řemesla s uměním. Byl totíž sám jeden z nich. [...] Když Opolský věc pojmenovává, jako by na ni sahal, opatrně, jemně a s jakýmsi něžným steskem na křehkostí krásy, jako by ji obracel v pozorných prstech a pak ji kladl přesně na místo, kam patří.[108]
Ivan Slavík 4 (1968)

Hervorgegangen aus der Dekadenz, besingt Opolský in symbolreicher Sprache Einsamkeit, Trauer, Enttäuschung, steigert sich bis zum Nihilismus und vermag weder in seiner Lyrik noch in den Kurzgeschichten den düsteren Pessimismus zu überwinden.[109]
Elisabeth Pribić (1975)

K Hlaváčkovi a Kvapilové se [...] druží Jan Opolský, nejpilnější prozaik českého symbolismu, jemuž zůstal věrný po celých čtyřicet let své tvorby. Je to autor z českých spisovatelů nejbližší Marcelu Schwobovi, který jako on přerušuje epický oblouk svých malých příběhů v momentě kolize nebo krize, a opatřuje je tak ironickou pointou. Tím-

---

106 Ivan Slavík, 'Básník miniatur a devadesátá léta', in Ivan Slavík (ed.) *Představení v soumraku* (Prague, 1968), p. 17; reprinted in Ivan Slavík, *Viděno jinak* (Brno, 1995), p. 121.
107 Ivan Slavík, 'Básník miniatur a devadesátá léta', in Ivan Slavík (ed.) *Představení v soumraku* (Prague, 1968), p. 17–18; reprinted in Ivan Slavík, *Viděno jinak* (Brno, 1995), p. 121.
108 Ivan Slavík, 'Básník miniatur a devadesátá léta', in Ivan Slavík (ed.) *Představení v soumraku* (Prague, 1968), p. 18; reprinted in Ivan Slavík, *Viděno jinak* (Brno, 1995), p. 121–122.
109 Elisabeth Pribić, 'Jan Opolský', in *Lexikon der Weltliteratur*, edited by Gero von Wilpert, 2 vols (Stuttgart, 1975), I, p. 214.

to způsobem portrétoval Opolský své současníky, historické a mytologické osobnosti a dokonce zvířata a věci. Básnicky nejsilnější je Opolský tenkrát, když bez historických a literárních rekvizit nachází symbol v reálné krajině, [...] a předkládá jej čtenáři zvláště vnímavému.[110]

Jiří Kudrnáč (1989)

Ein Charakteristikum von Opolskýs Stil ist die [...] ästhetische Sprache. Man kann darin eine spezielle Form der Antithese erkennen, die sich als zentrales Stilelement in verschiedenen Varianten wie ein roter Faden durch Opolskýs Texte zieht. [...] Andere frequente Stilmittel sind refrainartige Wiederholungen von Sätzen und semantischen Einheiten und Assonanzen. [...] Die Skizzen Opolskýs haben mit der symbolisch-dekadenten Literatur der neunziger Jahre die Subjektivität, den Pessimismus, die Desillusionierung sowie die Wahl der Stilmittel und die Typisierungen gemeinsam.[111]

Andreas Leben (1997)

Důsledkem měnící se a proměňované percepce je [...] fenomén tříštění a *fragmentarizace* celku, důsledky těchto estetických procesů následně vedou například právě k oblibě detailizovaného ornamentu nebo dekorativního bibelotu, který se stává nositelem estetické energie a napětí. [...]
Obdobné postupy, které vycházejí z principu iluzivní deformace, lze najít také v prózách Jana Opolského. Evokace chátrajícího objektu se v rámci tohoto typu imaginativní perspektivy mění téměř v ornamentální bibelot. Povšimneme-li se například způsobu, jakým Opolský pracuje s detailem právě v rámci fragmentarizované deskripce, jejímž předmětem je banální výsek skutečnosti, docházíme k zajímavým zjištěním – nahodilý objekt může prostřednictvím prizmatické interiorizace získat až halucinativní ráz. [...] [Ž]enský účes se stává dekorativním objektem manýristické evokace [...]. Sugestivní tragika až s existenciálním nápětím se prolíná s evokací podzimní scenérie.[112]

Hana Bednaříková 1 (2000)

Kategorie fragmentu, která zaujímá v rámci dekadentní estetiky jednu z ústředních pozic, bezesporu souvisí [...] s procesy, které směřují k dekompozici či decentralizaci. Základní představa celistvosti uměleckého díla pak jíž nebude vycházet se souborů usouvstažitelných prvků, [...] ale bude se jednat spíše [o] jisté řetězení (řady ornamentů, symbolů atd.) *dekomponovaných komponent*, jejichž možná interpretace bude odvoditelná od individualizované perspektivy subjektu.

---

110 Jiří Kudrnáč, 'Drobná próza české secese', pp. 4–34.
111 Andreas Leben, *Aesthetizismus und Engagement: die Kurzprosa der tschechischen und slovakischen Moderne* (Vienna, 1997), p. 109.
112 Hana Bednaříková, *Česká dekadence* (Brno, 2000), p. 70, 71.

Jednou z možností uplatnění tohoto typu estatizované fragmentarizace jsou akribistic-ké evokace, charakteristické především pro postupy Karla Hlaváčka, v próze se obdoba tohoto typu ulpívání uplatňuje ve velké míře například v textech Jana Opolského.[113]
Hana Bednaříková 2 (2000)

Paralelně s poezií psal O. krátké lyrické prózy s minimalizovaným dějem, v kterých směřoval od sevřených expresionistických obrazů, zachycujících propracovaným jazy-kem fantaskní a bizarní situace, scény násilí a katastrof, přezrálou erotiku a tesknou bezútěšnost *(Kresby uhlem)*, k traktování námětů z různých kultur a období, jednak pohádek a legend, jednak i osobitých vizí a evokací historie; často pro ně volil postavy výtvarných a řemeslných umělců, hudebníků a herců, jejichž duševní stavy, pocity a filozofii koncentroval na pozadí stylizované autonomní reality do poetické zkratky. Vzdálený a výlučný svět reprodukoval s bohatou imaginací, důrazem na detail a sna-hou objevit a postihnout tajemství vnitřní podstaty předmětů a věcí *(Muka a zdání, Visuté zahrady)*. V tvorbě O. se díky jeho zvláštním dispozicím také výrazně uplatnil dobový trend přelomu století, směřující k synkrezi slovesného a výtvarného umění a projevující se též sílícím zájmem o krásnou knihu a knižní grafiku; tomuto zaměření také odpovídaly bibliofilské edice většiny jeho prací.[114]
Jiří Zizler (2000)

[Opolský patřil k] nejtalentovanějším básníkům skupiny *Moderní revue* [...]. Svým de-butem *(Svět smutných*, 1899) a dalšími děma sbírkami *(Klekání*, 1900; *Jedy a léky*, 1901) zaujal pevné místo v české symbolistně-dekadentní poezii. Veškerá jeho básnická tvorba z přelomu století je prodchnutá adoracemi smutku a zmaru. Jeho poezie měla hudebností blízko k tvorbě K. Hlaváčka, svými autostylizačními převleky a bohatým využíváním pohádkových a romaneskních motivů (loupežníci, rytíři, vlkodlaci apod.) pak souzněla s touhou symbolistně-dekandentní literatury po co největší exotičnosti a bizarnosti. Trojice básnických knih z přelomu století představuje patrně vrchol veškeré Opolského tvorby. Další rozsáhlá literární činnost (převažovala v ní drobná próza) zůstávala poplatná atmosféře devadesátých let.[115]
Jaroslav Med (2001)

Comme dans tous les pays marqués par la sensibilité fin de siècle, on trouve en Bohème des poètes de la déception et la vanité, hantés par des désarrois sentimentaux, par une sexualité provocante et culpabilisante et par l'agnosticisme, voire par un nihilisme sans issue. [...] Chez certains, elle réprésente la dominante de leur création littéraire. Tel est le cas du poète, consideré comme le plus proche de Hlaváček et de Karásek, Jan

---

113   Hana Bednaříková, *Česká dekadence* (Brno, 2000), p. 105.
114   Jiří Zizler, 'Jan Opolský' in *Lexikon české literatury* (Prague, 1985–2009), edited by Jiří Opelík et al., 4 vols, vol. 3/1 (2000), p. 682.
115   Jaroslav Med, 'Česká symbolistně-dekadentní literatura', in *Česká literatura na předělu století* (Prague, 2001), edited by Petr Čornej et al., p. 87.

Opolský [...], auteur de nombreux recueils de poésie [...]. Dans le l'esprit de l'éclectisme de l'époque, il a publié également des oeuvres en prose.[116]
Hana Voisine-Jechová (2001)

Opolského hudebně laděné verše i prózy vyjadřovaly prostřednictvím symbolů a metafor pesimistický vztah k životu. I když se jich později zbavil, stále zůstával básníkem prchavých nálad. [...] Na jeho tvorbu měl vliv J. Karásek a K. Hlaváček.[117]
Václav Cílek (2011)

What emerges from this survey of critical opinion is that interpretations of Opolský are fundamentally unevolving. There is a clear concensus that Opolský is a late Decadent writer who has modelled himself on more significant literary precursors and may to that extent be described as a Decadent epigon. None of the commentators makes any significant distinction between the orientation of his prose and his verse in this respect.

Sometimes the Decadence (in the Czech context often identified with the Symbolist movement) is alluded to directly (Fraenkl, Píša, Kunc, Pribić, Bednaříková), sometimes it is referred to indirectly via its principal representatives Karel Hlaváček and/or Jiří Karásek ze Lvovic (Jelínek, Cílek), by its principal organ, *Moderní revue* (Med), or by its core period, the eighteen nineties/*fin-de-siècle* (Kunc, Med, Voisine-Jechová).

To substantiate this attribution, Opolsky's work is said to display features standardly associated with the Decadence. These include aestheticism, a cult of *l'art pour l'art*, withdrawal from reality, resignation, morbidity, and elements of an aristocratic pose.

Josef Čapek, possibly inspired by the colourful initials in the semi-bibliophile edition of *Demaskování* that he is reviewing, compares Opolský to a painstaking illuminator of manuscripts ('minuciosní malíř iniciál a iluminací'), creating beauty for its own sake ('vytváří tak kusy ryzí nečasové krásy a absolutní samoúčelnosti'). Novotný, following suit, describes him as an artist of the word sensitive to the finest nuances of style ('vzácný umělec slova a věty až do nejrafinovanějších odstínů') creating decorative images largely for their own sake ('zkrášlené obrazy, které mnohdy jsou samy sobě účelem'). Fraenkl too sees Opolský as an artist enamoured with the rhythm and melody of language ('zamiloval si slovo, s jeho těžkou, volně tekoucí krásou rytmované melodie'), as an engraver carefully chiselling away at the surface of a precious material ('pečuje o slovo básnické, stával se jeho ciselérem'). Píša, borrowing both the idea and the imagery, makes the same point more awk-

---

116   Hana Voisine-Jechová, *Histoire de la littérature tchèque* (Paris, 2001).
117   Václav Cílek, introduction to Jan Opolský, *Staré lesy*, edited by Václav Cílek and Pavel Kostiuk (Prague, 2011).

wardly, describing Opolský as an engraver of metaphor and rhythm ('cise-lér metafory a rytmu') and a jeweller of the word ('klenotník slova'). Jelínek, not be outdone, draws on both the image of the illuminator and the image of the engraver, comparing Opolský's skill to that of medieval copyists ('vieux moines enlumineurs') and his work to exquisite curios cut in ivory ('de rares bibelots taillés dans l'ivoire'). The image of the engraver comes up again in Skacelík ('slovní zlatotepec'). Götz sees Opolský as an aesthete who care more about art than life ('je to estetství, jež více cení umění než život'). This idea is echoed by Kunc, who sees Opolský as a writer so obsessed with beauty and form that he has lost contact with reality ('samou starostí o krásu věty a stavbu verše nechal však svět jít kolem'). The range of critical metaphor is only marginally extended by Sezima, who compares Opolský's attitude to beauty and language to that of old masters, medieval illuminators (again) and (rather puzzlingly) alchymists ('Opolský je v uctívaní krásy a v úctě ke slovu podoben starým mistrům, malířům iniciál i alchymistům'). Also avail-ing himself of the image of the painter, Slavík sees Opolský as a painter of words ('malíř slov') and a painter of miniatures ('volil malý prostor minia-tury'), adding that Opolský treats language like a painter, carefully choosing his words for their aesthetic effect and painting static scenes rather than developing action-filled plots. He points out that Opolský is not merely like an artist in his writing but frequently writes about artists, especially ancient illuminators, engravers, woodcarvers and sculptors who combine mastery of their craft with art ('dávní iliuminatoři, cizeléři, řezbáři, sochaři, [v jejichž] dílo, [...] se pojí dokonalost ovládání řemesla s uměním').

Much is made of Opolský's alleged pessimism and resignation. Both Holub and Cílek refer to his pessimistic attitude to life ('pesimistický [...] vztah k životu'). Fraenkl mentions his bitterness and never-ending sadness ('trpkost and věčný smutek'), his melancholy and loneliness ('samota a mel-ancholie'); Jelínek sees him as suffering from the same incurable sadness and bitter nostaglia that affected Hlaváček ('la même incurable tristesse, la même nostalgie amère dort au fond de ces deux poètes'). Kunc describes him as an embittered melancholiac ('hořký melancholik') and mentions the existential pessimism (životní pesimismus') and deep sadness ('smutek duše') coupled with nostalgia and helpless resignation ('k smutku [...] se pojí [...] stesk a resignace bez schopnosti vzdoru a výbojnosti') that he believes pervades Opolský's work. For Novotný, Opolský's prose expresses a nihilistic despair born of a sense of the vanity of earthly life and human yearning ('nevývratné poznání nicoty všeho pozemského a trpné vědomí marnosti i bláhovosti lid-ské touhy'). Pribić concurs when she says that Opolský's work escalates into nihilism ('steigert sich bis zum Nihilismus'). Sezima even endows him with a death wish motivated by a disappointment with worldly vanity ('unaven světskou marností vítá poselství smrti').

Possibly mindful of Huysmann's *À rebours,* which has its Decadent hero des Esseintes retreat from society into a solitary world of art and artificiality, and Fedor Soldan's characterization of the Czech Decadence as a rejection of social realities, Sezima sees Opolský as a writer who is so obsessed with the past, with dark spiritual states and visions that he is effectively turning his back on normal reality ('psychologicky to značí odvrácení od denního střízlivého světa'). Götz echoes this idea when he speaks of a creative stance that rejects immediate realities and engrosses itself in art ('stanovisko odvratu od bezprostředních realit a zahledění do světa umění'), as does Václavek when he describes Opolský's art as based on the portrayal of isolated and withdrawn characters ('lidí osamocených a odvrácených od života'), the creation of abstract musical figures ('odtažité hudební figury') suspended in thin air ('v zřídlém vzduchu'). Píša sees this withdrawal from social reality as a Decadent artistocratic pose ('dekadentní aristokratism'). For Fraenkl, Sezima and Kunc, it is more an expression of morbid sentiment and effete enervation. Fraenkl sees Opolský as immersed in a lethargic dream that has sapped his artistic health and crippled his creative imagination ('ponořen v [...] lethargický sen, který vypíjel jeho umělecké zdraví a dával zmrzati jeho rozběhu'). Sezima finds him too frail and feeble to engage with the outside world ('měl ruce příliš choré, než aby rozhoupal zvony světa'), while Kunc speaks of a morbid *fin-de-siècle* weariness ('morbidní únava z konce století').

Hartl points to an element of what George Ross Ridge in his study of the French Decadence has called 'cerebralism': a tendency to emphasize intellectual processes and abstract ideas over sensory and emotional immediacy ('Ulpívá proto na postřehu a analysuje jej s maniakální tvrdošíjností').[118]

For Bednaříková, what makes Opolský's work truly Decadent is more a matter of form than content. It is not just that Decadent writers had a predilection for the short prose form, but that Opolský uses a technique she calls 'fragmentizace' ('fragmentization'): the tendency to treat details as if they were dissociated from the whole of which they are an integral part. She considers this concentration on the fragment to be typical of the Czech and European Decadence ('Kategorie fragmentu [...] zaujímá v rámci dekadentní estetiky jednu z ústředních pozic'). Opolský's 'Ruce', which describes various types of human hand as if they were independent physiological entities, serves as her prime example.

Irony is not mentioned by any critics with the exception of Kudrnáč, for whom the prose pieces often have an ironic conclusion ('ironická pointa'). The kind of irony he seems to have in mind here is the typical Laforguian twist in the tail that comically emphasizes the Decadent message rather than

---

118   George Ross Ridge, *The Hero in French Decadent Literature* (Athens GA, 1961)

relativizes it. It is a far cry from the sustained structural irony that I shall be describing.

As we shall try to show in the following textual analyses, these opinions are fundamentally misguided because they fail to take account of Opolský's thoroughgoing irony. Admittedly, most of the critics do in part capture something of the character of the narrator whom Opolský is ironizing, particularly since this narrator, as will become apparent, has certain Romantic and Decadent characteristics, but none of them considers the possibility that the identity of the narrator might be different from the identity of the author, still less the possibility that the narrator might be an ironic construct. Though many of those quoted are leading critics (Fraenkl, Píša, Sezima), literary historians (Jelínek, Götz, Kunc, Václavek) or academics (Pribić, Leben, Bednaříková, Med), the standard of argument and the degree of imaginative engagement with the texts fails to impress. It is particularly disturbing to see critics slavishly copying off each other: Already Hanuš Jelínek had compared Opolský to a 'moine illumineur', which presumably inspired Karel Sezima to refer to him a 'malíř iniciál'. Antonín Píša coined the term 'klenotník slova', which Pavel Fraenkl converted into 'ciselér básnického slova', František Skácelík into 'zlatotepec slova', and Karel Sezima into 'brusič slovesných drahokamů', each time with only minor variations to the image.

Even leaving aside the question of irony, the case for the Decadent nature of Opolský's writing is rather lame. Much is made of his aestheticism, his inveterate pessimism and tendency to withdraw from life, but there is no reference to the neurotic sensibility, the sensual erethism, the appetite for perversion and sexual deviance that are also thought to characterize the Decadence.

4. IRONY

Having shown how Opolsky's prose has been understood by fellow writers, critics and academics alike, we are now free to engage on the dauting task of reinterpretation. Since the elusive and often treacherous concept of irony will be central to this quest, it seems advisable to begin by trying to develop a shared understanding of key terms.

After enquiring into the feasibility and usefulness of an overarching definition of irony, the present chapter examines the concept of *verbal* (or *rhetorical* irony) and its literary extension *narrative* (or *structural*) irony. It then considers how verbal irony is recognized and processed, and what pitfalls verbal irony presents to comprehension, exposition and critical appreciation. Finally, conventional verbal and narrative irony are distinguished from related phenomena, such as Romantic irony, sarcasm, satire, parody and the burlesque; and the relationship between irony and Decadence is briefly reviewed.

4.1 AN ELUSIVE CONCEPT

Cleanth Brooks believes that the concept of irony has been overused, and at times even abused.[119] D. C. Muecke speaks of its 'cancerous growth' from the end of eighteenth century onwards.[120] There is no doubt that we now confront a bewildering array of different types of irony: *verbal, dramatic, tragic, situational, cosmic, historical, nihilistic, Socratic, Romantic, postmodern, representional, visual, ambient*, etc. Muecke draws up an even longer list and adds a few more of his own devising: *irony of simple incongruity, irony of dilemma, irony of self-betrayal*. To the range of putative types comes the length of the concept's history and the variety of its literary practitioners. Irony has been used by authors as diverse and distant (both culturally and historically) as Aristophanes, Plato, Cicero, Horace, Boccaccio, Chaucer, Cervantes, Molière, Fielding, Swift, Voltaire, Ihara Saikaku, Flaubert, Gogol, Dostoevsky, Shima-

119 Cleanth Brooks, 'Irony as a Principle of Structure', *Literary Opinion in America*, New York, 1937, edited by Morton Zabel, pp. 729-741.
120 D.C. Muecke, *The Compass of Irony* (London, 1969), p. 1.

zaki Tōson, Ibsen, de Queiroz, Yi Kwang-su, Proust, Kafka, Thomas Mann and Lu Xun. What is more, the concept of irony exists in a field of tension among related concepts like the sarcasm, parody, and burlesque, each of which may be complex in itself.

To make matters worse, in their investigation of irony, literary theorists and linguists have largely gone their separate ways. While linguists have concentrated on the semantic and pragmatic properties of simple conversational ironies, literary scholars have been interested mainly in the structure of complex and sustained textual ironies. Questions which are the centre of linguistic debate, such as the relative merits of the 'echo mention' and 'pretence' theories of irony, find little or no reflection in the work of literary theorists.[121] Equally, linguists show little concern for the work of literary scholars and often fail to acknowledge the work of leading theorists like Wayne Booth or D. C. Muecke. To an extent, the lack of communication between the two disciplines is understandable and the result of fundamental differences in their intellectual agendas, but just occasionally literary theory might benefit from lending an ear to linguistics (as I hope to show).

Given the concept's seemingly intractable diversity, it has become almost *de rigueur* for literary theorists to preface their studies of irony with rhetorical gestures of desperation. D. J. Enright speaks of a general feeling among scholars that 'to talk seriously about irony is to lay one's head on the block' and reflects that 'it is unfortunate, even ironical, that for so ubiquitous and multifarious [...] a phenomenon there should be but one word'.[122] For Patrick Hanan, studying irony in the modern Chinese writer Lu Xun, the term 'escaped long ago from the fold of critical definition, and has since led critics on a wild and exhilarating chase; its recapture does not seem imminent'. Muecke jokes that 'getting to grips with irony seems to have something in common with gathering the mist; there is plenty to take hold of if only one could.'[123]

In the face of such (theatrically reinforced) despondency, two impulses seem to prevail: one is to assiduously avoid the question of definition;

121 On the echo mention theory, see Dan Sperber and Deirdre Wilson, 'Irony and the use-mention distinction', in Peter Cole (ed.), *Radical Pragmatics* (New York, 1981), pp. 295–318; Dan Sperber and Deirdre Wilson, 'On Verbal Irony', *Lingua* 87 (1992) pp. 53–76. On the pretence theory, see Herbert Clark and Richard Gerrig, 'On the pretense theory of irony', *Journal of Experimental Psychology. General*, 113 (1984), pp. 121–126; Gregory Currie, 'Why irony is pretence', in Shaun Nichols (ed.) *The Archictecture of the Imagination* (Oxford, 2006). On the debate between the two accounts see Roger Kreuz and Sam Glucksberg, 'How to be sarcastic: the echoic reminder theory of verbal irony', *Journal of Experimental Psychology. General*, 116 (1989), pp. 374–386; Sachi Kumon-Nakamura et al., 'How about another piece of pie: the allusional pretense theory of discourse irony', *Journal of Experimental Psychology. General*, 124 (1995), pp. 3–21; Deirdre Wilson, 'The Pragmatics of Verbal Irony: Echo or Pretence?', *Lingua* 116 (2006), 1722–1743.
122 D.J. Enright, *The Alluring Problem* (Oxford, 1986), pp. 3 and 7.
123 Patrick Hanan, 'The Technique of Lu Hsün's Fiction', *Harvard Journal of Asiatic Studies*, 34 (1974), pp. 53–96 (p. 76).

the other is to see an attempt at definition against the odds as a potential remedy.

4.2 TO DEFINE OR NOT TO DEFINE

Most studies of irony in an individual writer eschew any broader definition of the term. Erich Heller's failure to define irony in his landmark study of irony in Thomas Mann has become legendary, but it is by no means unusual.[124] Eleanor Hutchen's book on irony in Fielding's *Tom Jones*, which provides reasoned definitions of both verbal and dramatic irony, constitutes a notable exception.[125] Many generalized or theoretical studies of irony are equally unconcerned with definition. Leading theorists like Beda Allemann, Wayne Booth, Clare Colebrook, and Pierre Schoentjes contrive to avoid the issue more or less elegantly.[126] Some scholars expressly defend non-definition. J. C. Cuddon argues that irony is as undefinable as humour:

> No definition will serve to cover every aspect of its nature, just as no definition will serve to explain and describe mirth and why we find some things risible and others not.[127]

Hanan fears that an overall definition of irony would serve no useful purpose:

> There is [...] no advantage is trying to find the highest common factor in [...] current uses [of the term 'irony']; any meaning obtained will be so bland as to suit many different types of writing.[128]

Deidre Wilson, speaking of the wide range of phenomena to which the term 'irony' has been applied, says:

> There is no reason to assume that all these phenomena work in the same way, or that we should be trying to develop a single general theory of irony *tout court* [...]; in other words, irony is not a natural kind.[129]

---

124   Erich Heller, *The Ironic German: A Study of Thomas Mann* (London, 1958).
125   Eleanor Hutchen, *Irony in Tom Jones* (Alabama, 1965).
126   Beda Allemann, *Ironie und Dichtung* (Pfullingen, 1956); Wayne Booth, *A Rhetoric of Irony* (Chicago, 1974); Clare Colebrook, *Irony* (London, 2004); Pierre Schoentjes, *Poétique de l'ironie* (Paris, 2001).
127   John Anthony Cuddon, *A Dictionary of Literary Terms and Literary Theory* (Oxford, 1998), fourth edition.
128   Patrick Hanan, 'The Technique of Lu Hsün's Fiction', *Harvard Journal of Asiatic Studies*, 34 (1974), pp. 53–96 (p. 76).
129   Deidre Wilson, 'The Pragmatics of Verbal Irony: Echo or Pretence?', pp. 1722–1743 (p. 1725).

The principal advocate of a definition against all odds is Muecke. He realizes that his quest is unfashionable and is eager to to make light of his mission. Confessing a sneaking admiration for Heller's non-definition of irony, he quips:

> Heller has already successfully not defined irony, so there is no point in not defining it all over again.[130]

Muecke's bonhomie masks a serious concern. Elsewhere he explains what underlies this concern:

> Is there a single common feature or perhaps a set of family resemblances some of which show up in all instances of irony and only in irony? If we cannot show that there is, we cannot have a coherent concept of irony.[131]

In other words, if we cannot succeed in defining irony, the concept risks falling apart and becoming scientifically meaningless. Muecke then proceeds to provide a comprehensive definition on the following lines, itemizing three elements that he considers essential to the concept.

> In the first place irony is a double-layered or two-storey phenomenon. At the lower level is the situation either as it appears to the victim of irony (where there is a victim) or as it is deceptively presented by the ironist (where there is an ironist). At the upper level is the situation as it appears to the observer or the ironist. [...]. In the second place there is always some kind of opposition between the two levels, an opposition that may take the form of a contradiction, incongruity, or incompatibility. [...] In the third place there is in irony an element of innocence; either a victim is confidently unaware of the very possibility of there being an upper level or point of view that invalidates his own, or an ironist pretends not to be aware of it. The one exception to this is in very overt sarcasm, where the ironist does not pretend to be unaware of his real meaning and his victim is immediately aware of it.[132]

There are two problems with Muecke's reasoning here. The first is that, while he invokes Wittgenstein's theory of definition with its notion of family resemblances, he does not seem to understand it. Nowhere does Wittgenstein suggest that there is 'a set' of family resemblances that 'show up in all instances' of the phenomenon to be defined. The whole point of Wittgenstein's argument is that the Aristotelian reliance on the common denominator leaves us unable to explain the coherence of some of the simplest, most uncontro-

---

130 D. C. Muecke, *The Compass of Irony*, pp. 15.
131 D. C. Muecke, *Irony and the Ironic* (London, 1982), p. 33.
132 D. C. Muecke, *The Compass of Irony*, pp. 19, 20.

versial concepts. In his *Philosophical Investigations*, Wittgenstein challenges us to define 'table' and 'game' (he was probably thinking of German *Spiel*, which is even trickier), terms we happily use all the time without any sense of their imminent dissolution, and shows that the best we can do is to identify traits that some examples share with other examples and these examples in turn with yet other examples without ever achieving a closed and comprehensive list.[133] The second problem with Muecke's reasoning is that the elaborate definition that he has produced simply does not work. Consider only the classical example of cosmic irony (or irony of fate): the Olympic swimmer who drowns in his own bath-tub. According to Muecke's definition, for this event to be ironic there needs to be a lower-level situation 'as it appears to the victim of the irony' and a victim who 'is confidently unaware of the very possibility of there being an upper level or point of view that invalidates his own'. But this is clearly absurd. When the irony here takes effect, the swimmer is dead and, as such, he does not have a perspective: no situation, lower-level or otherwise, can appear to him and, by the same token, he cannot be confidently unaware of the situation he is in.

It is striking, and symptomatic of the theoretical confusion surrounding the concept of irony, that a leading theorist should provide a definition of it that is as elaborately crafted as it is obviously flawed. Of course, the failure of this definition in no way suggests that a definition of irony is impossible, but it does suggest that any adequate definition would have to be more carefully developed and involve more substantial argument than is possible within the confines of this chapter. I therefore propose to follow Hanan's example and confine myself to examining verbal irony, since this is the type of irony I am concerned with. The purpose of this examination will not be to create a definition but to obviate confusion and achieve clarity on central points. Like Hanan, I shall take Quintilian as my starting point.

4.3 THE NATURE OF VERBAL IRONY

The notion of irony as a rhetorical trope goes back to Cicero and Quintilian. Both offered elements of definition that have remained influential to the present day.

In *De oratore*, Cicero speaks of irony as a play on words in which meanings are reversed ('invertuntur verba'), or as a form of mockery in which, behind a pretence of seriousness ('severe ludas'), you say something different to what you are thinking ('quom aliter sentias ac loquare') (II, LXVII, 269). Similarly,

---

133 Ludwig Wittgenstein, *Philosophical Investigations* (Oxford, 1953).

Quintilian, is his *Insitutio oratoria*, characterizes irony as a trope in which an utterance assumes an opposite meaning ('qua contraria ostenduntur, iro-nia est') (VIII, 6, 54), or as an utterance whose literal meaning is different to that intended by the speaker ('nam si qua earum verbi dissent, apparet diversam esse orationi voluntatem / quae diversum et quod dicit intellectum petit') (VIII, 6, 54 and VI, 2,15).

It is often alleged that Quintilian produced two different definitions of irony. This discrepancy has been overworked. Since Quintilian also made it clear that irony was used to express blame through counterfeit praise and praise under pretence of blame ('laudis adsimulatione detrahere er vitupera-tionis laudare') (VIII), it seems likely that his notion of an opposite meaning had more to do with the valuation attached to the meaning (praise is the op-posite of blame and vice versa) than with the precise meaning of the words. There is no reason to suppose that he intended to define the ironic meaning of an utterance as a logical negation of its non-ironic meaning, though this is precisely how he was often undersood. The strangely simplistic idea that irony is a figure of speech in which the meaning is the opposite of what is said still informs many current dictionary definitions.

While Quintilian's definition provides a useful starting-point for the un-derstanding of verbal irony, it is at once too wide and too narrow.

It is too wide because because it allows both the expression of blame through praise and the expression of praise through blame. That irony often involves blame through praise is beyond dispute, but it is legitimate to doubt whether praise through blame constitutes irony at all. At the heart of irony, there is always a negative moment, a sense of a meaning being devalued or undercut, a sense of gentle mockery. As Pierre Schoentjes has remarked:

> Il manque à la louange par le blâme cet élément négatif ou critique qui est inhérent à l'ironie et que les définitions cherchent à souligner quand elles parlent de plaisante-rie ou de raillerie. Le moment négatif est indissociable de l'ironie verbale.[134]

For Schoentjes, using blame to express praise is not a form of irony but a form of urbane politeness.

> La maîtresse de maison qui, recevant un bouquet de roses des mains d'un invité, s'écrie «Oh, je vous gronde, il ne fallait pas... » fait peut-être preuve d'une délicatesse exquise qui témoigne de beaucoup d'éducation, mais certainement pas d'un sens très dévelop-pé de l'ironie.[135]

---

134   Pierre Schoentjes, *Poétique de l'ironie*, p. 85.
135   Pierre Schoentjes, p. 85.

On the other hand, the definition is too narrow because it limits the positive utterances that can be undermined by irony to instances of praise. In conversation, it is often the case that irony involves the subversion of praise, but in more developed ironies of the kind we find in literature, the meaning subverted may be almost any meaning to which we attach a positive valuation. In Swift's *Modest Proposal*, for example, the surface meaning conveys well-meant advice rather than praise. Though there are elements of praise (it is difficult to forget the narrator's revolting eulogy of well-cooked infants' flesh), the apparent focus of the narrative is the recommendation of cannibalism as a rational means of solving the problem of hunger and overpopulation in Ireland. Sometimes it is not praise or advice but agreement that is undermined by irony. The best known example is probably the famous opening sentence of Jane Austen's *Pride and Prejudice*:

> It is a truth universally acknowledged that a single man in possession of a good fortune must be in want of a wife.

As D. C. Muecke points out, Austen's narrator here confidently presupposes our unquestioning agreement to an assertion that is obviously misguided. Given our knowledge of social realities, we are quick to understand that it is not rich young men who desire a bride but young women who seek to improve their status by marrying a rich husband.[136] What is undercut by irony may also be an apology or defence. A good example is Montesquieu's mock defence of slavery in his *Défense de l'ésprit des lois* (1750).[137] But irony can equally well subvert expressions of hope, desire, reassurance, encouragement etc. As André Hallay has argued, verbal irony may even subvert forms of expression that appear to be free of any explicit valuation. The neutral, detached, matter-of-fact tone so characteristic of Flaubertian realism provides a narrative surface that can veil the whirls and eddies of authorial irony every bit as well as the most profuse praise.[138]

Consequently there is much to be said for Hamon's simpler characterisation of verbal irony as a figure of speech in which:

> on exprime explicitement une positivité [...] ou une neutralité [...] pour signifier implicitement une négativité.[139]

---

136   D. C. Muecke, *Irony and the Ironic*, p. 17.
137   D. C. Muecke, *Irony and the Ironic*, p. 57.
138   André Hallay, 'L'ironie', Revue politique et littéraire 9 (1898), No. 17 (23 April); quoted in D. C. Muecke, *The Compass of Irony*, pp. 68–69.
139   Philippe Hamon, *L'ironie littéraire. Essais sur les formes de l'écriture oblique* (Paris, 1996), p. 30.

Though this definition certainly represents an advance on Quintilian, it is still has shortcomings. Its main deficiency lies in a quality of verbal irony that, as far as I can see, has not been pointed out in the literature, even though it is of primary importance in the study of literary irony. Consider the following remark:

Oh, what lovely weather. I do so hate it when it's warm and sunny [said in bad weather].

This is a simple conversational irony but it illustrates the fact that irony can not only take the form of movement from a positive or neutral meaning to a negative meaning ('Oh, what lovely weather'), but also movement from a negative meaning to another, quite distinct, negative meaning that undermines the credibility of the first ('I do so hate it when it's warm and sunny'). There can hardly be any doubt that 'I do so hate it when it's warm and sunny', however we contrive to understand it, expresses a meaning that is negatively charged: the surface meaning is negative and the ironic meaning also. The ability to proceed from a perceived negative meaning to an alternative negative meaning is an important feature of verbal irony, and not understanding this may make obscure the recognition of literary ironies in cases where the surface meaning is also negatively charged.

Second, it makes the mistake of identifying the non-ironic meaning with an explicit or literal meaning, and the ironic meaning with an implicit or non-literal meaning. The French semanticist Robert Martin has repeatedly tried to point out why this view is fundamentally flawed but but has received little recognition for his efforts.[140] His leading example is as simple as it is cogent:

Nos amis sont toujours là, quand ils ont besoin de nous.

As Martin points out, the ironic meaning of this statement does not involve rejecting the literal meaning in favour of a non-literal meaning. On the contrary, it is precisely the literal meaning that the speaker is emphatically asserting. What makes the assertion ironic is not that the literal meaning is rejected but the fact that the literal meaning deviates from what we would

---

140 Robert Martin, *Pour une logique du sens* (Paris, 1983), pp. 269–274; Robert Martin, 'Irony and the Universe of Belief', *Lingua* 87(1992) pp. 77–90. As far as I can see the only person to have picked up on Martin's point is Katharina Barbe, who re-states the argument adapting an example from Alice Myers Roy: 'I love peope who signal' (said by someone annoyed that a driver did not signal on making a left turn), but fails to acknowledge her debt to Martin (she merely includes his English-language article in her bibliography). See Katharina Barbe, *Irony in Context* (Amsterdam and Philadelphia PA, 1995), pp. 25, 26 and Alice Myers Roy, 'Towards a definition of irony' in Ralph Fasold and Roger Shuy, *Studies in Language Variation* (Washington, 1977), pp. 171–183 (p. 172).

reasonably have expected to hear, namely 'Nos amis sont toujours là, quand *nous avons besoin d'eux'*. The ironic point is that the people in question are not true friends; they are not there for us when *we* need *them* but descend on us whenever *they* need *us*.

4.5 PROCESSING VERBAL IRONY

As I have suggested, understanding verbal irony involves making an inference from one level of meaning to another. In other words, ironic meaning needs to be actively reconstructed from a surface meaning that the listener or reader is prompted to reject. Wayne Booth describes the reconstruction of the ironic meaning as a sequence of four steps:
1. Rejection of the literal meaning
2. Consideration of alternative interpretations and explanations
3. Decision about the author's beliefs and values
4. Reconstruction of the ironic meaning
   These steps are presumably meant to be understood as stages in a logical argument rather than stages of a psychological process. Booth admits that they often occur almost simultaneously. He exemplifies what he means by the four steps with an example from (an English translation of) Voltaire's *Candide*:

> When all was over and the rival kings were celebrating their victory with Te Deums in their respective camps [...].[141]

Correct interpretation of this statement, he asserts, presupposes an argument of this kind:
1. The literal meaning is rejected: we know that both sides cannot win a war.
2. Alternative explanations are tried out: the author may have made a mistake, may be crazy etc.
3. Appeal to what we know of the author from the work as a whole: it is highly unlikely that this formulation is due to carelessness or foolishness
4. Reconstruction of the ironic meaning: both sides believe God is on their side and pander to the self-serving belief that victory is theirs whatever

---

141 Booth's example will serve, although it is marred by the fact that the English translation he is using does not correspond to the French original. What Voltaire wrote was: Enfin, tandis que les deux rois faisaient chanter des Te Deum chacun dans son camp [...]
There is no explicit mention of celebrating victory although this is certainly implied: the *Te Deum* was a prayer said after battle to thank God for victory. Voltaire's remark is certainly ironic and the import of the irony is much the same, but an analysis of interpretative process using the original wording would have had to have been constructed differently.

the truth may be (Booth does not actually make the ironic meaning explicit, but it would presumably be something like this).

Booth's analysis has received widespread recognition but has been cri-
tized for saying that the non-ironic meaning should be *rejected*. Bredin objects
to the view that the listener should ignore or discard the surface meaning,
stressing that:

> Irony is produced, not by way of a process in which what is said is *replaced* by what is
> meant, but by a process in which they *interact* with one another.[142]

and that

> [...] irony depends upon, and is a product of, an interaction between the stated and the
> unstated meanings, rather than a process in which we ditch the former in favour of
> the latter.[143]

A similar point is made by Schoentjes:

> L'ironie met [...] nécessairement en présence deux sens contradictoires dans une aire
> de tension: l'écart ironique naît du fait que l'ironie exprime toujours l'un *et* l'autre, le
> oui *et* le non.[144]

That verbal irony always involves a dual perspective is surely correct, but
as an objection to Booth it is beside the point. Booth never suggests that the
non-ironic meaning somehow disappears into thin air or 'vanishes unwanted
from the scene' (Bredin). Saying that the ironic meaning is based on a rejection of the surface meaning is not the same as saying that the literal meaning
is discarded. All it means is that the literal meaning is not a constituent of
the ironic meaning; and as long as 'literal' is taken to be synonymous with
'non-ironic', this is no more than a truism.

What Booth can and should be criticized for, however, is his equation
of literal meaning with non-ironic meaning, and ironic meaning with non-
literal meaning, a shortcoming he shares with other theorists and which we
have already commented on.

He might, I suppose, also be criticized for not elaborating on the ways in
which the non-ironic meaning comes to be rejected. From his analysis, it is
not entirely clear what, aside from obvious contradiction, might trigger the

142 Bredin, H. 'The Semantic Structure of Verbal Irony', *Journal of Literary* Semantics 26 (1997), vol. 1,
     (pp. 1–20), p. 13.
143 Hugh Bredin, p. 17.
144 Pierre Schoentjes, pp. 93, 94.

process of ironic interpretation. Of course, Booth may be right to avoid this issue. As Hamon points out:

Il n'y a pas de signaux fixes et specialisés de l'ironie.[145]

While fully accepting this, I think it may be possible to divide ironic cues into three broad theoretical types:

1. There is a conspicuous mismatch between an utterance and its context. This is the case with the conversational ironies of the kind often discussed by linguists:

He's a fine friend [said after the person in question has just rendered you a major disservice] (Grice)

Qu'est-ce qu'il fait beau [said while it is raining] (Martin)

Alors ça c'est agréable [said after spraining one's ankle] (Martin)

In such cases the ironic meaning is reconstructed against the background framework of common sense assumptions about what someone may reasonably assert. If someone who clearly knows that it is raining says that it is lovely weather, we have considerable difficulty taking his assertion literally. Short of considering the speaker raving mad or hopelessly eccentric, we have little option but to conclude that his assertion is not meant to be understood in the same way such assertions normally are. Utterances of this kind are unremarkable in themselves and become ironic only against the background of a context into which the surface meaning does not fit. The literary counterpart of such conversational ironies would be an assertion that undermines expectations raised elsewhere in the text or runs subversively contrary to agreed and established norms beyond it.

2. There is a conspicuous mismatch between elements of a given utterance:

What the hell, it's only cancer.

Наш уважаемый сержант владел всеми языками, кроме иностранных
[spoken by Ershov in Vassilii Grossman, *Žizn' i sudba*]

The machine dispensed a liquid that was more or less exactly unlike tea
[spoken by the narrator in Douglas Adams, *Hitch Hiker's Guide to the Galaxy*]

---

145 Philippe Hamon, pp. 87 and 107.

The expected continuation of 'What the hell, it's only ...' would be a reference to an asset normally considered incidental to human happiness like 'money'. Ershov's pronoucement that their sergeant knew every language, which seems to require no amplification, is at odds with the exception made for foreign languages, since we had assumed it was foreign languages that were at issue. The description of the beverage dispensed by the vending machine in Douglas Adams confronts us with the incongruity of using 'more or less' in combination with 'exactly', and 'exactly' in combination with 'unlike'. In each case, the ironic message is obtained by comparing what we have before us with what we might have expected to hear and drawing appropriate conclusions. The precise nature of the inference will depend on our knowledge of the specific realities concerned. 'What the hell, it's only cancer' shows itself to be a self-mocking reflection on the futility of trying to make light of a life-threatening disease. The remarks about the sergeant strongly suggests that his linguistic mastery consisted in little more than an unusually broad repertoire of foul language. 'The machine dispensed a liquid that was more or less exactly unlike tea' conveys initial puzzlement and ultimate disappointment at the receipt of an indiscriminate swill that bears little or no comparison to the original.

3. The inferential process is triggered by the presence of compromising ambiguity or adverse connotations:

> A smashing time was had by all [said of football fans on the rampage].

> Ask for me tomorrow and you shall find a grave man
> [spoken by Mercutio in Shakespeare, *Romeo and Juliet*]

> We wommen han, if that I shal nat lye,
> In this matere a queynte fantasye
> [spoken by the wife of Bath in Chaucer's *Wife of Bath's Tale*]

In the first case, the ambiguity of 'smashing' ('splendid' vs. 'destructive') provides an ironic indication that the fans were perhaps more interested in satisfying their destructive urges than in enjoying a game of football. The speech of the dying Mercutio in Shakespeare's *Romeo and Juliet* poignantly highlights the ambiguity of 'grave' ('serious' vs. place of burial) to suggest that the interlocutor should expect to find someone who is not just sombre but deceased. In the *Wife of Bath's Tale*, the licentious narrator's 'queynte fantasye' may be taken to insinuate that her imaginings are not so much quaint as sexually explicit ('queynte' also meant 'cunt').

4.6 NARRATIVE IRONY AND THE UNRELIABLE NARRATOR

When verbal irony is sustained over a whole narrative, we may speak of *narrative* or *structural* irony in the core sense established by Booth.[146] According to Booth, in conventional narrative irony the author puts forward an *unreliable narrator* (sometimes also referred to as a *fallible* or *discordant* narrator) whose function is to mislead the reader but, at the same, to betray his own unreliability in such a way and to such an extent that the reader is able to overcome the narrator's deception and understand the ironic message conveyed by the author.

Booth knows that the figure of the unreliable narrator is not peculiar to irony. It can be used to create suspense and keep the reader in the dark, as it does in Wilkie Collins's *Moonstone* and *The Woman in White* or Agatha Christie's *The Murder of Roger Ackroyd*. It can be used to allow the author to disassociate himself from the narrator, because he does not and cannot share his values, as in Vladimir Nabokov's *Lolita*, with its disturbed paedophile narrator, or Jonathan Littell's *Les Bienveillantes*, written from the point of view of a Nazi officer involved in the Holocaust. It can also be used to generate psychological depth and authenticity as in D. J. Salinger's *Catcher in the Rye* or Mark Twain's *Huckleberry Finn*. The same is true of Franz Kafka's *Verwandlung*, where the use of a narrator who relates supernatural events with the same objective detachment as everyday ones allows the author to achieve a haunting sense of mental suffering.

Nevertheless, Booth considers the notion of an 'unreliable narrator' to be an essential prerequisite for the analysis of narrative irony, which he believes is best understood in terms of an opposition between the voices of narrator and author. For Booth, both narrator and author are narrative constructs, based on levels of meaning in the text. On this understanding, 'author' cannot simply be equated with the biographical author.

Booth has been criticized for introducing the notion of an author's voice deemed separate from the voice of the biographical author.[147] However, he is right to do this for several reasons. First, narrative intent cannot simply be attributed to the biographical author. As Morson has pointed out, the biographical author is not automatically the best interpreter of his own writings. What is more, trying to speak of narrative intent in the depersonalized

---

146 Wayne Booth, *A Rhetoric of Fiction*, pp. 158–159.
147 See Ansgar Nünning, 'Multiperspektivität aus narratologischer Sicht', in Vera Nünning et al. (ed.) *Multiperspektives Erzählen* (Trier, 2000); Gérard Genette, *Nouveau discours du récit* (Paris, 1983); Mieke Bal, *Narratology: Introduction to the Theory of Narration* (Toronto, 1985); Shlomith Rimmon-Kennan, *Narrative fiction: contemporary poetics* (London, 1983). For a sustained defence of the implied author, see Seymour Chatman, 'Defence of the implied author', *Coming to Terms* (London. 1990).

language of implicit norms is forbidding. It is unclear how we can articulate something that is always referred to in personal terms in a language that studiously avoids the personal. Second, there are cases where real author and implied author are clearly not identical. Consider Italo Svevo's *La coscienza di Zeno*, where the unreliable narrator is endowed with several of the real author's personal characteristics. Here the author who stands against the narrator in the text is not the real author but an implied author who is more unlike the narrator than the real author is. Third, as Booth rightly points out, belief in the existence of literary irony is inconsistent with full-scale acceptance of the so-called 'intentional fallacy'. First formulated by Wimsatt and Beardsley, the doctrine of the intentional fallacy states that we cannot legitimately interpret texts in terms of the biographical author's intention because that intention can never be reliably established.[148] If we accept this, we can no longer speak of irony in a text, because a text can only be ironic if the person who wrote it meant it to be. It makes no sense to say that a text is ironic although the biographical author may not have intended it to be, any more that it makes sense to say that someone made an ironic remark but did not intend it to be ironic. Verbal irony presupposes intention.[149] But there is an extension to this argument that makes it clear why it is necessary to separate the author as a textual voice from the biographical author of the text, and it is this: once the biographical author has created his unreliable narrator and set up the ironic perspective that will pervade the text, there will be meanings within that structure that are fully intended (otherwise it would not be possible to speak of irony), but there may also be meanings within that structure that, while they fit the ironic perspective exactly and help to develop it, may not have been consciously intended.[150] Ultimately, in

---

148 William Wimsatt and Monroe Beardsley, 'The Intentional Fallacy', *Sewanee Review* 54 (1946), pp. 468–488: revised and republished in *The Verbal Icon: Studies in the Meaning of Poetry* (Lexington KY, 1954), pp. 3–18.

149 An exception needs to be made for utterances that have become severed from the context in which they were originally made. A good example is the 'horrible ironía de los nombres' ('awful irony of names'), described by Bénito Peréz Galdós in his sombre realist novel *Doña Perfecta* (1876). Here (at the beginning of chapter two) he talks about the attribution of poetic names ('nombres poéticos') to ugly places ('sitios feos'), for example *Valleameno* ('Pleasant Valley') to a barren and desolate landscape, *Villarica* ('Rich Town') to a wretched mud-walled village, *Valdeflores* ('Vale of Flowers') to an arid and stony ravine, and comments: 'todo aquí es ironía. Palabras hermosas, realidad prosaica y miserable' ('everything here is irony. Beautiful words, a prosaic and wretched reality'). In these cases, clearly, the undeniable irony of the names does not derive from any recognizable ironic intention on the part of the name-giver. The name-giving may have been purely euphemistic or straightforwardly bombastic, or it may have been a faithful reflection of an entirely different, historically distant and now extinct geo-physical and economic context.

150 Perhaps the best account of how consciously intended and not consciously intented meanings may cohere and form the basis of a valid interpretation has been given by E. D. Hirsch Jr., *Validity in Interpretation* (New Haven CN and London, 1967), pp. 51–57.

analysing an ironic text it makes little sense to distinguish the two since there is no reliable way of doing this (as the 'intentional fallacy' correctly predicts). It is precisely for this reason that it is wise to speak of the author's voice in the text without necessarily implying that this voice is in all respects the voice of the biographical author.

Though it has become a standard term, 'unreliable narrator' still needs to be used with care. As James Wood has pointed out, calling a narrator unreliable does not mean that he is completely untrustworthy.

> In most novels, unreliable narrators tend to become a little predictable, because they have to be reliably unreliable: the narrator's unrealiability is manipulated by the author. Indeed, without the author's reliability we would not be able to 'read' the narrator's unreliability.[151]

In fact, unreliable narration involves a degree of regularity that makes it almost mechanically repetitive.

> Unreliable narration is almost entrepreneurially efficient: once the novelist has set up his stall, he can franchise out his technique in chapter after chapter.[152]

One point that Wood does not make nonetheless deserves to be made. An unreliable narrator must not only be reliably unreliable, he must also have a residual honesty or a fundamental lack of guile that prevents him from trying to deceive us outright. Though he intends to mislead us, he cannot engage in straightforward, shameless lying. Since the role of the unreliable narrator is ultimately to betray himself, he can only lie and cheat in a way that remains minimally consistent with the truth he is seeking to hide.

Given this understanding of the role of the unreliable narrator, we may now consider how this device functions within the context of narrative irony. Generally we can say that in narrative irony, the non-ironic meaning is a based on a reading that takes what the unreliable narrator is saying at face value, while the ironic meaning is based on a reading that recognizes the narrator's unreliability and makes allowances for it.

However, we cannot simply identify the non-ironic meaning with the narrator's voice and the ironic meaning with the (implied) author's voice. Sometimes the ironic meaning may lie in what the narrator has really said as opposed to what he appears to have said or what he would like us to think he has said. This follows from my earlier point about the relationship of ironic meaning and literal meaning.

---

151   James Wood, *The Irresponsible Self: On Laughter and the Novel* (London, 2005), p. 84.
152   James Wood, p. 85.

When the narrator's unreliability is reliably sustained, the narrator himself becomes a natural focus for the ironic perspective. For this reason, narrative irony may turn in on itself, relativizing the narrator's viewpoint as an end rather than as a means. The externalities that the narrator describes may vary as the story progresses but the narrator's idiosyncratic psychological makeup remains largely constant. This means that the ironic text may in the end tell us more about the narrator than about the story he relates.

As details of the narrator's idiosyncratic perspective unfold, an interesting interaction between ironic and non-ironic meaning can come into play. Some indications of the narrator's idiosyncratic makeup may be conveyed by the non-ironic meaning while others emerge from the ironic meaning. In this way, the ironic meaning can reinforce or intensify the characterization of the narrator provided by the non-ironic meaning, magnifying certain traits and turning overt image into covert caricature. We shall refer to the resulting phenomenon as the ironic stylization of the narrator.

4.7 THE PITFALLS OF IRONY

Vladimir Jankélévitch devotes a third of his book on irony to what he calls 'les pièges de l'ironie', by which he means the pitfalls of irony for both writers and readers.[153] I acknowledge the need to talk about pitfalls of irony as a separate issue but I shall limit myself to the pitfalls of verbal and conventional narrative irony for readers and critics, emphasizing the challenges this type of irony presents to comprehension, exposition and critical appreciation. The points I make are materially different from those made by Jankélévitch.

4.7.1 CHALLENGES TO COMPREHENSION

Understanding irony is a good deal trickier than we often imagine. As Booth appositely observes:

> There is reason to believe that most of us think we are less vulnerable to mistakes with irony than we are. If we have enjoyed many ironies and observed less experienced readers making fools of themselves, we can hardly resist flattering ourselves for making our way pretty well, But the truth is that even highly sophisticated readers often go astray.[154]

---

153   Vladimir Jankélévitch, *L'ironie* (Paris, 1964).
154   Wayne Booth, *A Rhetoric of Irony*, p. 184.

The history of the reception of irony bears witness to the fact that even the most blatant ironies can be overlooked. The widespread indignation which greeted Swift's *Modest Proposal* is a good example. Subtler literary ironies can be overlooked for generations. The irony in Dostoevsky's *Bednye Liudy* was not recognized for more than a century and is sometimes still ignored today. The reason for this may be a lack of literary sensitivity, political ideology, the unquestioning preference for a sentimental or straightforwardly moralistic reading, or the lure of the familiar. We might assume that highly sophisiticated readers would be immune from these failings but Booth is right to point out that they are not. I think we might even go a step further. It seems to me that it is precisely the 'highly sophisticated readers' who go often astray and that literary scholars are not the least vulnerable among them. The truth is that narrative irony is resistant to many of the habits of mind that literary scholarship inculcates. There is much that could be said on this subject but I will limit myself to three points. First, literary scholarship works on the understanding that if we study carefully what others have written and continue to deploy the numerous critical 'tools' at our disposal, we will, in a collective effort of approximation, gradually come closer to a full understanding of the text in question. Unfortunately, irony does not work like that. With irony – to put it bluntly – you either 'get it' or you don't. Of course, once the ironic intention in a text has been recognized, working out the details of the ironic message may take a while; but we are talking hours or days, rather than years or generations. Second, since literary scholarship is often in the service of literary history, putting works in (a literary, historical, social, biographical) context is of paramount importance. With narrative irony, preoccupation with context can obscure the message. Narrative irony requires us to focus on the structure of an individual text and the only context it requires is normally provided by the sort of knowledge accessible to any educated reader of the time. This will include some information about the author, but only enough to be able to answer questions of a rather basic kind like: 'Could the author have seriously intended a 'straight' reading?', 'Could what appears to be irony be due to nothing more than poor style?', 'Was the writer of sound mind?'.[155] Third, verbal irony is understood with reference to a standard of 'normality' (conventional usage/common sense/shared knowledge, values and expectations) against which the surface meaning is found wanting. It is the resulting disparity that leads the listener/reader to reconstruct an

---

155   Doubts about the writer's sanity may have prevented Robert Walser's *Jakob von Gunten* (1909) from being securely identified as ironic. In this story, the narrator praises the uninspiring private boarding school he attends (called Benjamenta, presumably from *Benjamin* + Lat. *mens, mentis*) for promoting ignorance, small-mindedness and blind obedience as a safeguard against vanity and disappointment. Walser went mad and was committed to a psychiatric clinic for the last twenty-five years of his life (1929–1954).

alternative reading more in line with the implicit standard. This is as true of simple conversational ironies as it is of sophisticated literary ironies. Literary scholars, knowing from extensive experience that almost anything is possible in a literary text and that a writer's expression often reflects not only the conventions of his period but also the idiosyncracies of his individual poetic vision, can easily feel that to compare what a text says with a standard of 'normality' is intolerably naïve.

4.7.2 CHALLENGES TO EXPOSITION

We all know that you can kill a joke by explaining it, and the same is true of irony. With a joke, we are meant to 'get it' and a significant part of what makes a joke funny depends on that moment of realization when we do finally 'get it', and do so alone and unaided. When we have ask for a joke to be explained, we are usually resigned to the fact that, even if we now come to understand it, it will have ceased to be funny. Similarly, much of the joy of irony lies in our own recognition of the underlying incongruity and in our own successful reconstruction of the ironic meaning. Explaining irony takes that element of enjoyment away. What is more, as Booth says, 'explaining an irony is usually even less successful than explaining an ordinary joke' because of the unspoken beliefs on which it rests, the inferential processes involved in reconstructing the ironic meaning, and not least because:

> there is always an implied claim to superiority of total vision in the final view of those who see the irony and thus a potential look downward on those who dwell in error.[156]

The feeling of being overwhelmed and browbeaten that readers may have when irony is explained to them can be aggravated by matters of style. While we are normally careful to avoid apodictic assertions by using downtoners like *seems/appears/would seem* etc., this is liable to cause confusion when describing narrative irony with its contrast of apparent and hidden meanings, with its distinction between what the narrator seems to be saying and what he is really saying. When glossing the putative ironic meaning academic hedges of this kind are therefore best avoided but their absence should not be taken as an expression of certainty. Reconstructions of ironic meaning are always tentative and ultimately a matter of opinion.

However, perhaps the largest challenge to exposition is the fact that there is mostly no right way to enter an ironic text and no set path for the reader to follow. Different readers will respond to different ironic cues and make

---

156   Wayne Booth, *A Rhetoric of Irony*, p. 5.

their own way through the text, often retracing their steps and reassessing the situation as they go, reading and re-reading critical passages. In the case of a complex ironic text, reading through once only will rarely suffice. This creates a problem for exegesis that is largely insoluble. If there is no right way into an ironic text and even the most discerning reader will have to go back and forth to work out what is going on, how can the insights gained in such a process be set out convincingly in a linear fashion?

4.7.3 CHALLENGES TO CRITICAL APPRECIATION

Literary scholarship naturally expects a critical reading to be supported by convincing argument based on clear textual and extra-textual evidence. Yet all the interpreter of irony can ever hope to offer is a web of hints and implications whose convincingness may be more dependent on the skill of the ironist and the transparency of his design than it is on the insight of the interpreter. To make matters worse, in conventional narrative irony, the ironic meaning is meant to be recognized, not as one meaning amongst others, but as *the* meaning of the text, as its *real* meaning. To claim a text is ironic in this sense is therefore to lay oneself open to the charge of presumption and unscholarly neglect of other people's insights.[157]

    This situation is made worse by the fact that there is no wholly satisfactory criterion or set of criteria for judging the appropriateness and adequacy of an ironic reading. Booth has suggested that the ultimate criterion for the success of an ironic interpretation might be whether or not it enhances the literary value of a work:

> the test of whether a given interpretation – however plausible in itself – destroys or enhances a work is sometimes the only final arbiter of disputes about irony.[158]

He realizes that this standard is problematic. Critics may succumb to the temptation of imposing an ironic interpretation on a work in order to enliven a dull text or buff up the reputation of a third-rate writer. But Booth believes that without a final touchstone of this kind, we have no way of combatting

---

157   Richard Gregg's defence of his interpretation of *Mednyj Vsadnik* in 'The Nature of Nature and the Nature of Eugene in the Bronze Horseman', *Slavic and East European Journal*, 21 (1977), No. 2 (summer), pp. 167–179 (p. 175) provides a striking illustration of the mindset from which such charges issue. 'The proposed reading', he says, referring to his own interpretation of the poem, 'does not presume to nullify its predecessors (the presumption would be considerable) or to foreclose future interpretative forays'. In this view, apparently, it is a virtue if an interpretation does not rule out any other, past or future, real or potential. The interpreter of classical irony, who must of necessity rule out all other interpretations, thus exposes himself to the starkest condemnation.

158   Wayne Booth, *A Rhetoric of Irony*, p. 184.

excesses of interpretation, no way of preventing critical ingenuity from leading us astray.

I would like to suggest an alternative criterion but I do so with similar
misgivings. I think it is possible to argue that an ironic reading, like any other
reading, is ultimately vindicated by its ability to explain why a text is exactly
the way it is. In other words, the more an interpretation can explain, the better it is.[159] This criterion is also not without its drawbacks. It could mislead us
into valuing micro-reading more than genuine insight and it may privilege
elaborate ingenuity over sensible simplicity, but as Booth suggests every criterion will have its shortcomings.

4.8 IS THERE SUCH A THING AS A PRIVATE IRONY?

Some commentators assume not only that ironic meaning is intentional but
also that the ironist must wish for his irony to be understood. Booth speaks
of a meaning:

> deliberately created by human beings to be heard or read and understood with some
> precision by other human beings.[160]

But is this necessarily the case? Can we not imagine an ironist who is
unconcerned whether his irony is understood or even prefers his irony to remain largely undetected? Indeed, is it not possible that every serious ironist
is quite happy to see at least part of his audience taken in? Muecke acknowledges the possibility of private irony, i.e. irony which is not intended to be
preceived by the victim or anyone else.[161] Schoentjes is undecided. One the
one hand, he admits that:

> Alors que les ironistes s'adressent en majorité à un public et que l'ironie participe habi-
> tuellement d'une stratégie de communication, il peut arriver que l'ironiste désire res-
> ter le seul interprète de ses paroles. Seul gardien du sens, il entend en défendre l'accès
> aux autres. Cette ironie privée ne considère plus la langue comme moyen d'entrer en
> contact avec les autres, mais comme manière de ne se livrer qu'à soi-même.[162]

But at the same time he seems to be claiming that irony is always meant to
be recognized

---

159 A similar criterion is currently in favour in the philosophy of science, see Peter Lipton, *Inference
     to the Best Explanation* (London, 1991).
160 Wayne Booth, *A Rhetoric of Irony*, p. 5.
161 D. C. Muecke, pp. 59, 60.
162 Pierre Schoentjes, p. 188.

[...] l'ironiste [...] veillera [...] à ne jamais verouiller complètement l'accès à la signi-
fication de ses propos. L'ironie demande d'être percée à jour: elle ferme la porte mais
laisse une clé suspendue à côté de l'encadrement, voire engagée bien visiblement dans
sa serrure, elle invite celui qui fait route derrière elle et le guide en lieu montrant comment procéder pour la rejoindre. Son sourire et son clin d'oeil signifient: Suis-moi.[163]

To which one might add that private irony may also serve to protect the
writer's artistic integrity from the unreasonable demands of society, be it
those of state censorship or of an indiscrimate audience on whose taste he is
financially dependent.

Schoentjes provides an interesting example of a literary character con-
templating the advantages of private irony, taken from short story called
'Nikushimi' [Hatred] (1914) by the early modern Japanese writer Jun'ichirō
Tanizaki.[164] In this story, the hero expresses the belief that the most exquisite
way to express hate for someone would be to dissimulate the hate one felt for
him and to engage in praise and flattery instead, thereby constantly mocking the victim without his knowing. Muecke points equally convincingly to
Jane Austen's Mr. Bennett, who enjoys seeing his wife or Mr Collins take his
remarks at face value.

Muecke considers private irony to be 'very much like hoaxing' and sees
its principal attraction in 'contemplative enjoyment at the expense of fools'
and 'as a means of release' for those 'unwilling or unable to express their
bitterness or contempt, their anguish or indignation'.

The truth of the matter is surely that most ironies are to some extent private ironies. Much of the pleasure of irony lies in knowing that a part of your
audience may be fooled at least some of the time. Few ironists will want all
their audience to be fooled all of the time, because this would lead to creative
solipsism. But how much an ironist desires to be understood, and by whom,
will naturally vary, and it may vary considerably.

4.9 VERBAL IRONY AND RELATED PHENOMENA

This section differentiates verbal irony and conventional narrative irony
from a range of other concepts that occasionally cause confusion. My selection lays no claim to completeness and is based on pragmatic considerations.

---

163 Pierre Schoentjes, p. 148.
164 Pierre Schoentjes, p. 188–189. 'Nikushimi' was first published alongside 'Neppū ni fukarete'
     [Caught in a hot wind] in Jun'ichirō Tanizaki, Iraka [Tiled roof] (Tokyo, 1914). It was republished
     as 'Zōnen' [= Zatsunen, 'Idle/Stray Thoughts'] in Tanizaki Jun'ichirō Zenshū, 28 vols (Tokyo, 1966),
     vol. 2, pp. 287–300; and translated into French as 'La haine' in Jun'ichirō Tanizaki, Oeuvres, 2 vols
     (Paris, 1998), vol. 1, pp. 91–100. Schoentjes refers to the story by the later title 'Zōnen'.

4.9.1 ROMANTIC IRONY

Romantic irony is a concept that goes back to the German philosopher and critic Friedrich Schlegel (1772–1829), for whom it seems to have been little more than a matter of passing interest.[165] The idea was disseminated mainly by his fellow Jena Romantics Adam Müller, Karl Solger and Hermann Hettner,[166] but it did not become popular until the late twentieth century. In the Romantic period itself Romantic irony was never attributed to individual works. This means that, in applying it to works of the Romantic period, we are using it largely in retrospect. It is therefore hardly surprising there has been scant objection to extending its use even further backwards (to Sterne, Cervantes, etc.) and forwards (to Brecht, Pirandello, Thomas Mann, etc.). Perhaps for this reason, Romantic irony is now often understood archetypally rather than purely historically. The term has only been applied to a small number of Romantic texts, but to many more not considered to be Romantic.

Romantic irony is often ascribed to works that deliberately fail to maintain their own illusion of fictionality. They set up a fictional illusion only to deconstruct or demolish it more or less openly. As Gary Handwerk has pointed out, Romantic irony frequently refers to works that are in some sense self-reflexive, that contain within themselves a sense of their own construction, and in some cases even their own reception.[167] Ludwig Tieck's dramas, *Der Gestiefelte Kater*, *Die Verkehrte Welt*, and *Prinz Zerbino*, are often held up as prototypical examples. Here audience, critics, actors and director argue with each other about the merits of the individual scenes and and debate about how the action is to proceed. Laurence Sterne's *Tristram Shandy* is another example often cited, because of the way it reflects the writer's motivation and situation in writing.

Rüdiger Safranski has recently provided a good account of the way Romantic irony is related to verbal irony. He says that Friedrich Schlegel romanticized the familiar figure of irony, developing its potential in unexpected ways.

> Schlegel [...] knüpfte an der bisher bekannten Grundfigur der Ironie an, dass nämlich eine bestimmte Aussage in eine andere, eine umfassendere Perspektive gerückt wird und dadurch relativiert oder gar dementiert wird. Der Trick mit dem Schlegel die Iro-

---

165   Friedrich Schlegel, *Athenäums-Fragmente und andere Schriften* (Leipzig, 1986), edited by Andreas Huyssen.

166   Adam Müller, *Vorlesungen über deutsche Wissenschaft und Literatur* (Dresden, 1807); Karl Solger, *Erwin: Vier Gespräche über das Schöne und die Kunst* (Munich, 1971), edited by Wolfhart Henckmann, and *Vorlesungen über Aesthetik* (Darmstadt, 1980), edited by Karl Heyse; Hermann Hettner, *Kleine Schriften* (Braunschweig, 1884), edited by Anna Hettner.

167   Gary Handwerk, 'Romantic irony', *The Cambridge History of Literary Criticism* (Cambridge, 1993–2001), 9 vols, vol. 5, pp. 203–225.

nie zur theoretischen Goldader macht, besteht darin, dass er für die jeweils bestimmte Aussage das Endliche setzt und für die Perspektive der Relativierung und Dementierung das Unendliche.[168]

Having done this, Safranski says, the game can begin – a game that pulls the carpet from under any clear and definite assertions and causes them to be suspended in what Schlegel called a state of *Schweben*. Since all assertions are necessarily finite they are bound to involve a reduction of complexity. By showing you are aware of this reduction of complexity, you can ironically subvert your inevitably under-complex assertion.

According to Booth, the difference between conventional irony and romantic irony and lies in the fact that:

> [in the] one kind of all or most of the ironies are resolved into relatively secure [...] perceptions or truths; in the other, all truths are dissolved into ironic mist.[169]

He therefore characterizes conventional irony as *stable, covert* and *finite*, as against Romantic irony which he describes as *unstable, overt* and *infinite*. By saying that an irony is *stable*, Booth means that, once the ironic meaning has been reconstructed, the reader is not invited to undermine it any further. By *covert*, he means that the irony is meant to be reconstructed with meanings different from those on the surface. Finally, by calling an irony finite, he means that the reconstructed meanings are local and limited, that is enacted in a field of discourse that is narrowly circumscribed.[170]

An unusually clear account of the relationship between the two types of irony is provided by Lilian Furst.[171] According to Furst, traditional irony allows veiled incongruities and ambiguities to be resolved into a determinate meaning, while Romantic irony makes the reader realize that truth is unattainable and paradox prevails; the signals the implied author gives are 'loud and manifold' but ultimately 'conflicting and confusing'. In traditional irony there is a knowing complicity between the implied author and at least a part of his audience; in Romantic irony it is the reader who is the disconcerted and disoriented victim of the irony. Gone is the 'sense of dissembling that is meant to be seen through'; instead 'the mask merges with the persona in a displacement meant to generate disorientation.' 'While traditional irony is *between* the lines, Romantic irony is *in* the lines'.[172]

---

168 Rüdiger Safranski, *Romantik: eine deutsche Affäre* (München, 2007), p. 62.
169 Wayne Booth, *A Rhetoric of Irony*, p. 151.
170 Wayne Booth, *A Rhetoric of Irony*, pp. 3-4.
171 Lilian Furst, *Fictions of Romantic Irony in European Narrative* (London, 1984), pp. 225-239.
172 Lilian Furst, p. 131.

4.9.2 SATIRE

Dryden famously said that 'the true end of satire is the amendment of vices by correction'.[173] This view has remained influential, although it is legitimate to doubt whether all satire is ameliorative. As Gilbert Highet has pointed out, there are two different types of satirist and therefore two different types of satire:

> The optimist writes in order to heal, the pessimist in order to punish. One is a physician, the other is an executioner.[174]

Depending on the writer's purpose, satire can be playful, witty and amusing; or malicious, abrasive and denigrating. Humour is a frequent element in satire but it is not a necessary one.[175]

According to Matthew Hodgart, the keynotes of satire are *lampoon* (personal attack) and *travesty* (fantastic vision of the world). For him, 'all good satire contains an element of aggressive attack and a fantastic vision of the world transformed: it is written for entertainment but contains sharp and telling comments on the world in which we live'.[176] Northrop Frye, on whose analysis of satire Hodgart's claim seems to be based, agrees that 'essential to satire [...] is an object of attack' and that it is distinguished from pure polemic by 'wit or humour founded on fantasy or a sense of the grotesque or absurd'.[177]

In addition to lampoon and travesty, the arsenal of satire includes raillery, diatribe, mimicry, pasquinade, parody, pastiche, caricature, irony and sarcasm. Perhaps not inappropriately, the term satire is often thought to derive from Latin *satura* 'dish of diverse fruits offered to the gods' (therefore also 'miscellany' or 'pot-pourri').[178]

The relationship between satire and irony, especially verbal irony, is complex and has received comparatively little scholarly attention. The most sub-

---

173 John Dryden, 'To the Reader' [preface], *Absalom and Achitophel* (London, 1966), edited by James and Helen Kinsley.

174 Gilbert Highet, *The Anatomy of Satire* (Princeton NJ, 1962), p. 237.

175 However, some scholars do claim that humour is an essential element of satire, Paul Simpson even attempts to integrate a theory of satire into an overarching theory of the comic, see his *On the Discourse of Satire* (Amsterdam and Philadelphia PN, 2003). This approach is open to numerous objections. The poisonous laughter we often find in satire bears little relation to comedy. Also, there is no evidence that someone who fails to be amused by a satirical text is therefore unable to recognize and appreciate its satirical intent. What is more, the claim that some form of comedy is always subliminally present is so vague as to be virtually irrefutable.

176 Matthew Hodgart, *Satire: Origins and Principles* (New York, 1969).

177 Northrop Frye, *Anatomy of Criticism: Four Essays* (New York, 1968), p. 224.

178 This is most widely accepted of the derivations suggested by Diomedes Grammaticus, the fourth-century Latin grammarian. For the text with translation and commentary, see C. A. Van Rooy, *Studies in Classical Satire and Related Literary Theory* (Leiden, 1966).

stantial treatments of this topic are those of Dustin Griffin, George Test and Zoya Pavlovski-Petit.[179] To my mind, Griffin's account is largely invalidated by his unqualified rejection of Booth's concept of 'stable irony' that is at the centre of modern thinking about literary irony, while Test's account is marred by his failure to make any meaningful distinction between irony and satire. My own account below broadly follows and develops that of Pavlovski-Petit.

Irony and satire are often closely associated, though 'few have been willing to fully sanctify the relationship'.[180] Indeed irony and satire sometimes merge, as they do in Erasmus' *Encomium moriae* (In Praise of Folly) or Swift's *Modest Proposal*, but when they do the irony in question is normally blatant (that some of Swift's readers still managed to misunderstand the irony in his *Modest Proposal* is not an argument against its blatancy). Since the satirist wishes his message to be clearly understood, he does not normally retreat into subtler forms of irony except when subjected to external pressure. The ironic satire in the short stories of Mikhail Zoshchenko is conditioned by the need to navigate the strictures of Stalinist censorship.[181] Satire may also tolerate subtler ironies when they are no more than occasional ironies within a broader overtly satirical context and are therefore most unlikely to be misunderstood.[182]

But though satire and irony sometimes come together, they are essentially different in focus, tone and temper. The satirist offers moral criticism and seeks to reform or punish, while the ironist may have no greater concern than to distance himself from what he is describing (to safeguard his intellectual and artistic integrity). The satirist is out to mock and deride, while the ironist is usually happy to tease and enjoy a quiet laugh at someone else's expense. The satirist wishes to stir emotion, while the ironist is concerned to avoid it, because 'irony is a mental pleasure, and our feelings may militate against a sense of irony where objectivity and distance are difficult to achieve'.[183] The satirist is intent on conveying a militant message, while the ironist is often more interested in playing an elaborate cat-and-mouse game with the reader (there is no such thing as private satire, but irony is often to some degree private). The satirist, when misunderstood, will most likely step in and interpret or rephrase his message, making his point yet more emphatically, while the ironist is more or less honour-bound to step back and

---

179   Dustin Griffin, *Satire: A Critical Reintroduction* (Lexington KY, 1994), pp. 65–70; George Test, *Satire: Spirit and Art* (Tampa FL, 1991), pp. 150–185; Zoya Pavlovski-Petit, 'Irony and Satire', in Ruben Quintero (ed.), *Companion to Satire* (Oxford, 2007), pp. 510–524.
180   George Test, *Satire: Spirit and Art* (Tampa FL, 1991), p. 151.
181   Mikhail Zoshchenko, *Rasskazy i povesti* (Volgograd, 1983). See also Birgit Mai, *Satire im Sowjetsozialismus* (Bern, 1993).
182   Emil Draitser provides several good examples of such ironies in his *Techniques of Satire: The Case of Saltykov-Ščedrin* (Berlin and New York, 1994).
183   Zoja Pavlovski-Petit, p. 511.

let misunderstanding take its course. Though some satire may ultimately be motivated by self-criticism, as Leonard Feinberg has suggested,[184] and may even resort to self-deprecation as a rhetorical device to curry sympathy with the reader, as is the case with Horace, the satirist always attacks his victims from a position of moral superiority; the ironist, on the other hand, will often tolerate and acknowledge a degree of moral ambivalence (there is no such thing as self-satire, but many ironies are tinged with self-irony).

That here is a difference in temper between the ironist and the satirist also comes through in Josef Hrabák's reluctance to classify the medieval Czech *Podkoní a žák* as a work of satire because, in his view, the anonymous author lacks the belligerence and verve of the satirist:

> Nechce bojovat, chce jen bavit, a proto také úsměv neznámého skladatele není žlučovitý a nenávistný. Chybí mu pravá satirická verva, je spíš usmívajícím se divákem, než plnokrevným satirikem.[185]

Podkoní a žák, which reports a pub-house dispute between a stable-hand and a student in which each argues for the superiority of his state while simultaneously revealing the utter abjectness of his condition, is best described as a work of sustained narrative irony, perhaps the first work of this kind in Czech literature.

What Hrabák might also have pointed to in favour of his classification of *Podkoní a žák* as a work of irony is that in narrative irony the perspective of the fictitious narrator is undermined by the author and needs to be deconstructed in order to arrive at the truth, whereas in satire the perspective of the fictitious narrator is usually endorsed by the author who uses it as a means of heightening focus by defamiliarizing the familiar. Think only of the satirical device of the narrator as foreigner that we find in Lucian's *Dialogues* (second century AD), Montesquieu's *Lettres persanes* (1721), Voltaire's *L'ingénu* (1767) and Goldsmith's *Citizen of the World* (1762); and of the narrator as articulate domestic pet that we find in Natsume Sōseki's *Wagahai wa neko de aru* (*I am a Cat*) (1906), Tibor Déry's *Niki* (1956) and Alfonz Bednár's *Za hrsť drobných* (1970–1984).[186]

---

184 Leonard Feinberg, *The Satirist* (New York, 1965).
185 Josef Hrabák, *Starší česká literatura* (Prague, 1964), p. 85, 86.
186 Lucian *Selected Dialogues* (Oxford, 2006); Charles de Montesquieu, *Lettres persanes*, edited by David Galand (Paris, 2003); François Voltaire, *L'ingénu*, edited by Paule Andrau (Paris, 2002); Oliver Goldsmith, *Citizen of the World* (London, 2006); Natsume Sōseki, *Wagahai wa neko de aru* (Tokyo, 1962), translated into German by Otto Putz as *Ich, der Kater* (Frankfurt, 2001), and into English by Aiko Ito and Graeme Wilson as *I am a Cat* (Clarendon VT, 2002); Tibor Déry, *Niki. Egy kutya története* (Budapest, 1956), translated into German by Ivan Nagel as *Niki. Die Geschichte eines Hundes* (Frankfurt, 2001), and into English by Edward Hyams as *Niki. The Story of a Dog* (New York, 2009); Alfonz Bednár, *Za hrsť drobných*, 3 vols (Bratislava, 1970, 1974 and 1981). See also Donna

4.9.3 SARCASM

Though some scholars use 'irony' and 'sarcasm' interchangeably, there is surely a partial distinction between the two terms. Perhaps the most obvious difference is that, as Haiman has pointed out, situations can be ironic but only people can be sarcastic.[187] Another important distinction seems to be that irony is generally considered to be at its best when subtle and veiled, whereas sarcasm (often referred to as 'the lowest form of wit')[188] strives to be maximally overt and forceful. The reason for this may be that, while irony is often collusive, hoping to extract a knowing chuckle or smile from the listener/reader, sarcasm tends to mordant and aggressive. Already George Puttenham in his *Art of English Poesie* (1589) distinguishes between the 'merry skoff' or 'drye mock' of irony and the 'bitter taunt' of sarcasm.[189] Rockwell characterizes sarcasm as 'cutting and contemptous';[190] Behler describes it as 'bittere, höhnende, vernichtende Ablehnung';[191] and, though we should beware of etymologizing, we can hardly ignore the fact that 'sarcasm' comes from Greek *sarkazein*, 'to tear flesh'.

We might even go a step further and argue that irony enriches communication while sarcasm aims to disrupt it. A good example of sarcasm's natural tendency to rebuff are the remarks of hotel manager Basil Fawlty in the popular TV comedy series *Fawlty Towers*. It is perhaps for this reason that Basil is often referred to as 'the king of sarcasm'. When a fastidious guest complains about the view from her bedroom window, Fawlty famously counters: 'And what did you expect to see out of a Torquay hotel bedroom window? Sydney Opera House perhaps? The Hanging Gardens of Babylon? Herds of wildebeest sweeping majestically across the plain?'.[192] But delight as we may in such rhetorical extravagance, we must be careful not to overstate the case. Sarcasm is usually only disruptive if it is directed at the listener; sarcasm directed at a common adversary can create a far stronger bond between speaker/writer and listener/hearer than the most engaging irony. Conversely, a particularly

---

Isaacs Dalnekoff, 'A familiar stranger: the outsider of eighteenth century satire', *Neophilologus* 57 (1973), No. 2, pp. 121–134.

187   John Haiman, *Talk Is Cheap: Sarcasm, Alienation and the Evolution of Language* (Oxford, 1998).

188   This remark is often attributed to Oscar Wilde, but there seems to be no evidence for this.

189   George Puttenham, *The Art of Poesie* (Amsterdam, 1971), pp. 166, 218, 318; quoted in Burkhard Meyer-Sickendiek, *Was ist literarischer Sarkasmus? Ein Beitrag zur deutsch-jüdischen Moderne* (München, 2009), p. 71.

190   Patricia Ann Rockwell, *Sarcasm and Other Mixed Messages: The Ambiguous Ways People Use Language* (Lewiston NY, 2006), p. 6.

191   Ernst Behler, 'Ironie/Humor', in Ulfert Ricklefs (ed.), *Fischer Lexikon Literatur* 3 vols (Frankfurt, 1996), vol. 2; quoted in Burkhard Meyer-Sickendiek, p. 87.

192   John Cleese, 'Communication problems' in *The Complete Fawlty Towers* (London, 1998), pp. 159–186 (p. 166).

cruel or insidious irony directed at the listener may be as effective in putting an end to a conversation as the most overt sarcasm.

Meyer-Sickendiek, who has written the most comprehensive study of literary sarcasm to date, claims that while irony merely breaks the rules of conversation, sarcasm breaks cultural and moral taboos:

> Für den Sarkasmus ist nicht allein entscheidend, dass er die Regeln der Konversation bricht, wie dies die Ironie tut. Der Sarkasmus übertritt zudem auch kulturelle Verbote, er bricht moralische Tabus.[193]

He goes on to claim that sarcasm is socially corrosive:

> Der Sarkasmus zerstört soziale, kulturelle und moralische Werte. Er zerbricht und schwächt den kollektiven Frieden, die kulturelle Harmonie und den sozialen Zusammenhalt.[194]

Again, this is to overstate the case. Swift's *Modest Proposal* is usually regarded as a work of sustained irony, even though it breaks one of the most deep-seated cultural and moral taboos there is: the proscription of cannibalism; and sarcasm directed at attitudes and practices deemed socially harmful can hardly be considered socially subversive at the same time.

Perhaps the greatest overstatement of the distinction between irony and sarcasm can be found in an article by American psychologists Lee and Katz, who claim that 'in sarcasm, there is a specific victim who is the target of ridicule, whereas in irony, there is no one in particular who is the victim', basing their simplistic and apodictic assertion on an article by Kreuz and Glucksberg, which neither claims nor proves anything of the sort.[195] Kreuz and Glucksberg merely argue, on the basis of a small empirical survey, that American college students are more likely to identify a remark as sarcastic if there is a specific victim and as ironic if there is not. We may grant this conclusion without in any way accepting the generalisation that sarcasm always has a specific victim and irony does not. Some ironies are inconceivable without a victim (irony of fate, dramatic irony) and victims play such a central role in all forms of irony that leading theorist D. C. Muecke considers the existence of a victim to be a necessary condition of irony, as we have already seen. Sarcasm may be directed a 'specific victim' but it may equally well

---

193 Burkhard Meyer-Sickendiek, p. 14.
194 Burkhard Meyer-Sickendiek, p. 16.
195 Christopher Lee and Albert Katz, 'The Differential Role of Ridicule in Sarcasm and Irony', *Metaphor and Symbol* 13 (1998), pp. 1–15; and Roger Kreuz and Sam Glucksberg, 'How to Be Sarcastic: The Echoic Reminder Theory of Verbal Irony', *Journal of Experimental Psychology: General*, 118 (1989), No. 4, pp. 374–386.

be directed at a group, a set of social practices, an ideology – even something as impersonal as the weather. If I come out of my office to find it pouring with rain, I may exclaim: 'Brilliant. That's all I needed. Just when I forgot my umbrella'. Unless we take a strangely anthropomorphic view of the elements, it is hard to see who the 'specific victim' of this remark might be.

However, the difference between irony and sarcasm may sometimes be understated. Some scholars view sarcasm as a mere sub-category of irony because the interpretation of sarcastic utterances often involves a reversal of meaning or valuation typical of irony. Kaufer argues against this tendency to subsume sarcasm under irony, stressing that:

> Sarcasm designates a general *tone* of utterance while irony, the opposition of meaning. Wed together, irony enhances a sarcastic effect by increasing its bite but sarcasm is no more dependent on irony than irony on it. The widespread confusion of irony with sarcasm results from the frequency with which sarcasm is encoded ironically.[196]

Schoentjes provides an example of sarcastic remark that he believes is not encoded ironically:

> Ce n'est pas vous qui allez nous tirer de là.[197]

He considers this remark sarcastic although its interpretation does not involve any revision of meaning. The question, of course, arises as to whether such a remark should be considered merely caustic rather than truly sarcastic. However, it is quite possible that the concept of sarcasm is not precise enough to allow us to arbitrate on this matter satisfactorily.

The whole issue is further confused by the fact that some languages appear to use terms pertaining to sarcasm considerably less frequently than English does (e.g. 'Don't be sarcastic' is a far more common rejoinder in English than the literal equivalent in Russian, Czech or Polish) and some languages fail to observe the distinction between irony and sarcasm entirely (e.g. Arabic *sakhriya*, Sanskrit *kila*, Chinese *fengci* and Japanese *hiniku* translate both 'irony' and 'sarcasm'). There may even be a difference in the way sarcasm is conceptualized in languages as closely related as English and German. Recently perusing Adam Fletcher's bilingual *Wie man Deutscher wird/How to be German*, I was struck by the fact that the chapter heading 'Fail at Sarcasm' was rendered into German as 'Mit Ironie scheitern'.[198] As a bilingual speaker of

196   David S. Kaufer, 'Irony, Interpretative Form, and the Theory of Meaning', *Poetics Today*, 4 (1983), pp- 451–464 (p. 453).
197   Pierre Schoentjes, p. 228.
198   Adam Fletcher, *Wie man Deutscher wird/How to Be German* (Munich, 2013), pp. 55–55 and 58–60.

these languages myself, I felt that his translation was spot-on. An explanation of why it may sometimes be appropriate to translate English 'sarcasm' with German 'Ironie' has been provided by Meyer-Sickendiek. In the pioneering study cited above, Meyer-Sickendiek shows how the concept of sarcasm, introduced into Germany by Wieland in the late eighteenth century, became attached to specific manifestations of a German-Jewish tradition of satire running from Heine over Kraus and Tucholsky to Döblin and Broder. If he is right about this, then the concept of sarcasm may well be significantly narrower in German than in English.

To make matters worse, it is not only the interlingual boundaries that may be unclear. Attardo and others have argued that irony and sarcasm cannot reliably be differentiated not only because sarcasm is 'a folk concept and has fuzzy boundaries',[199] but also because 'a shift in meaning for the word irony seems to be taking place with sarcasm occupying what was previously the semantic space of irony'.[200]

4.9.4 THE GROTESQUE

Philip Thomson defines the grotesque as 'the unresolved clash of incompatibles in work and response' and as 'the ambivalently abnormal'[201] – 'ambivalent' because the grotesque combines the comic and the terrifying. He repeatedly emphasizes the unresolved nature of the grotesque conflict and considers it a distinguishing feature. The same point has been made by Michael Steig, who speaks of the 'state of unresolved tension' that results from our contemplation of the grotesque.[202]

Thomson's account of the difference between irony and the grotesque is so accurate that I can do no better than quote it at length. First, he points to intellectual nature of irony compared with the emotional nature of the grotesque:

Irony is primarily intellectual in its function and appeal, and the grotesque is primarily emotional. [...] The impact of the grotesque is characteristically one of a sudden shock, which is likely to stun, bewilder or nonplus – the mind takes a few seconds to function dispassionately again. Irony, on the other hand, depends very much for its

---

199 Salvatore Attardo et al., 'Multimodal markers of irony and sarcasm', *International Journal of Humor Research*, 16 (2003), pp. 243–260 (p. 243); quoted in Patricia Ann Rockwell, p. 7.

200 Salvatore Attardo, 'Humor, irony, and their communication: From mode adoption to failure of detection' in Luigi Anolli et al., *Say not to say* (Amsterdam, 2001), pp. 159–179), p. 171; quoted in Patricia Ann Rockwell, p. 7.

201 Philip Thomson, *The Grotesque* (London, 1972), p. 27.

202 Michael Steig, 'Defining the Grotesque: An Attempt at Synthesis', *Journal of Aesthetics and Art Criticism*, 29 (1970/1971), p. 260.

effect on the reader's being given the chance to intellectually to make distinctions and connections. In the extreme case, the grotesque writer will deliberately prevent a rational and intellectual approach to his work, demonstrating that the intolerable and inextricable mixture of incompatibles is a fact of life, perhaps the most crucial one. The ironist places the incompatible also in some kind of relationship, but it is always a relationship that can be 'worked out'. Much of one's pleasure in irony comes from detecting it.[203]

Second, coming back to his initial point, Thomson makes it clear that the clashes and tensions of irony are necessarily resolvable whereas the incompatibilites of the grotesque are ultimately unresolvable.

> [...] irony depends on the resolvability, intellectually, of a relationship (appearance/reality, truth/untruth, etc.), while the grotesque presents essentially the unresolvability of incompatibles.[204]

Ultimately the distinction between irony and the grotesque rests on the question of resolvability. Irony may use striking incongruities and marked deformations or distortions to make its point, but these are always resolvable by recourse to the implied meaning.

4.9.5 PARODY AND THE BURLESQUE

The burlesque is based on an incongruity between style and object. Joseph Addison first divided the burlesque into a low and a high variety. In the low burlesque, a vulgar style is used for an exalted object while in the high burlesque, elevated style is used for an lowly object. Richmond Bond extended this view of the burlesque by defining specific and general forms for each variety.[205] According to Bond, the specific form of the low burlesque is travesty, while the specific form of the high burlesque is parody. Both travesty and parody are directed against specific literary works, while general forms of the burlesque are directed against overall literary movements or stylistic fashions. This categorization has subsequently been adopted and popularized by David Worcester, John Jump, and others.[206]

There is clearly a connection between irony and the burlesque. Both irony and the burlesque aim to deflate and debunk. Irony is particularly close in

203 Philip Thomson, p. 49.
204 Philip Thomson, p. 50.
205 Richmond Bond, *English Burlesque Poetry 1700–1750* (Cambridge MA, 1932).
206 David Worcester, *The Art of Satire* (Cambridge MA, 1940); John Jump, *The Burlesque* (London, 1972).

intention to the high burlesque, both in its specific form of parody and its general form that, for want of a better word, we may call the 'mock-heroic' (to include the mock Romantic, the mock sentimental etc.). Just as the parodist uses elevated style for a lowly object, the ironist uses praise for the blame-worthy. But there are obvious differences, as I shall try to show.

The relationship between irony and parody has often been discussed. Wayne Booth accepts parody as a form of irony because in his view both parody and irony require the reader to make an inference to an unfavourable meaning from a favourable one, and both have the function of mockery. Linda Hutcheon, who has made a special study of this issue, believes that irony and parody are intimately connected because they have the same structure of semantic superimposition and interreferentiality: in parody, the parodying text refers beyond itself to the parodied text; in irony, the non-ironic meaning refers to the ironic meaning in the text.[207]

When it comes to the distinction between irony and parody, Margaret Rose is surely correct when she says that irony is 'more cryptic' than parody.[208] Linda Hutcheon seems to be making a similar point when she says that irony is 'the rhetorical minor of parody'. Irony prefers the covert and the subtle. But there is another issue. Rose again hits the nail on the head when she says that irony uses one code while parody inevitably involves a combination of two codes: the code of the parodied work and the code of the parody. For this reason, recognizing parody requires specialist knowledge of the kind that understanding irony normally does not. Of course, to understand historically distant ironies, we may have to reconstruct contemporary meanings and associations, but in doing so we are merely trying to compensate for our own remoteness from the context: the touchstone for irony remains normal usage, common sense and generally available knowledge of the world.

4.10 IRONY AND DECADENCE

Since we are dealing with irony and we also have cause to refer to the Decadence, it is perhaps appropriate to make it clear that the Decadents, like the Romantics, often made use of irony. However, despite the inflation of ironies we have already lamented, as far as I know, nobody has ever seriously proposed 'Decadent irony' as a type.

The Decadents' use of irony has never been examined in a systematic way. We have no study of the relationship between Decadence and irony, not even within the confines of a single literary tradition; all we have are occasional

207 Linda Hutcheon, *A Theory of Parody*.
208 Margaret Rose, *Parody: ancient, modern and postmodern* (Cambridge, 1993).

studies of, and more frequently transitory references to, the use of irony in writers associated with the Decadence.

Like the Romantics, the Decadents often refused to take themselves completely seriously, perhaps because the Decadence was an anti-bourgeois movement and taking oneself seriously was seen as a characteristically bourgeois trait, perhaps also because of a need to relieve the gloom and blunt the extremes in order to retain the reader's sympathy.

Already Flaubert has been suspected of 'grafting irony on to the uncanny'[209] There is a clear ironic strategy in Jules Laforgue, whose pessimistic poems almost always end with a sardonic twist. In Léon Bloy's Le désesperé, and in Octave Mirbeau's Abbé Jules and his Journal d'une femme de chambre, there is a 'tristesse qui rit' (to use Mirbeau's own phrase), a humour which shines through in an attempt to relieve the abject misery. Morton Gurewitsch has generalized this point by suggesting that aestheticism, by its very nature, ultimately eschews anguish and tragedy, preferring to sublimate the dramatic into the ironic.[210] This may also explain what Robert Pynsent sees as the 'ironic tone' of Karel Hlaváček's Mstivá kantiléna, a poem based on the rebellion of the Gueux in the Spanish Netherlands whose title may be thought to paradoxically combine the idea of vengefulness with that of melodious singing, thereby, according to Fedor Soldan, intimating a 'podivné spojení sociální nenávisti s melancholickou touhou po kráse'.[211]

In several Decadent writers, there is a sense of the dangers and ultimate absurdity implicit in a sustained Decadent stance. In Joris-Karl Huysman's A rebours, Rémy de Gourmont's Sixtine and Jean Lorrain's Monsieur Bougrelon, the authors acknowledge the paradoxality and human cost of the 'vie cérébrale' (to use de Gourmont's phrase), of an existence entirely given over to detached aesthetic contemplation and the indulgence of an unfettered imagination.[212] Schoentjes has gone so far as to suggest that the Decadent use of irony is based on and shaped by the Decadent love of paradox. Developing Michael Riffaterre's observation that paradox is constantly present in Decadent texts and D. C. Muecke's comparison of Romantic irony to the reflections in a hall of mirrors, Schoentjes argues that:

---

209   Charles Bernheimer, The Decadent Subject, preface.

210   Morton Gurewitsch, The Ironic Temper and the Comic Imagination (Detroit MI, 1994), chapter 2.

211   Robert Pynsent, 'Desire, Frustration and Some Fulfilment: A Commentary to Karel Hlaváček's Mstivá kantiléna', Slavonic and East European Review, 72 (1994), pp. 1–37 (p. 3); Fedor Soldan, Karel Hlaváček. Typ české dekadence (Prague, 1930), p. 47 (quoted in Robert Pynsent). Pynsent's case is not entirely convincing because, like Soldan, he seems to be unware of the fact that cantilenes often related tales of combat, cf. Cantilène de Saucourt, Cantilène d'Hildebrand. He also makes scant reference to instances of irony in the text.

212   Basing himself on de Gourmount, Ridge coined the term 'cerebralism'. He considers cerebralism to be one of the principal defining characteristics of the Decadence, see John Ross Ridge, The Hero in French Decadent Literature.

L'ironie de la décadence n'est pas une ironie de dédoublement: son image n'est pas celle du miroir mais bien celle du labyrinthe d'un palais de glaces où des miroirs, face à face, se réfléchissssent à l'infini. Le dédoublement du miroir offre encore l'image d'une ironie stable; au palais des glaces correspond une ironie instable.[213]

This view of Decadent irony assimilates it to Romantic irony and therefore removes it from the realms of stable irony that is our principal concern here.

---

213 Pierre Schoentjes, 'J.-K. Huysmans et l'ironie d'*A rebours*', in Perrine Galland-Hallyn (ed.), *Les Décadents à l'école des Alexandrins* (Valenciennes, 1996); Michael Riffaterre, 'Paradoxes déca-dents', in Mary Shaw and François Cornilliat (eds), *Rhétoriques fin de siècle* (Paris, 1992); and D. C. Muecke, 'Images of Irony', *Poetics Today*, 4 (2003), no. 3, pp. 399–413.

5. INTRODUCTION TO THE READINGS

I have chosen the following five texts for analysis: 'Poledne', 'Pláč Nioby', 'Rubensova Zahrada lásky', 'Čínská povídka' and 'Zrada'.

'Poledne' is from Opolský's earliest period as a prose writer. First published in the journal *Rozhledy* in 1903, it was included in *Kresby uhlem* (1907), Opolský's first volume of prose. 'Pláč Nioby' and 'Rubensova Zahrada lásky' were both written in the middle of Opolský's prose-writing career and were published for the first time in *Malé prósy* (1926). 'Čínská povídka' was first published in the newspaper *Národní politika* in 1940, shortly before the writer's death in early 1942, and was included in the posthumous collection *Hranolem křišťálu* (1944). 'Zrada' appeared in the same volume, but there is no previous record of publication. Since *Hranolem křišťálu* brings together prose written over a twenty-year period (1921–1941), this leaves us without any reliable indication as to its precise time of origin.

Though I have tried to achieve a reasonable spread in terms of chronology and subject matter, I am not claiming that the texts can be considered representative for this reason. Five texts can never be statistically representative of a total of three hundred and more, no matter how they are selected. The best I can hope for is to establish representativeness *ex post facto*, by demonstrating that the narrative structure of each text is so similar and so consistently sustained, so idiosyncratic and sophisticated in its artistry, that it is virtually impossible to believe that this mode of composition is not an essential part of Opolský's creative project, at least as far as his prose is concerned.

Each analysis takes the form of a running commentary. To this end I divide the text into short passages, some equal to, some longer, and some shorter than a paragraph, and comment on each passage in turn. To make it clear where paragraphs in the original text begin, quotations are indented at that point; a quotation without an indentation belongs to the same paragraph as the previous quotation. In the interests of concision, a few minor omissions in the texts have been made but these are signalled and do not in any way affect the interpretation. The exposition is strictly linear and makes no attempt to mirror the psychological process by which an individual reader might come to recognize the ironic meaning. Since there is no way of predicting what path a reader may take and there is no straighforward path that the reader should take, linear exposition is the only way to provide an account of the irony that is both efficient and non-arbitrary. The price that has to be paid for this mode of exposition may well be a lack of 'convincingness', especially in the early stages. The reader of a linear commentary is effectively 'thrown in at the deep end', finding himself suddenly confronted with a multitude of ironic implications that he could not possibly have worked out for himself at such an early stage. This places a considerable burden on the reader, and one which is aggravated by the act of explanation itself. Since we are meant to 'get' irony by ourselves, having irony explained to us is naturally disconcerting, even demeaning. Caught between bewilderment and belittlement, the reader's first impulse is almost certainly to rebel. I must ask the reader to resist this impulse and to go along with the interpretation as far as he reasonably can, before stepping back to judge.

The only thing that may ease the reader's burden is that there is no compelling need to read all the analyses all the way through, nor is there any compelling need to read all of them in exactly the same way or in the order given. The reader may choose to begin at the beginning but skip to the conclusion if satisfied that the argument is broadly correct. Alternatively, the reader may choose to begin by reading several analyses of his own choice, and then attempt to interpret the remaining texts largely unaided, turning to the commentary only where required.

6. POLEDNE[214]

We might, at first, be tempted to read 'Poledne' as a piece of social criticism perhaps not entirely dissimilar to the social criticism of Czech Decadent writers like Jiří Karásek and Arnošt Procházka. Describing a lunch-hour in an unnamed, and therefore potentially typical, small town, the writer seems to be lamenting the decline of provincial life to its contemporary desolate banality and to be scathing the local inhabitants particularly for their vulgarity and depravity.

Below the surface, however, sustained authorial irony is drawing a different picture. The text opens with the narrator giving his first impressions of the town and trying to explain them to himself.

> Stalo se, jakoby městečko pozbylo svého půvabu i jeho staleté zvony promluvily ke mně řečí konvenční a hluchou. Viděl jsem srdce jejich tlouci jako v mánii, ale nemělo to ušlechtilého významu z doby dříve minulé. Bily, bily, ale duši to nepozvedalo a nebylo jim rozuměti ničeho.
>
> Přemýšlel jsem o možném zhrubnutí mysli. Ale viny jsem na sobě nenalézal!
>
> O nepřiznané zášti. Ale nebylo jí a nebude!
>
> Stalo se, jakoby městečko pozbylo svého půvabu, ač jsem se já k tomu nepřičinil.

The main ironic insight here lies in the gradual realization that this description is telling us very little about the town and a great deal about the narrator himself. What is more, the more vigorously the narrator denies his involvement in what he observes, the clearer it becomes his perceptions are merely a projection of his aberrant sensibility. The irony begins almost imperceptibly at first. In the opening 'stalo se, jakoby' there is a covert semantic tension between 'stalo se' and 'jakoby', because 'jakoby' normally collocates more satisfactorily with verbs of appearing than verbs of occurring. By allowing this tension, the author is providing a first gentle hint at the narrator's tendency to confuse appearance and reality while at the same time suggesting that the experience the narrator is reporting may be no more than a unique occurrence. Even 'jakoby' itself is compromising, because it allows

---

214 Jan Opolský, 'Poledne', *Rozhledy*, 13 (1902–3), pp. 1232–4; reprinted in *Kresby uhlem* (Prague, 1907), pp. 53–6.

the author to imply that the narrator's claim about the town's loss of appeal is mere supposition. The narrator's lament that the church bells are speaking to him in an uninspiring manner mockingly reveals his overweening religiosity, his perverse self-centredness, and his tendency to engage in flights of wild fancy. This implication is underscored by 'staleté zvony' and 'řeč konvenční a hluchá'. At first, we are inclined to understand 'konvenční' as 'conventional' in the derived sense of 'commonplace', 'prosaic'; and 'hluchý' as 'idle', 'empty'. The author, however, is prompting us to understand 'konvenční' as 'conventional' in the root sense of 'established by convention', 'based on accepted standards'; and 'hluchý' as 'dull of sound'. Read in this second way, 'konvenční' and 'hluchý' would now normally be thought virtually redundant with regard to 'řeč' and 'staleté zvony' respectively, so that we can hardly adequately explain their use in this meaning other than by considering the narrator so divorced from reality that he does not understand that all speech is based on accepted norms, and that the centuries-old, doubtless heavily patinated, bells cannot be expected to ring out as new. That the narrator compares the normally ponderous motion of old church bells to manic beating suggests that he is so lacking in vitality that he sees even slow activity as a frenzy and is so unbalanced mentally that manic states are especially familiar to him. The cunning overlap between the literal and the metaphorical engineered in '[viděl jsem] srdce tlouci (*srdce* 'clanger' or 'heart'; *tlouci* 'to bang' or 'to beat') acts as a covert indication of the narrator's tendency to conflate the real and the imaginary. The implicit assumption that manic excitement is normally related to spiritual refinement that underlies the narrator's disappointed 'ale' brings out his perverse sensibility even further. The apparent tautology '[z doby] dříve minulé' implies that he is so engrossed in the past that he feels that 'minulý' alone, without a duplicating 'dříve', is not sufficient to convey genuine historicity. The expression 'duši to nepozvedalo' hints at his inveterate melancholy. By having 'duši to nepozvedalo' be followed directly by 'nebylo jim [zvonům] rozuměti ničeho', the author is suggesting that the narrator's understanding of things is heavily emotionally biased. This implication is all the stronger since the narrator's claim that he could not understand anything the bells were saying strictly speaking contradicts his previous characterization of the bells' message. At the same time, the narrator's claim not to to have been able to understand the bells implicitly exposes the illusoriness of his belief that they were speaking to him. That the narrator goes on to ask himself whether his impression has been influenced by a coarsening of the mind or by unacknowledged hate only to flatly deny any part in either suggests that he is a person who is ravaged by preposterous self-doubt which he counters with bursts of blustering self-righteousness. That he denies three times, like Peter denying Jesus or Jesus defying Satan, is a further comic hint at his importunate religiosity. His 'zhrubnutí mysli', which reminds us of the commoner 'zhrubnutí mravů/chování' that it simultaneously eclipses, mockingly suggests that his idea of refinement is of an unusually abstract and rarefied kind. The following 'viny jsem na sobě nenalézal' conveniently allows for the possibility that, in the narrator's opinion, said refinement may well be lacking in others. The second denial, 'nebylo jí [zášti] a nebude', compromises the narrator by the conspicuous omission of the present tense form 'není'. The repetition preceding the third denial that appears to be a sort of poetic refrain for the author reflects merely the narrator's embarrassment at his lack of convincing excuses. Finally, seen against this background, we can appreciate that the narrator's use of trite romantic language ('půvab') and his quest for refined significance ('ušlechtilý význam') are just further indications of the nature of his ironic make-up.

> Sklánělo se k poledni.
> Prudce pnul se kostel sv. Mikuláše a všude kolem něho kupily se holé ševcovské stánky. Do značné výšky vznášela se také morová boží muka tučně fermeží natřená a čtyři svatí nuceni byli nésti glorii v podobě mosazného víčka.

By allowing 'sklánělo se', that in this temporal sense metaphorically reflects the setting of the sun, to be followed rather oddly by 'k poledni', the author is implying that the narrator regards noon not as the highest but as the lowest point in the day, presumably because he is averse to the warmth and brightness of the midday sun. That the narrator continues his description of the town by mentioning a church and a passion column surmounted by figures of saints hints again at his religiosity. In 'prudce pnul se [kostel]', the combination of 'prudce' with 'pnout se' suggests that the narrator is intimidated by tall objects, as, in a milder way, does the only seemingly trivial 'do značné výšky' referring to the plague column. The use of 'všude' and 'kupit se' with regard to the shoemakers' stalls implies that the narrator is exaggerating, because it is unlikely that a small town should have so many shoemakers, and unlikelier still that they should all chose to set up stall in the same place. The reason for the narrator's exaggeration is, we suspect, his annoyance at what he considers a profanation of sacred soil. The narrator's 'holé stánky' betrays irrational criticism of these stalls for not being elaborately decorated and so covertly testifies to his aesthetic oversensitivity. The disgust we sense behind 'tučně' in '[muka] tučně fermeží natřená' is similarly unreasonable, because wood standing outside in all weathers obviously needs to be well protected. The remark about the saints' haloes compromises the narrator further. Since brass discs would normally be thought an unexceptionable means of representing haloes particularly on figures standing outdoors, we are led to suspect that the narrator is dissatisfied simply because the haloes are not genuine.

Suchý vítr severovýchodní zdál se míti uloženo cloumati lazebnickou miskou, pokud se dalo, nemohl také míti ve své svědomitosti a houževnaté snaze žádného soupeře.

Ráz na ráz skřípala miska na svém železném háku a v tomto zpěvu bylo něco horšího, nežli suché loupání v kostech.

The seemingly unnecessary specificness of 'suchý vítr severovýchodní' suggests that the narrator distinguishes oversensitively between different kinds of wind, rather like an old woman who feels the weather in her bones. The narrator's claim that the bowl is being shaken about is subverted in a number of ways. First, his '[vítr] zdál se' may be taken to relativize not only the metaphorical 'míti uloženo' but the dependent verb 'cloumati' as well. Second, 'pokud se dalo' leaves it open whether the movement was extremely vigorous or heavily restricted. Third, the claim that the wind was unrivalled on reflection reveals itself as platitudinous, since it is clear that nothing and nobody else would be trying to shake the sign in this way. Finally, the concentration on the wind's conscientiousness and assiduous effort suggests its ultimate ineffectiveness, since we often emphasize application to excuse failure. Noteworthy is also 'lazebnická miska'. At first we take 'lazebnický' to be an old-fashioned reference to the barber's trade. However, a bowl is not a sign for a barber's shop (in some countries marked by poles with spiral stripes) but for a chemist's (in the form of a pestle and mortar or the bowl of Hygeia surmounted by the serpent of Epidaurus). Since 'lazebník' can also be a derogatory term for a member of the medical profession ('quack', 'medico'), we begin to suspect that the narrator may be so bound up in superstition and prejudice that he regards scientific medicine as humbug. The reference to the creaking of the sign on its iron hook compromises the narrator further because it implicitly confirms that what is at issue here is not so much the vigorous swaying of the sign as the narrator's neurotic dislike of metallic grating sounds. The sense of dynamism the narrator is trying to create continues to be subverted by 'ráz na ráz', which indicates irritating successiveness rather than inordinate speed while at the same time leaving it open how frequent the offending noise was. By calling the noise 'zpěv', the narrator is betraying a curious understanding of song, one that may have been influenced by the monotony and slowness of ritual chanting. That the narrator compares the grating to a sort of rheumatic pain not only implies that he believes himself a sufferer but also encourages us to think of this rheumatism rather comically as a grating of bones. The inclusion of 'něco [ve zpěvu]' ironizes the narrator's tendency to vagueness and suggests also that it was only some minor aspect of the noise that was felt to be unpleasant in the way described. Contributory to the ironic stylization of the narrator are the elements of personification in 'míti uloženo', 'svědomitost', 'houževnatý' and 'soupeř', which are meant to prepare us for the realization that the narrator is inclined to see the world in childishly animistic terms.

> U paty pomníku, který svým způsobem diskreditoval představu národního hrdiny, strojily se ob den psí námluvy a horký písek vymršťován byl na všecky strany.
>
> Vítězství chýlilo se zdánlivě na stranu nepokrytého hnusu a malá slečna zavřela hlučně knihu v kterémsi okně prvního poschodí. Malá slečna přezvána byla Jane, sirotek Lowoodský, [...]. Jane, chorobné milovaná! Jane, pětkráte do roka čtená!

By 'svým způsobem' the author is hinting again at the narrator's tendency to vagueness and is also questioning whether the monument was discrediting in any normal sense. The insertion of 'představa' is meant to suggest that it was not the national hero himself who was at all discredited, merely some unspecified conception of him. At the same time, the preference of the formerly still rather exalted foreign borrowing 'diskreditovat' to a more traditional 'zneuctívat (památku)' brings out the narrator's affectation and social snobbery. His dissatisfaction with this monument covertly testifies to the idealistic nationalism and hero worship that we are invited to see as part of his romantic outlook. That the national hero in question is most likely Jan Hus provides a further hint at the narrator's religiosity.[215] The only seemingly sarcastic use of 'strojit se' and 'námluvy' to describe the behaviour of dogs who were presumably only sniffing at each other in passing covertly mocks the narrator's formalism and prudish conventionality, while 'ob den' suggests that the putative disturbance was not unduly frequent. The mention of the dogs also leads us to wonder whether their occasional presence is not the only reason why the narrator considers the monument discrediting. The subsequent '[písek] vymršťován [byl]' and 'na všecky strany' are implicitly affected exaggerations, because we can hardly imagine either the dogs or the wind described in the previous passage to be producing such a tremendous whirl of sand or dust. The narrator's claim that disgust was prevailing or gaining the upper hand, which begins the next paragraph, is undermined already by 'zdánlivě'. The formulation 'vítězství chýlilo se [...] na stranu [...] hnusu' for the author is not sarcastic, as it may appear to be, but reflects the narrator's tendency to express himself in a turgidly pompous and ludicrously fanciful way. For the author too, the adjective 'nepokrytý' does not intensify, as it seems to be doing, but simply reveals the narrator's dislike of openly displayed emotion. The reference to the girl in the window that seems to have been made in illustration of the allegedly prevailing disgust is variously subversive. The shutting of a book, even if it is done loudly, is hardly an ex-

---

215   In the main square of Opolský's native Nová Paka there is, besides a passion column of the kind described, also a monument to Jan Hus.

emplary sign of unreserved disgust, and what disgust it may have expressed would anyway be thought to have been directed more at the contents of the book than at the scene the narrator has been criticizing. That the narrator uses 'hlučně' to describe the shutting of a book at first-floor level above him suggests that he is oversensitive to noise. The smallness of the woman, her reading and therefore presumably sitting behind a first floor window, and the suspiciously vague 'v kterémsi okně' together imply that the narrator could not and did not see her, except in his mind's eye. That this presumably nonexistent woman is said to be nicknamed 'Jane, orphan of Lowood' consequently shows not the local inhabitants' but the narrator's affection for, and preoccupation with, the romantic figure of Jane Eyre. His saying 'Jane, chorobně milovaná! Jane, pětkráte do roka čtená!' therefore implies that it is he who loved her morbidly, not Rochester or a sentimental readership, and he who read the novel five times a year, not the local inhabitants. It is also revealing that 'čtená [Jane]' is attributed to the same subject as 'milovaná [Jane]' in these last two sentences, because this can suggest that the narrator is unable to distinguish satisfactorily between books and fictional characters, between the real and the unreal.

> Poledne přišlo a počaly se odmýkati dveře kanceláří. Adjunkt berní, nově povýšený, ztrácel se úplně v oblaku vysněné blahovůle své, figura soudního sekretáře, tučná, z těsta syrového, lící ustavičně zrosených tak jako oči mladého telete, pohybovala se krokem stokráte zjinačeným.
> I strážník vyšel, přizrzlý, dobrácký, jehož pysky ohledávaly se ustavičně v nevýslovně pokorném ševelení. Kdo ho viděl, rozuměl. Ve jménu jeho veličenství, císaře...

The expression 'poledne přišlo', though not unidiomatic, has ironic value because it comports with previous evidence of the narrator's tendency to personify indiscriminately. Telling is also the supposition that the office doors had to be unlocked, not just opened, before the employees could come out for lunch, since it may be taken to imply that the narrator considers ordinary paid work tantamount to imprisonment. The characterisation of the tax official develops the irony. That it is benevolence the narrator believes the tax official to be affecting prompts us to suspect that he is projecting his own moral aspirations and priorities into the mind of this character. The narrator's conviction that his supposed benevolence is merely affected, however, suggests that he is prejudiced by seeing the man as a servant of mammon, as a publican and sinner. The use of 'vysněný' in this connection provides another hint at the narrator's romanticism. His '[adjunkt] ztrácel se úplně v oblaku [vysněné blahovůle]' compromises the narrator further. The metaphorical use of 'ztrácet se (úplně) v čem' and even 'oblak čeho' each on its own is not unusual. In this combination, however, the metaphors are stretched beyond their conventional bounds and so come to evoke a comically graphic picture. The ironic effect is heightened by 'nově povýšený', because we may think of 'povýšený' in this connection as meaning not only 'promoted' but also 'elevated', 'uplifted'. We are thereby finally left with the ridiculous background image of this man ascending to the sky and disappearing in a cloud. Besides covertly mocking the narrator's tendency to confuse abstract and concrete, this subversive picture indirectly pokes fun at the narrator's religiosity. The use of 'tučný' for 'tlustý' in describing the clerk of court suggests that the narrator is secretly disgusted by human flesh. This suggestion is covertly supported by 'z těsta syrového', that, as a comic dislocation of the stock phrase 'z jednoho/z jiného těsta', mocks also the narrator's squeamishness and daintiness. The word 'zrosený' hints at the narrator's romanticism. The same is true of 'jako oči mladého telete', which is also rather ridiculous, because 'tele' is often used to express stupidity, as in 'dívat se jako tele na nová vráta'. In the description of the clerk's gait, 'stokrate' prompts us to infer that the narrator is grossly exaggerating, while the euphemistic and vague 'zjinačený' both secretly mocks the narrator's preciosity and leaves it open to what extent the man's walk may really be considered at all abnormal. The narrator's vision is ironically characterized also by the formulation 'figura [...] pohybovala se krokem' that is unduly abstract and lacking dynamism. That the narrator in portraying the policeman singles out his reddish hair from all other physical attributes and follows immediately with 'dobrácký' suggests that he fancifully imagines there to be a connection between reddish hair and kindness, presumably because he associates reddishness with a warm glowing and this warm glowing with kindness, in accordance with the central imagery of *Jane Eyre*,[216] the expression '[jeho] pysky ohledávaly se', by its conspicuous deviation from the standard 'ohrnovat pysky' and by the comic incongruity of the picture it presents, covertly ridicules the narrator's eagerness to personify. The narrator's belief that the movement of the man's lips is deferential implies that he sees it in analogy to prayer; indeed, even 'pokorný' itself hints at a religious scale of values. That the narrator imagines the man he has said is good-natured to be expressing devotion to the emperor suggests that he is not being sarcastic about this subservience, as we might think, but recording it approvingly. This prompts us to suspect that the narrator is a smug bourgeois whose loyalty to this system is at least as strong as, and by no means at odds with, his religious commitment. That the narrator did not hear what the man really said and is therefore putting his own tendentious interpretation on it is implied by 'kdo ho viděl, rozuměl' and also, secondarily, 'nevýslovně'.

---

216   On this point see the chapter 'Fire and Eyre: Charlotte Brontë's War of Earthly Elements' in David Lodge, *The Language of Fiction* (London, 1966), pp. 114-143.

[...] Fabričky s prsama zakrslýma utvořily po silnici kratší i delší řetězy, stavíce se oplzlejšími, než kdy byly a přivykajíce si v chůzi jistému methodickému pohybu křivou kyčlí. Rozrušovaly se osudem zatčené kuplířky, která od plodu pomáhala a vyhlížely ve svých lačných skupinách tak jako mouchy na čerstvém neřádu shluklé.

Jste-li vy sestry moje? rozpakoval jsem se v duchu, ale obával jsem se řádné odpovědi. Sestry, o nichž jsem snível a jejichž bídě věnovány byly znamenité idey věku?

Ucítil jsem hořkost a v ústech pachuť vlastního jazyka.

The narrator's claim that the women factory workers had stunted breasts suggests that he is rigorously applying a false and unattainable standard. In view of his religiosity, we are inclined to suspect that this standard is probably some ideal conception of the buxom madonna. By specifying 'po silnici' and 'kratší a delší [řetězy]', the narrator is betraying his annoyance that the women were walking not on a pavement but on the open road, and that the rows they formed were of uneven length. This shows up the narrator's comically small-minded bourgeois views on propriety and also his formalistic obsession with order. The use of the word 'řetězy', moreover, shows up the narrator's fear of the massed appearance of these women. His allegation that the women were pretending to be lewder than they ever had been by this very formulation gives us reason to suppose that they were not lewd at all. The impression of sexual provocativeness and deformity the narrator is trying to create is undermined also by '[fabričky přivykajíce si] jistému methodickému pohybu křivou kyčlí', because any walk involves systematic, and therefore in a sense methodical, movement of the hips; and 'křivý' can mean just 'curved', 'rounded' instead of 'crooked'. We note that the use of 'methodický' here not only allows a deceitful impression of intentionality to be created but also reflects the narrator's over-rationalized, formalistic view of reality. The word 'jistý', that seems to be a euphemistically oblique reference to an aspect of indecency, for the author merely shows up the narrator's obsessive predilection for vagueness. Implicitly characteristic of the narrator is also his affected use of the rare feminine form '[pohyb] kyčlí' in place of the normal '[pohyb] kyčlem'. The formulation '[fabričky] rozrušovaly se osudem [kuplířky]' leaves it open whether the women were annoyed at the arrest of a procuress and abortionist on whose services they had been dependent, as the narrator would like us to believe, or whether they were simply talking animatedly about the latest subject of local gossip. Consistently with this, the attribution of 'lačný' to 'skupina' implies that it is less that the women were really lascivious than that the narrator is intimidated by women in groups. The simile of the flies is likewise more a reflection of the narrator's antipathy than a reliable account of the behaviour of the women, who were, after all, said to have been proceeding in an orderly manner in rows. The euphemistic 'pomáhat od plodu' for 'vyhánět plody' or 'dělat potraty', and 'neřád' for 'výkal', bring out also the narrator's preciosity and prudishness. That the narrator says he fears an answer to the question 'jste-li vy sestry moje' that he asks himself with regard to the women is ironic because he is pretending that it is a negative answer he fears whereas we suspect that it is an affirmative one. The only seemingly superfluous adjective in 'řádná odpověd'' suggests, moreover, that the narrator is secretly aware that the answers he gives himself are often improper, insincere. In addition, the narrator's very choice of the here rather curious 'řádný', that normally means 'proper' more in the sense of 'decent', 'respectable' and also 'regular', 'orderly', for the author shows up again his preoccupation with propriety and obsession with order. By letting the narrator say 'sestry, jejichž bídě byly věnovány znamenité idey věku', the author is suggesting that the narrator's only reason for showing interest in the utopian socialist doctrines of his time, to which 'znamenité idey věku' presumably alludes, is that they have to do with the poverty he idealizes for religious reasons. The expression 'pachuť vlastního jazyka' is another hint at the narrator's preciosity and neurotic oversensitivity.

> Cihláři pojídali čtvrtinu svého bochánku, ulévajíce polačkou kapitální sousta a na jezeře jejich očí zračil se malý život bez nuancí. Bez ohně a beze všech tajných záblesků, ačkoliv tito lidé byli chvalně známými rváči a jejich manželská plodnost ničím nezadržitelná.
>
> Dojedli a svalili se do písku jako trámy. Polačkou zharmonisovány byly přikrosti světla i zvuku a chrápání cihlářů neslo se až na konec křižovatky.

By saying '[cihláři pojídali] čtvrtinu svého bochánku' the narrator is trying to persuade us that these workers were eating gluttonously. But since we know that round flat loaves of the sort called 'bochánek' are most easily broken up by halving and rehalving, 'čtvrtina' fails to impress in the way intended, and we are given to suspect that what disturbs the narrator is that the men did not cut the bread into neat little slices with a knife. The use of 'ulévat' with 'sousto', where we would normally tend to use 'zapívat' with 'sousto', and 'ulévat' with 'hoře' or 'smutek', hints at the narrator's tendency to confuse abstract and concrete, and also at his basic melancholy. The word 'kapitální' is ironic not only because it is somehow too weak to convince us that the bites the men took were truly enormous, but also because, being a trendy bourgeois term of the time, it helps to identify the narrator's social standing and attitude. The combination of 'malý život' with 'bez nuancí' suggests that for the narrator greatness in life lies only in minor finesse. His use of the then still fairly recent foreign borrowing 'nuance' also shows up his affectation. His assumption that there should be a secret gleam in the eyes of pub-brawlers and fire in the eyes of potent husbands reveals the narrator's childishly romantic attitude still more strongly than the comparison of eyes to lakes. The phrase 'chvalně známí rváči', moreover, deviously allows for the possibility that the men were not so much esteemed for their rowdyism as simply esteemed by everyone else and considered rowdies only by the narrator. The attribute 'manželská plodnost nicim zadržitelná' can hardly shock us either, since 'manželský' makes it seem likely that they were ordinary faithful husbands, and we can anyway scarcely imagine what force it could be that is meant to restrain their potency. The comparison 'jako trámy' suggests that the narrator is intimidated by the stature and proportions of these workers. It also reminds us of his religiosity because 'trám' is also the beam in the eye of the sinner referred to in Matthew 7: 3–5 and Luke 6: 41–42 ('Jak to, že vidíš třísku v oku svého bratra, ale *trám* ve vlastním oku nepozoruješ?').[217] His use of the cumbersome loan word 'zharmonisovat' shows up his affectation once again, while his 'přikrosti světla a zvuku' provides another hint at his oversensitivity to light and noise. The narrator's assertion that the snoring of the men now sleeping after lunch carried right to the end of the crossroads leads us to suspect that this is where he was standing, not daring to come any closer.

> Nevrle tloukl zvon poledník, z povinnosti závazného slibu, tak jako člověk za mzdu, na kteréhož se možno spolehnouti, učiní ve své jednotvárné práci dvojí zastavení.

The use of 'nevrle' with regard to the ringing of the bell and the mention of a vow or promise in this connection brings out once again the narrator's tendency to personify indiscriminately. The ambiguity of 'tloukl zvon poledník' can even provide a further ironic rationale for the narrator's personification here. Since 'tloukl zvon poledník' can be taken to mean not only that the noon-bell rang, with 'poledník' being understood as a descriptor of 'zvon', but also that a so-called 'poledník' rang the bell, 'poledník' in this sense being independent of 'zvon' and designating a mythological being believed to appear at noon, this expression may be thought to provide an additional hint at the narrator's involvement in the supernatural. The criticism for surliness also suggests that the narrator detests any mode of behaviour that is not genteel. The interpretation of the supposed surliness as an expression of reluctance to perform a moral duty is meant to reveal the narrator's own view

---

217 See Matthew 7: 3–5 and Luke 6: 41–42. The full text in Matthew is: "Jak to, že vidíš třísku v oku svého bratra, ale *trám* ve vlastním oku nepozoruješ? Anebo jak to, že říkáš svému bratru: ‚Dovol, ať ti vyjmu třísku z oka' – a hle, *trám* ve tvém vlastním oku! Pokrytče, nejprve vyjmi ze svého oka *trám*, a pak teprve prohlédneš, abys mohl vyjmout třísku z oka svého bratra." In Luke it is: "Jak to, že vidíš třísku v oku svého bratra, ale *trám* ve svém vlastním oku nepozoruješ? Jak můžeš říci svému bratru: ‚Bratře, dovol, ať ti vyjmu třísku, kterou máš v oku,' a sám ve svém oku *trám* nevidíš? Pokrytče, nejprve vyjmi *trám* ze svého oka, a pak teprve prohlédneš, abys mohl vyjmout třísku z oka svého bratra (my italics)."

and experience of morality as constraint to the disagreeable. The only apparently superfluous adjective 'závazný' is intended to imply that the narrator
to suit his own purpose distinguishes unscrupulously and with formalistic
prevarication between vows or promises that are binding and such that are
not. His 'člověk za mzdu' and 'jednotvarná práce' reveal bourgeois disdain for
the ordinary working man, to which the elaboration '[člověk] na kteréhož
se možno spolehnouti', by invoking an exception, adds a strong hint of basic
mistrust. The formulation 'učinit dvojí zastavení', used instead of the normal
'dělat dvě přestávky', not only betrays ludicrous affectation but may also be
taken to suggest a certain conversancy with 'zastavení' as a religious term
denoting pictures of Jesus carrying the Cross to Calvary.

> [...] Vždy nechutné a bláhové bylo zarmucovati se nicotou těchto lidí!
> Přišel bys jako přítel, hluboko se nahýbaje ke dnu jejich srdcí a oni by pokryli tvoji
> botu slinou z užvýkaného tabáku a obnažili by v úsměšku žluté svoje tesáky. Někteří
> požádali by tě o malou zapůjčku ve jménu boha trojjediného a v kruhu svých známých
> doporučili jako ťulpasa prvního řádu. Ano příteli, ku kterému mluvím, zařiď ty se po-
> dle nabytých zkušeností!

The narrator's 'nechutné [...] bylo zarmucovati se' implies that he normally enjoys melancholy, while 'vždy' suggests that he rather masochistically
repeats experiences he has found unpleasant. By 'bláhové [bylo]' the narrator
is expressing regret at having devoted himself to what he believes were the
wrong people, whereas the author is insinuating that the narrator's whole attitude has been foolish. The word 'nicota', with its metaphysical background
associations, also helps to show up the narrator's standpoint. The use of the
conditional tense in the following paragraph invites us to conclude that the
narrator's claim about his intentions and the men's reaction are mere conjecture. In '[přítel] hluboko se nahýbaje ke dnu jejich [cihláčů] srdcí', the author
is overstretching the standard metaphors 'hluboko v srdci' and 've dně / ze
dna srdce' to creat a comically immediate and graphic picture. That the narrator expects the men to spit on his shoes and fleer at him with bared yellow
teeth exposes his squeamish affectation and fear of derision. The strength
of his aversion particularly to the bodily is brought out and mocked by the
contrast between the expansive 'pokrýt slinou' and the restrictive singular of
'bota'. It is meant to come through also in the for the author exaggerated and
distorted, because as expressed here falsely direct, connection made between
the saliva and the tobacco in 'slina z užvýkaného tabáku', as well as in the use
of the here not merely colloquially pejorative but implicitly also threateningly
bestial 'tesáky' for 'zuby'. In 'malá zapůjčka', the narrator wishes us to understand the adjective as reporting sarcastically what the men themselves would
be saying, while the author is implying that the men would probably be ask-

ing for truly no more than some small change. Similarly, 've jménu boha troj-jediného', that seems to tell us that the men were exhorting like beggars, is implicitly only the narrator's tendentious and religiously inflated rendering of the common expletive 'proboha'. When the narrator says that the men would tell their friends that he is a dupe of the first order, the narrator would like us to believe that it was out of spite at his refusing the loan, while the author is implying that the narrator knows from experience that most people consider him a prime fool. This is implicitly confirmed by the subsequent 'zařiď […] se podle nabytých zkušeností'. That the narrator addresses this last remark to a hitherto unmentioned friend he claims to have been talking to suggests that he is used to carrying on imaginary conversations, so divorced is he from reality.

> Ustalo zvonění, ustala i hokynářka v hlasité persifláži andělského pozdravení […]
> Náměstí se vyprázdnilo, jenom některá služka blížila se k výčepu se skleněnou kon-vicí.
> Bylo poledne, chvíle kusého odpočinku, který zde neposílí a neblaží…

The narrator's curious and unconvincing assertion that the woman grocer was parodying an angelic greeting is an ironic reminder of his importunate religiosity. This religiosity is meant to be implicit also in the use of anaphora in 'ustalo zvonění, ustala i hokynářka', reminiscent as it is of the style of the Beatitudes. Consistent with the social snobbery imputed to the narrator is his use of 'hokynářka', with its potential strong negative connotations, for 'zelinářka' or 'ovocnářka'; and his use of the at the time still rather distinguished foreign borrowing 'persifláž' for 'posměšné napodobení'. The adjective 'hlasitý', pointing out seemingly unnecessarily the wholly usual loudness of the woman's call, hints again at the narrator's oversensitivity to noise. That the narrator imagines the woman fetching beer to be a maidservant, not just an ordinary housewife, brings out his bourgeois perspective again. His use of 'skleněná konvice' for 'džbán' supports this by suggesting that he is familiar only with jugs of the smaller, more elegant sort that are made not of glass but often of choice materials like silver or pewter. The closing remark '[poledne] chvíle kusého odpočinku, který […] neblaží' is meant to show up and mock the narrator's longing for profound spiritual repose and beatitude that we are to assume has provided the incongruous standard here. The eccentricity of the narrator's position is ironically emphasized by his use of 'kusý', a word which normally collocates far more strongly with terms like 'vzpomínky', 'znalosti', and, crucially, 'práce'. It is precisely the standard collocation 'kusá práce' that provides the ironic counterfoil to 'kusý odpočinek', suggesting that when it comes to work and rest the narrator's priorities are oddly inverted.

Examining 'Poledne', we have seen authorial irony gradually reveal the narrator as a comic figure divorced from the reality of life. The particular characteristics exemplifying this basic attitude of the narrator include an obsessive religiosity tending towards asceticism; a rigid formalism not excluding a childishly fanciful romanticism; an extreme timidity and oversensitivity both physical and aesthetic; and a presumably bourgeois affectation. The small town and its inhabitants, which are the object of the narrator's attack, are by comparison ultimately normal and unexceptionable.

7. PLÁČ NIOBY[218]

The Niobe legend reaches back to earliest antiquity. Achilles recounts it to the mourning Priam of Troy in the *Iliad* (Book XXIV). It inspired tragedies by Aeschylus and Sophocles and a poem by Sappho, of which only fragments survive. After Latin versions by Hyginus and Parthenus of Nicaea, it was cast in its most authoritative form by Ovid in the Metamorphoses (*Metamorphoses*, VI, 146–313). Niobe has remained a significant motif in art, music, and literature ever since. It was popular in the painting of the Italian Renaissance (Tintoretto) and the Dutch Golden Age (Bloemaert, Lemonnier, Jombert).[219] It is the subject of an opera by Agostino Steffani, an essay by Shelley and a dramatic poem by Leconte de Lisle. In Bohemia, a statue of Niobe can be found in the colonnade of the Květná zahrada in Kroměříž in southern Moravia and a painting of the death of her children (Smrt dětí Niobiných, ca. 1590) by Jacopo Negretti is kept in Prague castle. In Czech literature, it figures as the subject of an occasional poem Jaroslav Vrchlický dedicated to a mourning mother.[220]

According to Ovidian tradition, Niobe was the daughter of Tantalus, and wife of King Amphion of Thebes, by whom she had seven sons and seven daughters. She boasted her progenitive superiority to the Titaness Latona, who had only two children, the twin deities Apollo and Artemis. To avenge the insult to their mother, Apollo and Artemis took their bows, hunted down and killed all Niobe's children. Niobe mourned her children incessantly and was metamorphosed into a column of stone on Mt. Sipylus in Lydia which continued to shed tears.

Opolský's 'Pláč Nioby' apparently follows this outline. It differs from Ovid's version in that the story seems to be told exclusively from Niobe's point of view, whereas in Ovid it is related from the standpoint of an independent narrator who quotes Niobe and Latona at length, and also Apollo. There is considerable divergence, too, in the elaboration of the above outline. We notice, for example, that, although the names of the sons in 'Pláč Nioby'

---

218 Jan Opolský, 'Pláč Nioby', in *Malé prosy* (Prague, 1926), pp. 19–25.

219 K. Stark, *Niobe und die Niobiden in ihrer literarischen, künstlerischen und mythologischen Bedeutung* (Leipzig, 1863); M. Guptil, *Niobe and the Niobids in Greek and Roman Art and Literature* (Chicago, 1928) and Elsbeth Wiemann, *Der Mythos von Niobe und ihren Kindern: Studien zur Darstellung und Rezeption* (Worms, 1986)

220 Jaroslav Vrchlický, 'Niobe', *Nové zlomky epopeje* (Prague, 1895), pp. 54–57.

are taken from Ovid, the description of the children coincides only in a few details. Of all parts of the narrative, Niobe's self-portrayal in the two versions apparently corresponds most closely in substance, but here order, combination and formulation of the utterances differ conspicuously.

The choice of what is on the surface a single narrative standpoint and the noticeable divergence in details from the Ovidian original can be readily explained once Opolský's ironic intention is recognized. The position of a single speaker or narrator is easier to relativize than that of several speakers, and the appreciable idiosyncratic adaptation of the subject matter gives Opolský the room he needs to develop his alternative view.

We shall elucidate the irony in 'Pláč Nioby' in the same way as we did with 'Poledne', examining the text passage by passage. We shall make reference to the Ovidian version only where this contributes to a fuller understanding of the irony.

Niobe's soliloquy begins with her reflecting on the causes of her conflict with Latona.

> Byla jsem z míry pyšná, neboť ve mně vířila dymná krev otce, kterýž hodoval s bohy. Moje matka byla ze sedmi Hyad, jež byly vřazeny mezi hvězdy.
>
> Théby a Helespont byly mi poddány a jeho moře se na můj kyn zkonejšilo, jako by bylo zakleto v lazuritu.

By allowing 'z míry', which more than the commoner 'příliš' can suggest the assumption of a fixed measure, the author is beginning to imply that the narrator's view of things is coldly formalistic. This hint is followed up in '[Hyady byly] vřazeny [mezi hvězdy]' with its connotations of ordering, classifying. In 'byla jsem [...] pyšná', the ambiguity of 'pyšný' is being used to imply that the narrator is not admitting to having been vain, as we initially suppose her to be doing, but claiming to have looked magnificent. This is a first hint at her obsession with her own appearance. The description of her father's blood within her takes the irony further. The movement 'vířit' conveys can be thought of as rapid and therefore as a sign of vigour, as the narrator intends it to be, but also as uncontrolled and therefore unnatural. Expanding on this in 'dymná [krev]', the author, implicitly reducing the apparent metonymy to literality and exploiting the available connotations, is insinuating that this blood is not fuming hot, as the narrator is pretending, but is itself a vapour, heavy and lingering like smoke, and maybe even cold like fog. Given this ambiguity of perspective in the description of the blood, we are then also tempted to see Niobe's father's feasting with the gods as a sign not so much of eminent nobleness as of a lack of physical being. That Niobe's mother is referred to only as a star is meant to suggest that she is similarly remote from life. By letting the narrator in her subsequent claim to power combine Thebes so directly with the Hellespont, the author is mock-ingly suggesting that she mentally assimilates the political power she has as Queen of Thebes to the ostensibly supernatural power she believes she has over the Hellespont. The conjunction 'a', moreover, by its vagueness can ac-commodate both the narrator's pretence that the behaviour of the waters is merely an example of her power and the author's implication that it consti-tutes her sole reason for believing in it. The use of 'moře' to describe the wa-ters of a narrow channel like the Hellespont carries with it a faint suggestion that the narrator is exaggerating, possibly out of fear. We are also meant to understand that the occurrence Niobe witnessed was not supernatural. The author here is expecting us to infer that Niobe, having travelled from Thebes to the Hellespont across the Aegean and entered the straits through the tur-bulent western mouth, interpreted as obedience to a gesture of hers the sud-den abatement of the waters under the lee of the bounding promontories. That Niobe imagines using her power to subdue activity and not to stimulate it is intended to show up again her alienation from life. The personification in '[moře] se [...] zkonejšilo', though perhaps not inappropriate to the mental world of a prehistoric personage, is nonetheless meant to have ironic value here by comporting with the view of the narrator as detached from what the author would have understood as normal reality. The formulation '[moře] jakoby zakleto v lazuritu' compromises the narrator further. By letting the idea of enchantment be included within the unreal comparison, the author is implicitly dismissing as mere supposition the operation of magic forces that the narrator's claim assumes. Furthermore, the preference of the static 'v lazuritu' to 'do lazuritu' implies that the alleged enchantment is anyway independent of Niobe's agency here. Also, the choice of lazulite as an object of comparison introduces connotations of coldly lustrous ornamentality and celestial azure depth that subversively point up the narrator's remoteness from life.

> Moje líc byla nade všecky vznešená, aniž by v ní proto bylo méně sladkosti pro muže Amfiona. Byla mi dána nebezpečná krása a všichni frygičtí flétisté hráli takové písně k mé cti, jako by tonuli v slzách. Byla jsem předurčená lásce a štěstí se střelo přede mnou jako hebký koberec dusící hrubé kročeje života.

We may understand 'vznešený' as meaning 'noble' or 'dignified', or else as suggesting some sort of elevation above living reality. By 'sladkost', we take the narrator to be meaning erotic lust, while the author is suggesting that she means only slushy sentiment. The negative comparative construction 'aniž [...] bylo méně' even heightens this irony, because it leaves it open how much, if any, of this 'sladkost', in whichever sense, was ever there. As a result, we begin to suspect that Niobe is not only disturbed sexually but also gener-

ally incapable of more than very feeble emotion. Developing this line, the
formulation 'pro muže Amfiona', coming as it does from Niobe herself, suggests extraordinary emotional distance. Pointing in still the same direction
is 'nebezpečná krása', behind which the author sees not knowledge that these
looks will ensnare, but fear that they may attract unwanted male passion. This
implication paves the way for the later revelation of Niobe's lesbianism. The
description of the flautists and their music takes the irony further. By letting
the narrator say 'k mé cti' instead of the usual 'mně ke cti', and by taking ad-
vantage of the fact that 'čest' means 'honour' not only in the sense of 'esteem',
'reverence', 'glory' but also in the sense of 'chastity', 'virginity', the author is
implying that the allegedly tearful songs are not songs of despairing love or
adoration played in Niobe's honour but songs played to lament the virginity
she must have lost in marriage. The admission that the flautists are Phrygian
suggests that they were not playing because they were overcome by emotion,
as the narrator would like us to think, but because they had been ordered to
play, since they were slaves like most of their compatriots in Greece. Given
the implication that Niobe is disturbed sexually, we suspect that she herself
ordered the musicians to play because it was she herself who regretted, and
regrets, the loss of her virginity. The suggestion that the flautists were not
playing out of emotion receives covert support from the construction '[flé-
tisté] hráli takové písně, jakoby [tonuli v slzách]', because the insertion of
'takový' surreptitiously transforms what appears to be an adverbial simile
into an adjectival one and thereby transfers the attribute of tearfulness from
the playing of the musicians to the song. That even this tearfulness of the
songs is not genuine is meant to come through in the simile 'jako by [flétisté]
tonuli v slzách' itself, because 'jako by' can be thought of as relativizing not
only '[flétisté] tonuli' but also 'v slzách'. At the same time, the high-pitched,
hollow sound we think of flutes as producing contrasts subversively with the
depth and intensity of feeling 'tonout v slzách' seems to want to convey, and
so mocks the narrator's shallow and feeble emotionality. The same disturbed
emotionality comes through in '[Byla jsem] předurčena lásce', where the associations of cold mechanicalness that attach to 'předurčeny' run counter to
any normal understanding of 'láska'. The narrator's assertion that happiness
lay before her can suggest that she never experienced happiness, and may
also lead us to wonder whether her saying that she was preordained to love
does not mean that this love too was always only a future prospect. The simile
of the fluffy carpet does more than comically trivialize Niobe's idea of happiness. That the narrator, as this simile reveals, considers happiness to lie not
in facing and overcoming hardship but in being protected from it is meant
to show up her unrealistic attitude to life. This perspective is developed in
'hrubé kročeje života', where the author, inviting us to read what appears
to be a possessive genitive as a genitive of definition, is implying that the

narrator is speaking not of the coarser aspects of life but of what she regards
as the coarseness of life in general. The ambiguity of the verb 'dusit' adds to
this. Since 'dusit', preferred here to the more usual 'tlumit', can mean not only
'to dampen', as 'tlumit' does, but also 'to stifle', we are led to suspect that the
narrator secretly desires the very extinction of life.

> Byla jsem matkou čtrnácti synů a dcer, což byl sedminásobný počet dětí Latoniných,
> při čemž moje krása s léty sílila jako pomerančový peň.
> Proto Latona, jež byla zplozena Titany a uzavírala podřadnou stupnici bohů, cítila
> se býti dotčenou ve své povýšenosti věčného božství a položila nepřátelství mezi sebe
> a mne, viníc mne z rouhačství a pomateného velikášství.

That the narrator uses the expression 'sedminásobný počet' in speaking
of her children is intended to show up once again her coldly formalistic way
of thinking. The same subversive impression is meant to be produced by her
later '[Latona] uzavírala podřadnou stupnici [bohů]'. Her choice of the verb
'sílit' to describe the alleged growth of her beauty betrays her conviction that
beauty is a form of strength and so reveals her exaggerated aestheticism.
In the simile 'jako pomerančový peň', 'peň' makes us think of this beauty as
being austere and desolate just like a tree-trunk without branches and foli-
age, while 'pomerančový', preferred to the expected 'pomerančovníkový' not
only for euphony, implicitly denaturalizes even this 'peň', suggesting that
the trunk of the image is not of an orange-tree, merely orange-coloured. The
narrator's immediate digression from her motherhood to her beauty, furthermore, provides another hint at her exaggerated aestheticism. Following on
from this, the narrator's 'proto' can be thought of as referring back to her
claim to be mother of fourteen children that forms the main clause of the
previous sentence, or else to her repeated overt and covert pretensions to
beauty that are continued in the subordinate clause with which this previous sentence closes. The resulting ambiguity not only ironically emphasizes
the narrator's obsession with beauty but also implicitly calls into question
the pivotal role Niobe's progenitive prowess traditionally plays in the story.
The congruence in the literal meanings of the ostensibly purely metaphorical
'dotčený' and 'povýšenost' allows the claim that Latona was offended in her
haughtiness to be underlaid with the comically concrete image of her being
touched while sitting on high. The potential connection with the simile of
the growing tree-trunk above adds the subversive possibility that it is this
trunk that is to be seen as touching her, rising up into her posterior from
below. In 'věčné božství', the only apparently redundant adjective suggests,
by implicit contrast with 'časné [božství]', that the narrator, contrary even to
the assumptions of Greek mythology, believes also in a divine principle that
is temporal, so divorced is she from reality. The same deficient sense of reality

is meant to come through in the unusual combination of the concrete 'položit mezi koho' and the abstract 'nepřátelství' in '[Latona] položila nepřátelství mezi sebe a mne'.[221] Still in accordance with this, the only seemingly tautological phrase 'pomatené velikášství' is intended to imply that the narrator believes also in a sane form of megalomania.

> Tupila prý jsem oltáře, ohně nepozbývající.
>
> Zlehčila prý jsem osly, vlekoucí k jejím slavnostem věnce a chleby, neboť byli velmi netrpěliví pod svým břemenem, kopajíce kol sebe a nehezky hýkajíce. V pochybnost prý jsem uvedla panenství strážných děv, jež se k třicetileté službě Latoně zaslíbily.

The use of 'tupit' with regard to the altars shows up once again the narrator's tendency to personify. The phrase '[oltáře] ohně nepozbývající', particularly because of the stressed final position of 'nepozbývající', suggests that the narrator was alarmed by the fact that the fire on the altars kept on burning. This prompts us to suspect that her alleged insult was probably no more than openly displayed fear of the flames that Latona fatuously misinterpreted. The description of the donkeys carrying oblations takes the irony further. The addition of 'chleby' to 'věnce' prompts us to understand 'věnce' as meaning not garlands, as we are disposed to do initially, but pastries of a kind commonly used as a food offering in rural Bohemia. This gives the picture an incongruous touch of romantic Czech folkiness. The term 'věnec' is subversive also because of its symbolic connection with virginity that is ironically appropriate to Latona's cult of virginity mentioned in the next sentence. The euphemisticness of '[osli] netrpěliví' and 'nehezky [hýkat]', and the preciosity of the following '[osli] kopajíce' by the poetic contraction 'kol', reveal the narrator's squeamish aversion to the donkeys and so lead us to suppose that Latona may here again have mistaken a spontaneous expression of emotion for an insult. Subversive is also the combination of 'zlehčit' and 'pod [...] břemenem'. Playing on the covert semantic congruence between 'pod [...] břemenem' and the literal meaning of 'zlehčit', the author is implying that the narrator sees her alleged slighting of the donkeys in a comically concrete way also as a sort of physical act of disburdening. He is thereby hinting at her tendency to confuse abstract and concrete, metaphorical and literal. The narrator's account of the offence she is supposed to have given regarding Latona's votaries is no less revealing. By letting the narrator say 'v pochybnost

---

221 The expression 'položit nepřátelství mezi koho a koho' is unusual but not entirely unfamiliar: it occurs in Genesis 3: 15, where it over-literally translates an Ancient Hebrew idiom. The use of a biblical phrase in the present context might also be understood as a very remote hint that the narrator is ultimately not simply a fictional Niobe but a historically later figure casting him- or herself in the role of Niobe; but this perspective is not developed in the rest of the text and is therefore best neglected here.

[...] jsem uvedla [panenství děv], the author is implying that what happened was not that Niobe voiced doubts about the maidens' virginity, as we initially assume, but that she had homosexual intercourse with them, thereby making it unclear whether they could still be considered virgins. Besides helping to confirm our suspicion that Niobe is a lesbian, this implication leads us to infer that here again Niobe was not insulting Latona but merely succumbing to the impulses of her aberrant sensibility. It is ironic also that the virgins are said to have pledged themselves to thirty years' service, because this leaves it open whether they were attractive young girls or ugly old hags.

> Co však více, sama ubledlá tvář Latony nebyla prý ušetřena mrzkosti mého jazyka, neboť jsem prý v ní nalézala pouze mrtvolný půvab a živoucí nedostatky.
> Pohaněla jsem prý bytost i sochu jejího syna Apolona na odtoku kastalského pramene se vztyčující a dceři její Artemidě, jíž byla zasvěcena noční nebesa, podlomila jsem mnohé záměry, daleko do lidské zrůdnosti nemající.

For the author, 'mrtvolný půvab' is not meant sarcastically, as it appears to be, but betrays the narrator's liking for deathly pallor that we may see as another aspect of her alienation from life. Similarly, in 'živoucí nedostatky', the adjective 'živoucí' may be understood as stressing the reality of these faults or as reflecting the narrator's criticism of Latona's appearance for still having a certain liveliness. Revealing is also the expression 'bytost i socha'. By letting the narrator put 'bytost' in an unstressed position before 'socha', the author is implying that she considers Apollo himself less important than his statue. This is another hint at her exaggerated aestheticism. At the same time, her use of the term 'bytost' is meant to show up her metaphysical orientation. In the reference to the statue's position, the indication we have in 'na odtoku [...] pramene' that the statue is at the bottom of the lower end of a watercourse comically subverts the sense of imposing height normally conveyed by 'vztyčující se'. By 'lidská zrůdnost', the author is suggesting that the narrator means not a human kind of monstrousness, as we initially assume, but the monstrousness of what is human. This leads us to suspect that what Niobe reproached Artemis for is not that as Diana she cruelly transformed the deerstalker Actaeon into a stag and allowed him to be savaged to death by his own hounds, as we might have thought, but that as Selene she conceived a human passion for the mortals Endymion and Orion. This ironic interpretation is covertly supported by the brief characterizing phrase '[Artemis], jíž byla zasvěcena noční nebesa'. Considering the imputations as reported here, we can again see that Niobe did not intend to insult Latona. Not only are her remarks about Latona's appearance implicitly compliments in disguise, but her criticism of the statue was presumably purely aesthetic and her observations about Artemis simply the consequence of her lesbianism.

Běda, podlehla prý jsem nemocné žádosti, býti uctívána, jak jsou uctíváni pouze bohové nadsmyslní, nalézající pro to důvod pouze ve své fysické leposti a viditelnosti. Byla jsem jednoduše obviněna ze vzpoury proti bohům a moje vrozená, vznešená tvář nemohla mne přirozeně obhájiti.

A poznala jsem hrůzu a utrpení chvíle, ve které patří pomsta bohům.

In 'nemocná žádost', the author is using the associations of the concept of illness to imply that this desire was perhaps less perverse than simply feeble, and would therefore not have been much of a threat to the authority of the gods. The for the author only apparently otiose adjective in 'bohové nadsmyslní' suggests, by implicit contrast with its opposite, that the narrator believes also in gods who are confined to the sensual, just as she believes in a divine principle that is temporal. Also, we may conjecture that if Niobe wanted to be adored in the sense mentioned, it was not because she wanted to be considered a god, as seems to be believed, but because she wanted to be thought of as detached from the sensual. The term 'důvod' can cover both the surface meaning of objective reason or justification and the underlying ironic meaning of subjective reason or motive. In 'fysická lepost a viditelnost', the seemingly redundant addition of 'viditelnost' to 'fysická lepost', and also the normally superfluous attribution of 'fysický' to the already conventionally only physical 'lepost', suggests that the narrator has no adequate conception of the concrete. The insertion of 'jednoduše' is meant to convey the implication that the narrator is annoyed not so much at the rashness of this indictment as at its lack of ceremony and prolixity. This brings out her formalistic way of thinking again. In 'vrozená [...] tvář', the only apparently redundant adjective is meant to suggest that the narrator knows herself to have also a face that is not natural to her, a face that she merely puts on as a sort of mask. At the same time, the attribution of 'vrozený', that is normally used only abstractly of traits of character and illnesses, to the concrete 'tvář' shows up the narrator's tendency to confuse abstract and concrete. The term 'vznešený', as before, can be understood to mean 'noble' or 'dignified', or else to suggest some kind of elevation above living reality. Following on from this, the adverb 'přirozeně' may be read as 'obviously', or else ironically as 'in a natural way', 'by its naturalness'. The addition of 'chvíle' to 'hrůza a utrpení' implicitly trivializes it by severely reducing the length of time involved, while the use of 'poznat' suggests that the narrator's experience of this horror and suffering was more intellectual than emotional. The phrase 'chvíle, ve které patří pomsta bohům' makes us think of a legalistic allocation of turns to take vengeance and so brings out both the narrator's formalism and her emotional immaturity.

Miláčku můj, Ismene, [...] kterýž jsi byl jezdcem bez sedla i třmenů, dávaje se v trysku jízdy doháněti pouze vichřicemi, kterýž jsi byl polaskaný sluncem, vyhlížeje na

svém bílém koni jako zleštěná bronzová socha; padl jsi a smrt nemohla ti vzíti otevře-
ného úsměvu, který byl jako koruna, vsazená na čelo tvé mladosti.

This son's riding without saddle and stirrups may indicate that he is skilful enough not to need them, or else that he is too small to fit in them, as
the author is suggesting. Apart from this, the absence of saddle and stirrups
helps to begin to create also in the present picture that sense of abstraction
from concrete reality which is to be considered characteristic of the narrator's vision. This implicit perspective is developed in 'v trysku jízdy', where
the author, prompting us to consider 'jízda' redundant only apparently, is
encouraging us to understand that the narrator means 'trysk' ultimately
more in the sense of 'jet' or 'spout' than simply 'gallop' since she sees this
riding largely abstractly as a spouting of energy. Consistently with this, her
claim that only gales could chase her son may be thought to reflect more
how insubstantially she perceives him than how fast he rides. The narrator's
view is ironically relativized also by the ambiguous 'dávat', which leaves it
open whether only gales were able to chase this son, as the narrator is asserting, or whether he allowed only gales to chase him, presumably for fear
of compromising himself. The expression 'polaskaný sluncem' reminds us
of the narrator's tendency to personify. The simile of the polished bronze
statue hints at her liking for artificiality that is another aspect of her alienation from life, and allows the covert stylization to move from abstractness
and insubstantiality to the implicitly equally lifeless contrary extreme of
inert solidity. That this son is said to look like polished bronze on his white
horse suggests also that his tan shows up only by contrast with the whiteness. The phrase 'otevřený úsměv' makes us wonder whether this smile is
not some sort of toothy grimace, since 'otevřený' is used in the abstract sense
of 'frank' usually only in such entirely abstract expressions as 'otevřená
povaha', 'otevřené slovo'. Indeed, already the remark that death could not
take this smile away intimates its lifeless coldness. The simile of the crown
shows up again the narrator's liking for artificiality and disturbs also by
bringing in the forehead in place of the mouth. Even the idea of a crown set
on the forehead is suspect, since it can make us think not just of a normal-
sized crown whose front rim touches the forehead but also of a comically
diminutive crown perched entirely on the forehead and ready to topple off.
The expression 'čelo […] mladosti' shows up once again the narrator's tendency to personify. We are also meant to understand that Niobe's address-
ing her remarks to a dead child, in this and the following cases, is for the
author not an example of rhetorical apostrophe, as she herself would like
us to think, but evidence of her conviction that the dead are somehow still
alive.

Jsi mrtev i ty, líbezný Sipyle, kterýž jsi byl dědicem mé krásy [...]. Mrtva jsi, moje
druhá duše, moje druhé tělo, ale nenajde se krkavce v božím povětří, který by se snesl
k tvé mrtvé hlavě, aby ji mohl oči vyklinouti.

Je hrůzno mysliti na vás, Faedime a Tantale, kteří jste nalezli smrt ve formě sladkého
podobenství. Neboť zapasíce před branami o větev vavřínu, ve kteréž bylo zpodobněno
nejsladší uznání života, hruď na hrudi protknuti jste byli jedním šípem, jako jsou dvě
jména hlasem smrti najednou vyslovená.

By introducing a sense of airy sweetness and delicacy inappropriate to
the portrayal of a young man, the use of 'líbezný' to describe the second son,
Sipylus, not only brings out the narrator's obsessive aestheticism and superficial sentiment but also suggests that this youth is rather effeminate. The
subsequent 'byl [jsi] dědicem mé krásy' hints at the narrator's lifelessness,
because in the legal sense basic to 'dědic' inheritance presupposes the death
of the previous owner. The apostrophes 'moje druhá duše' and 'moje druhé
tělo' implicitly confirms our suspicion that Sipylus was effeminate, because
they make us think that he had a womanly soul and a womanly body like the
narrator. At the same time, 'moje druhá duše' and 'moje druhé tělo' show up
once again the narrator's metaphysical perspective that is for the author as
much an indication of her alienation from living reality as is the religiosity
behind 'boží'. By going on to claim that no ravens would descend to peck out
this son's eyes, the narrator is trying to persuade us that he was too beautiful
for the ravens to disfigure him, while the author is suggesting that his body
was too flimsy to provide the ravens with solid sustenance. The expression
'je hrůzno mysliti na vás', referring to the third and fourth sons, Phaedimus
and Tantalus, is no less ambiguous, because it can be taken to mean that it is
gruesome to think of their sudden demise, as the narrator would like it to be,
or that it is gruesome to think of how they were while they were still alive.
The term 'sladké [podobenství]', just like the subsequent 'nejsladší [uznání]',
reveals once again the narrator's mawkish sentimentality, while 'podobenství', that can mean also 'parable', betrays her religious preoccupation with
hidden spiritual meanings and messages. Implicitly characteristic of the narrator is even the otherwise wholly standard expression 'nalézt smrt', because
it can serve as a further example of her tendency to confuse abstract and
concrete. The following formulation '[Faedimus a Tantalus] zapasíce před
branami o větev vavřínu' is vague enough to leave us in doubt whether these
sons were grown athletes wrestling in an official contest held outside the city
gates, as we are at first inclined to assume, or whether they were perhaps
only children scrambling playfully to pick up a laurel branch lying before the
gates of the palace in which they lived. There is subversive ambiguity also in
'uznání života', where the author, prompting us to read what appears to be a
possessive genitive as a genitive of definition, is suggesting that these sons

were striving not so much for one of the forms of recognition that life has to offer as for the existential recognition that is life itself. Even the sons' being chest to chest and pierced by a single arrow acquires in the present context an ironic significance absent in the here similarly worded Ovidian original.[3] Given the implications of sentimentality and insubstantiality in the text so far, the phrase 'hruď na hrudi' comes to suggest more an affectionate embrace than a violent clinch, and the transfixion by a single shaft loosed from a rudimentary prehistoric bow is made to imply that the victims were not sturdy athletes, as the narrator would like us to think, but slight to the point of being almost insubstantial. The personification of death and its voice are additional hints at the narrator's metaphysically embroidered lack of realism, which her fanciful conception of a voice uttering two names simultaneously is meant to bring out even further.

> Mrtev jsi, Alfenore, jehož jméno sládlo v mých ústech jako umleté ovoce fíku, vnořené do storaxu. Když jsem tebe celovala, bývalo slyšeti prchlivý svár hamadryád, které se přely o barvu tvých vlasu v uzel spletených, o šíři tvých ramen, na nichž pevně sedělo železné krzno, o tvé černé oči, jež polykaly jejich nahotu i o tvou vášnivost a dobrotu, jež spolu ode vždy zápasily. Tvoje jméno zanechá nyní palčivou hořkost hysopu, kdykoliv bude už vysloveno!

In the first sentence we are reminded of the narrator's love of sweetness that belongs to the ironic characterization of her. The description of this sweetness takes the irony further. The preference of 'sládnout' to 'být sladkým' invites us to suppose that this name was never really sweet because it was always only becoming sweet without ever having become sweet. That the crushed figs of the simile are said to have been immersed in storax, which is not a foodstuff but a balm or incense, implies that the narrator did not eat this mixture but inhaled it as a balmy vapour. Her preferring to savour figs in this ludicrously rarified form and her appreciating the benumbing effect of balm mockingly reveal her alienation from life. The use of 'mlít' instead of the normally more appropriate 'mačkat' to describe the crushing of the figs suggests that the narrator perceives the soft pulpiness of the figs as hard, so great is her oversensitivity. By telling us that when she kissed Alphenor the hamadryads used to be heard quarrelling, the narrator is trying to convince us that the hamadryads were jealous of her maternal privilege, while the author is hoping to suggest that she merely imagined their squabbling voices on hearing the shrill, intermittent, irregularly modulating sound she herself produced by sucking through moistened and tightly pursed lips in the course of an exaggerated, theatrical kiss. The word 'prchlivý', because cognate with 'prchat' and 'prchavý', has faint associations of volatility and vaporization that comport with previous hints that narrator's vision of the world is tending towards the insubstantial. The reason why the hamadryads allegedly quarrelled about the colour of Alphenor's hair may be that they were sexually attracted to him, as the narrator would like us to believe, or that the colour of the hair was so weak as to be practically indeterminate. It is even ironic that the young man's hair is said to have been tied up in a bun, because this hairstyle may be thought indicative of youthful nobility and sportsmanliness, if considered purely historically, or else of effeminacy, if more modern associations are allowed to prevail. That the hamadryads supposedly argued also about the width of this son's shoulders may be explained by assuming that he was unusually broadly-built, as the narrator would like it to be, or by assuming that there was no way of ascertaining how broad the shoulders really were because he kept them hidden under his coat. In 'železné krzno', the author, who expects us to remember that the military coat referred to as 'krzno' is typically leathern, is implying that the narrator by 'železný' means not 'made of iron', as we initially take her to be doing, but 'hard as iron', as an expression of her ludicrously oversensitive reaction to the stiffness of leather. This same reaction comes through also in 'pevně', that therefore only apparently commends the young man's stature. The use of 'polykat' and 'nahota' in the description of Alphenor's putative erotic interest in the hamadryads is meant to reveal the narrator's barely concealed disapproval of normal sexual passion. In 'vášnivost a dobrota', the compliancy and meekness we tend to associate with 'dobrota' are subversively set off against the recklessness and even violence we would normally want to associate with 'vášnivost'. This brings out once again the narrator's feeble emotionality. Exploiting two similar contrasts in 'palčivá hořkost hysopu', the author is suggesting that the narrator is so oversensitive that she perceives the mere mintiness of the hyssop plant as bitter, and bitterness exaggeratedly as a burning sensation. The addition 'kdykoliv bude [tvoje jméno] už vysloveno' leaves it open whether this name will ever be uttered again.

> Padl jsi i ty, jemňoučký Damasichtone, tesknější měsíčného paprsku, křehčí nad květ plovoucí po vodě a zavírající i otvírající se podle závanu větru! Jehož krok byl lehoučký, podobný tanci svatého listí na pěšině hajní, jehož hlas, matku oslovující, byl jako melodie svitá z bolesti a blaha. Nikdy tebe nemoho oželeti, jest mi, jako bych tebe znovu a znovu ztrácela!

By letting the narrator use 'jemňoučký', that can mean not only 'very sensitive', 'very tender-hearted' but also 'very delicate', 'very tenuous', and also 'křehčí [nad květ]', that can mean not only 'more tender' but also 'more frail', 'more fragile', the author is implying that this son, Damasichton, was not so much just sensitive or tender as exceptionally flimsy. Pointing in the same direction is 'lehoučký [krok]', which can mean 'very nimble', 'very fleet', but also 'very light-weight'. When the narrator then says that she feels as if she were losing this son again and again, we are led suspect that this is not out of grief but because of his exceptional flimsiness. At the same time, 'jemňoučký' and 'křehčí [nad květ]' suggest that this son was effeminate, because 'jemňoučký' associates with 'jemňoučká dívenka' and 'křehký' with 'křehká dívčinka' and 'křehotinka'. Since 'křehký' is used also of character to mean 'inconstant', the subsequent comparison of this son to a blossom at the mercy of water and wind suggests also that he is spineless and fickle. The simile of the leaves encourages us to think that his legs whirled about as the leaves are said to be doing and so reflects back ironically to 'padnul jsi'. The reference to the gloominess of ray of moonlight, to a drifting blossom and to fallen leaves in an autumn grove brings out in a recognisably exaggerated and trite way the narrator's melancholic romanticism. The terms 'tesknější [paprsku]' and 'tanec [listí]' as well as the treatment of a voice as an independent agent in 'hlas [matku] oslovující', testify with similar comic intensity to the narrator's tendency to personify. The word 'svatý' shows up once again the narrator's religiosity, while the following 'bolest a blaho' hints at her perhaps mystically sublimated masochistic enjoyment of pain. The narrator's tendency to confuse abstract and concrete comes through in 'melodie svitá z bolesti a blaho', where the standardly only concrete 'svinout' is implicitly at odds with the abstract 'melodie' and 'bolest a blaho'.

> [...]. Jsi mrtev, [Ilioneus,] můj nejmladší, rozhlížející se ještě zdiveně na prahu života, kterýž jsi přijal smrt s malou a zvědavou rozkoší, nemoha ničeho z její záhadnosti pochopiti! Umírals, domnívaje se v čistotě své mysli neznámy život počínati.

By saying that this youngest child was still on life's threshold, the narrator is trying to convey his infancy, while the author is suggesting that he never came to life properly. This implication finds an ironic echo in 'zdiveně', which may be thought of as expressing less wonder at the excitingly new as astonishment at the incredibly alien. The child's delighted acceptance of death is therefore for the author due not to his innocence, as the narrator is alleging, but to his lifelessness. In 's malou a zvědavou rozkoší', the use of 'malý', that seems to betoken the child's smallness, on a deeper level reflects the inability of this lifeless boy to experience the intense delight of which small children are usually capable. The use of 'zvědavý' in the same phrase supports this implication by suggesting that this emotion is heavily intellectualized and is anyway hardly much stronger than an inquisitive itch. The term 'záhadnost' hints at the narrator's romantic or mystic liking for the mysterious and reveals too her difficulty in understanding life itself. Her 'čistota' is meant to reveal an underlying scheme of religious values. The boy's false expectation with regard to life that the narrator goes on to mention is for the author due not to ignorance of his fate but to ignorance of his own nature, and the unknown quality of life for him therefore not to its futurity but to its otherness.

> [Artemis usmrtila] i sedmero dcer mých [...].
> Nejstarší, podpírající ještě stydnoucí mrtvolu Ilioneovu. Druhá, která by pouze pro přespřílišnou krásu směla být souzena v dykasterii. Další, tonoucí v nejčistším milostném snění uprostřed platanového stromořadí, tající v sobě tolik vášnivosti, jakou by snesl obraz, malovaný zlatem a krví.

The eldest daughter's attempt to prop up her brother's corpse for the author indicates not desperate grief but indifference to the distinction between life and death. That 'ještě' may be thought of as modifying not 'stydnoucí', as it appears to do, but 'podpírající' implicitly supports and emphasizes this point. When the narrator says of her second daughter '[ona] by pouze pro přespřílišnou krásu směla být souzena v dykasterii', the author, relying on a certain ambiguity of the verb 'smět', is suggesting that what lies behind this remark is not that this daughter is so virtuous that she could not lawfully be tried on any other charge, as we initially assume, but that the narrator as Queen of Thebes would not allow her to be. The exception the narrator makes for excessive beauty therefore leads us to suspect that she is secretly very envious of her daughter's appearance and would seriously consider having her tried on this very charge. This brings out once more her obsession with beauty. The claim that the third daughter is passionate is subversively weakened by 'milostné snění', which makes us think of pubertal day-dreaming rather than mature passion; and also by the surreptitious substitution of 'vášnivost' for 'vášeň' after 'tajit v sobě', which confronts us with the ironic truth that what is at issue is not a concealment or suppression of passion, which is common, but a concealment or suppression of passionateness, which is unusual, and, because unexplained, suspicious of being a construction to vindicate a false attribution of emotionality. The simile of the painting undermines the claim further by evoking lifelessness in the place of emotional vitality. In '[obraz] malovaný zlatem a krví', the author is accordingly stressing 'zlato', with its connotations of artificiality, not 'krev', as the narrator seems to be doing. The use of 'snést', besides hinting at the narrator's tendency to personify, shows up her basic rejection of sexual passion, indeed passion in general. The same attitude to passion comes through also in her use of 'nejčistší [snění]' and her assumption that passionateness would be suppressed. The mention of a colonnade of plane trees mockingly reflects the narrator's love of formalism by suggesting that she prefers the cold geometrical shape produced by the arrangement in rows of these trees with their bare, tall straight trunks to the natural unconstrained growth and leafiness of a normal forest. Contributory to the irony is also the syntactic structure of this whole passage. The exclusive use of relative clauses dependent on a main verb in the previous paragraph and punctuated as separate sentences brings out the narrator's lifelessness on this level too. The preponderance of participles even enhances this effect.

> Čtvrtou, tak něžnou, aby ji mohla býti zůstavena přezdívka Erhefory čili nositelky rosy. Dvě jiné, které se v životě od sebe nikdy neodloučili, nacházejíce zalíbení v tunice téže barvy, ve voňavce téhož omamujícího odstínu, jehož se získává v době pučící limby, v téže lahodné hybnosti těla a v těmž smyslném usmání, jež bylo jako kynutí rozkvětlou růžovou větví. Jedné lásky, která se odnášela k mladému Achajci, jenž vrhal disk a tančil nahý uprostřed věncoví z horských květin a čerstvě položeného sena.

This passage largely preserves the ironic syntactic structure of the previous one. In other ways too the description of these next three daughters is not what it seems. Since 'aby' in the first sentence may be thought of as introducing either a clause of effect or a clause of purpose, it is left open whether this girl was already tender enough to deserve the nickname, or whether she was, comically, merely trying to be. The use of 'zůstavit' amusingly suggests that this nickname was not spontaneously coined but passed on from person to person. What is more, the connotations of abandoning and also bequeathing that 'zůstavit' has makes us wonder whether the present holder of the nickname has not had enough of it or is not perhaps even on her last legs. Also, the very appellation 'nositelka rosy' in connection with 'něžný', if we visualize what the narrator would prefer us not to, suggests the ludicrously ginger movement of someone trying to carry a handful of dewdrops without them bursting. The narrator's assumption that the inseparability of the next two daughters has to do not with emotional intimacy, as we might have expected, but with a certain uniformity of taste brings out her superficial aestheticism no less strongly than her use of 'lahodný' to describe bodily movement. The narrator's approving use of 'omamující', with its connotations of narcotizing, reminds us of her hostility to the starkly sensual. The attribution of 'omamující' to 'odstín', which allows the fineness implicit in 'odstín' to contrast subversively with the heaviness we tend to associate with 'omamující', suggests that the narrator is oversensitively exaggerating the strength of the perfume. The insertion of 'v době' between 'odstín' and the mention of the stone-pine, moreover, undermines the connection between this perfume and the scent of the tree that the narrator is arguing for. In 'smyslné usmání', the author is using the connotations of tameness and superficiality that attach to 'usmání' to trivialize the narrator's 'smyslný', that we anyway suspect reflects largely only her disapproval of the erotic. The comparison of the smile to a wave with a rose-branch betrays again something of the narrator's sentimentality. There is also a strong hint of personification, because we feel it likely that what the narrator is interpreting as a beckoning sign is merely the swaying in the wind of a branch of a rose-bush. This picture in turn suggests that what lies behind this allegedly inviting smile is quite nasty, like the thorny middle to which the rose-bush would be thought to be beckoning with its branch. The coupling of the abstract 'odnášet se' to 'láska' is another hint at the narrator's emotional coldness and tendency to think formalistically. That the youth the girls are allegedly in love with is said to throw the discus at first recommends him as an athlete, but the subsequent description of him prancing about among garlands of flowers and on a fresh bed of hay probably put down to prevent him hurting his delicate feet on the hard ground provides a suitably delayed ironic corrective. The specification 'nahý' is meant to reflect once again the narrator's underlying moral censure.

> Usmrtila mi nejmenší, která se nevzdalovala ještě příliš od mého klína, hrajíc si s bílým kozletem, jako by sobě rovným v něze a prostomilosti.

The narrator, taking 'klín' literally, would like us to understand that this youngest daughter was killed only a short distance from her mother's lap or knees, while the author, reading 'klín' metaphorically, is implying that she met her death before distancing herself very much from her mother's womb. This is a hint at her virtual lifelessness. In the comparison of the daughter to the white kid she was playing with, the author is suggesting that 'jako by' relates not to 'sobě rovným', as the narrator would like us to think, but to 'v něze a prostomilosti', and hopes we may infer from this that she was the goat's equal in another respect, namely stupidity.

> Jsem nyní sama jako balvan, o který se vlny Archerontu s obzvláštní němosti rozrá-
> žejí. Jsem sama jako podym, který se vznesl do prázdna z navždycky uhaslého obětiště.
> Sama jako opuštěné dlaždice chrámu, jichž se lidský krok po celé století nedotýká.
> Vítr nepohne mým rouchem, nezčeří mého vlasu, nedostojí srdce rythmicky povin-
> nosti své k vyznění poslední životní stanze, neboť umlklo uprostřed nejživějšího tepo-
> tu, jako by zkamenělo.

By comparing herself to an isolated boulder washed by a silent river, to a last cloud of smoke rising from the ashes of an abandoned fire-place, and to the untrodden paving of a deserted temple, the narrator is merely trying to illustrate her sense of dereliction and solitude. The author, on the other hand, is using the associations of cold inertness and inanimacy that attach to 'balván' and 'dlaždice', the related associations of complete rarefaction and total extinction that attach to 'podym, který se vznesl do prázdna' and 'navždycky uhaslé [obětiště]', and the evocation of death in the reference to the River Acheron to bring out once again the lifelessness of the narrator's vision and sensibility. He is also, in the same comparisons, using 'obětiště' and 'chrám', together with 'lidský', implicitly distinguishing between human and divine, to show up the narrator's religiosity that he sees as concordant with this lifelessness. The expression 's obzvláštní němostí' hints at the narrator's lack of realism, because the absence of sound denoted by 'němost' would normally be thought incapable of intensification. The extravagance of her imagination is meant to come through also in 'vlny [...] [se] s [...] němostí rozrážejí', where the use of forceful 'rozrážet se' in place of the expected neutral 'lámat se' contrasts subversively with 's [...] němostí'. The narrator's observation that the wind will no longer play in her clothes and in her hair ironically emphasizes her lifelessness, because the author is hinting that her conception of life is wholly denaturalized if this is what she will mainly miss in departing. The ambiguity produced by the negation of 'pohnout' and 'zčeřit' takes this irony further. On the surface, we are to see the choice of these verbs as dependent on the negative form of the narrator's statement and to understand that death will take away even the minimal motion they express. On a deeper level, however, it is implied that the choice of 'pohnout' and 'zčeřit' has not been dictated by the negative meaning to be conveyed, but reflects the narrator's preference for feeble waftings that cause only the slightest movement. The narrator's use of 'dostát povinnosti' to describe the working of her heart is a teasing reminder of her coldly formalistic way of thinking, while 'vyznění poslední životní stanze' brings out once again her exaggerated aestheticism. The only apparently redundant 'rhythmicky' suggests, by implicit contrast with its opposite, that the narrator believes her heart could work properly also in an arhythmical way, so divorced is she from reality. At the same time, the use of 'rhythmicky' alongside 'vyznění [...] stanze' mockingly implies, by association, that the narrator thinks of her heart as a sort of percussion instrument beating time to the verses of a song. That the narrator claims her heart stopped beating at its liveliest is a further hint at her lifelessness and her melancholy, because it suggests that she felt herself most alive when all had become dead around her. The use of 'tepot' instead of the usual 'tlukot' introduces a hint of metallic artificiality that accords with the implication of lifelessness. The verb 'umlklo [srdce]' compromises the narrator further. Since 'umlklo [srdce]', is past tense and the narrator still speaking, therefore presumably still alive, we are led to infer that the narrator by this characteristically personificatory expression means not that her heart has stopped beating, but that it has stopped talking to her. The simile 'jako by zkamenělo' provides another irony. By allowing the mention of petrifaction to be included within the unreal comparison, the author is implicitly dismissing it as mere conjecture or supposition, thereby calling into question the traditional version of the legend that ends with Niobe's being turned to stone.

[...]. Jako čerň prázdná a propastná je pojmuto zrakem mým všecko to, co se kdy ve světle radovalo, kvetlo, formy nabývalo a vyvíjelo se pro potěšení smyslů.

Sama ruka Zevova formuje z někdejšího mého úsměvu kamenný obraz, omývaný bezvolnými přívaly slz, které ho nemohou rozleptati. Neumírám, Latono, ale přijímám z jeho rukou toto tajemné a ulevné zakletí života, kterýž jsem tolik milovala!

The narrator's claim that everything is like blackness to her sight, in its present formulation implicitly a ludicrously inflated variant of the common phrase 'dělá se mi černo před očima', leads us to suspect that she is merely fainting and so calls the traditional petrifaction into question again. That the narrator considers the blackness she sees to be empty and abysmal is meant to show up her fanciful romantic imagination. At the same time, the disparity between the expression of emptiness and immeasurable depth in '[čerň] prázdná a propastná' and the sense of grasping and encompassing basic to the verb 'pojmout' provides another hint at the narrator's unrealistic metaphysical perspective. Implicitly characteristic of the narrator is also her '[co] se [...] radovalo, kvetlo, formy nabývalo a vyvíjelo se'. By letting the narrator describe what she believes she will no longer be able to see in this sequence of verbs degressing from an expression of exuberant human emotion to an expression of mere development, the author, working against our expectation that a sequence should progress, is once again covertly mocking her alienation from life. The addition 'pro potěšení smyslů' may be understood as a further hint at her shallow aestheticism. The phrase 'sama ruka Zevova' suggests that the narrator, far from wanting to challenge the authority of the gods, is flattered by divine attention and recognition. The use of the verb 'formovat' only shortly after the use of the noun 'forma' in '[co] formy nabývalo' helps to bring out the narrator's obsession with form that is as much a sign of her aestheticism as it is of her formalistic way of thinking. The only apparently redundant '[z] někdejšího [úsměvu]' is meant to imply that what is happening is not that Niobe's smile is being turned to stone and therefore in some trivial sense no longer a smile, but that a former smile of hers is being used as a model for an independent likeness. Our suspicion that the traditional ending of the legend is not being enacted here is thereby implicitly confirmed. That the narrator should think of the likeness in question as being made up only of a smile shows up the ludicrous abstractness of her vision. The preference of 'kamenný obraz' to the more usual 'obraz z kamene' develops the irony by suggesting that this smiling likeness was not made of stone, merely stony in expression. By then letting the narrator say that this smiling likeness was covered in tears, the author goes on to imply that she is known to enjoy crying and being miserable. In '[obraz] omývaný [...] přívaly [slz]', the word 'příval', that normally calls to mind a falling torrent, is subversively weakened by being linked to 'omývat', that we tend to associate with the lapping of water on a shore. This subversive weakening not only brings out the narrator's inadequate sense of dynamism but also suggests that the tears are not as profuse as she would like us to think, and presumably therefore as little an expression of deep, heart-felt emotion as her implicitly stony smile. Following on from this, the only seemingly superfluous 'bezvolný' suggests that tears for the narrator are more often than not histrionically forced. That the tears cannot eat away the likeness is for the author explained not by Zeus's having supernatural powers and intending to keep Niobe in stone crying for ever, as the traditional legend relates, but by the tears being an integral part of the likeness Zeus had made. In accordance with this, the assertion 'přijímám z jeho [Zevových] rukou' ultimately indicates not that the narrator is acquiescing to petrifation but that she is being given the likeness Zeus had made. By 'zakletí života', we now consequently understand the narrator to mean not the entrancement of life in stone, as we at first wanted to, but the entrancement of life in the likeness in question. This ironically emphasizes the narrator's exaggerated aestheticism. The word 'tajemný', describing this entrancement, reflects the narrator's romantic or mystic liking for the arcane, while the parallel 'úlevný' hints at her relief in considering herself freed not from grief, as we might suppose, but from life itself. That the narrator, finally, claims to have loved life, after all the hints at her alienation from life, provides a culminating irony that conceals also the indirect truth that life for the narrator could not have been more than an external object of desire.

Our examination of 'Pláč Nioby' has shown it to be similar in ironic structure to 'Poledne'. The only differences in the ironic characterization of the narrator and his or her perspective are that in 'Pláč Nioby' the aspect of lifelessness comes through more strongly, the element of religiosity less strongly, than in 'Poledne'; and that instead of covert mockery for bourgeois prejudice we have insinuations of homosexuality. It seems reasonable to suppose that these differences merely reflect incidental adaptation to the given subject matter. It is of course also true that the narrator in 'Pláč Nioby' is female and not male as in 'Poledne', but this is clearly no more basic to the ironic structure that the fact that they both speak in the first person and not the third.

Through ironic subversion of the narrator's point of view the Niobe legend is transformed. The changes affect even central parts of the plot. The conflict between Niobe and Latona is no longer the result of Latona taking offence at defiant insults from Niobe, but the result of Latona fatuously misinterpreting what are on Niobe's part harmless expressions of eccentricity and deviant sensibility. Niobe's traditional pride at her progenitive virtuosity effaces behind an obsession with imaginary beauty. Finally, Niobe is not turned to stone in this version, but is presumed to faint on seeing some statue or painting of herself.

8. RUBENSOVA ZAHRADA LÁSKY[222]

'Rubensova Zahrada lásky', as the title indicates, deals with the painting 'The Garden of Love' (1630–32; now in the Prado, Madrid) by the Flemish Baroque artist Peter Paul Rubens (1577–1640). Manifestly, it is not a critical technical or historical study but a kind of descriptive essay largely devoted to the literary evocation of the scene conceived and portrayed by the artist.

As with 'Poledne' and 'Pláč Nioby', we shall try to explicate the irony inherent in the narrative structure of the text. In doing so, we shall not need to rely on any independent information about Rubens and his painting, since knowledge of this kind is not presupposed.[223]

The narrative begins with a comment on Rubens's temperament and the nature of his undertaking.

> Naplněn byl po dlouhý čas jakýmsi pokojným tempem flanderského smíchu, neo-třásajícího přespříliš lidskou bránicí a svěřil svým rukám, jež byly stvořeny pouze k tomu, držeti ve svých prstech růže, práci těžkou, ač rozkošnickou.

The phrase 'po dlouhý čas' tends to weaken the metaphorical meaning of 'naplněn byl', because 'naplnit' in this sense is standardly used of surges or fits of emotion, by their nature short-lived, as in 'událost ho naplnila hněvem/nenávistí/rozhorlením'. Exploiting the consequent compensatory strengthening of the literal meaning of 'naplněn byl', the author is encouraging us to see the artist as a mere vessel and to suspect that the narrator is used to seeing people as mere vessels, perhaps also in a religious sense. The following 'jakýsi' provides a first hint at the narrator's tendency to vagueness. The use of 'pokojný', that is hardly appropriate to describe laughter, is intended to reflect the narrator's preoccupation with spiritual peace. The incongruous combination of the normally dynamic 'tempo' with the static 'naplněn byl' reveals no less subversively the narrator's inadequate sense of dynamism. By attributing 'tempo' to 'smích', the author is implying that

---

222 Jan Opolský, 'Rubensova "Zahrada lásky"', in *Malé prosy* (Prague, 1926), pp. 13–18.

223 On the motif of the garden of love in Rubens, see Gustav Glück, *Rubens Liebesgarten* (Vienna and Leipzig, 1920); Annegret Blang-Süberkrüb', *Der Liebesgarten eine Untersuchung über die Bedeutung der Konfiguration für das Bildthema im Spätwerk des Peter Paul Rubens* (Berne, Frankfurt, 1976); and Elise Goodman, *Rubens: the garden of love as conversatie à la mode* (Amsterdam, 1992).

the laughter in question was not melodious, as the narrator would like us to think, but monotonously rhythmic, that is, forced and hollow. The modification of '[smích] otřásající [bránicí]' by 'přespříliš ne' prompts us to infer that the narrator is squeamishly averse to the shaking of the diaphragm any heartier laughter would cause. In 'lidská bránice', the only apparently redundant adjective is meant to suggest that the narrator wishes to allow for the possibility that the laughter mentioned might shake more strongly the diaphragms of some more delicate similarly disposed non-human beings, such as, perhaps, angels. The description of the artist's hands and the task he sets himself develops the incipient irony. The use of 'svěřit' in this connection shows up the narrator's tendency to personify. That the hands are said to have been created, and created for a purpose, provides another hint at the narrator's religious orientation. By claiming that the hands were meant only for holding roses, the narrator is trying to convince us in a symbolic way of the predominance of the artist's aesthetic sensibility, while the author is concluding more soberly that these hands were therefore not meant for painting. The only seemingly superfluous addition of 've svých prstech' to 'ruce' in connection with the holding of the roses calls to mind the picture of someone squeamishly holding the stalks of roses between his fingertips to avoid pricking himself on the thorns. In 'práce těžká, ač rozkošnická', the term 'rozkošnický' is meant as a first hint that the narrator basically disapproves of the task the artist has set himself. In accordance with this, the concessive 'ač' in the same phrase suggests that the narrator hesitates to qualify as hard work any activity involving gratification of the senses, presumably because he regards such gratification as frivolous and therefore incompatible with the sombre dignity the same moral severity leads him to associate with hard work.

> Thema o zahradě lásky, jež bylo od předchozích mistrů zužitkováno, vracelo se jako nové a nevyžité do jeho snů a představ: lidské tělo, sycené proudy ohnivých šťáv, nezhublé temnými vášněmi, ale napjaté a zhlazené vřelými vánky života, oděné pletí, jež může byti malována pouze smíšením mléka a krve, objevilo se před jeho uměleckým zrakem, svrhujíc se své nahoty poslední trochu roucha, v něž je konvence ukrývala.

By letting the narrator say 'thema o zahradě lásky' instead of the expected 'thema zahrady lásky', the author, playing also on the associations of 'thema', is implying that what is at issue is not the garden of love as a subject but some formalistic construction based upon it. In '[thema] bylo od předchozích mistrů zužitkováno', the author is exploiting the ambiguity of 'od' and the connotations of 'zužitkovat' to suggest that it is not simply a case of the subject's having been used by previous masters but of its having been treated in a purely utilitarian way from these masters onwards by other presumably less masterly artists here unnamed.[224] This is a further hint at the degeneracy of the conception available to Rubens. Continuing with '[thema] vracelo se jako nové [do jeho představ]', the narrator is trying to convince us that the artist kept on imagining the subject in new ways, while the author, allowing the imperfective to convey not repeated but incomplete action, is suggesting that the artist found the subject novel as it started to come back to him, presumably after he had forgotten it for a while. The artist's lack of interest and emotional involvement in his subject is being hinted at also in '[thema] nevyžité', which can mean 'fresh', 'unused', as the narrator would like to, or 'not lived out', 'not experienced fully'. The combination of 'sny' and 'představy' in 'do jeho snů a představ' is meant to suggest that the artist's ideas are dreamily vague and disconnected. In '[tělo] sycené proudy [šťáv]', the sluggishness we tend to associate with saturation or satiation contrasts subversively with the dynamism normally conveyed by 'proudy', and so brings out once again the narrator's inadequate sense of vitality that is here, by extension, also the artist's. There is a similar pespective in '[proudy] ohnivých šťáv', because the connotations of inertness and viscosity that attach to 'šťáva' implicitly discredit the alleged fieriness. Even the claim that the body in question is full of streams or currents of fiery humours is ironic, because it can mean that the body was brimming with vitality, as the narrator would like us to think, or else that it looked somewhat like an illustration in a contemporary anatomy book. In this way, the author is hinting at the artificiality of the artist's conception. In '[tělo] nezhublé temnými vášněmi', the adjectives for the author do not have objective reference but mirror the narrator's religiously prejudiced view of passion as sinister and destructive. In 'vřelé vánky', the author is subversively contrasting the heat or ardour normally conveyed by 'vřelý' with the gentleness and mildness we usually associate with 'vánek' to mock the narrator's lifelessness once again. The formulation '[tělo] napjaté a zhlazené [...] vánky života' contains several interacting ambiguities. The genitive '[vánky] života' may be read as a conventional possessive genitive or, alternatively, as a genitive of definition. In close connection with this, '[tělo] napjaté a zhlazené' may be thought of as describing the bulging and slackening of muscles or the bloating and smoothing out of a sort of inflatable skin. To complete the picture, the instrumental 'vánky' may be taken to refer back just to '[tělo] zhlazené' or to '[tělo] napjaté a zhlazené' as a whole.

---

224 Although not necessary for an adequate interpretation of this point, it is perhaps helpful to know that the theme of the garden of love, from the Middle Ages onwards a courtly theme involving the portrayal of a refined *societé élégante*, is considered to have its origins in the pastoral, arcadian conceptions of Classical antiquity. The historical development of the theme from natural to artificial may well have influenced Opolský in writing 'Rubensova Zahrada lásky'. Knowledge of this background is, however, not assumed and might, if brought to bear without very careful discrimination, make understanding of the irony more difficult.

As a result of these interacting ambiguities, it is left open whether it was that life's breezes relaxed an already tensed muscular body or that breezes considered to be the stuff of life pumped up like a balloon a previously slack and crinkled skin in an attempt to make a living body out of it. The only apparently rhetorical or poetic '[tělo] oděné pletí' takes the implication of artificiality further by suggesting that the complexion has been put on like a layer of clothing. The claim that the body could be painted only with milk and blood is meant to be understood as an ironic dislocation and extension of the stock phrase '[děvče je] krev a mléko'. That the narrator in this phrase puts 'mléko' before 'krev' and not after it suggests, moreover, that the complexion was not fresh and healthy, as we at first assume, but uncommonly pale. The expression 'před uměleckým zrakem' hints at the narrator's metaphysical perspective, because it associates with 'před duševním/duchovým/vnitřním zrakem'. The description of the divestment adds to the irony. The addition of 'se své nahoty' to '[tělo] svrhujíc [poslední trochu roucha]' is strictly speaking contradictory, because from nakedness no clothing can be thrown off. This underlying inconsistency is being used to suggest that what is at issue is not that the body is stripping naked, as we initially assume, but that the narrator is prudishly disgusted by the degree of exposure the clothing still allows. This leads us to infer that the narrator is criticizing convention not for being unduly conservative, as he appears to be doing, but for being unduly liberal. The irony is even taken a step further. By putting 'poslední [trocha]' in a medial position between '[tělo] svrhujíc' and '[konvence] ukrývala', and connecting it syntactically to both, the author is suggesting that the narrator is deceitfully leaving it open whether it is the last piece of undermost garment that is being cast off, as we understand from associating 'poslední' more closely with '[tělo] svrhujíc', or the last piece of uppermost garment, as follows from associating 'poslední' more closely with '[konvence] ukrývala'. This ambiguity is supported by the use of 'roucho', which can mean both clothing in general and ceremonious outer clothing in particular.

> Tělo vesničanek z okolí slunečného Elevytu, povalující se s ňadry a hýžděmi koulovitými na břehu lučního potoka, těla děcek, živená a nakypřená jakousi zázračnou živototvornou kaší, i těla mužská, brunátná, s vysokým odstíněním žil a svalů.

By punctuating the relative clauses of which this passage consists as a separate sentence and even starting a new paragraph with them, the author is bending normal syntax to bring out the narrator's lifelessness also linguistically. The use of the singular form 'tělo' in 'tělo vesničanek' in contrast to the plural 'těla' in 'těla děcek' and 'těla mužská' allows the author to suggest a correspondence between the 'tělo' in 'tělo vesničanek' and the 'tělo' in 'lidské tělo' in the previous passage. He is thereby trying to imply that Rubens has rather effeminately taken as his paradigm not a male body but a female one. By following the nouns '[tělo] vesničanek' and '[těla] děcek' in the same phrases by the adjective '[těla] mužská' instead of the congruent noun '[těla] mužů', the author is suggesting that the bodies in this case may be male but are not the bodies of proper men. The phrase '[vesničanky] z okolí slunečného Elevytu' leaves us free to conclude that the place these country women are from is not itself sunny. Even 'slunečný Elevyt' will be shown to be deceptive; the alleged sunniness and the Greek-sounding 'Ele-' in 'Elevyt' initially tend to make us think of a Greek landscape, but the later introduction of recognisably Flemish names into the text will prompt us to infer that 'Elevyt' can only be referring to a place in Rubens's native Flanders.[225] For the time being, however, the narrator can maintain the illusion and even develop it by going on to speak of gods and goddesses. That the artist is said to imagine country women to be lazing about in the sun instead of working hard on a farm leads us to suspect that the artist, and maybe also the narrator, sentimentally idealizes country life, probably from a safe bourgeois distance. This implication will be developed. At the same time, the use of 'povalovat se' suggests that the narrator secretly disapproves of the inactivity imputed to the women. By following 'povalovat se' with 'koulovitý', that is particularly appropriate to the literal meaning of 'povalovat se', the author goes on to imply that the women imagined by the artist are not so much simply lazing about as rolling to and fro because of the roundness of their parts. In 's ňadry a hyžděmi koulovitými', the author is contrasting the concrete, plain anatomical 'hyždě' with the loftier, comparably emotive 'ňadra' and the geometrically abstract 'koulovitý'. By implicitly isolating 'hyždě' in this way as the only concrete neutral physiological term, the author is hinting at the narrator's inability to come to terms with the physical reality of life. The term 'luční potok' can suggest lack of dynamism, since a stream of this kind may do no more than trickle feebly. By using 'nakypřený', the author is able to imply that the bodies of the children are not well-rounded, as the narrator would like us to think, but lifelessly bloated, since the verb 'nakypřit' is equivalent to 'učinit kyprým' only where 'kyprý' means 'loose', 'airy', 'puffy', as in 'kyprá půda' or 'kypré těsto'; but not when it means 'full', 'well-developed', 'buxom', as in 'kyprá postava' or 'kypré tělo'. As a result, the narrator's 'živený' is implicitly discredited. The use of 'zázračný' and 'živototvorný' hints again at the narrator religious, metaphysical perspective. The attribution of these adjectives

---

225   The reader who happens to know that 'Elevyt' is the French name for Elewijt, the Flemish village in which Rubens often resided in Steen Castle, may appreciate the irony already now, provided that this knowledge does not lead him to ignore the impression of Greekness that the form 'Elevyt' can create in this connection. Significantly, Opolský has preferred the form 'Elevyt' at this stage to the recognisably Flemish 'Elewijt'.

to 'kaše', that usually designates the gruel that is the staple food of peasants, helps to confirm our suspicion the artist and narrator are bourgeois who sentimentally idealize country life. This conjecture receives further support from '[těla] brunatná', which for the author does not mean that the bodies of the men were swarthy, as we might first think it does, but that they appeared to the artist to be made of russet, a coarse homespun material often used by peasants. It is thereby also implied that the artist, instead of imagining real bodies that he tries to convey on to the canvas, starts by imagining already canvas-like bodies. In 's vysokým odstíněním', the author is using the associations of fineness and subtlety that attach to 'odstínění' to belie the sense of bright or high contrast normally conveyed by 'vysoký' in this sense, thereby covertly mocking the narrator's oversensitivity. That both veins and muscles are said to be visible can indicate that the bodies in question were bulging with muscular tension, as the narrator would like it to, or else that they too looked somewhat like illustrations in an anatomy book. The use of 'odstínění' with regard to the veins and muscles suggests, moreover, that this coldly physiological conception of the bodies was not even scientifically clear but faint and vague.

> Byla to určitá a jasná synthesa pozemského zdraví, na němž nehlodá ani červ smutné předtuchy. Jako by i sama duše těchto těl byl jenom neutuchající veselý plamen, jejž není možno z moci světa uhasiti.

We initially take 'určitý' to mean 'definite', but the author is encouraging us to read it as 'a certain', in accordance with previous hints at the narrator's tendency to vagueness. At the same time, he is allowing 'jasný' to equivocate betwen the apparent meaning 'bright' or 'radiant' and the here subversive meaning 'evident' or 'obvious'. There is a parallel ambiguity in 'synthesa', by which the implicitly metaphysically oriented narrator means some kind of sublimating fusion into oneness, the author however merely an artifical compounding of naturally unconnected parts. The narrator's metaphysical orientation comes through also in his use of the terms 'pozemský', 'duše' and 'z moci světa'. The expression '[zdraví] nehlodá ani červ smutné předtuchy', by suggesting commoner variants of the same figure like 'koho hlodá červ špatného svědomí/skepse/závisti' betrays the narrator's religious moralism. The phrase 'smutná předtucha', in which the author is implying that the adjective is for the narrator not a contingent but a defining attribute of the noun, is meant to show up the narrator's tendency to romantic melancholy. The use of 'hlodá červ' in connection with this 'smutná předtucha' therefore suggests that the narrator has a bad conscience because of this melancholy since his religious beliefs commit him to optimism. The attribution of 'veselý' to 'plamen', that seems to be no more than a case of transferred epithet, is meant to bring out the narrator's tendency to personify, while the attribution of the usually only abstract 'neutuchající' is intended to reveal again his inability to distinguish satisfactorily between abstract and concrete.

> A vycházeje z této synthesy, i vraceje se k ní tisícerými myšlenkovými pěšinami, obdechoval tato těla se zjevnou tvůrčí rozkoší, kupil je k tanci, pojil v přilnavá objetí a připravoval k tělesným zásnubům a rozhýřením.

By following 'vycházeje' with 'vraceje se', and attaching the mention of the thousands of paths to 'vraceje se' and not to 'vycházeje', the author is implying that the artist did not elaborate his basic notion in a multitude of ways, as the narrator would like us to think, but in his attempt to develop it kept getting lost, straying about and ending up back where he started. In 'myšlenkovými pěšinami', 'myšlenkový' suggests that it was more cold intellect than imagination which was involved, while 'pěšina', that unlike 'cesta' is rarely used abstractly, helps evoke the comically concrete image of thoughts strolling along. The verb 'obdechovat' may convey the idea of a symbolic transfer of energy to the scene, as the narrator would like it to, or of the artist literally breathing on these bodies in an attempt to bring them to life. The adjective 'zjevný' in 'zjevná tvůrčí rozkoš', that seems to convey the irrepressible strength of this pleasure, for the author reveals the narrator's basic incredulity at the thought that someone might find such an occupation pleasurable. The use of 'pojit' and 'kupit' hints at artificiality of conception. In 'přilnavá objetí', the adjective for the author is not objectively intensifying but betrays the narrator's disgust at the thought of close bodily contact. In 'tělesné zásnuby a rozhýření', the ideality and tame conventionality suggested by 'zásnuby' contrasts subversively with the physicality and sensual abandon normally conveyed by 'tělesný' and 'rozhýření'. In this way, the author can show up both the narrator's inability to come to terms with the concrete reality of life and the tendentiousness of 'rozhýření' that implicitly does no more than reveal the narrator's religiously motivated moral disapproval of what he is describing.

> A vžívaje se celou svou mužnou, otevřenou myslí do svého sujetu, vytvořil ovzduší zahrady lásky, ve kterém dospívá k aktu mezi bohy a bohyněmi.

By contrasting the total involvement indicated by 'vžívaje se' with the purely intellectual effort suggested by 'myslí', the author is again hinting at the artist's lack of emotional response to his subject matter. The word 'mužný' can be taken to mean 'masculine', as the narrator intends, or 'courageous', in implicit confirmation of the artist's inadequacy to his task. Ambiguous is also 'otevřený', which the narrator would like us to read as 'broad-minded', 'liberal', the author however as something more like 'uncertain', 'indecisive'. The loan word 'sujet', that seems to add a note of distinction, for the author intimates the trivial, superficial fashionableness of the theme. By letting the relative clause following 'zahrada lásky' refer back not to 'zahrada lásky' itself but to 'ovzduší', the author is implying that what is said in this clause applies not to the subject as represented on the canvas but to some atmospheric abstraction of it the artist has created for himself. Moreover, since 'akt' can mean both 'sexual intercourse' and 'nude portrait', we are left in doubt whether the figures in question are engaged in erotic foreplay or whether they are simply undressing to pose in the nude. This ironic ambiguity is developed in 'mezi bohy a bohyněmi', which can accommodate both the idea of intercourse between gods and goddesses and the idea of other figures undressing in the midst of gods and goddesses who may therefore be no more than statues surrounding the scene. In addition, the use of the imperfective 'dospívat' leaves it tellingly open how far the action in question has progressed.

> Bílá bříza tu jaksi přemoženě šepce a šelestí a kde jakou pevnou oporu ovíjí sladká ipomea. Sloupy a vchody zahradního úkrytu rovnají se v přepychu báchorce viděného kdysi paláce mantovského.

By letting the narrator follow the word 'zahrada' that in the previous passage occurred in the text for the first time by the description of a tree and a creeper, the author is suggesting that the narrator shares our expectation that a garden should contain vegetation. The brevity of his inventory contrasts subversively with this expectation and so helps bring out the unnaturalness of the scene. This implication is supported by the use of 'tu', which encourages us to think that the narrator is picking out a relatively minor detail to salvage his case. The term 'přemoženě' hints at the narrator's sentimentality. The only seemingly unnecessary addition of '[bříza] šelestí' to '[bříza] šepce' suggests that the narrator in his fancifully personified view of reality considers the whispering of the tree to be something other than the rustling of its leaves. By using the formulation '[ipomea ovíjí] kde jakou pevnou oporu', the narrator is trying to persuade us that the ipomoea is rampant, while the author, considering 'kde jaký' indicative more of desperate quest than abundant result and 'pevný' redundant only apparently, is suggesting that the ipomoea cannot proliferate because it cannot find enough sufficiently firm supports. The attribution of sweetness to the ipomoea plant, which is known to contain a powerful narcotic and hallucinogenic substance, betrays the narrator's liking for drug-induced detachment from reality.[226] The transi-

---

226 The substance in a question, a derivative of D-lysergic acid, is very similar in chemical composition and physiological effect to the well-known synthetic drug LSD. The here only implicit drug

tion from the ipomoea to allegedly magnificent pillars and entrances without any explicit connection being made allows a compromising ambiguity. The narrator would like us to believe that there is a connection, and that the pillars and entrances are magnificent because the ipomoea entwines them. The author, however, wishes us to realize that there is no connection and that the narrator is trying to mislead us into thinking there is one so that he may surreptitiously change the subject and escape from the embarrassment the scantiness of the vegetation is causing him. The compromising unnaturalness is implicitly at issue also in 'sloupy a vchody zahradního úkrytu', because the idea of monumental architecture suggested by 'sloupy a vchody' contrasts subversively with the idea of a natural hide-out in or behind bushes that would normally be conveyed by 'zahradní úkryt'. The contrast is all the stronger if we accept that the alleged magnificence of the pillars and entrances is not due to the ipomoea but structural. The use of 'rovnat se', which is commonly used also in arithmetic, comports with previous implications that the narrator thinks formalistically. In the remainder of the sentence there is a complex play of meanings. The word 'přepych' can mean not only 'splendour', 'magnificence' but also 'extravagance', 'pomposity'. There is parallel ambiguity in 'báchorka paláce', which can be taken to be equivalent to 'báchorkovitý palác' or to 'báchorka o paláci'. As a result of these two last ambiguities, we are left in doubt whether the pillars and entrances are being compared in splendour to a fairy-tale palace, as the narrator would like us to think, or in extravagance to a fairy-tale about a palace. The irony is heightened by the fact that 'báchorka' can mean not only 'fairy-tale' but also 'old wives' tale', 'cock-and-bull story'. The use of 'kdysi' suggests that the palace in question is anyway only a hazy memory and, at the same time, brings out once more the narrator's liking for vagueness.

A delfín, z jehož široké tlamy voda se hrne, zdobí vrchol kašny, stávaje se bezděky účastným všeobecného smyslného[227] uneseni. Najada, sedící obkročmo na jeho hřbetu, tiskne mezi prsty hroty svých ňader, vypuzujíc odtud dva stříbrné pruty vody, která v nádrži pleští. Zemi pokrývají pivoňky a zlatý písek.

The basic arrangement of the description of the fountain reveals the narrator's continuing preoccupation with the compromising unnaturalness of

motif is explicit in Opolský's 'Narkotikum', *Lumír*, 59 (1932–3), pp. 186–8; reprinted in *Visuté zahrady* (Prague, 1935).

227 The only extant text has 'smylného [sic]'. We correct to 'smyslného', but not without certain misgivings. It is hard to ignore the appropriateness of the apparent misprint to the irony. In view of the basic censure imputed to the narrator, it is tempting to see the form 'smylný' as an attempt to cross 'smyslný' with 'smilný'. Could it be that Opolský originally wrote 'smyslného' and took the opportunity to conserve the useful misprint when correcting the proofs?

the scene. The sentence openings 'A delfín [...]' and 'Najada [..]' suggest that the narrator is interested in the fountain not because he thinks it particularly beautiful but because the figures at its head give him the opportunity to continue trying to convince us that the scene is not as unnatural as he knows it is. The initial focus on the dolphin can temporarily create an illusion of naturalness; an illusion that is not yet spoilt by the content of the first relative clause, since we can also think of a live dolphin as spouting water. The disruptive effect of 'kašna', when the clarifying word finally falls, is all the stronger for this brief suspension. The irony is heightened by the expression 'zdobit vrchol', which would normally be used to describe a relatively insignificant decoration on top of a towering object, like an ornamental weather-vane on a church steeple. The appeal to 'zdobit vrchol' here enhances the implicit debunking effect of 'kašna' by producing an instantaneous optic switch from the still favourable zoom on the dolphin to a compromising wider shot revealing the dolphin's comparative unimportance. Secretly aware of his failure to sustain the desired illusion, the narrator tries again with 'Najada [...]'. Throughout the first relative clause and the subsequent main clause of this next sentence, there is nothing to prevent us assuming that the naiad is alive, and given the earlier promise of a mythological environment we might well so assume. It is only when we learn of the water spouting out of her breast into the basin of the fountain that we are driven to conclude that she is also merely part of the stone figure-head. This makes us feel that the narrator has once more tried to mislead us for as long as he could before having to capitulate before the reality he would like to, but cannot, deny. That the narrator's embarrassment at the scene's unnaturalness remains with him unallayed is brought out by his attempted return to the question of vegetation in the third and last sentence of this passage. His assertion that the ground is covered with peonies and sand, however, only compromises the artist further, and this not merely because of the mawkishness of taste this combination suggests in the present ironic context. The mention of sand cancels what reparative effect the reference to peonies alone might have had, since it leads us to infer that these flowers are not rooted in this barren ground but loosely strewn over it. The rest of the irony in this passage is moving in a similar direction. The express reference to the width of the dolphin's snout, implying departure from the normal beak-like form, prompts us to suspect that the artist, unable to make the fall of a narrower stream of water seem sufficiently dynamic, has compensated by artificially extending the dispensing orifice. The same underlying tendency is present in 'hrnout se', which the narrator is using in the standard sense of 'to rush', while the author, working against this surface dynamism, is looking to the less common but more basic meaning 'to pile up' that may be arrived at by reading 'hrnout se' as a simple reflexive of 'hrnout'. The subordination of 'stávat se' as a transgressive to 'zdobit', implicitly reversing the normal order which would give priority as main verb to the more dynamic term, helps lend further ironic emphasis to the staticness imputed to both the narrator's language and to the reality described. The description of the dolphin's supposed erotic involvement in the scene is variously subversive. The narrator's idea that a stone figure can be enraptured shows up his ludicrously animistic view of reality. That the narrator speaks of a general feeling of rapture when his account of the emotionality in the painting, as distinct from the artist's imagination, has so far included only an overwhelmed birch-tree suggests that he is deceitfully concealing a compromising reality. By now adding to the overwhelmed birch-tree an enraptured stone figure of a dolphin, the narrator, conspicuously avoiding for the time being any mention of the feelings and behaviour of the sentient beings we would expect to have been given pride of place, is betraying his uncomfortable awareness of the fact that the activity of these sentient beings, divine or human, is not what it should be. What is more, the cold abstractness of 'stávat se účastným' and 'všeobecné unešení', and the automatism suggested by 'bezděky' contrast subversively with the depth of feeling the narrator is trying to convey. At the same time, the use of the terms 'smyslný' and 'unešení' helps to bring out the narrator's basically critical attitude to the sexuality he thinks he is describing. The description of the naiad compromises the narrator further. The word 'obkročmo', because of its closeness in form to other adverbs of the '-mo' -type used predominantly in gymnastics, is not without subversive background associations of the coldly athletic that accord with the general implication of unnaturalness. The expression 'hroty ňader' does more than ironically enforce this sense of artificiality. The revelation that the naiad is part of the stone figure-head of the fountain makes us realize that this 'hroty', which seems to be merely a poetic variant of 'bradavky', is comically appropriate in a more concrete way, since the nipples of the fountain-head figure that serve as spouts are likely to be exactly the sharp metal points that 'hroty' would otherwise call to mind. The use of the potentially also mechanical 'tisknout', and the combination of 'stříbrné [pruty]' with 'zlatý [písek]' below, also contribute to maintaining a background sense of artificiality. The preference of 'prut' to the commoner 'proud', 'trysk' or 'pramen' again hints at a lack of dynamism and is supported in this implication by the construction '[pruty] vody, která v nádrži pleští'. By making the relative pronoun refer back to 'voda' instead of 'pruty', and using 'v nádrži' instead of 'do nádrže', the author is implying that the sound described is not that of the two jets from the nipples of the naiad hitting the surface, indeed not that of falling water at all. If the noise that is heard is consequently only the lapping of water already in the basin, we are bound to conclude that the streams of water falling into the basin must be exceptionally feeble if the sound of their impact does not drown it.

A snášejí se tu porůznu, proti všem zákonům možnosti a pravdy, amoreti, kteří jsou našeptávači neklidných myšlenek a v jejich neskrytém dříku spočívá význam udrženého smyslného půvabu života.

Těžci, masití, s růžovými peroutkami ze zad vyrůstajícími, baví se přínosem květin, vypouštěním bílých holubic, které jsou ustanoveny poslicemi, a přeletem z místa na místo, jako by nemohli nalézti ukojení.

In 'snášejí se [...] porůznu [amoreti]', the author, playing on the ambiguity of both verb and adverb, is suggesting that the amoretti are not flying down in various places, as the narrator would like us to think, but in isolated cases putting up with each other. In this way, he can mock the behaviour of the amoretti and also subvert the surface dynamism of the narrative. The narrator's appeal to invented laws of possibility and truth betrays not only his tendency to think formalistically and legalistically, but also his fancifulness and irrationality. The connotations of malicious incitement in 'našeptávač' help to bring out the narrator's basic disapproval of the sexually provocative. The same underlying attitude comes through in 'neklidné myšlenky', which suggests that the narrator regards this stimulation as a hindrance to peace of mind. That the narrator makes special mention of the entirely usual nakedness of the amoretti reveals his prudish annoyance. The preference of 'neskrytý' to the more usual 'nezakrytý', moreover, betrays his conviction that nakedness should be not only covered up but hidden away as something shameful and embarrassing. By allowing 'dřík' for the commoner 'trup', the author is introducing a hint of artificiality, because 'dřík' can also mean 'shaft (of column, anchor, screw, etc)'. The insertion of the concrete term 'v dříku' into the abstract structure 'v čem spočívá význam' is meant to bring out once again the narrator's tendency to confuse abstract and concrete. In '[význam] udrženého smyslného půvabu', the mildness and refinement we associate with 'půvab' contrast subversively with the stark physicality normally conveyed by 'smyslný'; and the deliberate effort conveyed by 'udržený' is comically at odds with the natural ease normally suggested by 'půvab'. By then allowing the narrator to attribute 'půvab' to 'život', the author is hinting at his superficial aestheticism. At the same time, the statement that these naked torsos show the importance of preserving attractiveness that we take the narrator to be making here prompts us to suspect that he is secretly criticizing them for being out of shape. This interpretation is borne out by '[amoreti] těžci, masití' at the beginning of the second paragraph. This description also suggests that the narrator is squeamishly exaggerating the conventional chubbiness of amoretti. The use of 'peroutka' for the more usual 'peruť' provides a further comic hint of artificiality, because 'peroutka' can mean also 'feather-brush', both in the sense of 'feather-duster' and as the name of the kitchen utensil used for painting dough with egg yolk. The adjective 'růžový' helps to bring out once again the narrator's shallow aestheticism and insipid sentimentality. That the term 'vyrůstající' occurs in the stressed final position in its clause prompts us to infer that the narrator is secretly repelled by the thought of wings growing out of these bodies instead of being hung onto them as he presumably considers to be the case with angels. By letting the main verb of this second sentence be the static 'bavit se', and the movement to be expressed by noun phrases subordinated to 'bavit se', the author is again trying to show up the narrator's lifelessness also syntactically. That the first activities to be included in the narrator's account of what is happening in the painting itself are the bringing of flowers and the releasing of what we first take to be messenger-pigeons is ironically out of keeping with the earlier promise of libidinous abandon. The contrast becomes stronger when we understand better what the role of the birds is meant to be. By letting the narrator use not 'holub', which associates with 'poštovní holub', but 'holubice', which associates with 'mírová holubice', the author is prompting us to infer that these birds are not messenger-pigeons but doves as messengers of peace. The reason why the narrator does not describe the birds' message is therefore not that the message is obviously an invitation to sexual activity, as the narrator would still like us to think, but that the birds are their own message. The choice of the verb 'ustanovit' helps to confirm this view of the birds, because it suggests that the narrator considers their role divinely ordained. The expression 'z místa na místo' leaves it open how much flying about was done in this scene and so helps to subvert the surface dynamism of the narrative still further. Following on from this in 'jako by nemohli [amoreti] nalézti ukojení', the author is implying that the amoretti are not flying about apparently insatiably or relentlessly, as the narrator is trying to make us think, but simply in a way that suggests they cannot find a single instance of sexual satisfaction in this scene.

> Tady se naklání jeden z nich k sličné paní, jejíž prsa převysoko z korsetu kypí, jejíž hlava je zvrácena těžkostí smilného snu a ruce jako by se malátné vzpíraly o pelest lůžka. Násilné moci a hrubé síly vyžaduje její bledé a kypré tělo, aby nasytilo svou podvědomou lačnost a utišilo sténající touhu.

That the first person to be mentioned as being part of the scene in the painting is not a god or goddess but an ordinary woman implicitly confirms our suspicion that the artist has not realized on the canvas what he imagined for himself. The refinement of 'sličný' and the propriety of 'paní', moreover, are comically at odds with the uninhibited lustfulness we were led to expect. The adverb 'převysoko', that seems to indicate that the breasts are swelling up very high, for the author merely reveals the narrator's prudish conviction that their exposure is excessive. The use of the verb 'kypět' makes us think more of a frothing or puffing up than a firm bulging of the flesh, consistently with previous hints at the airiness of the bodies the artist conceived. The mention of a corset, that the narrator hopes will persuade us of the boldness of the portrayal, is for the author comically in conflict with earlier promise of nakedness or near-nakedness, especially since this corset may still be under layers of clothing. By allowing '[hlava je] zvrácena' to be followed by 'těžkostí', which can take on also a literal meaning, the author is suggesting that the narrator sees this dream not just as an oppressive experience causing the head to drop languidly but also as a heavy weight pressing the head back. In this way, the author is again mocking the narrator's tendency to confuse abstract and concrete. At the same time, the author is allowing the term 'zvrácen' to equivocate subversively between the literal meaning of 'bent back' and the figurative meaning of 'perverse' to bring out the narrator's basic disapproval of the behaviour he is describing. The only apparently intensifying 'smilný' reveals the same underlying censure. In 'jako by se [ruce] malátné vzpíraly [o pelest lůžka]', the author is implying that 'jako by' does not relativize 'malátně', as the narrator hopes we will think, but 'vzpírat se'. This prompts us to infer that the woman's arms are genuinely sickly or puny and that the narrator's claim that her arms are braced is mere supposition, presumably based on another barely visible detail. The very introduction of a bed-frame into the narrative is ironic, because it enforces our impression of the garden's unnaturalness. The only apparently intensifying adjectives in 'násilná moc' and 'hrubá síla' for the author reveal the narrator's attitude to power and strength as such. The verb 'vyžadovat', preferred here to the more usual 'žádat', suggests more requesting or demanding than desiring or craving and so helps to bring out once again the narrator's tendency to think in a coldly formalistic way. In 'bledé a kypré tělo', the adjective 'bledý' implicitly confirms the point made with regard to 'malátné' and also disappoints the expectations of healthy rustic swarthiness raised earlier. The use of 'kyprý' in the same phrase supports the implication that this body is not buxom but airy and puffy. The term 'lačnost' that seems to indicate the strength of this desire for the author merely reflects the narrator's basic censure. By calling the desire a subconscious one, the narrator is trying to convince us of the depth of this woman's feeling, while the author is suggesting that the desire was hardly felt. The preference of the verbs 'nasytit' and 'utišit' to the standard neutral 'ukojit' is meant to impart the gentle hint that the narrator tends to think of satisfaction either as an unnatural sating or as a mere assuaging or placating of desire. The expression 'sténající touha' is a mocking reminder of the narrator's trite romanticism. The direct attribution of 'sténající' to 'touha' in this phrase, apparently only a case of transferred epithet, reveals, moreover, the narrator's tendency to personify even the abstract.

Není tučný amoret zobrazením této síly, ale jest její nápovědí. Není jím ani jiný, který lascivním způsobem spojuje paži muže a ženy, ale všichni, pozbyvše mythičnosti,
utvrzují zde nahou reálnost zobrazeného lidského prostředí.

By continuing to refer to the force the woman allegedly needs to satisfy
her only to say platitudinously that neither of the two amoretti represents
it, the narrator is betraying an embarrassed awareness of its absence. The
content of the clauses following the opening denials reveals and subverts
the narrator's attempt to cover up this absence. The assertion that the first
amoretto prompts this force cannot offset the subversive effect of the preceding denial, since it is equally platitudinous. The reference to the activity
of the second amoretto and the statement that all the figures in the scene
bear witness to stark realism only heightens the disruptive effect of the now
already more disturbing second negation, since together they suggest that
the narrator is trying to avoid the ultimately central issue by first digressing
and then completely changing the subject. The irony is enhanced by the use
of the 'ne ..., ale ...' construction, which, given the narrator's apparent intention to praise, we may think of as the framework for rhetorical negation.
Because we expect this figure, we prepare to stress the adversative statement
introduced by 'ale' it would normally highlight, only to discover that this
statement is ironically the unworthier of emphasis. There are also several
other more specific points of irony in this passage. The use of 'tučný' as a par-
ticularizing attribute among amoretti who only a while ago were described
without distinction as heavy and fleshy implicitly confirms our suspicion
that the earlier descripton was a tendentious exaggeration. In 'zobrazení
síly', the abstractness of 'síla' contrasts subversively with the tendency to
concreteness to 'zobrazení' and so helps bring out once more the narrator's
inability to distinguish abstract and concrete. The word 'nápověd' introduces
a further subversive hint of artificiality, since it calls to mind also prompting
in the theatre. The mechanical 'spojovat' and the coldly anatomical 'paže' do
more to undermine the natural eroticism the narrator would still like us to
believe in and at the same time show up once again the narrator's detached
formalistic way of thinking. The same is true of the preference of 'lascivním
způsobem' to 'lascivně', because the introduction of 'způsob' not only helps to
make the expression drily abstract but also suggests that the lasciviousness
was merely outward appearance. Because of its breadth of meaning, 'paže'
also leaves it tellingly open whether the amoretto was making the couple
put their arms round each other's shoulders or simply hold hands. The word
'lascivní' itself, like several related terms before, is for the author not objectively intensifying but reflects the narrator's underlying prudish censure.
The insertion of '[všichni] pozbyvše mythičnosti' compromises particularly
the artist. We have already been led to suspect that the vision of gods and

goddesses making love that the artist is supposed to have begun with has not been realized on the canvas. By letting the narrator address this crucial matter that clamours for explanation merely parenthetically and with extreme terseness, the author is suggesting that the narrator is uneasily aware of the fact that this discrepancy is due to simple artistic failure. The narrator's preference of 'mythičnost' to the expected 'mythologičnost' is meant to reveal his disdain for a religious conceptuality he considers primitively heathen. The only apparently intensifying adjective in 'nahá reálnost' is intended to betray also his underlying disapproval of all that realistic. In 'zobrazené lidské prostředí', the term 'zobrazený' that seems to be redundant since we know that what it describes is part of the picture for the author serves to weaken the sense of reality that would normally be conveyed by 'lidské prostředí'. The use of 'prostředí' in the same phrase subversively turns our attention away from the bodies we expected to be most important to incidental aspects of the environment.

> Uchvacující kráska, manželka vlažného purkmistra Rockosce, jejíž sněhové tělo vystupuje s příkrostí z černorudého brokátu, není sličnější manželky Gewaertsovy, kterýž se kromě svého sběratelství mincí zanáší prokletou žárlivostí.

That the narrator follows his claim that the picture is realistic by mentioning various Flemish names, but without making a connection explicit, suggests that he knows, but is reluctant to admit, that the alleged realisticness of this picture consists solely in its being a copy of a scene staged with models the artist has recruited from among local acquaintances. In 'uchvacující kráska', the rather precious bourgeois 'uchvacující' contrasts subversively with the popular 'kráska' that associates strongly with rusticality. This helps to confirm our suspicion that the narrator is a bourgeois who sentimentally idealizes country life. A related point is made by 'manželka [...] purkmistra Rockosce' and 'manželka Gewaertsova'. By identifying both women alone through their role as wives and by mentioning Rockosc's office together with his name, the narrator is betraying an attitude to women and an awareness of status that the author would like us to see as typically bourgeois. The narrator's use of the word 'vlažný', that normally conveys more lack of zeal or fervour than lack of passion, and associates with such expressions as 'vlažná víra' and 'vlažná zbožnost', mockingly reveals also his religiosity. The attribute 'sněhový', more than 'bledý' in the case of the woman on the bed, prompts us to infer that the artist has not been able to paint the rustic swarthiness we assumed he had imagined or even the rosiness normally suggested by '(vesnická) kráska'. Given that the woman now being described is said to be a mayor's wife and, a little further on, to be wearing brocade, we begin to realize that the reason for the pallor of the women is that the artist has based his portrayal of the bodies not on the peasant girls leading a healthy outdoor life that were mentioned before but on bourgeois women perhaps residing in the country but used to sitting around indoors. In '[její tělo] vystupuje s příkrostí [z brokátu]', the author is using the ambiguity of both terms to suggest that what is at issue is not so much that the body contrasts boldly in its whiteness with the blackness of the brocade, as the narrator would like us to think, but that it sticks out abruptly from under the brocade whose constraining stiffness causes the bloated flesh to swell up over the edges of the material. The author is thereby developing his general implication that the women in this scene are not attractively buxom with nicely rounded breasts and buttocks, as we were led to expect they would be, but hideously out of shape. What is more, the mention of brocade that can hardly be anything other than the material of outer clothing goes further than the earlier reference to a corset towards suggesting that the nakedness or nearnakedness the artist is supposed to have imagined has not been realized on the canvas. The adjective 'černorudý' adds to the irony. Since genuine brocade is normally variegated with gold or silver thread, we are led to suspect that this material, offering only a contrast of red and black, might be no more than a cheap imitation. This can suggest that the woman is making a snobbish false display of wealth. The use of the negative comparative in the pivotal '[manželka Rockosce] není sličnější [manželky Gewaertsovy]' suggests that the narrator, having had difficulty vindicating his 'kráska', is now anxious to avoid any more direct affirmation of beauty. That the narrator mentions Mrs Gewaerts's appearance only to turn immediately to her husband prompts us to suspect that he is eager to avoid describing her presumably also ugly figure. The abruptness of the digression is ironically emphasized by the use of the strictly speaking ungrammatical subordinating construction 'manželka Gewaertsova, kterýž...', in which a relative pronoun is made to refer to a possessive adjective. The description of Gewaerts himself is no less ironic. By letting his jealousy be mentioned together with his coin-collecting, the author is suggesting that his possessiveness is less consumingly passionate than pettily hoarding. Consistently with this, the adjective in 'prokletá žárlivost' is for the author not objectively intensifying but merely reflects the narrator's sternly moralizing condemnation of jealousy as such. The sylleptic use of 'zanášet se' to refer to both coin-collecting and jealousy, as if jealousy were an outward activity like coin-collecting and not an inward state, is meant to bring out the narrator's tendency to confuse inward and outward, states and activities. At the same time, the application of 'zanášet se' to 'žárlivost' hints at the narrator's emotional coldness, since 'zanášet se' would normally be considered appropriate to 'myšlenka' or 'úmysl' but not to an expression of feeling. The characterization of both Rockosc and Gewaerts also provides the basis for a later irony. Being told that Rockosc is indifferent and Gewaerts jealous, we initially suppose that their wives have left them to their stuffy occupations, Rockosc to his mayoralty and Gewaerts to his coin-collecting, and are seeking or have sought sexual relations with other men. We note, however, that the narrator has not said that this is the case and that another, more compromising, interpretation therefore remains possible.

> Oběma ženám pak záleží na tom, neochladiti plamene mužské žárlivosti, ale čekati stále na břehu života s vnadidly do vody vrženými. Je také roucho paní Gewaerts v záhybech proměnlivé jako šat rosničky, naznačujíc tajnou možnost rozkoše, která je proto, aby byla vznícena a zmizela.

The adverb 'pak' leaves it open whether there is a connection between the preceding reference to Gewaerts's jealousy and the present claim that the women wish to rouse jealousy, because it can be read as a connecting 'however' marking the contrast between its being only Gewaerts who is jealous and its being both women who wish to rouse jealousy or, alternatively, as an indifferent 'besides' that assumes no connection. This ambiguity will be exploited presently. The use of the expression 'komu na čem záleží' is ironically out of keeping with the supposedly erotic context, since it conveys more superficial rationalistic interest than deep sexual feeling. The preference of 'neochladiti' to the expected 'nenechat ochladiti' prompts us to conclude that the women, said to be concerned not to cool down the men's jealousy, may well be unconcerned about letting it cool off. That 'neochladiti' is followed not just by 'žárlivost' but by 'plamen žárlivosti' allows another irony. We may read the verb 'ochladit' in the minimal sense of 'to make less hot', but also in the maximal sense of 'to cause to become cool' that brings it into conflict with our knowledge of the hotness of flames. The author is using this underlying inconsistency to bring out the narrator's inadequate understanding of physical reality and also to trivialize the women's alleged concern, whose object, on this level, is merely the avoidance of what we know is impossible. Developing the ambiguity opened up by 'pak', 'mužská žárlivost' may be thought of as referring to the husbands' jealousy, as we initially assume it to be, or to the jealousy of men in general. In this way, the author is insinuating that the women are interested more in being emptily provocative than in seeking satisfaction, or at least that the narrator secretly considers them so to be. This hint finds support in 'stále čekat', which for the author conveys not the intention to make an amorous conquest at all costs, as it seems to do, but the intention to go no further than idle coquetry. The phrase 'na břehu života' hints at the women's lifelessness by placing them metaphorically on the edge of life. The term 'vnadidlo' is meant to bring out once again the narrator's basic condemnation of the sexual. There is also a deeper irony in this first sentence. That it is only the intention of the women which is described and that this intention is described only figuratively by the implictly passive image of their waiting with their lures cast prompts us to suspect that they are not actively doing anything concretely provocative in the picture and that the narrator has imputed to them a sexual intention not deducible from their behaviour. This in turn leads us to conclude that the narrator considers the sexual behaviour of women in general, not specifically only these women, to be merely provocative and not directed at sexual satisfaction and personal fulfilment. This implication will find confirmation later. The mention of Mrs Gewaerts's garment with its folds ironically eclipses her figure even more strongly than the previous abrupt digression and helps to confirm our suspicion that the persons in this scene are not naked or nearly naked as we were led to expect. What is more, since 'roucho' can be taken to refer not merely to an unspecified item of apparel but also to a ceremonious robe, we also begin to suspect, particularly after having come across 'brokát', that the women are even formally dressed for what they regard as a special social occasion. At the same time, we realize that the word 'roucho', which is also used to describe a monk's habit and a priest's cassock or chasuble, recommends itself to the narrator also through its religious associations. The remark about the changeable colour of the garment adds to the irony. The narrator would like us to believe that the material is shimmering exquisitely like shot-silk, while the author, particularly attentive to 'v záhybech', is suggesting that the varying hues are due, not to any sophistication of the weave, but very ordinarily to the different depths of shadow thrown by the folds. This prompts us to infer that the women, though perhaps formally dressed, are not expensively dressed. No less ironic is 'jako šat rosničky'. The narrator has chosen this simile because he feels that the variability of the tree-frog's skin illustrates the changeability of the colours on the dress. The author's interest in the expression, however, lies more in the associations of repulsive sliminess attaching to the object of comparison and the implications of infantilism deriving from the naive imagery of 'šat' that allow him to subvert the surface eroticism and develop his covert stylization of the narrator. The claim that the dress is seductive is also undermined by the sequence 'naznačovat', 'tajný' and 'možnost'. The narrator, preferring the vague and the elusive to the determinate and the concrete, regards these terms as intensifying, while the author considers them merely obscuring and devaluing. By letting the narrator say that the lust he thinks the dress promises is meant to be aroused and to disappear, the author is suggesting the narrator considers that it is not meant to be satisfied.

Však ani paní Gewaerts není krásnější, nežli žena tiskaře Plantina, jenž je poněkud hloubavý a roztržitý, zapomínaje na krásu své paní a na četné něžné nutnosti jejího života. Mnoha dobré vůle a ohnivosti je proto zapotřebí mladému kytaristovi, aby bylo zklamání paní Plantinové lepším způsobem odčiněno.

The use of the negative comparative again allows the narrator to avoid making any more substantial and committing statement about the women's beauty. That the next woman mentioned is introduced as 'žena tiskaře Plantina' is meant to remind us of the narrator's bourgeois attitude to women and social standing. The narrator's curious and unconvincing attempt to explain Plantin's indifference to his wife by saying that he is somewhat broody and absent-minded or distracted mockingly reveals his religious preoccupation with the distinction between faith and sceptical brooding and between contemplation and distraction. By letting the narrator say that Plantin forgets his wife's beauty, the author is implying that she may have been beautiful long ago but is so no longer. The phrase 'četné něžné nutnosti' that seems to be just a gallant euphemism for the author reflects both the narrator's disgust at the frequency and compulsiveness of sexual desire and his tendency to sublimate this desire into a romantic feeling of tenderness. In '[mnoho] dobré vůle a ohnivosti', the meekness and compliancy we associate with 'dobrá vůle' contrast subversively with the vehemence and recklessness we would normally want to associate with 'ohnivost'. The expression 'je zapotřebí', furthermore, leaves it tellingly open whether the guitarist already has the qualities mentioned or whether he is still in need of them. That the narrator now refers to disappointment without yet having mentioned satisfaction helps confirm our suspicion that the scene is not as lustful as we were led to expect. The narrator's 'lepším způsobem' betrays his snobbishness, because in the sense in which he would like us to understand this phrase 'lepší' has the value of 'higher', 'more refined', 'more cultivated', as in 'lepší kruhy společnosti'. At the same time, it is hinted, in connection with the ambiguity in 'je zapotřebí', that what the narrator really means by 'lepším způsobem', as distinct from what he would like us to think he means, is that the guitarist ought to be doing better. This, in turn, leads us to suspect that Mrs Plantin's disappointment has been caused not by her husband's neglect but by the inept endeavours of the guitarist. In this way, the inadequacy of the scene is brought out even more strongly. More important still, the description of the guitarist's activity by its vagueness leaves us in doubt whether the musician is seducing Mrs Plantin or just playing her a tune. The narrator's religiosity is hinted at also by the use of 'odčinit', that can mean 'to expiate', 'to atone for'.

Snažení tohoto hudebníka v alonžové paruce dochází uznalosti: černé oči paniny se třpytí jako vroucí smola, její rty jsou ovlhly a chtivě porozevřeny jako slezový květ, bílé zuby vyhlížejí ze svého sladkého žaláře, jako by chtěly smyslnost úsměvu rozhojniti a její plné ruce se zabývají v uměle stoudné rozpačitosti mošničkou z barevné kůže, v níž je uschován rozkošný amulet, klíč a miniaturní šitíčko.

The use of the vague 'snažení' betrays the narrator's continuing reluctance to make it clear whether the musician is seducing Mrs Plantin or just playing her a tune. The mention of the musician's allonge wig helps to confirm our suspicion that the figures in this scene are not naked or nearly naked but formally dressed. The phrase '[snažení] dochází uznalosti' hints at the narrator's emotional coldness, since it calls to mind more intellectual recognition than affective response. The simile of the boiling pitch reveals the narrator's religiously conditioned moral condemnation of the behaviour he is describing, since pitch is an Old Testament symbol for sinfulness and divine retribution, and popular religious fantasy often pictures hell as being full of burning pitch and brimstone. The same comparison also subverts 'třpytit se', because pitch when hot does not have the lustre it has when cold and set. The narrator's assumption that moistened lips are characteristic of sexual excitement shows up his indiscriminate loathing for the fleshly. The same disgust comes through in 'jako slezový květ', because we can hardly imagine the woman's lips being like the flower of the hollyhock without picturing the rest of this repulsive man-sized plant with its hairy stem, downy leaves and cheese-shaped fruits. The assertion that the teeth seem to want to make the smile more sensuous is undermined by the intervening metaphor of the jail which suggests that they are not free to do what they may seem to want. The narrator's supposition that a showing of teeth can make a smile more sensuous suggests that he equates sexual desire with bestial voracity. The statement about the teeth characterizes the narrator also in other ways. Since it has been implied that the narrator is repelled by the woman's mouth, the adjective 'sladký' in 'sladký žalář' comes to be understood as conveying not the rapturousness of the woman's smile, as we initially suppose it to be doing, but the narrator's romantic idealization of dungeons. The linking of 'rozhojniti' to the abstract 'smyslnost' shows up the narrator's tendency to confuse abstract and concrete. The portrayal of the teeth as prisoners, moreover, provides further evidence of a tendency to personify. The description of the woman's hands and their activity is variously subversive. By 'plné [ruce]' it is implied that this woman is not pleasantly rounded in the right places, as we were led to expect the women would be, but is unshapely with fat where a normally buxom woman would not have any. In 'v uměle stoudné rozpačitosti', the qualifying terms for the author do not have objective reference but merely reflect the narrator's moral condemnation of the behaviour he is imputing to the woman. That the narrator describes the woman's bag unusually as 'mošnička z barevné kůže' is meant to suggest that what he started by thinking of is a sort of bag referred to more appropriately as 'mošna' or 'mošnička' than 'měšec', 'kabelka' or 'taštička' and normally neither dyed nor leathern, that is, the kind of plain cloth bag that would be carried by pilgrims, itinerant monks and homeless beggars. This provides a hint at the narrator's religiosity but also allows the implication that the narrator as an opinionated bourgeois regards this artisan's wife as rather beggarly. The list of the bag's contents is ironic not only because it suggests that the woman is sentimental and well-domesticated, but also because it prompts us to infer that the real reason for her embarrassment is that she has forgotten her purse and does not know how to remunerate the musician.

> [...J]e [...] neméně krásná Helena, choť Rubensova, jež má jasný vlas lesku mosazné pánve, kadeřící se na oblém zátylku jako ohnivé chmýří; která má ubledlé silné tělo svaté živitelky, sestoupivši divem mezi rybářské děti se svého oltáře v Bruggách, kterouž poznamenalo mateřství jako jabloň odkvětu, smetnuvší k jejím nohám všechen zardělý, sladkostí chabnoucí květ.

The use of the negative comparative with regard to Helena's beauty has the same ironic function as in the previous cases. That the narrator immediately identifies Helena as Rubens's wife and uses the genteel term 'choť' reminds us of his bourgeois attitude. Telling is also 'jasný [vlas], because it can have the value of a commendatory 'radiant' or of a subversively trivial 'clear'. The hair's being said to have the gleam of a copper frying pan not only creates a sense of comic banality but also shows up the narrator's bourgeois familiarity with pans of the more expensive sort. At the same time, by virtue of the metallic quality suggested, the comparison provides a further compromising hint of artificiality. In '[vlas] kadeřící se [...] jako ohnivé chmýři', 'chmýří' with its associations of feeble fluffiness tends to subvert both 'ohnivý' and 'kadeřící se'. By letting the narrator mention the rotundity of the normally flat nape, the author is implying that Helena too is not attractively buxom with curves in the right places but generally fat and unshapely. That the narrator can see the form of the nape implies, moreover, that this hair is not flowing seductively, as we might have thought, but is primly tied up in a bun. The comparison of Helena's body to that of the Virgin Mary or, more accurately, to that of a Flemish madonna, brings out the narrator's religiosity once again. The reference to the body's pallor supports previous implications that the artist has not painted the rustic swarthiness we were led to expect. The choice of the term 'silný', that in the present euphemistic sense is commonly used to describe overweight bodies broad also round the waist, helps to confirm our suspicion that this woman is not attractively buxom with curves in the right places but hideously out of shape. In using the designation 'svata živitelka', the narrator would like us to think of the Holy Mother suckling her child, while the author is discreetly mocking the lucrativeness of the madonna cult. That the Madonna, or the Flemish statuette of her, is said to have descended among children is meant to intimate the unreliability of the witnesses' reports on which belief in this alleged wonder was based.

By letting the narrator specify that these children were the children of fisher-men, the author is mockingly revealing his belief in the religious significance of fishermen. The addition of 'se svého [svaté živitelky] oltáře v Bruggách' produces a suitably delayed ironic switch from the picture of the Virgin Mary descended from Heaven which we have on reading '[tělo] svaté živitelky, sestoupivší divem' to the picture of a Flemish madonna that has come down from a local altar which we end up with. The comparison of Mary, and there-fore indirectly also Helena, to an apple-tree out of bloom not only reveals the narrator's melancholic romanticism but also goes further than previous hints towards suggesting that the women in this scene are plain. Moreover, the fact that the motherhood mentioned is attributed directly only to Mary leaves us free to conclude that Helena's lack of beauty is not the effect of pregnancy and childbirth but innate.[228] The description of the blossom as 'sladkostí chab-noucí' brings out the narrator's morbid sentimentality and, together with 'zardělý', his tendency to personify. The phrase 'sladkostí chabnoucí' is ironic also in other ways. Since 'sladkost' can mean not only sweetness but also sexual rapture, we are led to suspect that the narrator also has in mind the erotic ecstasy he associates with closeness to the feet of the Virgin Mary. It is also ironic that 'sladkostí chabnoucí', which is the only part of the descrip-tion that can convey erotic feeling, is applied not, to a person in the alleg-edly lustful scene of the painting, but to the blossom of a metaphorical tree.

> Helena, choť Rubensova, která jako Betsabé hříšně by roznítila smysly judského krále, jsouc věnčena svity a stínem této zahrady, kde bílá bříza jaksi přemoženě šepce a šelestí, po štíhlých oporách ipomea šplhá a země je pokrytá zlatým pískem a pivoň-kami. Kde šustí a blýskají se sukně krasavic zrádnými refleksy aksamitu, staré zlato prstenů a řetězů třeští, všeobecný šum převyšuje melodický hlas kohosi předčítajícího z Plata a ze Senecy, a jako pukání strun ozývá se v nádrži čirý prut vody, jež byla z prsu Najady vypuzena. Kde svítí na temném pozadí silné a v gestu klidné ruce, krmící pávy.

The straining of normal syntax and narrative logic provides the basic irony here. After the apparent subject 'Helena', there is no main verb, only a phrase in apposition followed by a sequence of relative clauses already the third of which no longer refers back to 'Helena' but to 'zahrada' in the second clause. The three clauses referring to 'zahrada' are together over four times longer than the two clauses referring to 'Helena', and, from the second on, are punctuated as if they were separate sentences. This structure is doubly

---

228 It is perhaps worth pointing out in this connection that Rubens is believed to have painted 'The Garden of Love' immediately after his marriage to Helène Fourment in late 1630 and to have largely completed it by the time she bore him the first of their five children in early 1632. Opol-ský's irony here is therefore by no means flatly contrary to fact.

subversive. By allowing a main verb to be done without and relative clauses to be given token independence, the author is again implicitly devitalizing the narrator's language. At the same time, by allowing the narrator to forget Helena syntactically and digress lengthily on the surrounding garden, the author is suggesting that the narrator is eager to avoid further mention of her for fear of compromising his argument. Contributory to the irony is also the recapitulaton of earlier detail: we come across the rustling birch tree again, the ipomoea entwining its supports, the sand and peonies covering the ground, and the jet of water squirting from the naiad's breast into the basin of the fountain; we are even reminded that Helena is Rubens's wife. This repetition allows a dual interpretation. It may be thought of as conveying in prose an effect of poetic recitation or else, less impressively, as betraying the narrator's embarrassment at not being able to find anything more to say in favour of what he is describing. The sometimes slightly altered wording allows the author to accommodate a few additional points of irony. The preference of '[ipomea] šplhá' to the more usual '[ipomea] popíná se' can show up the narrator's tendency to personify, while '[po] štíhlých [oporách]' discreetly reminds us of the lack of sturdier supports hinted at before. The formulation 'jako pukání strun ozývá se v nádrži [prut vody]' not only adds a subversive hint of metallic artificiality but also suggests that the basin so echoing must have been largely empty, the water flow therefore inadequate. The new information we are given yields as much. The narrator's comparison of Helena to Bathsheba is ironically self-defeating, because the wording makes Helena's alleged seductiveness dependent on her becoming somebody else. The comparison also shows up again the narrator's religiosity, and, as 'hřišné' in particular indicates, his underlying censure. In '[Helena] věnčená svity a stínem [zahrady]', the author is exploiting the connotations of 'svit', and the discrepancy between the plural 'svity' and the singular 'stínem', to suggest that the shadow is a basic encompassing whole broken only here and there by faint spots of light. This in turn prompts us to understand 'věnčený' as meaning 'wreathed' rather than 'festooned'. The description of the women and their dresses takes the irony further. The effect of 'krasavice' is subverted by juxtaposition to 'sukně', that directs our attention away from bodily attributes. There is also the suggestion that the dresses are made of a cheaper fabric than they appear to be. The phrase 'refleksy aksamitu' can be understood as meaning that the reflections have been produced by samite or that they are merely such as samite produces. Consistently with this, 'zradný' may be taken as meaning that the reflections are deceptive by the changing colour they make us see, or else that they are deceptive by the false impression of samite they create. In support of this same implication and in covert mockery of the narrator's tendency to personify, the author is exploiting also the ambiguity of the verb 'blýskat se', which can be read as 'to flash', but also as 'to show off', 'to flaunt', 'to brag'. The description of the women's jewelry is no less revealing. That the gold the rings and chains are made of is said to be old suggests that the women, not possessing any more recently acquired jewelry, have put on their family heirlooms for the occasion. It is thereby again implied that the women are not as wealthy as they would like to seem. The use of 'řetězy' for the more usual 'řetízky' is meant to reveal the narrator's secret condemnation of jewelry as spiritually entrammelling. The expression 'zlato […] třeští' conceals a further mocking hint at the narrator's tendency to personify, since the verb form 'třeští' is the third person singular both of 'třeštět' meaning 'to clink', 'to clang' and of 'třeštit' meaning 'to rave'. The narrator's claim that the general noise drowns the voice of someone reading aloud from Plato and Seneca undermines his position further. The author intends us to infer that the narrator, in an attempt to convince us of the worldliness of this scene, has invented the argument that the people in this scene are, to his mind reprehensibly, indifferent to the Idealist and Stoicist teachings he himself admires and which, forcing home his point, he puts in the mouth a figure that, as '[hlas] kohosi' suggests, is not even sufficiently visible to be recognized. The irony in this case, however, lies not only in the implication that the narrator's claim is spurious but also in the comicality of the idea that someone in a garden of love should be reading a book, let alone a philosophy book of this kind. We even feel disinclined to believe that the general noise the narrator refers to can be loud enough to drown a voice. For the rustling of the dresses, the alleged clinking of the gold, and the twang of the water falling into the basin of the fountain to be distinctly audible, the noise-level must be relatively low. This leads us to suspect that the narrator is exaggerating in an attempt to convince us that this garden is livelier than it is. The narrator's assumption that the voice of someone reading aloud should be melodious tends to suggest religiously conditioned association with ritual chanting. The reference to the hand feeding the peacocks reveals more. That it is the hand that is said to be shining and not the normally brilliant feathers of the peacocks discreetly mocks the weakness of Rubens's colouring and reminds us of the pallor of the figures in the scene. The mention of a dark background implicitly confirms our suspicion that it is shadow and not light that is predominant in this picture. In 'v gestu klidné ruce', the inclusion of 'klidný' suggests that the narrator is so afraid of these animals that he considers calmness in their presence worthy of special note, while 'v gestu' implies that he is unwilling to believe that this calmness can be more than only superficial.

Kde i mužové vlažní a hloubaví stávají se bezděčnou hračkou prostředí, do něhož byli uvedeni. Kde se zdá, jako by v podivném tání a jihnutí ocitlo se srdce purkmistra Rockosce i sběrače mincí Gewaertse, rušeného občasně slepou žárlivostí. Pokládají těžké své ruce na pasy svých paní s přespříliš zřejmou výmluvností.

By allowing the sequence of detached relative clauses begun in the previous passage to be continued even into a new paragraph, the author is developing his implicit devitalization of the narrator's language. The terms 'hloubavý' and 'vlažný', as before, hint at the narrator's religious orientation. Pointing in the same direction is 'bezděčná hračka', which for the author is not objectively intensifying but reflects the narrator's basic condemnation of sexual incontinence. The assertion that the passive men are stimulated by the surroundings reveals for the first time that they have not been left behind, as we initially supposed, but are part of the scene. The addition '[prostředí] do něhož byli [muži] uvedeni' takes this irony further, because we may take it to refer to the men's having been introduced into the painting by the artist, as the narrator would like us to, or to their having been brought along by their wives. This is the first hint that the passive men are not spectators but principal performers in the scene. The description of the men's reaction as a melting and thawing of the heart is comically inappropriate to the portrayal of what is still supposed to be lustful eroticism and thereby mocks not only the tameness of the picture but also the narrator's sentimentality. The adjective 'podivný' not only brings out the narrator's obsession with the wondrous and fanciful but also insinuates that the men's apparent warming is simply peculiar. What is more, the existence of even this emotion is called into doubt by the use of the relativizing 'zdát se, jakoby' construction. The narrator's 'ocitlo se srdce' is a further hint at his tendency to personify gratuitously. The characterization of Gewaerts as a 'sběrač mincí' develops the irony. When used of persons, 'sběrač' can be applied only to someone who gathers in or picks up, as in 'sběrač ovoce' or 'sběrač míčků'. Used in place of 'sběratel', it therefore implies that Gewaerts's hobby is not so much numismatics as picking up coins dropped in the street.[229] Subversive is also 'rušený', which may be thought of as an imperfective of 'vzrušený', 'roused', or of 'vyrušený', 'disturbed'. Consistently with this, the apparently intensifying 'slepý' for the author merely reflects the narrator's secret condemnation of jealousy as such. That the men are said to be putting their hands on their wives' waists now confirms our suspicion that they are not only part of the scene but their wives' partners in it. This revelation is also ironic in connection with the statement that the men are stimulated by the surroundings, because it leads us to infer that it is therefore not their wives who are doing the stimulating. The reference to the heaviness of the hands that the narrator would like us to see as evidence of a firm manly grasp is for the author simply an indication that the men too are fat. In accordance with this, 'výmluvnost' may be thought of as referring not to the seductiveness of this gesture but to its harmlessness.

---

229 It is amusing to note that in the entry *sběrač*, the *Slovník spisovného jazyka českého* (Prague, 1971) adds: zř. [rarely] *s. mincí* (Opol.) [Opolský], sběratel.

[...] Petr Pavel Rubens, jejž věk svírá, nemůže činiti výčitek svým smyslům, neboť ho nikdy v životě nezradily. A třeba ze ruka života, sejmuvši s jeho hlavy široký klobouk, zvískala stříbrnými prsty jeho kadeře, třeba ze se usadil jeden strašně hořký tah mezi ostatními rysy grandseigneurského obličeje, třeba se začal klásti na jeho oči zjevně jakýsi mystický stín, jako by to za sivým sklem rudly pochodně života, na jeho paletě nevadne sladká pohoda odstínů, jímiž je zahrada lásky naplněná.

By having the narrator say that Rubens is oppressed by age with out at-tributing this feeling to a possible cause like infirmity or isolation, the author is prompting us to suspect that Rubens is oppressed not by any such conse-quence of age but by age itself that he regards as an undesirable prolonga-tion of life. The irony here is consolidated and heightened by the fact that the narrator is made to use the plain, neutral 'věk' instead of the more expressive and evocative 'stáří' and, in implicit contrast to it, the in this context unusu-ally intense 'svírat' in place of the broader and milder 'skličovat'. The claim that Rubens's senses never failed him conceals a subversive ambiguity, since it may be true because they were uncommonly reliable, as the narrator would like us to think, or because he never really used them, as the author is sug-gesting. The inclusion of 'v životě', that appears to be merely emphatic, may be interpreted as a further hint at the narrator's metaphysical perspective, because it can suggest that he distinguishes between what happens in life and what happens beyond it. The use of 'činit výčitky' and 'zradit' brings out once again the narrator's tendency to personify, as does the following reference to the hand of life. That this hand of life is thought to have had to remove Ru-bens's wide-brimmed hat before being able to run its silver fingers through his hair covertly mocks both the narrator's tendency to confuse metaphorical and literal and Rubens's habit of wearing this unwieldy, obstructive hat. The choice of the verb 'zvískat' to describe the action of the hand allows amusing associations of de-licing. In 'strašně hořký tah', the modification of 'hořký' by 'strašně' mockingly suggests that the narrator is daunted by any expres-sion that is not pleasant and affable. The unexplained appearance of such a look of bitterness in Rubens's face, moreover, makes us wonder whether he has not finally come to recognize his own artistic failure. The term 'grand-seigneurský' not only reminds us of the narrator's preoccupation with social status but also covertly ridicules Rubens for his pomposity. The use of 'usadit se' is yet another hint at the narrator's tendency to personify. In '[začal se klásti na jeho oči] zjevně jakýsi mystický [stín]', the incongruous combina-tion of 'zjevně' with 'jakýsi' and 'mystický' mockingly exposes the defective attitude to reality which underlies the characteristic liking for the vague and the mystical that we are meant to attribute to the narrator. The metaphor of the torches is variously subversive. Since all that is said about the posi-tion of the torches is that they are behind the grey glass that represents the clouded surface of Rubens's eyes, we are left in doubt whether the light of life shed by the torches is in Rubens's eyes and perceived as dim by the narrator, as the narrator himself would like us to think, or, on the contrary, in the world outside and perceived as dim by Rubens himself. In this way, the author is again hinting at the artist's lifelessness. There is also an ironic ambiguity of emphasis in this metaphor, because the narrator is stressing the continued visibilty of the torches, the author their having been obscured. This ambiguity is significantly enhanced by the use of the verb 'rudnout', that in the present connection can be taken to mean not only 'to be red', as the narrator would like it to be, but also 'to fade'. The description of the colours on Rubens's palette adds to the irony. By 'sladká pohoda odstínů', the author is implying that the colours are slushily soft, bland and lacking fullness. He is thereby inviting us to conclude that the reason why they will not fade is that they could not possibly grow any weaker. The mention of Rubens's palette in this connection makes the assertion ironically platitudinous in also another way, because colours may fade on the canvas but hardly while still on the artist's palette.

> A bůh dopřál umělci, aby ji [zahradu lásky] bez muk a vnitřní hořkosti vyměnil pro svoji osobu, dříve než by se toho jiní nadáli, za zahradu smrti...

The use of 'bůh' and 'muka' brings out once again the narrator's religious conceptuality. The assertion that Rubens exchanged the garden of love for the garden of death without distress implicitly confirms the previous suggestion that Rubens wanted to die. That this exchange is said to have taken place earlier than others expected, moreover, leads us to suspect that what happened is not that Rubens died suddenly while apparently still in good health, as the narrator would like us to think, but that he was inwardly dead before he died in reality. The implication is supported by 'pro svoji osobu', which, since it is normally used only with expressions of attitude and not with expressions of action, prompts us to infer that the exchange was a matter of personal belief or feeling. The attribution of 'vnitřní' to 'hořkost', given the previous reference to a very bitter trait established in Rubens's face, suggests that Rubens now always looked so bitter that the narrator has to relegate the lack of bitterness he postulates in this connection to an unobservable inner realm.

Our interpretation of 'Rubensova "Zahrada lásky"' has evinced its structural affinity to 'Poledne' and 'Pláč Nioby'. The ironic characterization of the narrator follows the already familiar pattern with only minor elaboration.

As the narrator's standpoint is subverted, the subject matter is comically transformed. What is initially meant to be a sort of pastoral scene in which gods and goddesses with naked, well-proportioned, sun-tanned bodies are in the course of making love gradually turns out to be the contrived staging amidst furniture and monumental architecture of a formal social gathering of ostentatiously dressed, pale, fat, passive bourgeois spouses recruited from the artist's neighbourhood. The ostensibly original, bold, libidinous Rubens is ultimately revealed as unimaginative, effeminate and lifeless.

9. ČÍNSKÁ POVÍDKA[230]

On the surface, 'Čínská povídka' tells the story of an old Chinese nobleman renowned throughout China for his wealth, wisdom and happiness, but known especially for his possession of a lacquer cabinet containing many valuable works of art in compartments ceremoniously opened at intervals one by one. The story consists mainly of detailed descriptions of these works of art, among them an antique codex, a shimmering silk kakemono and a pagoda in silver filigree. The tale ends pointedly with the disclosure that the last compartment opened only on the old man's death contains not a further work of art but a cob of maize and an ear of rice as symbols of prosperity.

At first sight, 'Čínská povídka' seems to follow in the late Romantic tradition of Julius Zeyer's novellas 'Zrada v domě Han' and 'Blaho v zahradě kvetoucích broskví' with their highly idealized and extravagantly aestheticized view of China.[231] This tradition prominently includes 'Sen o říši krásy', in which Decadent Jiří Karásek uses China as the backdrop for a tale about an empire of aesthetes in which the emperor is elected for his beauty and is forced to abdicate when age disfigures him.[232] 'Sen o říši krásy' takes the form of a play that Karásek believed could only be adequately staged in the stylized world of the puppet theatre.[233] Far from being limited to eccentric writers, the unrealistic attitude towards China displayed by Zeyer and Karásek

---

230 Jan Opolský, 'Čínská povídka', *Národní politika*, 1 March 1940, p. 2, reprinted in *Hranolem křišťálu* (Prague, 1944), pp. 10–14.

231 Julius Zeyer, 'Zrada v domě Han. Čínská legenda', *Lumír*, 9 (1881), pp. 289–292, 306–309, 323–326, reprinted in *Amparo a jiné povídky* (Prague, 1896) and *Obnovené obrazy*, 3 vols (Prague, 1906), vol. 2; 'Blaho v zahradě kvetoucích broskví. Podivná povídka', *Lumír*, 10 (1882), pp. 146–149, 161–165, 177–182, reprinted in *Novely*, 2 vols (Prague, 1879 and 1884), vol. 2. Also set in China is 'Bratři. Čínská komedie ve dvou jednáních', *Lumír*, 10 (1882), pp. 513–516, 531–535, 550–552, 561–563, reprinted in *Tři komedie* (Prague, 1894).

232 Jiří Karásek ze Lvovic, *Sen o říši krásy. Čínská pohádka o dvou dějstvích* (Prague, 1907).

233 Karásek argues that puppets are the original dramatic protagonists and therefore superior to human actors ('Herec jest surrogát za loutku. Loutka byla dříve než herec. Je původní. A proto jest víc než herec'); they embody the characters they represent more fully because they always are what they represent ('[...] herec není nikdy pouze tím, co má hrát. Loutka však, jež představuje císaře, jest vždycky a zůstane císařem'); and they do not bring the action down to the level of everyday banality because they incorporate an element of charm and mystery ('[...] herec sen básníkův snižuje ke skutečnosti. Loutky [...] berou z reálnosti jen to, což jest jejím půvabem. [...] A jaká tajemnost je v loutce'). See *Sen o říši krásy*, pp. 6, 7.

even affected the judgement of professional orientalists, as can be seen from Rudolf Dvořák's lavish praise for the cultural accuracy of Zeyer's novellas, and remained influential right through to the nineteen-forties, as sinologist Jaroslav Průšek's cloyingly sentimental *Sestra moje Čína* (1938) demonstrates.[234] The celebration of Bohumil Mathesius, a man who produced several translations of classical Chinese poetry without knowing a word of Chinese, as an expert on Chinese language and literature, and his own willingness to embrace this role, reflects a similar lack of professionalism and objectivity.[235] The image of Japan, similarly distorted by Zeyer and Karásek, fared slighly better, due to the influence of writers like Josef Kořenský, Joe Hloucha and Jaroslav Havlasa. Kořenský had travelled the length and breadth of Japan, and Hloucha and Havlasa had an intimate knowledge of the country based on extended stays and personal involvement.[236] However, this did not prevent Kořenský from idealizing Japan nor did it prevent Hloucha from writing his first and most influential travelogue before actually visiting Japan. Hloucha also went to considerable lengths to make his later experiences fit in with his early fantasies.[237]

However, to see 'Čínská povídka' as a work in the tradition of Zeyer and Karásek would to ignore the sustained structural irony that subverts the surface reading throughout. By examining 'Čínská povídka' in as much detail as the previous texts, we shall try to trace the working of this irony here as well.

---

234 Rudolf Dvořák (1860-1920) is known for several works works on Confucian ethics, especially *Číňana Konfucia život a nauka*, 2 vols (Prague, 1887 and 1889) and *Čína. Popis říše, naroda, jeho mravů a obyčejů* (Prague, 1900). Early works by Jaroslav Průšek (1906-1980) include *Sestra moje Čína* (Prague, 1938) and *Trojí učení o společnosti v Číně* (Prague, 1940).

235 Bohumil Mathesius (1888-1952). His collections include *Černá věž a zelený džbán* (Prague, 1925); *Zpěvy staré Číny* (Prague, 1939); *Nové zpěvy staré Číny* (Prague, 1940).

236 For Zeyer on Japan, see *Gompači i Komurasaki. Žaponský román* (Prague, 1884); 'Píseň za vlahé noci', *Lumír*, 13 (1885), pp. 5-10, reprinted in *Obnovené obrazy*, 3 vols (Prague, 1906), vol. 2; 'Lásky div. Žaponská komedie o jednom jednání', *Květy*, 10 (1888), pp. 505-520, reprinted in *Tři komedie* (Prague, 1894); 'Večer u Idalie. Hrstka tradic, legend a pohádek z nejkrásnějšího východu', *Stratonika a jiné povídky* (Prague, 1892), pp. 1-66; 'O velkém bolu bohu Izanagi', *Lumír*, 19 (1891), pp. 373-374, reprinted in *Obnovené obrazy*, 3 vols (Prague, 1906), vol. 2, and incorporated in 'Večer u Idalie'. For Karásek on Japan, see 'Japonerie', *Zazděná okna* (Valašské Meziříčí, 1894). For Josef Kořenský (1847-1938), see *Žaponsko* (Prague, 1899). For Joe Hloucha (1881-1957), see *Sakura ve vichřici* (Prague, 1905) (fictional travelogue); *Zátopa* (Prague, 1906) (novel); *Vzpomínky na Japonsko* (Prague, 1906) (travelogue); *Moje „paní Chryzantéma"* (Prague, 1910) (short story); *Polibky smrti* (Prague, 1912) (short stories); *Pavilón hrůzy* (Prague, 1920) (short stories); *Dopisy neznámého* (Prague, 1923) (novel); *Prodavačky úsměvu* (Prague, 1929) (travel sketches); *Mezi bohy a démony* (Prague, 1929) (travel sketches); *Japonečky* (Prague, 1931) (travel sketches). For Jan Havlasa (1883-1964), see *Okna do mlhy* (Prague, 1918) (novel); *Japonská pohádka o dvou dědcích* (Prague, 1919) (short story); *Japonským vnitrozemím* (Prague, 1924) (articles); *Cesta Bohů. Japonské potulky* (Prague, 1926) (articles); *Bloudění duše* (Prague, 1931) (short stories); *Japonské jaro* (Prague 1932) (articles); *Roztříštěná duha* (Prague, 1932) (short stories); *Přízraky a zázraky* (Prague, 1934) (short stories); *Schody do podvědomí* (Prague, 1939) (short stories).

237 On early and contemporary images of Japan in Bohemia see also Jan Lukavec, *Od českého Tokia k exotické Praze* (Prague, 2013), pp. 12-36.

The narrative begins with a brief portrayal of the protagonist.

Živ byl jeden prastarý, vznešený Číňan a mohlo se říci, že už docela na sklonku žití, s tímto přirozeným během světa usmířený. Byl hnědý a svraštělý jako pečené jablíčko a bradu měl takovou dlouhou a říďounkou jako z bílých koňských žíní.

From the outset, the narrator is trying hard to paint a quaint and endearing picture of his hero, while the author is doing everything he can to devitalize and dehumanize him. This implicit devitalization already begins with 'Živ byl jeden ….'. This opening is suspiciously close to the conventional 'Žil jednou jeden.....' but conspicuously deviates from it both by turning the main verb ('žil') into a static combination of adjective and copula ('živ byl'), and by suppressing 'jednou', that expresses the temporality essential to a life lived. This initial implication of lifelessness finds immediate support in the use of 'prastarý', which is more readily applicable to the inanimate than the animate; and also 'vznešený', which can suggest that the hero is not so much 'noble' as somehow 'up in the air', elevated above the physical reality of life. This same ironic tendency comes to the fore in 'na sklonku žití'. By allowing the narrator to replace the biological 'život' with the comparatively rarefied 'žití', the author is again edging the protagonist out of the realm of the concretely physical. The ambiguity of 'docela' points in a different direction. Since 'docela', like English 'quite', can be understood as meaning 'wholly' or simply 'fairly', the author is able to imply that the narrator, though he pretends otherwise, is basically unwilling to claim without reservation that this very old man has reached his declining years. The author is thereby suggesting that the narrator too is senile, at least in his outlook on life. That the protagonist is said to be reconciled to the natural run of the world for the author means not that he is full of mature wisdom but that natural impulses are something fundamentally alien to him that he has considerable difficulty accommodating. The lateness of the alleged reconciliation, moreover, may be understood as a measure of the initial hostility. In addition, the preceding 'mohlo se říci' implicitly calls into question the reality of even this reconciliation. The description of the man's appearance is no less subversive. The comparison to a baked apple suggests that he is not healthily tanned and naturally wrinkled but somehow scorched and shrivelled. That the description of him is limited to his head and that his beard is said to be sparse and like white horse-hair can also make us think of him as a puppet of the kind Czech puppeteers traditionally used, with detachable heads and beards made of a few strands of white horse-hair glued on.[238] At the same time, the reference to

238 A good example of a such a puppet is the Devil by Josef Mádle ml., Nová Paka (1919), held by the Moravské zemské muzeum, Brno. Opolský's home town, Nová Paka, was a puppet-making cen-

a baked apple, in Bohemia customarily a children's dish, together with the childlike portrayal of the man as if he were a puppet, following incongruously upon the supposedly enlightened philosophical comment in the previous sentence, develops the earlier hint at the narrator's senile perspective by suggesting that he tends to alternate between philosophical pretentiousness and infantility. This ironic impression is enforced by the equally incongruous use of the familiar expressive 'jablíčko' and 'říďounký' immediately after and alongside such bookish terms as 'na sklonku žití','přirozený běh světa' and 'brada'.

Měl mnoho výstavností, dobře zavodňovaných polí, a dobytka rohatého i bezrohého, vzácné drůbeže, a jeho nemovité vlastnictví nikdo nemohl přepočísti.

We can use 'výstavnost' as an abstract noun to refer to appealing archictecture (as in 'výstavnost a krása města') and as a concrete noun meaning simply 'building'. So when we read 'měl mnoho výstavností' our initial impression is favourable, partly because the positive connotations of the first meaning inevitably spill over into the second meaning that is at issue here, partly because the archaic quality of 'výstavnost' in this second meaning lends it an air of loftiness and distinction. But it is the very loftiness and vagueness of 'výstavnost' that is suspicious here. We cannot help feeling that the narrator's is using 'výstavnost' as a euphemism for edifices he hesitates to classify

---

tre. Its illustrious tradition was founded by Jan Sucharda st. (1770–1820) and his son, Antonín Sucharda st. (1812–1886). Carvers and weavers by trade, they supplied puppeteers throughout Northern Bohemia, including the Nová Paka branch of the famous Majzner family. Jan Sucharda ml. (1797–1873) and Antonín Sucharda st. (1812–1886), inspired by Klicpera's plays, were the first to open a dedicated puppet-making worshop, training other well-known puppet-makers such as Jan Mádle st. (1820 – ?) and Jan Mádle ml. (1843–1911). This workshop was continued by Antonín Sucharda ml. (1843–1911). Nová Paka puppets were visually striking and technically sophisticated, and are generally considered to rank above those produced by other leading puppet-makers, such as Mikoláš Sychrovský in Southern Bohemia and Josef Alessi in Prague. The puppets were up to a metre high, with eyes that moved and mouths that opened (giving rise to the popular characterization 'i ty packá otevřhubo, i ty packá vyjevena otevřtlámo'). Opolský's local contemporary, Vojtěch Sucharda (1884–1968) and his wife, Anna Suchardová-Brichová (1883–1944), founded the Říše loutek, a well-known puppet-theatre in Prague. Anna Suchardová went on to become a prominent puppet designer, noted for her use of unconventional designs and materials (rubber, paper boxes, steel springs). Collections of locally-made puppets are exhibited in Suchardův dům and the Městské muzeum (formerly Podkrkonošské muzeum), Nová Paka. On puppet-making and the puppet-theatre in Nová Paka, see Jaroslav Blecha and Pavel Jirásek, *Česká loutka* (Prague, 2009), pp. 71–75, p. 152; Alice Dubská, *Dvě století českého loutkářství* (Prague, 2004), pp. 51–52, 175, 183–186; Marie Jirásková and Pavel Jirásek, *Loutka a moderna* (Brno, 2011), pp. 74–79 (chapter entitled 'Barokizující Suchardové'); Milan Knížák, *Encyclopedie výtvarníků loutkového divadla v českých zemích a na Slovensku od vystopovatelné minulosti do roku 1950* (Hradec Králové, 2005), pp. 875–883; and Bedřich Slavík, *U Suchardů* (Prague, 1973).
Opolský uses the puppet motif overtly in his prose piece 'Opera s loutkami', *Muka a zdání* (Prague, 1921) and in his contributions of verse to the journal *Loutkář*.

as 'budova / stavba' and is any case unwilling to describe in greater detail. Our misgivings are heightened by the fact that 'výstavnost' reminds us of closely cognate 'výstavní', prompting us to ask ourselves whether the edifices in question are not in fact makeshift constructions put up purely for show. This implication will receive support later on. By telling us that the farmer's fields are well-irrigated, the narrator is again trying to impress us, but we are quick to understand that extensive irrigation is more likely to be evidence of poor soil and an arid climate than exemplary agricultural wealth. Of course, we can avoid this uncomfortable implication by telling ourselves that this is China and that the fields in question would be paddy-fields whose cultivation normally requires extensive flooding. However, this does not save us from the underlying irony because it merely replaces worrying intimations of poverty with an equally disturbing hint that the narrator, substituting the idea of being well-irrigated for the reality of being completely flooded, is engaging in euphemistic understatement. So if we opt for the paddy-fields, we find ourselves confronted with a narrator who is embarrassed by a superabundance of water that in his opinion and limited experience also falls critically short of being a reliable sign of agricultural prosperity. The description of the livestock fares no better. That nothing more is said about the livestock than that there are both horned and unhorned animals prompts us to suspect that the narrator is unwilling to be more explicit for fear of compromising himself. What is more, the linking of 'rohatý', not to the expected congruent 'nerohatý', but to 'bezrohý', that unlike 'nerohatý' can mean not only 'unhorned' but also 'hornless', invites us to suppose that the old man does not even have any unhorned livestock, merely horned livestock that has lost its horns, perhaps out of decrepitude. Similarly, in 'vzácné drůbeže', the ambiguity of the adjective leaves us free to assume that this poultry is less fine or exquisite than simply rare or weird. It is also significant that in the itemization, '[mnoho] výstavností, dobře zavodňovaných polí, a dobytka rohatého i bezrohého, vzácné drůbeže', '[mnoho] polí' is suddenly and unexpectedly followed by 'a' instead of another comma. This creates the ironic impression that the narrator was about to run out of things to say when fresh inspiration came to his rescue ('oh, and...'). That the term 'nemovité vlastnictví' occurs after the narrator has already finished mentioning the buildings and fields that would normally be thought the principal constituents of real estate is meant to suggest that these makeshift buildings and watery fields are not solid enough to fulfil the condition of immobility that the phrase 'nemovité vlastnictví' makes it clear is an essential attribute of real estate. The expression 'nikdo nemohl přepočísti', besides amusing us with the idea of simply counting rather valuing real estate, leads us to suspect that the problem is not immeasurable wealth but universal innumeracy.

Viděl děti svých dětí stoupati opatrně do šlépějí jím samým vyhloubených, byla v něm mírná důvěra ve všechen další osud, trpné sklonění přede vším, co by se kdysi mohlo posupného a neodvratného dostaviti, a nenapodobitelný stoický klid při představě jakékoliv fysické smrti.

Normally we come across 'děti svých dětí' as part of the stock phrase 'své děti a děti svých dětí'. Standing on its own like this, it is strange enough to irritate and provoke reflection. Given the consistent implications of devitalization that have accompanied the portrayal of the protagonist so far, we begin to wonder whether the narrator is not using 'děti svých dětí' to avoid a biologically unequivocal 'vnuci', because he knows that the largely lifeless protagonist is not surrounded by his own grandchildren, only by people toward whom he has a fatherly disposition – or perhaps a typically Confucian paternalistic attitude. The implication that the protagonist has no progeny will receive support later on in the story. In 'stoupati opatrně do šlépějí jím samým vyhloubených', we have another thought-provoking deviation from standard usage, and again this deviation acts as the vehicle for an ironic message. The expression 'stoupati do šlépějí [koho]' is a cliché and the tired image it evokes has become fixed as a metaphor. So when we hear that someone has followed in someone's else footsteps, we do not think of a physical act of following or treading in footprints left behind. However when the stereotypical image of 'stoupati do šlépějí [koho]' is extended beyond its conventional bounds by the unexpected addition of 'opatrně' and '[do šlépějí] jím samým vyhloubených', the tired image is suddenly regenerated and a sense of its literal significance restored. Now we do see people stepping from footprint to footprint and are amused to find that they do so with caution and are even more amused to discover that the footprints have not simply been left behind but have been worn out of the ground by repeated action (cf. 'kapka vyhloubí kámen') or even deliberately hewn out of it (cf. 'sedlák vyhloubil jámu'). This gives us the impression that the children are not so much carefully emulating the protagonist as stepping vigilantly from hollow to hollow, as if engaged in some overly tentative game of hopskotch, and suggests that the aged protagonist has had trouble making his mark, perhaps because he finds it hard to make substantial inroads into physical reality of life. There may even be a subsidiary irony here. Given the the protagonist's implicit similarity to a puppet, we may wonder whether the children's slow and emphatic gait is not somewhat like the controlled and ponderous movement of a puppet, and whether the hollowing out of the footsteps is not suggestive of the heavy-footed walk of large puppets with leaden or lead-weighted feet.[239]

---

239 Vojtěch Sucharda's brother, Bohuslav Sucharda (1878–1927), pioneered the use of leaden and lead-weighted feet in puppets to improve control of movement.

The irony in 'mírná důvěra' is created by simple ambiguity. Since 'mírný' can mean not 'calm/quiet' but also 'moderate', we are given to understand that the protagonist's trust in fate may be less complete than we initially imagine. This is followed up in 'důvěra ve všechen další osud', which suggests that what is at issue here is not straightforward trust in fate ('důvěra v osud') but an aggrieved feeling that fate will continue to strike in a multitude of ways. This implication is enforced by 'trpné sklonění'. Since 'trpný' can mean 'passive/ stolid/imperturbable' but also 'painful/suffering/agonized', 'trpné sklonění' leaves it tellingly open whether what we have here is genuine acquiescence to fate or simply aggrieved, teeth-gritting capitulation. In much the same vein, 'co by se [...] mohlo [...] neodvratného dostavit' prompts us to conclude that the fatalism we suppose the narrator to be projecting into his main character is ill-founded and nothing more than a sham. True fatalism, the author is expecting us to reason here, cannot admit contingencies, nor can it distinguish inevitable events from avoidable ones, still less can it, contradictorily combining the two, speak of contingent inevitabilities. Disruptive is also 'kdysi', and this not only because its indeterminacy combined with the conditional tense of the verb makes the events to which the old man is said to be acquiescing recede into comic remoteness. Since 'kdysi' is more at ease with its commoner past meaning, it also threatens to subvert the future meaning apparently conveyed by it, exploiting to this effect the possibility of reading '[co] by se mohlo [dostavit]' as synonymous with '[co] by se bylo mohlo [dostavit]'. This leaves us with the disturbing feeling that the old man may be concerned not so much about what might happen as about what might have happened but did not. That the events the protagonist is submitting to are described as surly or sullen ('posupný') quietly mocks the narrator not only for indiscriminate personification but also for childlike timidity. By 'nenapodobitelný', the author is hinting that the narrator, because of this timidity, would like to be able to imitate the protagonist's alleged stoic calm but finds he cannot. Even 'stoický' is ironic, since it can imply that the narrator believes peace of mind to involve formidable self-discipline. We may assume, however, that the reason why the old man is calm at the thought of death is not self-discipline but fear of life. The use of 'fysický', implicitly distinguishing between the bodily and the spiritual, is meant to bring out once again the narrator's metaphysical perspective. The expression '[představa] jakékoliv [...] smrti' adds to the irony. Given that the protagonist is very old and that he is implicitly utterly set in his ways, listless and extremely broody, we can hardly imagine him dying of any other than natural causes. The unlimited range of spectacular and dramatic possibilities evoked by 'jakýkoliv' is therefore comically superfluous.

> Říkalo se tudíž o něm: Lao je nejbohatší, Lao je nejmoudřejší a Lao je nejšťastnější
> člověk na této zemi.

Vskutku, mnoho zevních okolností k tomuto všeobecnému úsudku opravňovalo. Neboť jemu se urodila rýže sněhobílá a moučnatá, saki z ní dobyté připravilo pijákovi nejsladší oblouznění. Indigo a cukrová třtina dosáhly vzhledu vzrostlého šumného a chřestícího lesa a čajové keře hýřily prašnými květy ve velikosti plané růže. Lýkové ošatky byly stále plné vajec, jak je bez únavy kladli jeho kury, bažanti, krocani a pávi.

In view of what we have just learnt, we can hardly believe the extravagant claim about Lao at the beginning of this passage, and the author is careful to allow us the verbal leeway we need to develop our sceptical stance. By having the narrator preface his assertion by 'říkalo se', the author is leaving us free to conclude that it is based on nothing more than idle gossip. This implication is cunningly followed up by 'tudíž', which can be read as 'therefore' but also as an old-fashioned and ultimately trivial 'here'. No less significant is 'na této zemi', which he might be referring to the whole earth, the whole country, or some conveniently undefined area of land that might be very small indeed. The narrator further compromises himself by asserting that there was considerable evidence for the claim about Lao and proceeding to set it out, because he initially led us to believe that the claim was adequately substantiated by what went before. By letting the narrator start out once again to justify what he appeared to have justified already, the author is implying that the narrator is uncomfortably aware of his previous failure. The ironic ambiguity of 'tudíž' is thus implicitly confirmed. The dubiousness of the claim about Lao is hinted at also in 'vskutku', which can be emphatic, but also simply concessive, in this case expressing a certain measure of understanding for a judgement held to be mistaken. The phrase 'zevní okolnosti' mockingly betrays the narrator's characteristically religious conviction that material assets of the kind he goes on to mention are not an essential part of true richness. On a different level of irony, 'zevní okolnosti' suggests also quite simply that the evidence provided by this list of assets is merely superficial and incidental. Pointing in the same direction is the expression 'všeobecný úsudek', because 'všeobecný' can accommodate both the narrator's contention that the judgement is popular opinion and the author's insinuation that it is an untenable generalization . The imperfective '[mnoho] opravňovalo', moreover, can convey a sense of continual justification or, on the contrary, a sense of incomplete, inadequate justification. That the rice Lao cultivates is said to be snowwhite and floury hardly recommends it. The milled short-grained rice eaten by the Chinese is normally white, and while white rice can be ground into flour, its texture would be more favourably described as sticky or flaky. That the narrator describes the sake as '[z rýže] dobyté' rather than '[z rýže] vyrobené' is still within the bounds of normal usage but we cannot help registering the connotations of laborious extraction that attach to 'dobyté'. The narrator's use of 'připravilo' to describe the giving of the pleasure is also within the bounds of normal usage but again we cannot ignore the sense of merely preparing rather than actually giving that 'připravilo' allows to creep in. That the pleasure in question is referred to as 'oblouznění' is unusual. We are familiar with 'blouznění' ('yearning', 'phantisizing') and 'obluzení' ('stupor', 'delusion'). In the present context it is tempting to see 'oblouznění' as a semantic hybrid that affects rakish approval of the ensuing drunkenness ('blouznění') while concealing severe moral censure ('obluzení'). The pretence of approval is evident in the adjective 'nejsladší' that the author would have us realize is yet another indication of the narrator's sentimentality. That the narrator secretly disapproves of drinking and drunkards is also brought out by his use of the pejorative 'piják'. At the same time, and on another ironic level, '[saki připravilo] pijákovi [oblouznění]' can suggest that the sake is so weak that it only induces drunkenness if consumed in large quantities. The description of the indigo and sugar-cane is no less suspicious. In 'dosáhly vzhledu vzrostlého […] lesa', the narrator is arguing for towering height while the author is asking to consider that similarity of appearance does not guarantee size. That the forest is described as 'šumný a chřestící' conceals a double irony. First, the fact that in this metaphor the attributes are attached to the target rather than the source can suggest that the sounds in question are purely imaginary.[240] Second, the use of 'chřestící', where we would have expected 'chrastící' in line with the cliché, subversively implies that the sound the narrator is imagining is more a rattling or jangling noise than a rustling of leaves in the wind. This is a sly hint at his predilection for artificiality and the lifelessness of his vision. It may even be a hint that what the narrator is imagining is more like a scene in a puppet-theatre where plants might be depicted using coloured paper on wire frames. That the flowers on the tea bushes are said to be the size of dog-rose ultimately fails to impress us, because we know the size of the leaves does not correlate with the quality of the tea. With black and green tea alike, it is the smaller top leaves that are thought to make the best tea. The use of 'prašný', moreover, leaves it open whether the flowers are polliniferous or simply dusty. The statement about the eggs and the fowl adds to the irony. That the egg-laying fowl is of the specified kinds suggests that the old man was more interested in wondrous variety than agricultural utility, and maybe particularly in the optic appeal of elaborate or exotic plumage. The use of the term 'kury', that covers all gallinaceous fowl

240 I am using George Lakoff's terminology. According to Lakoff, the *source* of a metaphor is the subject from which the attributes are borrowed, the *target* the subject to which attributes are ascribed. I. A. Richards uses *tenor* for *source* and *vehicle* for *target*. See George Lakoff and Mark Johnson, *Metaphors We Live By* (Chicago, 1980); George Lakoff and Mark Johnson, *Women, Fire, and Dangerous Things: What Categories Reveal about the Mind* (Chicago, 1990); and I. A. Richards, *The Philosophy of Rhetoric* (London, 1936).

wild and domestic, even leaves us in doubt whether the old man has such a thing as ordinary farm-hens. What is more, since 'kury' includes the species named after it, its occurrence here can imply that part of the fowl is not identifiable in terms of familiar species. The hint in 'vzácné drůbeže' earlier is thereby implicitly confirmed. Taking the irony still further, the phrase '[ošatky] stále plné' encourages us to think that the baskets were more continuously full than continually filled. In close connection with this, 'jak' may be taken to mean not that the eggs were gathered as soon as they were laid, as the narrator wants us to believe, but that they were merely of the sort laid by the old man's fowl. This, in turn, prompts us to suspect that the eggs in the baskets are not fresh home produce awaiting distribution but ornaments on display that may well have been acquired elsewhere.[241] The implication of ornamentality ties in with the fact that eggs of this kind, with often unusual patterning and coloration, would normally be considered more interesting visually than in taste, and also with the old man's predilection for hoarding supposed artistic treasures that will be described . Consistently with the ambiguity of 'jak', the phrase 'bez únavy' may be understood as meaning that the birds laid tirelessly, incessantly, or else that they laid without getting tired, presumably because they did not do so very often. Contributory to the irony is also the mention of 'krocani' and 'pávi'. These terms can be read as unmarked for gender but they can also be read as the masculine complements of the marked feminine 'krůta' and 'pávice'. This leaves us free to conclude that the narrator may be letting male birds lay eggs, so alienated is he from the realities of life. In line with the ironic implication of ornamentality is even the reference to baskets made of bast. In China baskets were almost always made of bamboo, a material ideally suited to splicing and weaving. Bast baskets make us think of Russia, the Ukraine and areas of Eastern Europe, where bast was commonly used for this purpose. This leaves us wondering whether the baskets are not foreign imports exhibited for their unusualness. But there is an implication even beyond this. The baskets described as 'ošatky' are the small, flat bread baskets commonly found on the Czech breakfast table. Are we to assume that these baskets are perhaps no more than makeshift props in an amatuerish puppet-theatre production. This may seem a fanciful

---

241 The reference to the peacock along with the implication of its purely decorative function may be interpreted as a jibe at the English Aesthetic Movement, which elevated the peacock to symbolic status. We need think only of Aubrey Beardsley's print 'The Peacock Skirt', used as an illustration in Oscar Wilde's *Salome*; James Whistler's 'Peacock Room' in Frederick Leyland's house in Prince's Gate (1867–8); Edward Burne Jones's lacquered painting 'The Peacock'; and the menagerie of blue peacocks Dante Gabriel Rossetti kept in his garden (1864–71). Vases of peacock feathers and stuffed peacocks became popular features of interior decoration. See Lionel Lambourne, *The Aesthetic Movement* (London, 1996); Christine Jackson, *The Peacock* (London, 2006); and Karen Zukowski, *Creating the artful home: the aesthetic movement* (London, 2006).

association until we remember that bast was a favourite material in the Czech puppet-theater (the words 'lýko' and 'loutka' are cognates).

> Nu, a ženu měl takovou úslužnou a poddajnou jako kobereček, jaký se prostírá bílým nohám, vystupujícím z lázně. Ale co ho činilo nade vše jiné proslulým v této nesmírné zemi mezi dvěma mořskými proudy, to byla skříň z nejjemnějšího laku, nanášeného ve třiceti vrstvách a plasticky zlatem zvýšeného, která měla mnoho uzamčených příhrad, z nichž každá skrývala klenot vždy drahocennější a nenahraditelnější, jak byla jedna po druhé postupně odmykána.

That the reference to the man's wife follows immediately upon the listing of his fowl makes us think of her as just another item of domestic chattel. Matters are not improved by the narrator's 'Nu, a...', which makes this late mention feel like a coy afterthought. Even 'žena' is potentially compromising. Though it is often used as conversational equivalent for 'manželka', we cannot help wondering whether the woman in question is not more of a maidservant than a wife and therefore as little a family member as the curious 'dětí svých dětí' mentioned earlier on. That the narrator commends her for servility and submissiveness is somewhat irritating but might be explained as a reflection of an oriental preference for female subordination. However, when he goes on to say that she is like a bath-mat, the balance is irrevocably tipped and we find ourselves revolting against the narrator's admiration, just as the author intends. That the legs stepping on to the bath-mat are said to be white irritates us further, since the legs of fair-skinned person getting out of a bath would normally be rosy with heat. This makes us wonder whether the beings that people the narrator's imagination are not bloodless phantoms, or maybe even puppet-like figures with crudely painted limbs. That the legs are spoken of as if they were independent agents mockingly reveals the narrator's tendency to personify no less poignantly than his attribution of servility and submissiveness to the bath-mat. When we first read 'v této nesmírné zemi mezi dvěma mořskými proudy', we imagine the narrator to be talking about the vast expanse of land between the Huang Ho and the Yang-tse Kiang, the two majestic rivers that cut right across the Chinese mainland from west to east. However, by having the narrator omit all reference to unique geographical landmarks ('země' can refer to any piece of land and 'proud' to any body of moving water) and by having him use language that is in any case visibly hyperbolic (land is never truly measureless and rivers are never truly oceanic), the author is effectively severing this description from any reliable perspective. If we now remember that the narrator considered fields of sugar-cane and indigo to be like towering forests, we cannot help suspecting that the narrator's perception of size is aberrant. If he perceives small objects as unnaturally large, as we suspect he does, the dimensions of the landscape he is describing may be nothing like as impressive as he would have us believe. The narrator's preference of 'proslulý' to 'slavný' suggests that he is secretly aware that the old man is more notorious than famous and, in his embarrassment, tries to hide this behind a word that covers both. The irony behind the description of the old man's lacquer cabinet is more difficult to unravel. There is lacquering technique, developed in Heian-dynasty Japan (794–1185) and later imported into Song-dynasty China (960–1279), called *maki-e* ('sprinkled picture').[242] In *maki-e*, a wooden, leather or paper base is standardy covered with twenty-five layers of ordinary lacquer, then with up to fifteen layers of lacquer into which gold or silver dust is sprinkled. In a variant of *maki-e* called *takamaki-e* ('raised sprinkled picture'), developed in Muromachi Japan (1336–1573), the lacquer is raised by the insertion of gold or silver leaf or plate to produce a relief pattern. This is what the narrator seems to be describing and his description is technically accurate, so we may ask ourselves where the irony is supposed to be. It lies in a cunning switch of narrative focus. The narrator's description is technically accurate but it confuses the end with the means. The whole point of *maki-e* is that it allows the artist to achieve a highly decorative pattern exploiting the striking contrast between the black lacquered surface and the gold or silver inlay. Of this all-important pattern, whose elegance is meant to justify the painstaking effort involved, we learn absolutely nothing, as if the aesthetic effect were of no importance. This prompts us to see the technique of piling on layer after layer of lacquer and raising the lacquer with gold as an end in itself, as a desperate attempt to add substance to something that is embarrassingly insubstantial. That it is physical elevation rather than artistic enhancement that is the cabinet-maker's principal objective is hinted at in 'plasticky [...] zvýšeného'. That the cabinet might be exceptionally flimsy also hinted at in 'z [...] laku'. Normally 'z laku' means 'lacquered' (cf. 'střevíce/kabelka z laku'), but read in accordance with the commoner $z(e)$ + *material* paradigm (cf. 'z dřeva/ze zlata/ze skla') it can suggest that the article in question is virtually made of lacquer. Notice also that the material to which the lacquer has been applied is not mentioned, leaving us wondering how substantial the base actually is. Another hint at the cabinet's lack of substance is contained in the hidden opposition between 'skrývat' and 'odmykat'. When the compartments are opened, we would expect their contents to be revealed, not hidden. Prompting us to seek a rationale for this disparity, the author is hoping that we may consider the possibility that the contents are hard to see at first glance. That

---

242 Opolský may well have become familiar with technique of *maki-e* from the numerous examples contained in the outstanding collection of Japanese art held by the Northern Bohemian museum in Liberec since 1873. See Filip Suchomel and Oldřich Palata, *Japonská sbírka Severočeského muzea v Liberci* (Prague, 2000).

there is something suspicious here also comes through in '[klenot vždy] drahocennější a nenahraditelnější'. To say that something is irreplaceable may be to do more than to say it is valuable but it may also be to do considerably less. What is more, the use of the comparative form of 'nenahraditelný' can also suggest that the irreplaceability in question is merely subjective, since objective irreplaceability would, strictly speaking, be absolute and not relative. Another hint that something is amiss is to be found in the apparent tautological '[příhrada] jedna po druhé postupně [odmykána]' as well. The author is prompting us to realize that 'postupně' is not simply duplicating the foregoing phrase as it seems to be doing, but is giving expression to the slowness with which each lock is turned. Why the lock might need to be turned so slowly becomes clearer when we consider the previous hints at the cabinet's frailty. For the time being, however, the implication that there is something untoward about the cabinet is still very weak. It is only with the progression of the irony in what follows that we will slowly be pushed further towards the realization that this is not a normal piece of furniture but itself a diminutive *objet d'art*.

> Jednou za dlouhý čas, za některé obzvláště slavné příležitosti v kruhu rodiny a nejlepších přátel, byly zásuvky skříně pohledům zpřístupněny. A tu, kdo měli oči k vidění, nemohli než rozkoší oslzeti, a kdož měli srdce na svém místě, dlouho je nemohli poté utišiti. Dálo se vše velmi pomalu, s účelnou odměřeností, nikoli bez jakéhosi příjemného ceremonielu.

The phrase 'jednou za dlouhý čas' has a disparaging note, since it is often used to express annoyance at the insufficient frequency with which something happens or is done. In '[za] některé obzvláště slavné [příležitosti]', the indeterminacy of 'některý' subversively relativizes the strong claim to particularity in 'obzvláště slavný'. The surreptitious substitution of 'slavný' for the expected 'slavnostní' in 'slavná příležitost' makes us wonder whether the old man is celebrating a festive occasion or simply making the best of a capital opportunity; 'slavný' can extend to 'solemn' (as in 'slavná mše') and 'festive' (thus overlapping with 'slavnostní'), but it can also mean 'illustrious', 'glorious', and, more colloquially, 'great', 'capital', 'smashing', while příležitost can encompass both 'occasion' and 'opportunity'. The subsequent 'v kruhu rodiny a nejlepších přátel' is no less compromising. It is unusual that the circle of friends should be greatly restricted and that of the family not at all, especially since Chinese families are traditionally very large. This not only betrays a curious attitude to friendship but also implicitly confirms previous hints that the old man's family is not what the narrator is pretending it to be. It is also curious that the formal, elevated 'kruh [rodiny a přátel]' should be followed by a colloquial 'nejlepší' instead of a correspondingly formal, elevated 'nejdůvěrnější' or 'nejužší'. The author is using this apparent discrepancy to suggest that 'nejlepší' here does not mean 'best' in the colloquial sense of 'closest', as we at first think it does, but 'best' in the stylistically neutral and therefore here more readily compatible sense of 'most suitable'. This echoes the sense of opportunism in 'slavná příležitost'. The expression '[zásuvky byly] pohledům zpřístupněny' brings out the narrator's tendency to treat the abstract as if it were concrete even to the extent of personification. By allowing 'kdo měli oči k vidění', which is strongly reminiscent of a similar expression involving ears and hearing that occurs nearly a dozen times in the New Testament, the author is showing up the narrator's religious preoc-cupations.[243] The parallelism of 'kdo měli oči k vidění' and 'kdož měli srdce na svém místě' also has a biblical ring, this time reminding us more of the itera-tive conventions of Old Testament style. The irony goes even further. The nar-rator's 'měli srdce na svém místě' is decidedly odd. We normally speak about someone having his heart in the right place, 'na pravém místě', but not simply in its place, 'na svém místě'. By allowing this deviation from normal expres-sion, the author is prompting us to suspect that what is at issue is not whether the members of the audience are right-thinking but whether they, literally, have a heart where the heart should be. Since the reference to the eyes can also be taken literally, we find ourselves moving off on a new semantic tack. Thinking literally, we begin to wonder how it could possibly be that members of the audience might not have eyes to see and might not have hearts where the heart normally is. What the author would like us to consider is not just the possibility that the narrator may be picturing the audience as puppets, in line with previous implications in this direction, but that some of those said to be attending were present only as spirit tablets harbouring the souls of deceased ancestors, in line with the Chinese custom of placing such ancestral tablets on household altars and including them in family rituals.[244] There is yet another implication available here. Given the narrator's tendency to per-sonify, we may even ask ourselves whether the expression 'na svém místě' in 'měli srdce na svém místě' is not also being used in the sense of 'capable' or 'competent', as in 'člověk na svém místě', suggesting that what is at issue here, and implicitly in doubt, may be not so much the rightness of attitude of those

---

243 See the parable of the sower (Matthew 13: 18–32; Mark 4: 3–19; Luke 8: 4–15).

244 Spirit tablets (Chin. *paiwei, shenwei, shenzhupai*) are plaques of wood inscribed with name, age and date of birth of the deceased. Often adorned with silk, they are displayed on the household altar. Normally they reach back five generations (Chin. *wu fu*) and are often included in family rituals. The Chinese believe that when someone dies, one of the souls remains with the body in the grave (the *yin* soul or *white* soul, referred to as *po*), while another leaves the body to inhabit the ancestral tablet (the *yang* soul or *cloud* soul, referred to as *hun*). See James Thayer Addison, 'The modern Chinese cult of ancestors', *Journal of Religion*, 4 (1924), pp. 492–503, and William Lakos, *Chinese Ancestor Worship* (Newcastle, 2010), pp. 28–30.

present as the strength of their presumably aged hearts. In addition, there is a minor irony in 'nemohli než [rozkoší oslzeti]' and 'dlouho je [srdce] nemohli poté utišiti', which together can suggest that in the narrator's opinion unsettling emotion should be suppressed. Implicitly characteristic of the narrator is also his sentimental conviction that rapture would manifest itself in tearfulness. Equally subversive is 'dálo se to vše velmi pomalu', because 'vše' can imply that for the narrator it is not only the actions that would be very slow but the reactions too. The addition of 'nikoli bez [...] ceremonielu' forces us to review our initial interpretation of 'účelná odměřenost'. At first we thought that the reason for the studied movement was precisely ceremoniousness, but now we learn that this ceremoniousness was merely incidental, no more than a side-effect. This prompts us to seek another explanation for 'účelná odměřenost', and this our knowledge of the tiny lacquer cupboard's extreme frailty readily provides. The use of 'jakýsi' hints once again at the narrator's tendency to vagueness. The attribution of 'příjemný' to 'ceremoniel' is meant to suggest that the narrator likes ceremony, presumably because it combines ornamentality with formalism.

> Co bylo v prvé zásuvce?
> Byla tam drobná kniha, psaná na papíře nejstarší samarkandské úpravy, silném, ale nedávajícím šelestu jako závoj. Obsahovala kodex sedmačtyřiceti zákonných pojednání o věrnosti. Psána byla přeostrým štětečkem z chlupu hranostaje a kreslířská tuš byla prudce napuštěna mošusem, kafrem a cinnameinem, v pohledu se strany pak mihotala se všemi odstíny starodávného zlata.

The opening question seems to be purely rhetorical but may also be taken to suggest that the object in the drawer is somehow hard to identify at first glance. This puzzlement finds its ironic continuation in 'drobná kniha'. When used of writings and without a following diminutive, 'drobný' usually refers to texts that are short/not full-length (as in 'drobné spisy', 'drobný článek', 'drobná korespondence'), so we struggle to accommodate 'drobná kniha' to this meaning. Just when we think we may have succeeded, we are thwarted by the revelation that the book contains forty-seven treatises, which hardly suggests lack of substance. We are thus driven to find another rationale for 'drobná kniha'. Initially this is difficult because there is little to go on. However, as we proceed through the story and find ourselves confronted with objects that are not just flimsy but minute, we will come to understand that 'drobná kniha' is an indication of the narrator's embarrassment at the size of the object in question. Unwilling to say 'drobná knížka' or 'drobná knížečka' for fear of giving the game away, the narrator compromises with 'drobná kniha', hoping that we will not inquire too closely into its true meaning. That the book is said to have been written 'na papíře nejstarší samarkandské úpravy' sounds impressive. Paper-making in Samarkand began in the mid-seventh century, so the oldest Samarkand paper would be a material of considerable antiquity. However, if we examine the wording carefully, we cannot help noticing that all we are guaranteed is paper made in accordance with the oldest Samarkand technique. Since the age of the technique says nothing about the age of the paper, we come to realize that this particular treasure may not be an antique at all. Problems accummulate with '[na papíře] silném, ale nedávajícím šelestu jako závoj'. That the narrator says the paper is thick and then compares it to a veil in respect of its lack of rustle strikes us as clumsy and far-fetched. Why compare something to its exact opposite in respect of some third characteristic that is only marginally relevant to either? This is precisely the question that the author is encouraging us to ask. What he would like us to understand is that the narrator is acutely embarrassed by the thickness of the paper and is desperate to find some way of commending it. The awkwardness of his comparison is a measure of his desperation. We sense that he is clutching at straws in order to square the thickness of the paper with his preference for fineness and delicacy. That the book is said to be a codex containing forty-seven treatises on loyalty is no less compromising. When we hear the number forty-seven combined with the idea of loyalty in an oriental context, we are reminded of the famous legend of the forty-seven samurai that is a paradigmatic story of loyalty in Japan.[245]

---

245 According to this famous Tokugawa legend, daimyo Asano Naganori, summoned to the court of shogun Tsunayoshi in Edo, refused to be suborned by the rampant bribery and corruption. Subjected to repeated insult and humiliation as a result, he once allowed himself to be provoked to an angry attack on one of the senior courtiers. The courtier was barely injured but Asano was forced to commit *seppuku* (ritual disembowelment) for assaulting a member of the court. His death was avenged by 47 of his most faithful retainers (who through his death became 'wandering samurai' or *rōnin*) in a cunning and protracted under-cover operation. In the end, they were caught and forced to commit *seppuku* like their master. See John Allyn, *Forty-seven ronin* (Rutland VT, 1970).

Like Julius Zeyer, Opolský may have known the story from Algernon Mitford's famous *Tales of Old Japan* (London, 1871), available also in German as *Geschichten des alten Japan* (Leipzig, 1875), in a translation by J. G. Kohl. Opolský may also have been familiar with it as one of the principal themes of Japanese *ukiyo-e* woodblock printing, used by masters like Utamaro, Hokusai, Hiroshige, Toyokuni and Kuniyoshi. See Basil Stewart, *Subjects Protrayed in Japanese Colour Prints* (London, 1922), pp. 230–291, and Julius Kurth *Geschichte des japanischen Holzschnitts*, 3 vols (Leipzig, 1925–1929).

Opolský may have drawn particular inspiration from the fact that the woodblock prints were based not on the legend itself but on its portrayal in the famous *bunraku* puppet play *Chūshingura* ('Treasury of Loyal Retainers'), penned by Izumo Takeda, Shōraku Miyoshi and Senryū Namiki, and first staged in 1748. Japanese *bunraku* puppet-theatre was popular in Bohemia and was later to inspire the creation of the *Laterna Magica* in Prague.

That the story of forty-seven samurai was well-known and widely discussed in contemporary Bohemia is evident from Richard Heise's *Über Loyalität in Japan: 47 ronin* (Böhmisch Krumau, 1931). Joe Hloucha in his hugely popular fictional travel diary *Sakura ve vichřici* (Prague, twelve editions, 1905–1948) describes a visit to the Sengakuji temple to see the graves of the 47 *rōnin* (entry for 9 April).

The irony here lies in the amusing discrepancy between the single-minded warriors with their ultra-sharp swords that come to mind when we think of the legend and the wordy disquisitions to which the emblematic number has been surreptitiously transferred. This ironic contrast finds a secondary reflection in 'zákonná pojednání', where the trenchancy and finality that we normally associate with 'zákon' is undermined by the sense of rambling speculation that attaches to 'pojednání'. Ironic is also the reference to a codex and the thickness of the paper. When we think of a codex written on thick paper, what we normally imagine is a massive volume sturdily bound in leather with iron-capped edges. However, if we have been able to pick up on the slowly developing implication that the cabinet and its contents are much smaller that we might anticipate, we can already see how the dimensions of this conventional image are being ironically subverted. That there is a problem with size also comes through in '[kniha] psána byla přeostrým štětečkem', because we may legitimately ask ourselves why the book had to be written with such an ultra-fine brush. The narrator compromises himelf in other ways too. His characterization of a fur brush as 'přeostrý' betrays a morbid oversensitivity that perceives even the softest of materials as extremely sharp. Even more telling is 'z chlupu hranostaje'. When we hear of stoat's hair, we normally think of ermine, the exquisite white fur provided by the animal's soft and fluffy winter coat, so we may ask ourselves why the narrator has not said 'z hermelínu'. What the author would like us to understand is that the narrator has avoided the apparently obvious 'z hermelínu' because he knows that the brush is not made of ermine at all, but of hair that was probably shed from the stoat's unspectacular and worthless summer coat. The description of the Indian ink takes the irony further. Indian ink usually has a pungent smell, usually of camphor or patchouli, so by telling us that this ink is permeated by musk, camphor and cinnamon, the narrator is hoping that we will be impressed by its unusually rich and refined bouquet. But this does not add up. Indian ink ('tuš') smells of camphor or patchouli because the oils of camphor and patchouli are commonly used as solvents to provide a liquid base for the pigments. In other words, the characteristic smell is a by-product of the chemical composition. By throwing in additional odours that would normally be considered extraneous, the narrator is making us wonder whether the ink-maker has not added further substances to the ink in order to create an exotic olfactory experience for the reader. That the dark scent of musk, the bracing odour of camphor and the sweet smell of cinnamon do not blend suggests that his attempt has not been overly successful. This irony owes its inspiration to the fact that the ancient Chinese added a whole array of substances to their inks largely to improve colour and solvency but sometimes also to mask the pungent smell of adhesive.[246] The author is clearly aware of this fact but has adapted the information in such a way that it ceases to be credible even to the culturally initiated reader, who may be expected to realize that any substance added to the ink as an odour would have been there to spare the writer's nostrils and not to titillate the senses of readers across the ages. Compromising for the narrator is also his use of '[tuš byla] napuštěna [mošusem, kafrem a cinnameinem]'. Normally 'napustit co čím' is used only of solids permeated by liquids ('napustit podlahu fermeží', 'napustit boty olejem'). By letting the narrator use 'napustit' of a liquid permeated by aromatic substances hints at his tenuous grasp of material reality. The modification of 'napustit' by 'prudce' makes matters worse because for anyone sufficiently grounded in physical reality a material that is soaked in another is close enough to saturation for 'prudce' to be virtually meaningless. That the narrator feels 'prudce' is necessary in this context suggests that he has difficulty appreciating what material saturation entails. But this is not the end of the irony here. If we cast our eye over '[tuš byla napuštěna] mošusem, kafrem a cinnameinem' again, we notice that something else is amiss. Musk is a scent; camphor is both a scent and a spice; but cinnamon is just a spice. By allowing the list to move gradually from scent to spice in this way, the author is mockingly suggesting that the narrator is as much concerned by the ink's taste as by its smell. That the narrator has used the exotic foreign borrowing 'cinnamein' for 'skořice' betrays his affectation. The description of the ink's alleged glimmer is no less disruptive. The looking from one side suggests a desperate attempt to catch the light at its most favourable and the likeness to old gold complete lack of lustre even then. Contributory to the irony here is also the narrator's strikingly detailed knowledge of the production process. We may put this down to the narrator's omniscience, but we may also chose to see it as further evidence that the object is a recent facsimile.

> Co bylo ve druhé zásuvce, uzavřené v rozích i ve středu pěti zlatými klíčky?
> Bylo to pečlivě a na drobno složené, s úžasnou uměleckou záludností malované hedvábné kakemono, jež by mělo splývati s cedrového obložení pokoje císařova. Rozvinuto jevilo se ve svém základním tónu proměnlivě jako fosforeskující voda, a všecky štíhlé květiny byly na ně namalovány tím způsobem, aby se jeho barevné hybnosti zúčastnily.

The introductory question can again be rhetorical or genuine, with the same ironic import as in the previous case. That the drawer is said to have as

---

246 See Thomas Höllmann, *Das alte China* (Munich, 2008), p. 221 and *Die chinesische Schrift* (Munich, 2015), p. 54–55. A comprehensive list of such additives (from aconite to walnut) is given in the eleventh-century *Mopu fashi*, an instruction manual for ink-making.

many as five locks seems to hark back to the narrator's attempt to convince us that the objects in the cabinet are inordinately valuable and his indication that they will be presented in order of ascending value. Our first instinct is therefore to put the large number of locks down to the added security needed for this new object. It is only on reflection that we come to realize that the extraordinary arrangement of the locks described here can hardly be functional. That the locks are therefore likely to be largely decorative compromises the narrator's argument, but even this decorativeness is questionable. When the narrator speaks of five golden keys, we are quick to assume that there must be five golden locks, and this is what we see in our mind's eye. The author, however, would like us to understand that golden keys do not guarantee golden locks, and hopes that we will be willing to revise our mental picture downwards once again. The number and arrangement of the locks also helps to develop another ironic perspective. That there are five locks may suggest that the narrator is again projecting his own attitudes into the story, because the number five can make us think of the pentagram or pentacle, a mystic symbol credited also with magic virtues, and of the five books of Moses. What is more, since the five locks are said to be at the corners and in the middle, therefore presumably arranged in the order two-one-two, we are also led to think of the Pythagorean pentad, conceived of as the sum of two plus one and two, that is supposed to symbolize the perfection of the microcosm.[247] By allowing this association, the author is not only hinting at the narrator's extravagant admiration for the object in the drawer but also suggesting that it too was no more than a miniature representation. In 'pečlivě a na drobno složené [kakemono]', the author is implicitly dissociating the meanings of the adverbial terms which the narrator would like us to associate.[248] We are thereby given to understand that the kakemono was not rolled up carefully because it had to be rolled up from large to very small, but was rolled up carefully because the material was tenuous and very delicate, and rolled up very small, not as a result of long and careful rolling, but because it was very small

---

247 According to Pythagorean numerology: 1 = macrocosm; 2 = microcosm; 3 = 2 + 1 = perfection; 5 = 3 + 2 = 2 + 1 + 2 = perfection of the microcosm.

248 That Lao is said to possess an *objet d'art* that is recognizably Japanese (the kakemono is a Japanese hanging scroll), together with the previous references to matters Japanese, may be seen as a sly dig at the European fashion of *japonisme* that affected European art from Monet to Matisse. See Lionel Lambourne, *Japonisme* (London, 2005); and Klaus Berger, *Japonismus in der westlichen Malerei* (Munich, 1980). The influence of Japanese art is also evident in Bohemia from 1880 onwards, influencing the work of painters like Alfons Mucha, Vojtěch Preissig, Emil Orlik, Walter Klemm and Carl Thiemann as well as designs across the Northern Bohemian glass industry from Nový Bor to Harrachov. Joe Hloucha ran a Japanese-style coffee-shop and tea-room called the *Jokohama* in the Lucerna just off Wenceslas Square from 1908 to 1924. He also built a Japanese-style villa in the Prague suburbs which became the model for the *Sakura* Japanese restaurant in Roztoky on the outskirts of Prague. See Markéta Hanová, *Japonismus v českém umění* (Prague, 2014).

to begin with. In this way, the author continues to mock discreetly the frailty and diminutiveness of Lao's ostensible treasures. The expression 'umělecká záludnost', apparently referring to a skilful deceptiveness of the painter in producing what is supposed to be an optical illusion of shimmering colour, for the author merely reflects the artist's perfidiousness in trying to pass this flimsy piece of shoddy workmanship off as an *objet d'art*. The ambiguity here is complemented by the addition of 'úžasný', which can convey marvel and admiration but also consternation and surprise. The claim that the kakemono should have been hanging in an imperial chamber takes the irony further, because we suspect that the reason why it was not hanging there may lie not in the circumstances of its ownership but in its prohibitive frailty and minuteness. The use of the verb 'splývat' ironically emphasizes the disparity, since flowing pre-supposes more substance and dynamism that simply hanging. That the narrator assumes an imperial chamber would have cedar panelling betrays his peculiar taste, because cedarwood is very pale and ethereally fragrant, and would therefore normally be considered rather unsuitable for panelling. The narrator's assumption also brings out his religiosity, since according to the Old Testament it is part of the rare splendour of the temple of Solomon, the house of Solomon and the house of Pharoah's daughter that they have cedar panelling on all walls from floor to ceiling.[249] The strange use of 'pokoj císařův' for the expected 'komnata císařská' can even suggest that the place where the narrator imagines the kakemono ought to be hanging is not an imperial chamber, as we had assumed, but just a normal-sized household room, that is probably also not inhabited by, only devoted or consecrated to, an emperor. In this way, the author is covertly mocking both the narrator's reduced scale of vision and the Confucian ideal and practice of piety towards elders and superiors. The expression 'základní tón' is rather odd here, because it is normally used more abstractly, as in 'základní tón romantiky'. The word 'tón' can be used of colours to mean 'shade' or 'tint', but if this is what we take it to mean here we have difficulty with 'základní', because it is hard to understand what exactly can be meant by saying that a painting has a basic shade or tint as distinct from a predominant or background shade or tint. This gives us the impression that the author is using 'základní' to deprive 'tón' of its concreteness, and 'tón' in this sense to avoid a definitive, to his mind hardly justified, 'barva'. The simile 'jako fosforeskující voda' develops this irony. By comparing the colour of the kakemono to phosphorescent water, the narrator is trying to make us believe that it is shimmering, whereas the author is suggesting that it is cold and feeble, as phosphorescent light is, and also watery. At the same time, the author is exploiting the background as-

---

249 1 Kings, 6 and 7.

sociations of rotting plankton to bring out the narrator's alienation from life. The implied weakness of the colours provides a further ironic explanation for the mention of cedar panelling, because we can imagine that only against a very pale background would they have a chance of standing out. The narrator's argument is also subverted by 'štíhlé květiny'. Since flowers would normally be considered very slender, at least if pictured with their stalks, these particular flowers, especially noted for their slenderness, are probably taking up only a negligibly small area of the painting. Their mention therefore implicitly disqualifies the colour effect the narrator is trying to exemplify. We note too that the use of 'štíhlý', though not uncommon with regard to plants, supports previous hints at the narrator's tendency to personify. Compromising for the narrator's case is also the construction 'tím způsobem, aby', that may be introducing the desired clause of effect or only a clause of purpose. It is thereby left open whether the painter succeeded in producing the effect he allegedly intended. The subsequent 'hybnost' can evoke both personification and, on a different level of irony, mechanicalness, since it may be thought of as meaning nimbleness, as in 'hybnost jinocha', and also the joint mobility of parts in a mechanism, as in 'hybnost uložení válce'. In either case, the narrator's attitude is being covertly mocked. The latter implication is perhaps the stronger, because of the formality of 'zúčastnit se', and the abstractness of 'barevný', which is being allowed to mean not 'colourful' but only 'pertaining to colour'.

> Při sebemenším dotknutí čarovně splývajícího kakemona se zdálo, že všecky větvičky, kalichy a traviny kolébá slabý vítr, přilétající od Žluté řeky, a mohlo se míti za to, že to není plocha hedvábí, ale část živoucí rajské země, kde se kmitají i motýli, a modraví brouci v nejmizivějších odlescích se předstihují.

By saying 'při sebemenším dotknutí', the narrator is trying to make us believe that only a very slight touch is needed to set the scene moving, while the author is suggesting that the kakemono is so delicate that nobody dares to do more than touch it very gently. The reaction described is therefore implicitly not the smallest the kakemono can be seen to produce but the greatest. The term 'čarovně', besides revealing the narrator's involvement in magic and the supernatural, also betrays his surprise in spite of himself that the tenuous kakemono has enough weight to hang at all. The narrator's renewed recourse to the verb 'splývat' takes the irony even further. On the surface, 'splývající' conveys a sense of dynamism, but its use here is impossible to reconcile with real motion, since the narrator has just told us that it took an external impulse to set the scene moving. As a result, 'splývající' is unmasked as an attempt to invest the static act of hanging with a false sense of movement. There is yet another irony in 'splývající'. Given the ambiguity of 'splývat' ('to

flow' but also 'to merge', 'to blend in'), 'splývající' can suggest that the kakemono is not so much flowing or hanging freely as merging or blending in with
its background. This provides a further hint at its watery indistinctness. This
implication is strengthened by 'čarovně', which insinuates that the merging
or blending in succeeds marvellously well. Ambiguous is also the import of
'zdálo se', because it may be thought of as qualifying only the assertion that
a wind is rocking the scene or also the more general contention that there is
movement at all. The use of 'kalich' prompts us to realize that the flowers in
the scene are not blooming colourfully, as they might have been expected to
do. Contrary to what we might assume, 'kalich' in its botanical sense does not
refer to the often brightly coloured cup-shaped corollae certain flowers have,
but merely to the inconspicuous green whorl of leaves forming the outer en-
velope of the bud. In this way, the author is bringing out the lifelessness of
the scene and providing an ironic explanation for the previous mention of the
flowers' slenderness. That the narrator should have chosen the unnecessarily
specific 'kalich' also reveals his religiosity, because it associates with 'mešní
kalich' and 'kalich utrpení'. Even 'travina' is ironic, because its preference to
the ordinary 'tráva' can suggest that the vegetation in question is not grass
but something only vaguely resembling grass. The reference to the twigs, calyces and grasses helps to undermine the narrator's claim about movement in
the scene. Since the items mentioned are presumably only details in a larger
landscape scene, we are led to infer that the alleged movement in the picture
has to be looked for extremely carefully. Subversive in this connection is also
the use of 'kolébat', because the movement of such small and flimsy objects
as twigs, calyces and grasses in only a gentle wind is hardly extensive or substantial enough to be described as rocking in any normal sense. In this way,
the author is reminding us of the narrator's inadequate sense of dynamism.
The narrator's preference of 'kolébat' to alternative verbs like 'houpat' or
'klátit' is also meant to be understood as a further hint at his predilection for
any lulling or appeasing of the senses. The subsequent 'přilétající', besides
showing up the narrator's tendency to personify, goes still further towards
revealing the staticness of the scene, because it is conspicuously weaker than
the normal 'dující', 'foukající', 'vanoucí' or 'vějící'. That the wind is said to have
come from the vicinity of the Yellow River suggests, furthermore, that it is
no more than an onshore breeze spent after a long journey inland. The same
assertion also mockingly reveals the narrator's tendency to confuse art and
reality, because in it the narrator is endowing the wind seen in the picture
with geographical attributes as if it were a real wind existing independently
of the picture. By 'mohlo se míti za to', in the next part of the sentence, the
author is implicitly distancing himself from the assertion that follows. It is
suggested, however, that he would still want to endorse 'to [kakemono] není
plocha hedvábí', the impression described being to his mind justifiable, if not

by any artistic merit of the painting, at least by the tenuousness and frailty of the material. The subsequent '[část] živoucí rajské země' provides another hint at the narrator's disturbed attitude to the reality of life, since the associations of spiritualization and transcendent immateriality in 'rajský' stand in implicit contrast to the physical vitality normally conveyed by 'živoucí' and to the immanent concreteness that is standardly part of the meaning of 'země'. Contributory to the irony here is also the conspicuous lack of congruence between 'to není plocha hedvábí', which refers to the painting as material, and 'ale [je to] část živoucí rajské země', which refers to the painting as a scene. By allowing this discrepancy, the author is suggesting that the narrator feels obliged expressly to exclude the manifest possibility that the painting considered as a scene might be thought no more than a piece of material. Deceptive is also 'kmitají se i motýli'. Since the narrator has just spoken of movement, we initially assume that the verb 'kmitat se' here means 'to flit about', and this reading is particularly appropriate to 'motýli'. When we then see that the narrator passes on immediately to talk again about colour, we realize that 'kmitat se' may well be meant more in the sense of 'to shimmer', 'to flicker'. This confronts us with the implication that in this painting even the normally so brilliant colouring of butterflies is as vague and watery as all the rest. When we first read '[brouci] v nejmizivějších odlescích se předstihují' we seem to understand that one beetle surpasses the other only negligibly in its colouring. More careful consideration of the wording here, however, leads us to conclude that the beetles are not one more scintillating than the other, but outdoing each other in the very negligibility of the mere reflection of colour they produce. This in turn enables us to see in the use of 'modravý' a hint that this colour is simply too weak to be called 'modrý'.

> Rovněž tak při malovaných pitvorných dracích dalo se zříti, jak v souladu s touto po-
> všechnou barevnou hybností stále střídají metalické zážehy svých krunýřů a šupin, ale
> ve svém výrazu nebudili děsu či hrůzy, jenom něco ze světu odcizené utkvělosti.

By continuing with 'rovněž tak' and adding 'v souladu s touto [...] barevnou hybností', the author is implying that the colouring of the dragons is just as indistinct and watery as that of everything else in the scene. The only apparently redundant 'malovaný' is suggesting that the dragons we would anyway have known are in the painting are themselves painted dragons, that is, models, presumably made of paper and held up on sticks, as Chinese model dragons usually are. This suggestion receives support from 'pitvorný', which leaves it open whether they are monstrous or simply grimacing. Similarly ambiguous is 'povšechný', which may be telling us that the colour effect is comprehensive, as the narrator would like us to believe, or merely vague and superficial. By using 'střídat', the author is implying that the flashes from the dragons are controlled and not particularly rapid. This tends to confirm our suspicion that the dragons are merely models held up on sticks. What is more, since the narrator says 'draci […] střídají', we are also given the comic impression that the dragons he has typically personified are taking turns to flash, as if they were anxious not to overdo it. The adverb 'stále', on this level, conveys rather the strictness of the alternation than the regularity of the flashing. In 'metalické zážehy', the warm soft glow evoked by 'zážeh' implicitly negates the cold harsh brilliance we would want to associate with 'metalický' and so discredits the narrator's argument. There is comparable ironic tension in '[zážehy] krunýřů a šupin', because 'šupiny' with its associations of flaky thinness and brokenness of surface conspicuously fails to match 'krunýře' in the massiveness and plate-like compactness its suggests. The mention of horror and dread in connection with the dragons makes us expect this to be what they might be inspiring in their beholders. The specification 've svém [draků] výrazu' ironically disappoints this expectation by letting us know that it is the expression of the dragons themselves that is at issue, not that of any onlookers. This is funny also because we would have expected the dragons to be showing, or trying to show, ferocity, not horror and dread, as if it was they who should be terrified. The phrase 'něco ze světu odcizené utkvělosti' is ambiguous, because the verb 'odcizit' can mean both 'to alienate' and 'to steal'. That the rigidity in the dragon's expression may be thought to be not alienated or divorced from the world but stolen from it discreetly mocks the narrator's view of the world as unbending and unyielding because, we presume, obstinate and set in its vicious ways. The use of 'něco', moreover, hints at the narrator's liking for vagueness.

> Středem tohoto kouzelného kakemona byla vedena tekoucí řeka, z níž vyplouvaly ryby s průsvitnými samaragdovými ploutvemi a nachovým podbřišším, a plavnost této řeky a mrštnost ryb mistrně byly přizpůsobeny chvějnému vlnění kakemona.

The narrator's 'kouzelný' is a further hint at his predilecton for magic and the supernatural. Compromising is also 'tekoucí řeka'. By attributing 'tekoucí' to 'řeka', the narrator wants us to understand that the river in the painting looks as if it were really flowing. The author, however, expects us to see the attribution of 'tekoucí' to 'řeka' as ultimately tautological if 'tekoucí' refers to the flowing of water, and invites us to eliminate this tautology by assuming that 'tekoucí' here refers more to runniness of colour. The use of the verb 'vyplouvat', whose aspect and prefix both create ambiguity, leaves it open whether the fish are continually jumping out and diving in again, or just gradually surfacing. This equivocality will be exploited presently. The wateriness of the kakemono's colours is hinted at once again in the combination of 'průsvitný' and 'samaragdový', where 'průsvitný' subversively attenuates the rich green normally conveyed by 'samaragdový'; as well as in 'nachový', which refers to crimson and purple, but often only that of crepuscular skies and maidenly blushes. It is ironic too that the narrator mentions the colour of only the fins and underbellies of the fish, not only because of the smallness of the area covered, but also because it is precisely these parts that are visible when dead fish float upside-down on the water. In this way, the ambiguity of 'vyplouvat' comes into its own. The dynamism the narrator is trying to convey is undermined also by his allowing nearly all expression of movement in the remainder of this sentence to be carried by a series of abstract nouns. This subversive effect is heightened by the fact that 'mrštnost' may refer only to potential movement, and that 'plavnost' in its present sense is normally used only metaphorically, as in 'plavnost chůze' or 'plavnost posunků'. In 'chvějné vlnění', moreover, the adjective implicitly reduces rather than elaborates on the movement described by the noun. As a result of this covert suppression of dynamism, the narrator's claim that the movement of the fish and the river corresponds to the movement of the kakemono reduces to the assertion that staticness corresponds to staticness. The irony goes still further, however. That the narrator speaks of a masterly adaptation of the movement in the scene to the movement of the material is ridiculous, because he has only just maintained that the movement in the scene is physically determined by the movement of the material.

> V zásuvce třetí?
> Byla pagoda o třinácti střechách, filigránsky ze stříbra vytvořená, neboť tento kov bohatců byl obvyklým uměleckým materiálem v chudinké zemi. Kolem každé ze střech byly útlé zvonečky, uzpůsobené na pouhé zavanutí, jejichž srdečka nebyla větší, nežli je makové zrnko, a každý z diváků byl tajně přesvědčen, že to ani není dílem rukou lidských, že to je pouze pavoučími nožkami vytepáno.

The introductory question here has the same ironic significance as the previous ones. That the pagoda is said to have thirteen roofs, suggests that the narrator, projecting his superstitions into the story, believes the pagoda to be perfect but doomed to destruction, because thirteen, according to an originally Babylonian tradition, is thought to augur not just general misfortune but specifically the destruction of perfection. This implication follows on from the allusion to the narrator's belief in the perfection of the kakemono and ties in with earlier and later hints at the precarious frailty of Lao's ostensible treasures. Another such hint is present in 'pagoda filigránsky ze stříbra vytvořená', because the preference of 'filigránsky ze stříbra' to the standard 'ze stříbrného filigránu' may be taken to imply that the pagoda is not made of silver filigree in the accepted sense, merely of silver that is unusually tenuous and delicate. By allowing the narrator to include 'kov bohatců' and 'v chudinké zemi' in his remark about silver being the usual artistic raw material, the author is suggesting that art in this country is a means of putting on a false show of wealth and also that the silver was made so thin because the artist could not afford to use any more of it. The narrator's use of the biblical 'bohatec' for 'boháč' betrays his religiosity, as, in a lesser way, does his use of the expressive 'chudinký', that reveals special sympathy with poverty. We note also that with 'v chudinké zemi' the narrator has for the first time admitted that this country is poor. This poverty reflects unfavourably on Lao's alleged reputation of wealthiness. The narrator's attitude is also brought out by the terms 'utlý' and 'srdečko' personifying the bells. In '[zvonečky] uzpůsobené na pouhé zavanutí', the author, implicitly depriving 'uzpůsobený' of the intentionality invested in it by the narrator, is suggesting that the wafting referred to as 'zavanutí' is not the least the bells have been made to respond to but the most they are capable of standing up to. The comparison of the clangers in size to poppy-seeds implies furthermore that the whole pagoda is not just tenuous but also minute. At the same time, the choice of the poppy-seed as an object of comparison is meant to suggest that the narrator, of whom it has been implied that he enjoys a dulling of the senses, is particularly familiar with the poppy because he cultivates it for opium. By letting the narrator say 'každý z diváků', the author is again implying that many of those present cannot see. The adverb 'tajně' hints that those who could see thought that they had better keep their opinion to themselves. The narrator's observation that they thought the pagoda was made not by human hand but by the legs of a spider compromises him still further. By confusedly using the verb 'tepat', appropriate only to human hands, of the spiders' legs, instead of a more suitable 'snout', 'příst' or 'soukat', the narrator is unwittingly admitting that the pagoda is more than just ordinarily thin, because what the legs of a spider can hammer out as distinct from merely spin out must be virtually devoid of substance. There is, however, another irony in this passage that is perhaps more significant than the hidden meanings that subvert the description of the pagoda. It resides in the fact that with this description the narrator has for the first time overtly admitted that one of Lao's *objets d'art* is small and delicate, something he has so far been at pains to hide.

> Ale největší světa div byl, že tyto zvonečky skutečně vyzváněly; bylo k tomu ovšem potřebí svatého ticha a sluchu na výsost vypjatého, postihnouti tuto plachou symfonii, jež byla spíše jen jakousi hudební mlhovinou. Na vrcholu stříbrné pagody byla ještě usazena figurka tučného, joviálního bůžka, svolna kývajícího hlavou sem a tam, jako ztělesnění věčného záporu a časné nicotnosti.

That the almost imperceptible ringing of these miniature bells is described as the greatest wonder of the world covertly mocks the narrator's drastically reduced scale of vision, because the concept of wonders of the world associates strongly with colossal monumental edifices and their herculean construction. The choice of the inverted 'světa div', moreover, is not merely poetic but is meant to allow a hint at the narrator's metaphysical orientation that the conventional 'div světa', with its standardly concrete reference, could not convey. The use of 'vyzvánět' in place of the neutral 'zvonit' gives rise to a subversive contrast between the resounding loudness it connotes and the assertion that the bells are barely audible, which the potentially concessive 'ovšem' implicitly heightens rather than tempers. The phrase 'svaté ticho' allows an additional hint at the narrator's religiosity, because the colloquial meaning of 'complete' for 'svatý' that first comes to mind here, familiar from such expressions as 'mít od čeho svatý pokoj', is stylistically incongruous and therefore meant to be discounted. Compromising for the narrator is also '[bylo potřebí sluchu] na výsost vypjatého'. By writing 'navýsost' as two words, and following it with 'vypjatý' instead of the standard 'napjatý', the author, exploiting the potential concreteness of 'vypnout nač' and the appropriateness of the prefix 'vy-' to 'výsost' in this sense, is suggesting that this hearing, as the narrator imagines it, is not so much highly strained as stretched up to great heights. The verb 'postihnout' contributes to this implicit shift from abstract to concrete, since it can mean not only 'to perceive' but also 'to catch up with'. There is, however, another irony behind 'vypjatý'. Since 'vypnout' can also mean 'to switch off', we begin to ask ourselves whether hearing the sounds in question involves not so much to straining our hearing to the limit as switching it off, leaving ourselves free to imagine what we cannot actually hear. The narrator's use of 'plachý' in 'plachá symfonie' provides another hint at the narrator's tendency to personify indiscriminately. His 'jakási hudební mlhovina' is ironic, not simply because the metaphorical comparison with a kind of mist suggests that this music is obscure and formless, but also because the vagueness of 'jakýsi' is comically compounded with the vagueness already in 'mlhovina' in its meaning of 'something resembling a mist'. That these vague sounds are referred to as a symphony heightens the irony because a symphony, as a fully-orchestrated composition, is normally considered to be particularly powerful and dramatic piece of music. The pagoda's inordinate frailty is being hinted at also in 'ještě', by which the narrator means 'also', the author 'still'. It is revealing too that the narrator should think of a god he describes as fat and jovial as representing a negative principle, because this suggests that he is being influenced in his imagination by the condemnation of these qualities his ascetic morality dictates. Indeed even the terms 'tučný' and 'joviální' themselves have pejorative connotations. Implicitly characteristic of the narrator's outlook is also his 'figurka [...] bůžka', which implies that to him 'bůžek' alone does not mean an idol but a real living little god and therefore has to be supplemented by a clarifying 'figurka'.

The rest of the descripton is no less subversive. On reading 'kývající hlavou' after 'joviální', we suppose that this god is nodding. When we came to 'zápor', however, we realize that this god must be shaking his head, not nodding. This makes us read 'kývat' more generally as 'to tilt', 'to swing', and leads us to suspect, now that we know of the pagoda's unusual frailty, that this head is wobbling because the neck is too tenuous to hold it. We are encouraged by 'svolna', which can mean 'slowly' or, in accordance with this implication, 'freely'; and also by 'sem a tam', which suggests irregular, erratic movement. The simile 'jako ztělesnění věčného záporu a časné nicotnosti' with its cumulation of metaphysical terms helps to bring out and covertly ridicule the narrator's attitude. Particularly compromising for the narrator is his inclusion of the conjunction 'a', because we would have preferred to read the simile without it, understanding that temporal nothingness is precisely what the god is eternally negating, not what he is embodying in addition to eternal negation. The surprising revelation that the god embodies also this nothingness reminds us teasingly of the extreme frailty of the pagoda. This irony is enhanced by the fact that 'časný' can mean not only 'temporal' but also 'early'.

> Srdce přátel starého Lao byla až po okraj naplněna mlčenlivou úctou k umění předků, kteří pradávno práchnivějí. Bylo ještě mnoho přihrádek neotevřených a čekalo se, že krása a hodnota dalších předmětů bude vystupňována téměř až do nemožnosti.
>
> Starý Lao dopřál svým přátelům v každém jednotlivém případě nutného časového odstupu, aby se mohli, nabravše dechu, znovu do hlubiny tajuplného v umění ponořiti. Přišlo se i na věci, které byly hotovými zázraky, vyšlými z práce manuální.

That only Lao's friends are mentioned here is odd, because we were told that the audience consisted of both friends and family. This oddity prompts us to suspect that the members of his family are not able to react in the way described, perhaps because they are not present as sentient living beings. This conjecture will receive support very soon. The modification of 'srdce byla [...] naplněna' by 'až po okraj' extends the metaphorical image beyond its conventional bounds and so reduces it to comic literality. By 'umění předků', the narrator means Lao's treasured objects, the author, having insinuated that what passes for antique is not, means an earlier art form. That the respect of Lao's friends for the art of their ancestors is said to be silent therefore leads us to infer that they kept quiet about this, to their minds, superior art in order not to offend Lao's pride in his lesser possessions. The expression '[předky] kteří pradávno práchnivějí', deviates conspicuously from the stock phrase 'či kosti už dávno práchnivějí' which means that someone died long ago. This invites us to suppose that what is meant is not so much that these ancestors died very long ago, but that they are literally taking a very long time to decay, perhaps because, as we suspected before, they are merely present in the form of spirit tablets, and as such have been mouldering away on the family altar for generations. This hint in turn prompts us to suspect that Lao's family may amount to no more than such a collection of ancestral tablets and so provides covert support for the previous suggestion that the members of his family are perhaps not present as sentient living beings. The main irony in this passage revolves around 'čekalo se', which can convey expectation or the simple act of waiting. Based on this ambiguity, what we understand may be that ever more valuable items were expected or that Lao deliberately had everyone waiting until the next item grew in value over time. The subversive picture that emerges makes a mockery of the claim about the value of the objects by showing it to be not a piece of conventional rhetoric but the literal reflection of an absurd strategy of deception. The expression 'krása a hodnota dalších předmětů' is no less subversive. By allowing 'hodnota' to follow 'krása', and 'krása' therefore to be in our minds when we read 'hodnota', the author is implying that 'hodnota' does not mean concrete, material value, as it normally does when used of objects and as the narrator would like us to think it does, but, like 'krása', abstract, immaterial value. This follows up the earlier suggestion that the alleged irreplaceability of Lao's objects is subjective rather than objective. In 'téměř až do nemožnosti', the inclusion of the restrictive 'téměř' makes it difficult to understand 'až do nemožnosti' in its standard hyperbolic meaning of 'extremely', 'to the hilt', and therefore tempts us to read 'nemožnost' here more in the colloquial sense of 'impracticability', 'ridiculousness'. The specification 'v každém jednotlivém případě' leaves it open whether Lao allows sufficient time between each showing, as the narrator wishes us to believe, or between any two invitations to the same individual, as the author is suggesting. This gives us the impression that Lao punishes with suspension anyone who was not sufficiently appreciative. By combining 'nabravše dechu' with 'ponořit', and 'ponořit' with 'do hlubiny', the author is overstretching each metaphor to produce another ironically concrete iamge. The terms 'tajuplný' and 'zázrak' bring out once again the narrator's metaphysical involvement. The same is true, if less directly, of 'hlubina', which associates with such expressions as 'hlubina pekelní', 'v hlubinách duše' and Komenský's famous 'hlubina bezpečnosti'. The inclusion of 'i' in 'přišlo se i na věci', introducing the claim that some of the remaining objects are miracles of craftsmanship, comically suggests that the narrator is secretly aware of the fact that the weird and wonderful objects encountered hitherto were by no means miraculous. The adjective 'hotový' has pejorative connotations because of its colloquial humorous emphatic use in phrases like 'hotový blbec' and 'hotový nesmysl'. It is worth noting too that in the phrase 'vyšlý z práce manuální', the abstract 'vyšlý' tends to belie the concreteness we would normally associate with 'práce manuální', and so mocks the narrator's lack of realism. What is more, the narrator's preference of the formal 'manuální práce' to the more common 'ruční práce', or even to some more appropriate expression like 'umělecká obratnost', mockingly reveals his condescending discriminatory attitude to manual labour.

> Byla to na příklad krátká bambusová tyč, do jejíhož povrchu byl vyryt ve znacích v podstatě celý obsažný výtah z mravouky Konfuciovy. Nebylo zase ovšem nikoho, kdo by se hodlal těmi kuriosními, posvátnými záznamy probíjeti, a přece měla tato hůlka v svém významu závažnost pěti knih thory, plných moudrosti a zasvěcení.

By allowing the seemingly redundant specification 'povrch', the author is hinting that the engraving is unusually superficial. The phrase 've znacích' may mean that the text is in code or that it is simply in Chinese characters. The ambiguity becomes relevant in our interpretation of 'kuriosní' and 'probíjet'. For the narrator both terms are meant to be explained by the text's being in code, while for the author, who knows that it is in ordinary writing, they are explained rather by the faintness, and probably also diminutiveness, of the inscription. In 'v podstatě celý obsažný výtah', the terms 'v podstatě' and 'vý-tah' contrast subversively with 'celý' and 'obsažný'. This reflects ironically on the length and import of the text and also brings out the narrator's peculiarly abstract understanding of content. The inclusion of 'ovšem' in the assertion that there was nobody who might decide to tackle the text implicitly refers back to the earlier insinuation of general illiteracy. The surreptitious conversion of the initial 'tyč' into 'hůlka' at this later stage prompts us to see the allegedly spiritually edifying significance of the cane not in the meaning of the moralizing text, as the narrator wishes us to, but in the fact that the cane represents a well-tried means of chastisement. The reference to the Torah, together with the use of 'posvátný' before it, covertly identifies the narrator's strangely eclectic religiosity. His attitude is ironized also in the combination 'moudrost a zasvěcení', which suggests that he cares most for wisdom of an esoteric kind.

> Ještě se [...] objevila před zraky obdivovatelů mnohá kouzla, vyšlá z lidského důmyslu a mravenčí přičinlivosti, jako byla maloúnká pětistrunná lyra, vydlabaná do kamenitého fíkového dřeva, jejíž struny nahradily převzácné rudé vlasy; nebo prsten z jediného kusu onyxu v podobě svinuté černé kobry, jejíž otrávený zub mohl se ihned vyprázdniti, jakmile byl prsten navlečen člověku podarovanému. Nikdy se však nevyskytlo ani nejslabší pomyšlení na tuto možnost a prsten odpočíval tiše a nevýhružně, jako je spánek skutečného jeskynního hada z pohádky.

By including '[před zraky] obdivovatelů', the author is implying that the alleged wonders were seen only by those already disposed to admire. The word 'kouzlo' shows up again the narrator's involvement in magic and romanticism. In 'mravenčí přičinlivost', the adjective, that seems to be only standardly symbolic of the industriousness at issue, is, particularly by virtue of the contrast with the previous 'lidský', hinting subsversively at the diminutiveness of the objects. The narrator's 'malounká [lyra]', we suspect, understates this diminutiveness here. This point will be developed. That the lyre, in '[lyra] vydlabaná do [...] dřeva', is said to be chiselled into wood, not out of it, as we would have expected, suggests that it is an abortive product. The use of 'vydlabaný' instead of an equally possible 'vyrytý' or 'vyřezaný' to describe the fashioning of the fig-wood covertly mocks the narrator's exaggerated sense of hardness, because in normal parlance 'dlabat' has strong associations of forceful chipping and hewing that are comically out of keeping with the unusual softness characteristic of fig-wood. The same oversensitivity comes through also in 'kamenité [fíkové dřevo]', which suggests that the narrator considers the zones of coarser fibre that alternate with the softer fibre in this wood to be like stones. That the narrator imagines the lyre to be made of fig-wood hints at his religiosity, because the fig-tree is an Old Testament symbol of Messianic peace and prosperity. The revelation that the string of the lyre were replaced by hairs is amusing, not only because it retrospectively overstretches 'pětistrunný', but also because we suspect that the reason for this substitution is probably that the lyre is too small for strings of whatever size made from normal material. The adjective 'převzácný' equivocates ironically between 'very exquisite' and 'excessively weird'. By telling us that the ring is made of a single piece of onyx and is black, the author, expecting us to know that onyx consists of very thin differently coloured layers, is leading us to conclude that this object too is unusually small. That the cobra is said to have one fang and not two implicitly confirms this conclusion, because it suggests that one fang is all there was room for. What is more, since cobras are both very long and quite large, the fang in question must be tiny in relation to the coiled body, the amount of poison it can contain therefore microscopic. This implication finds covert support in 'ihned', because the immediacy of the emptying may easily be ascribed to an extreme paucity of content. The reason why nobody ever thought to use the ring for its ostensible purpose is for the author not that everyone here is virtuous, as the narrator would like us to believe, but that the ring is obviously too small to be put on. The expression 'nevyskytlo se [...] pomyšlení', treating an intention as if it were a material object, covertly mocks the narrator's tendency to confuse abstract and concrete. Contributory to the ironic characterization of the narrator is also the personificatory '[prsten] odpočíval tiše a nevýhružně'. The simile of the serpent compromises the narrator still further. On careful reading, we realize that the reposing snake-formed ring is being compared not to a sleeping serpent, as we would expect, but to a serpent's sleep. This is comic, because it means that 'tiše' and 'nevýhružně' describe also this sleep, as if to say that the serpent in question is not having scary nightmares but dreaming sweetly. The implicitly contradictory combination of 'skutečný' and 'z pohádky' provides another hint at the narrator's disturbed attitude to reality.

> Lao však nezmalomyslněl ve chvilce smrti a díval se jí do očí mírně, ač neohroženě. Shromáždil své děti, praděti a přátele a dal jim nahlédnouti do přihrádky poslední. Nalezli v ní uzrálý, zlatový, mastný klas kukuřice a rozsochatý klas rýže. Neboť to bylo nejdrahocennější rukojmí za život a blaho této nesmírné a chudinké země.

The concessive 'však' subversively suggests that the narrator considers losing heart in the face of death to be the normal course of events. This is an ironic hint at his inability to achieve the stoic composure his religiosity would normally be thought to confer. His preference of 'zmalomyslnět' to the more common 'pozbýt odvahy' and 'klesnout na mysli' comports with this religiosity, because, unlike its alternatives, 'zmalomyslnět' can be used to mean 'to become faint-hearted' in the religious sense of 'to lose trust in God'. In 've chvilce smrti', the use of diminutive 'chvilka' is meant to suggest that Lao's supposed steadfastness was extraordinarily short-lived. The expression '[Lao] díval se jí [smrti] do očí' ties in with previous hints at the narrator's tendency to personify even the abstract. Implicitly characteristic of the narrator is also 'mírně, ač neohroženě', because the use of 'ač' in place of the expected 'a' prompts us to infer that the narrator is so timid that he considers boldness or dauntlessness normally inconsistent with peace of mind. Even 'shromáždit' is ironic here, because in view of the narrator's tendency to confuse animate and inanimate it is not without connotations of piling or heaping up. The use of the exceptional and potentially vague 'praděti' lends support to the implication that Lao has no progeny, because it suggests that the narrator is once more going to considerable lengths to avoid a geneologically definitive 'vnuci'.[250] When we read the description of the cob of maize and the ear of rice adds to the irony, we are initially seduced into believing that the maize and the rice are real. The image of ripe, succulent maize and rich ears of corn seems irresistible and we cannot help feeling that the ensuing contrast between the lofty aspirations of art and the biological and economic realites of life gives the story a persuasive final twist. But just as we are ready to embrace this sanguine philosophical message, we suddenly realize that something

---

250 The word 'praděti' is included neither in the four-volume *Slovník spisovného jazyka českého* (Prague, 1971) nor in the nine-volume *Příruční slovník jazyka českého* (Prague, 1935–57). We have found it only in *Allgemeines Handwörterbuch der böhmischen und deutschen Sprache*, edited by Josef Rank, ninth edition, 2 vols (Prague, Vienna, Leipzig, 1920), I; and in *Česko-anglický slovník*, edited by H.T. Cheshire et al. (Prague, 1935). Both these dictionaries give the meaning 'great-grandchildren'. This meaning can hardly be applied straighforwardly to the present context, because in the phrase 'děti, praděti a přátelé', 'praděti' immediately follows 'děti'.

is seriously amiss. If the cob of maize and the ear of rice have been locked away in a drawer for such a long time, how can it be that they are now ripe, instead of being completely dessicated and possibly even rotting? No sooner have we asked ourselves this question than we are driven to understand the author's inexorable conclusion: the cob of maize and the ear of corn are not real but themselves mere objets d'art. The seemingly so fitting punch-line is thus ironically relativized. What is more, the attributes of these objects fail to convince. Implicitly eclipsing 'zlatý', 'zlatový' insinuates that the maize is not truly golden even now. The seemingly so promising 'mastný' becomes something of an embarrassment, because we now find it difficult to imagine how the characteristic in question could be discerned from a mere representation. It therefore becomes more attractive to follow the author's implication that 'mastný' does not have objective reference but merely reflects the narrator's squeamish dislike of starchy food. The use of 'rozsochatý' implicitly exemplifies the narrator's reduced scale of vision, since 'rozsochatý' is normally used of much larger objects like trees. At the same time, it suggests that the rice too is of poor quality, since a single branching of the ear is not much and would not normally be considered worthy of special attention. The covert substitution of 'rukojmí' ('hostage') for the more natural 'záruka' ('guarantee') not only brings out the narrator's tendency to personify but also provides a stark hint at the sheer desperation to which the poverty in this land gives rise. The combination 'život a blaho', finally, tends to confirm our suspicion that the narrator's conception of life is religiously sublimated.

Our analysis has shown that 'Čínská povídka' evinces the same structural irony as the previous texts and makes use of a very similar ironic characterization of the narrator. The only new features in the narrator's ironic make-up are the extreme senility he shares with the protagonist and his drastically reduced scale of vision. It may, however, be assumed that the introduction of these features is merely a specific contextual response to the subject-matter.

Through the irony the central elements of the story are radically transformed. The old man is revealed as lifeless, extraordinarily timid and broody, illiterate and by no means wealthy. It is also suggested that he is childless, and possibly even without living relatives. His cabinet, that we first assume to be of normal size and material consistency, is gradually shown to be extraordinarily diminutive and fragile. Far from harbouring the spectacular artistic treasures the narrator would have us believe in, the drawers are seen to contain nothing more than a collection of weird and worthless objects.[251]

---

251 What Opolský is ironically referring to here is the traditional Chinese miniature curio cabinet (Chin. *duobaoge*, 'box of many treasures'), a casket with many drawers and compartments used to house tiny *objets d'art* that was first produced in the Jiangnan region of China (south of the Yang-tse) in the late Ming dynasty and popularized during the reign of the Emperor Qianlong (r. 1736–95) in the early Qing. This new mode of semi-permanent display replaced earlier habits

Many of the props in Opolský's story are reminiscent of Zeyer's 'Zrada v domě Han', with its fragrant woods and gentle breezes, its blue- and golden-scaled dragons, its silver snakes and swarms of butterflies, its fish with metalically flashing scales, its peacock and pheasant feathers, and its vases made of translucent porcelain; as well as his 'Večer u Idalie', with its kakemonos, black lacquer objects and diminutive model village. The oblique references to puppets and the puppet theatre are evocative of Karásek's 'Sen o říši krásy'. But Opolský is not imitating Zeyer or Karásek, but indirectly poking fun at them. However, it is doubtful whether Opolský intends his story to be read as a parody. Parody presupposes recogniton of the original in the reader and this seems unlikely given the time span between Zeyer and Karásek's productions and Opolský's. It is more likely that Opolský, like a true ironist, intends the reader to read the text on its own terms without reference to outside models. If there is an element of parody here nonetheless, it would mean that 'Čínská povídka' may to some extent be thought to share in a minor tradition of Zeyer parodies, some of which were specifically directed at his obsession with China, such as Bohdan Kaminský's 'Neštěstí v zahradě kvetoucích kaktusů' and Josef Svatopluk Machar's, 'Čína a Číňan'.[252]

of viewing collections only on specific occasions or the use of antiques as household furnishing. The *duobaoge* is presumed to have evolved from the travelling cases used by itinerant scholars to hold their brushes, inkstones, combs, perfume flacons, and other utensils. Opolský remains largely faithful to the Chinese context, though he anachronistically combines the use of the *duobaoge* with earlier viewing habits. It is worth noting that the irony is achieved not so much by deviating from the reality of the Chinese context as by allowing the reader to build up false expectations that the introduction of this less familiar reality then subverts.

252 Bohdan Kaminský, 'Neštěstí v zahradě kvetoucích kaktusů', *Verše humoristické a satirické* (Prague, 1893); Josef Svatopluk Machar, 'Čína a Číňan', *Rozhledy*, 4 (1884/1885), pp. 25–28.

10. ZRADA[252]

On the surface, 'Zrada' tells the story of an accomplished Venetian glass-blower of the Renaissance called Giacomo Tartaglio/Tartaglia (henceforth Tartaglio).[254] Despite the profound inspiration he derives from the distinctive beauty of his native city, the protagonist is deeply dissatisfied with the meagre professional opportunities afforded to him by a parsimonious and repressive regime. Braving the threat of imprisonment, he flees the country, taking with him the closely guarded secrets of his trade.[255] Having disclosed everything he knows to his eager foreign pupils, he commits suicide, plagued by pangs of conscience at his traitorous action. Below the surface, however, a rather different picture begins to emerge. Even the detailed descriptions

---

253 Jan Opolský, 'Zrada', *Hranolem křišťálu* (Prague, 1944), pp. 15–20.

254 The name has probably been borrowed from a real personage. Giacomo Tartaglio a. k. a. Tartaglia (1678–1751) was a carver and sculptor of the Settecento from Trapani, Sicily, who worked in wood, marble and alabaster (*pietra incarnata*). His best known work is a procession scene known as *Il Trasporto al Sepolcro*, including figures of Joseph of Aramathea, Mary, Mary Magdalen, St. John and Nicodemus. It is displayed every year in Trapani during *Settimana Santa* in the traditional *Processione dei Misteri*. He also produced a marble statue of Philip V, and figures of the dead Christ, St. Francis and St. Rosalia. It is generally accepted that his correct name is Tartaglio despite the fact that the street named after him in Trapani is the Via Giacomo Tartaglia. That Opolský equivocates between the forms 'Tartaglio' and 'Tartaglia' in this story indicates that he was aware of this historical namesake. For the sake of convenience I shall adhere to 'Tartaglio'.

What may also have recommended the name to Opolský is the fact that Tartaglia was the name of an outstanding comic character in the Italian *Commedia dell'arte*. Believed to have been created by Carlo Gozzi in Naples in 1610, the figure of Tartaglia, typically cast as an official of Spanish extraction, had a heavy stutter ('Tartaglia' has echoes of Sp. *tartamudear* 'to stutter'), spoke Italian badly and was hard of hearing. As a result, he invariably distorted the content of the messages he was entrusted with, often creating vulgar *double entendres* by stammering at strategic moments. Standardly bald, pot-bellied and shortsighted, he wore a large grey felt hat, a green robe with yellow stripes, an enormous cloak, oversized boots and overlarge green or blue spectacles. See especially Maurice Sand, *Masques et bouffons* (Paris, 1860). The plays of the *Commedia dell'arte* were popular in Bohemia from the eighteenth century onwards in both human and puppet-theatre versions.

255 This is an oblique reference to the historical fact that Venetian glassblowers were sworn to secrecy on pain of death. That the glassblowing industry was exiled to the island of Murano in 1291, ostensibly to protect the city's wooden buildings from fire, is generally thought to have been motivated by the desire to prevent glassblowers from fleeing. In 1295 a law was passed forbidding glassmakers from leaving the city. However, far from being poorly treated the artisans enjoyed a privileged social status with many benefits.

of the art of glass-blowing and its history contained in the piece take on a different complexion[256]

> Benátský stát kromě svých politicky i přírodně nejistých hranic žárlivě střežil svoje umění, plně rozkvetlé jako terč slunečnice v blahodějném záhřevu renesance. Zvon s kampanily chrámu Marie dei Frari, kde byl pochován Tizián v královské slávě, zněl do uší obecného měšťanstva, dožat i samotné Velké rady jako varovné volání, aby se umění domovu nezcizilo a jeho květní vůně za nechráněné duchové hranice nevyvanula.

We can understand '[kromě] svých politicky i přírodně nejistých hranic' in two ways, depending on the geographical perspective we adopt. If we focus on Venice's terrestrial borders, it seems reasonable to think of '[kromě] svých politicky i přírodně nejistých hranic' as referring to a lack of natural boundaries and the territorial disputes that frequently ensue. However, if we focus on Venice's more familiar maritime borders, we suddenly find ourselves wondering whether the problem might not be more a matter of watery instability and indiscernible location. The description of contemporary Venetian art as 'plně rozkvetlé jako terč slunečnice' harbours a more trenchant irony. Sunflowers may impress us with the length of their stems and the size and brilliance of their heads, but we should not allow ourselves to be taken in. The circular inner head referred to by 'terč' is nothing more than a cluster of tiny florets that later mature into seeds. As a result, the narrator's claim that Venetian art of the period is in full bloom is neatly undermined.[257] His case is also weakened by the connotations of artificiality that attach to the word 'terč', which standardly means 'target (disc)'. No less compromising for the narrator is 'v blahodějném záhřevu renesance'. With the Renaissance we as-

---

256 Originating from Northern Bohemia and being a professional craftsman, Opolský may well have felt a close connection with the art of glass-making. Glass-making in Northern Bohemia goes back to the late thirteenth century. It was popular under Rudolf II but did not reach industrial-scale production until the middle of the nineteenth century. The first area to develop was the region of Česká Kamenice, with important centres in Kamenický Šenov and Nový Bor, producing red, blue and yellow glass decorated with hunting scenes for a mass market. The first schools were set up here in 1856 and 1870 respectively. The Vienna Exhibition of 1873 gave the new industry international prominence. A second area developed in the Jizera Mountains (Jizerské hory), with centres in Jablonec, Smržovka and Tanvald. The northern Bohemian 'Glass Road' eventually also found its way to Harrachov, some twenty-five miles from Nová Paka, Opolský's home town. Later glass-making extended to the Bohemian Forest (Sázava) in the south and to Teplice and the western spas (Karlovy Vary, Mariánské Lázně, Františkovy Lázně). See Kurt Pittrof, *Böhmisches Glas im Panorama der Jahrhunderte* (Munich, 1987).
257 Opolský may also be poking fun at Oscar Wilde and the English Aesthetic Movement. Because of its flamboyance, the sunflower was one of Oscar Wilde's favourite flowers. He is said to have decorated his rooms with sunflowers, lilies and peacock feathers, and he famously wore a sunflower in his lapel on a visit to New York.

sociate a resurgence of vitality, a bursting of fetters, an explosion of creativity, an overflowing of sensuality, a celebration of Petrarchan *goia di vivere* and Boccaccian hedonism. That the narrator should speak of this dramatic and stimulating epoch as if it were akin to the experience of an old lady basking in the gentle warmth of the evening sun is the first poignant hint at his significant lack of vitality. The irony in the remainder of this passage is created mainly by a subtle skewing of the narrative line. The assertion that Venice jealously guarded its art, that forms the core of the previous sentence, gives rise to expectations about what will follow. We feel entitled to expect some further indication of the quality and value of Venetian art and some indication of how it was guarded. When we look at what actually follows, we can see that this expectation is both acknowledged and conspicuously undercut. The mention of Titian reminds us of a great Venetian painter and the reference to his majestic tomb emphasizes his importance. But this information is clearly unsatisfactory. Not only is there no mention of living artists, but the very reference to a solitary dead master makes us wonder whether the heyday of Venetian art is not long since past. It is only in his belated reference to its flowery scent that the narrator finally returns to the quality of contemporary Venetian art. But again we are sold short. His description tells us next to nothing, and the author's artful substitution of coldly botanical 'květní vůně' for the sensually more evocative 'květinová vůně' ironically emphasizes its vacuity. Similarly, the narrator's remark about the church bell ringing out its warning message both acknowledges the need to elaborate on the way Venice guards its art and fails to satisfy it. Initially we are seduced by the narrator's bold metaphor, but the author is hoping that we will see our way to questioning it. He would like us to see that the connection between the bell ringing and the complex socio-political message it is meant to be conveying is spurious. There is no reason for attributing this particular message to the bell beyond the fact that the bell belongs to the church in which Titian is buried. However, the imaginative gap between the alleged content of the message and the presence of Titian's tomb is difficult to bridge. The author is happy for us to try, perhaps by asking ourselves whether the idea behind the message is not that artists forsaking their country will miss the opportunity of a royal send-off, but he hopes that we will finally give up and accept the arbitrary nature of the narrator's attribution. To encourage us to do so, he has been careful to specify 'zvon z kampanily Marie dei Frari', making it as clear as he can without giving the game away that this particular bell is merely one of many and has therefore been arbitrarily singled out as the bearer of the message. But the irony does not stop with this skewing of the narrative line. That the narrator thinks of the sound of the bell as having to work its way up a social hierarchy of ears, from those of the common populace to those of the Grand Council, mockingly reveals his snobbish-

ness.[258] This implication is underscored by 'samotný'. In 'aby se umění dom-
ovu nezcizilo', the author is playing on the ambiguity of 'zcizit' to suggest that
what is really at issue is not that great works of art might be stolen but that
art might somehow become alienated, thus ironically begging the question of
the art's material value. In 'vyvanula', there is a similar equivocation between
the idea of the scent being wafted away and the more subversive notion of it
simply evaporating.

> Zemské pomezí bylo tudíž opatrováno valy a příkopy naplňovanými bahnitou
> vodou, hustě je přerývaly záseky a vlčí jámy, ale panovala krom toho též snaha, aby
> duchové hranice, pokud se dalo, byly ještě nepřestupnější.

By launching into a detailed account of boundary fortifications, the narrator is implicitly trying to make up for his failure to provide a satisfactory
explanation of how Venice guarded its art. He does so with a vengeance and at
first we are impressed by the imposing array of ramparts, moats, abatis and
wolf traps, but on reflection doubts begin to creep in. The main problem is
that the narrator, going on to mention the even greater impermeability of the
spiritual boundaries, has effectively admitted that the fortifications he has so
painstakingly itemized are all but irrelevant to his case. There is even a problem with some of the individual items. By letting the narrator say 'příkopy
naplňovanými bahnitou vodou' instead of 'příkopy naplněnými bahnitou
vodou', the author is prompting us to understand that the moats were not
filled with water which in time became muddy, as we would expect, but that
the moats were constantly being re-filled with water that was already muddy.
This is rather strange and suggests that in the narrator's opinion the principal
deterrent was not the forbidding depth of the moats but the horrible muddi-
ness of the water. Another difficulty here stems from the fact that moats were
standardly used as a fortification for castles. The use of the moats to protect
the frontiers of a whole state therefore seems oddly half-hearted. The narrator's claim that the border region was transsected by abatis and wolf-traps
also gives cause for concern. While 'přerývat' is literally appropriate to the
wolf-traps which have had to be dug out of the ground, it is only metaphorically appropriate to 'záseky', because abatis are not cut out of the ground but
erected on top of it. Given the difficulty of accommodating both literal and
metaphorical meanings in the same word, we automatically try to resolve the
contradiction. The only way to do this is to consider the possibility of reading

---

258   This may be a sidesweep at John Ruskin, who, in his *magnum opus The Stones of Venice*, 3 vols (London, 1898), not only celebrated the Doge's Palace as the apotheosis of Western architecture but
also proclaimed Venice's system of government with its election of the 'worthiest and noblest' to
be a perfect political system. Ruskin was popularized in the Bohemia by critic F. X. Šalda and the
group around *Volné směry*.

'záseky' literally as well. Of course, this is not possible in the sense of 'abatis', but it is possible if we read 'záseky' in its alternative meaning of 'notches', 'incisions', 'cavities', especially if we remember that in mining 'záseky' can refer to cuts made during the exploratory excavation of the rockface. This in turn prompts us to ask ourselves whether the 'záseky' here are not abatis but holes hewn into the ground, perhaps traces of exploratory mining or unsuccessful quarrying.[259] The connection with defence measures is thereby subtly undermined. The mention of the wolf-traps supports this irony in another way too. Since wolf-traps placed along a border would obviously be there to keep wolves out, not to keep them in, the orientation of the alleged defence efforts is subtly reversed, thus further subverting the narrator's argument. The allegation about the spiritual boundaries is also compromised. In 'panovala snaha', the author is using the implications of stability and invariance that attach to 'panovat' ('panoval/-a/-o pořádek/ čistota/ ticho') to undermine the sense of focused activity and will to change normally present in 'snaha'. This again brings out the lack of vitality that is a central element in the ironic stylization of the narrator

Jak můžeme však býti jasně poučeni dějinami světa, ztroskotávala v tom směru každá lidská povaha, neboť pro umění není žádných reálných ani pomyslných hranic. Položivé fantomy Giottovy a plaší cherubové Fra Angelika přeletují na všecka cizí duchovní území a architektury Sansovina a Paladia vrhají do budoucnosti svůj vznešený obrys a stín.

The narrator's revelation at the end of the last passage that Venetians tried to make the spiritual borders even more impermeable than the terrestrial ones is crying out for explanation. We would very much like to know how they went about this daunting task. The terrestrial borders have been dealt with in considerable detail, even though we could easily have imagined for ourselves how terrestrial borders might be secured. It is far more difficult to imagine what the Venetians might have done to secure their spiritual borders, but much as we may wish for edification on this point, details are conspicuously lacking. By allowing the narrator to default on our expectations in this way, the author is prompting us to suspect that he would have considerable difficulty substantiating his claim. It therefore makes sense for him to retreat to the safer ground of what appears to be a historical-philosophical truism. But even here the author will not allow him to escape

259 Built on a lagoon, the city of Venice famously lacked the stone needed for its construction. High quality stone was at a premium and most of it was quarried in Istria, both within the confines of the Venetian state (around Rovinj, Pula and Portorož) and beyond (around Triest). Stone of inferior quality of stone was quarried closer to hand, in the area around Brescia in Lombardy, also within the Republic of Venice.

unscathed. The pronouncement with which the narrator begins this passage is undermined in several ways. In 'jak můžeme však býti jasně poučeni', the author is exploiting the subtle semantic tension between the potentiality of 'můžeme [...] býti' and the emphatic assertiveness of 'jasně' to suggest that the narrator is not as convinced of the truth of this claim as he pretends to be. There is a similar ironic tension in 'ztroskotávala každá povaha', where the author is using the static 'povaha' to undermine the dramatic dynamism of 'ztroskotávala'. The main irony, however, comes in the narrator's assertion that for art there are no real or imaginary boundaries. What the author is trying to elicit from us here is not undivided assent but the realization that only someone who is completely alienated from reality would find it necessary to point out that something which is imaginary does not exist. The narrator's problematic relationship to reality also comes out in the metaphor of the flying phantoms and cherubs that now follows. That the narrator has chosen precisely those figures that would be able to fly not just metaphorically but also literally leads to a disorientating conflation of the metaphorical and the literal that implicitly characterizes the narrator's vision and leaves us wondering whether we should not take this literality further and think of the phantoms and cherubs as having absconded from the pictures they were in, leaving these sadly depleted. The seemingly innocent insertion of 'plaší [cherubové]' covertly supports this ironic interpretation by allowing for the possibility that the cherubs may have been frightened off. The author is also exploiting the ambiguity of 'položivé [fantomy]', which could express admiration for painted figures that seem to be almost alive or disappointment at representations that seem rather lifeless. Even the phrase 'přeletují na všecka cizí [...] území' is problematic because, by focusing on the direction of their flight, it leaves it open whether the phantoms and cherubs ever arrive at their foreign destinations. The narrator fares no better with his reference to the architecture of Sansovino and Palladio.[260] At first glance, the metaphor of buildings casting imposing shadows into the future is a striking expression of the timelessness of art. What undermines it is the way it allows the image of urban palazzi with elegant stucco facades that first comes to mind when we hear the names of the architects to recede behind a vision of chimerical black-and-white outlines. Matters do not improve with 'vznešený', which can be understood as meaning 'distinguished', 'sublime', but also as connoting airy elevation above concrete, physical reality. The narrator's sensibility

---

260 Jacopo d'Antonio Sansovino (1485–1570) and Andrea Palladio (1508–1580) were leading Renaissance architects who both left their stamp on Venice. Sansovino is famous for the Libreria Marciana opposite the Doge's Palace, Palladio for the churches of San Giorgio Maggiore on the island of San Giorgio di Castellone and Il Santissimo Redentore on the island of Guidecca. Palladio founded a style of architecture that remained influential well into the nineteenth century. Examples in Bohemia include the Villa Kačina near Kutná Hora.

is also being gently mocked in 'obrys a stín'. We can regard this expression as largely tautological, since, when you are talking about the silhouette of a building, contour and shadow are simply different aspects of the self-same thing. The author, however, would like us to consider the possibility that 'obrys' and 'stín' (shadow/shade) are independently meaningful, because the narrator is not only interested in the silhouettes of buildings but also in the shade they give. That the narrator secretly longs for relief from the heat of the southern sun is an implication which will be picked up again later.

> A že také jiným způsobem může býti umění odevzdáno do cizího duševního majetku, chceme následujícím způsobem osvědčiti. Benátské sklenářství mezi mnoha uměleckými odvětvími svým stářím temenilo až k mythické době Etrusků, kteří byli uměleckými praučiteli Italie. Vdechujíce ušlechtilou duši sklovinám, hlíně a alabastru, v pradávnu už stali se zvěstovateli benátského umění sklářského, jež bylo plno formového a světelného kouzla a výmluvnosti.

When the narrator now tells us that there are other ways in which ownership of art may be transferred, and offers to provide evidence of this, we are right to be perplexed. If his previous assertion is to be understood as a metaphorical expression of art's ability to overcome spatial and temporal boundaries, it makes little sense to talk about alternative scenarios. This only makes sense, if we consider the description of the activity of the phantoms, cherubs and silhouettes to be something more akin to a listing of literal examples. However, if we go down this interpretative route, the narrator's pronouncement about alternative ways of transferring ownership becomes ridiculous, because nobody in their right mind would assume that the only way art could be transmitted was through the agency of flying spirits and time-travelling shadows. The narrator's case is further subverted by the surreptitious substitution of 'sklenářství' for 'sklářství', creating the impression that the Venetian glasswork he is speaking about has less in common with the high art of the glass-blower than with the common craft of the glazier. There is a similar substitution in '[sklenářství] temenilo až k [...] době [Etrusků]'. When the verb 'temenit se' is used in connection with 'doba', the expression that unfailingly comes to mind is 'temenit z doby čeho'. By allowing the expected 'temenit z doby čeho' to be replaced by the wholly unexpected 'temenit až po době čeho', which relies on 'temenit' being read not in its usual sense of 'derive from', 'go back to' but in the rarer sense of 'rise up', the author is slyly mocking the narrator's infatuation with the ancient Etruscans. That this infatuation is based more on legend than fact is hinted at in '[k] mythické [době Etrusků]'. The narrator's case is further weakened by 'svým stářím', which makes it clear that it is age not stature that is at issue, and by 'mezi mnoho uměleckými odvětvími', which conspicuouly fails to make a reliable semantic connection between the art forms mentioned and the pedigree claimed for Venetian glass. The characterisation of the Etruscans as 'primordial teachers' implicitly reveals the narrator's occult hankerings.[261] The irony in 'vdechujíc [...] duši sklovinám, hlíně a alabastru' is dependent on the way the semantic structure of the metaphor changes as the series of dative complements progresses. When 'vdechovat duši' is read in relation to the initial 'sklovinám', the act of blowing in the source corresponds to a physical act of blowing in the target (glass is blown into shape). When 'vdechovat duši' is then read in relation to 'hlíně', the act of blowing in the source clearly no longer corresponds to a physical act of blowing in the target (clay is not blown but moulded), though it may be taken to correspond to a metaphysical act of blowing (the blowing of life into clay/dust according to Genesis 2:7 and the consequent blowing of life into a clay golem according to Prague Jewish legend). However, when 'vdechovat duši' is read in relation to the final 'alabastru', the act of blowing in the source now corresponds to nothing at all in the target beyond a generalized act of artistic creation (alabaster is not blown or blown into, physically or metaphysically, but carved). The effect of this gradually shifting perspective is subtle. By allowing the verb that gives the metaphor its force to be progressively reduced from the physical to the metaphysical to the purely notional, the author is slowly taking the wind out of the narrator's sails, thereby mocking his imagery and the imagination that produced it. What is more, the use of the imperfective 'vdechovat', which can convey not only repeated but also incomplete action, leaves it tellingly open whether the 'ušlechtilá duše' ever arrived at its destination. The narrator's claim that the Etruscans were the harbingers of the Venetian art of glassblowing is variously subversive. Since the relative clause 'jež bylo plno formového a světelného kouzla a výmluvnosti' can be both non-defining and defining, and its head 'Benátské umění sklářské', can be both a determinate and an indeterminate noun phrase, we are left with compromising possibility that what the Etruscan practices adumbrated was not so much the Venetian art that actually ensued and happened to have the qualities commended but

---

261 'Urlehrer' (primordial teacher) was one of the favourite terms of the Austrian anthroposophist Rudolf Steiner (1861–1926). According to Steiner, the 'Mondenmenschen', spiritual beings who in ancient times lived with mankind on earth and now observe everything we do from the spiritual sphere of the moon, are the 'Urlehrer der Menschheit'. Steiner's teachings were popular in Bohemia and several organizations (the 'Česká antroposofická společnost', the 'Česká společnost theosofická' and its 'Literární kruh') ensured a steady stream of translations from 1907 onwards; see Tomáš Zdražil, *Počátky theosofie a anthroposofie v Čechách* (Příbram, 1997). However, not a few Czech readers must have felt that Steiner's ethereal lunar beings were uncannily reminiscent of the ethereal aesthetes that populate the moon in Svatopluk Čech's famous satire *Výlet pana Broučka do Měsíce* (1888) and found it difficult to take such elements in Steiner's teachings seriously. Opolský may have come into contact with Steiner's teachings through his theosophically-minded friend and mentor Břetislav Jampílek.

a Venetian art that was to have these qualities but never came about. Even the qualities themselves are questionable. By allowing the narrator to insist on form and light, the author is leaving us free to suspect that there may be a corresponding lack of content and substance. The narrator's case is not helped by 'kouzlo', which threatens to relegate the aesthetic appeal to the realms of romantic fancy, and 'vymluvnost', which fails to make it clear whether this art is full of feeling or indicative of incompetence. In this way, one level of irony has been underlaid by another. Finally, let us note in passing that the covert stylization of the narrator has benefited from 'ušlechtilá duše', which suggests a preoccupation with aristocratic moralizing, and from the reference to its infusion into clay, which reveals the narrator's religious and metaphysical preoccupations.

> Křehké sklo jako tvárný materiál v rukou umělcových má mnoho shodných vlastností s kovy, ač se to zdá na první pohled pravdě nepodobno. Ve všech stavech změknutí žárem přivoděného dává se opracovávati jako kovy, jež svou vnitřní podstatu v plamenech proměnily.

The irony here is generated mainly by a discrepancy between banality of content and extravagance of style. It is common knowledge that glass and metal are moulded by heating, so the narrator's revelation falls resoundingly flat. What astounds and amuses us is the degree of affectation and redundancy in his language. We hardly need reminding that glass is brittle and could easily have guessed from the context that it is the brittleness of glass that is at issue. Still less do we need telling that glass and metal in the hands of the artist are 'tvárný materiál', because we would not have assumed otherwise. More importantly, 'sklo [...] má mnoho shodných vlastností s kovy' and 've všech stavech změknutí žárem přivoděného' are just a grossly inflated and unduly cumbersome ways of saying 'glass is a lot like metal' and 'when molten', respectively. The narrator's preference of the stilted 'pravdě nepodobno' over the more usual 'nepravděpodobno' bespeaks affectation. However, it is only when we come to '[kovy] jež svou vnitřní podstatu v plamenech proměnily', that we suddenly begin to see where the narrator is coming from and why he has been labouring the obvious. What we need to understand is that what seems to be merely a poetic metaphor is in fact an expression of the narrator's sincere belief that a change in the properties of a material cannot be due to an incidental change of temperature but must involve a change of its essence. This is a strong indication that the narrator's world view is not informed by science but by medieval doctrines of essence and accident.

> Možno je tekuté líti do nespalitelných forem, úměrným, vypočítavým tlakem lisovati, modelovati formovacími kalenými kleštěmi, dmychačkou vyfukovati v okouzlující

ampule a báně, v utuhlém stavu břitkým démantem rýti a kaliti do závoje jiskrných čar, či přísně tajenými metalickými přísadami barviti je žárnými duhovými záplavami.

Here we find more compromising redundancy of expression. There is no need for 'tekuté', because it is logically entailed by 'líti', just as there is no need for '[do] nespalitelných [forem]', because it is obvious that moulds into which red-hot molten material is poured need to be heat-resistant. Equally, there is no need for 'úměrným, vypočítavým tlakem [lisovati]', because it is clear that materials can only be pressed ('lisovat') using pressure ('tlakem') and that this pressure needs to be appropriate to the task ('úměrným') and carefully controlled ('vypočítavým'). We can happily dispense with 'formo-vacími' because tells us nothing that is not already contained in 'modelovati [...] kleštěmi'. Even 'kalenými' is suspicious because of its unusual position. If it were necessary for the tongs involved in this modelling process to be pre-heated, we would have expected the narrator to say '[modelovati] kalenými formovacími [kleštěmi]', putting 'kalenými' before 'formovacími'. His failure to do so weakens 'kalenými' by relegating it to a subordinate position and makes us suspect that if the tongs were hot, it is not because they needed to be hot from the outset, but because they had become hot by contact with red-hot material. However, if this is the case, 'kalenými' must join the ranks of the tautologically superfluous. The same is true of 'v utuhlém stavu břitkým [démantem rýti]', because it is obvious that only solids can be engraved and that diamonds used for engraving need to be sharp. However, the irony here goes beyond the effect created by simple redundancy. In 'do nespalitelných forem', 'nespalitelný', besides being logically superfluous, implicitly exagger-ates the standard 'nezápalný'. This covert hyperbole ironically emphasizes the narrator's inflationary rhetoric while at the same time revealing a hysterical fear of the heat involved in the production process. That the carefully mea-sured pressure is described as 'vypočítavý' hints at the narrator's tendency to personify indiscriminately. Contributory to the ironic stylisation of the narrator is also 'dmychačkou vyfukovat'. It is common knowledge that glass is blown using a blowpipe (píšťala) and not bellows (dmychačka/dmychadlo). The narrator's strange assumption to the contrary reveals an extraordinary ignorance of the mechanics of glass-making and suggests that the narrator is too squeamish to even contemplate the possibility that anyone would blow di-rectly into the molten mass. When the narrator then adds 'vyfukovat v okou-zlující ampule a báně', we are immediately struck by 'ampule'. Given the narrator's evident desire to demonstrate the amenability of glass to blow-ing, we would have expected him to begin with a more expansive example. This leaves us feeling rather disappointed and the belated addition of 'báň' cannot quite make up for what has been lost. On the contrary, 'báň' merely adds to our discomfort because we are not quite sure what sort of vessel it refers to and whether it refers to a vessel at all. Though it can be used as a somewhat unspecific word for 'receptacle', 'báň' mostly serves to denote things that are merely rounded in shape, like a domed roof or cupola. We therefore begin to suspect that the products of this act of blowing may not amount to very much. Even more compromising in this respect is 'kaliti do závoje jiskrných čar'. For the author, the intensely focussed light normally conveyed by 'jiskrný' is attenuated by extension into 'čáry' and blurred into indistinctness by 'závoje'. The verb 'kaliti', which can mean 'to temper' but also 'to muddy / to cloud', implicitly confirms this obfuscation. There is a parallel irony in 'žárnými duhovými záplavami', where the intensity of light normally associated with 'žárný' is weakened by juxtaposition with the ethereal 'duhový' and all but extinguished by the watery torrents we associate with 'záplavy'. That the metallic ingredients used for these attempts at colouring are said to be 'přísně tajenými' rather than 'přísně tajnými', as we might have expected, implies that what is at issue here is more obsessive secretiveness than carefully guarded secrecy. The greatest irony in this passage, however, derives from the way the narrative line has been manipulated. The narrator originally prefaced his remarks about glass-making by telling us that glass and metals had numerous similarities. He then went on to demonstrate this by telling us that both glass and metals can be moulded by heating, pressed into shape, and formed with the aid of tongs. This is a promising start but three examples are hardly enough to substantiate his argument that the similarities are numerous. However, instead of providing us with the additional examples we are eagerly awaiting, the narrator has now begun to fob us off with irrelevance. Clearly, being shaped by blowing and being coloured by the addition of metallic pigments is something that is done to glass, not metals. We can see the narrator becoming desperate in his attempt to maintain his argument. The phrase 'kaliti do závoje jiskrných čar' takes the irony a step further. The colour effect the narrator is describing is something we would associate with glass, not metals, so the connection to the argument is again lost. However, 'kaliti' is standardly used, not of glass, but of metals like steel that are hardened to make them suitable for use in tools and machine parts that need to be especially resistant to wear and tear.[262] This confusion can suggest that the narrator has not only lost control of his argument but may also be largely ignorant of his subject matter.

Může se také na ně konečně nanášeti rozplavené zlato či stříbro a navždy je s ním spojiti za znovu podstoupeného ohnivého křtu a očištění. Lze je také učiniti vláknitým

---

262 'Kaliti' may be used to describe modern procedures of toughening glass, making it resistant to cutting and drilling, but the normal word here is 'tvrditi'. In any case, it is out of place in describing Renaissance glass-making.

jako čarovné přádlo, z něhož hbité prsty znají vyvésti subtilní kabinetní kousky, složité světlo jímající a ve chvějných prismatech zase vypuzující.

There is a gentle irony in 'konečně', because 'konečně' can be used neutrally to designate the last stage in a process or emotively to signify a long-awaited outcome. The author, cleaving to the latter interpretation, is suggesting that narrator, though he is loathe to admit it, is secretly glad that the glass has been covered up, presumably because the precious metals do at least lend it a semblance of real colour that the narrator, despite his pretence to the contrary, knows it lacks. However, there is a strong implication that the narrator is not entirely satisfied with this solution. To pick up on it, we need to pay precise attention to the wording in 'nanášeti rozplavené zlato a stříbro'. We naturally assume that gold and silver applied to the surface of glass would most likely be in a molten state and so we expect to read 'roztavené' instead of the orthographically and acoustically similar 'rozplavené' that surprisingly confronts us. While 'roztavit (kov)' is 'to melt (metal)', 'rozplavit (roztlucenou rudu)' is 'to wash (crushed ore) with water to flush out impurities'. At first this meaning seems strange, since the gold and silver applied to the glass are presumably not unrefined ores that needs to be washed. The author intends us to be puzzled but is helping us with the subsequent reference to 'očistění', which not only brings out the narrator's expectation that the precious metals and the glass need to be fused but also his belief that the combination needs to be cleansed. What the author is trying to tell us is that the narrator believes precious metals like gold and silver to be impure in themselves and communicate their impurity to anything they come in contact with. The reference to the renewed baptism of fire is meant to bring out the narrator's obsessively religious perspective. The narrator's subsequent claim about the artistic potential of glass is subverted in a number of ways. Not only is the author playing on the everyday connotations of 'vláknitý' (cf. 'vláknité maso / vláknitá zelenina', 'stringy meat / vegetables') to produce a negative undertow, he is also using 'čarovný' in 'čarovné přádlo' to bring out the narrator's interest in magic and the occult. The narrator's surreal, metaphysical perspective is also at issue in 'hbité prsty znají' [vyvést kabinetní kousky]', which allows the fingers to be portrayed as if they were independent agents endowed with their own abilities. This subtle subversion continues in 'vyvésti subtilní kabinetní kousky', where the author is exploiting the ambiguity of 'vyvést' and the negative connotations of 'kabinetní kousky'. The verb 'vyvádět/vyvést' can not only mean 'to draw out' as here, but also 'to fool around, to lark about'; in this meaning it is normally intransitive, but it can also be transitive as in 'co vyvádíš?', 'what are you playing at?'; 'cos to zase vyvedl', 'now look what you have gone and done'; and 'vyvést komu co', 'to play a prank on sb'. The term 'kabinetní kousek' is often used derogatively to describe things that are flamboyant and over-wrought, even things that have gone preposterously wrong, while 'kousek' on its own can refer to a prank as in 'provést komu (uličnický) kousek', 'to play a prank on sb.' However, the brunt of the irony does not comes until we reach 'složité světlo jímající a ve chvějných prismatech zase vypuzující'. On the surface, this description of the play of light in glass in quite engaging, but it does not take long for us to realize that the narrator is throwing dust in our eyes. After his reference to skillfully-made cabinet pieces, we would have expected him to provide us with a suitably impressive example; instead all we get is an over-elaborate but ultimately banal account of the way light is refracted in a prism. That the process described here relates only to glass and not to metal further weakens the narrator's argument that glass and metals share numerous characteristics.

> Zejména pokud se týkalo leštění a rytí, potom přejemné pulérování skla zrcadlového na otáčecích stolech, to bylo primátem benátských sklářů mezi uznávanými odborníky světa, a starý sklář, umíraje, zanechával svému synovi vedle mnohomluvného požehnání i klíč pracovního tajemství, v zásadě často jednoduchý, ale nikdy nevyzrazený.

By going on to tell us what the Venetians were especially good at, the narrator is again trying to pull the wool over our eyes. What reveals the falsity of his argument is the lack of a suitable antecedent to his perky 'zejména'. In looking for an antecedent, our first instinct is to think back to the descriptions of glass-making we have just been given, only to realize on reflection that these were not accounts of Venetian glass-making at all, only examples of what can be done with glass, as part of a general argument aiming to show that glass has much in common with metal when it comes to artistic potential. The logical connection necessary for 'zejména' to function properly is therefore missing. Matters are not improved by the narrator's reference to 'leštění' and 'pulérování'. The narrator is hoping that we will interpret these terms as trade-specific colloquialisms for the technically correct 'broušení'. The author, however, is relying on standard usage to make it clear that these glass-makers are not cutting glass but merely polishing it, as one might polish floors, furniture or shoes. The reference to mirror glass is impressive until we realize that 'zrcadlové sklo' it is just an alternative term for ordinary plate glass. The surreptitious substition of 'otáčecí stoly' for 'otočné stoly' prompts the comic realization that what we have here are not lathes ('otočný stůl' < Ger. *Drehbank* means the same as 'soustruh') in the normal sense but, quite literally, revolving tables (cf. 'otáčecí dveře', 'revolving doors' / 'otáčecí jeviště', 'revolving stage'). Together with 'přejemné', this creates the ridiculous image of glass-makers polishing glass with a minimum of physical exertion, applying only the gentlest of pressure and making use of the automatic motion of the tables to avoid having to move. No less compromising is 'to bylo primátem benátských sklářů' because 'primát' leaves it open whether this activity was the supreme accomplishment of Venetian glass-blowers or merely something they claimed as a privilege. Similarly, 'mezi uznávanými odborníky světa' fails to make it clear whether the specialists in question were world-renowned authorities or merely persons from somewhere in the world recognized only by the Venetians themselves. What adds to the irony here is the fact that no sooner has the narrator begun to tell us something about the accomplishments of Venetian glass-blowers than he veers off this potentially compromising subject by suddenly telling us about the way trade secrets were passed on from father to son. This new argumentative tack does not help matters. The narrator's assumption that each craftsman would have only one secret and that he would have to wait until his death-bed to impart it hardly argues for a rich and vigorous artistic tradition. What is more, the narrator's admission that the secret was in principle often simple ('v zásadě často jednoduchý') surely requires a more convincing follow-up than the disclosure that the secret was never divulged ('nikdy nevyzrazený'); we would have expected something along the lines of 'basically simple, but ingenious' or 'basically simple, but highly effective'. Finally, 'mnohomluvné požehnání' makes us wonder whether the dying artist's final blessing was loaded with meaning or merely verbose.

> Giacomo Tartaglia byl sklář-umělec tak vyspělý jako občan a patriot, nezapomínající ani na své umělecké tajemství, ani na své vlastenecké povinnosti.

The principal irony here is created by the discrepancy between what we believe the narrator to have said and the actual meaning of the words used. Given the terms 'sklář-umělec' and 'občan a patriot' bound together as they are by the comparative 'tak...jako...', we assume that what the narrator is telling us is that Tartaglio was as mature as a citizen and patriot as he was as an artistic glass-blower. However, on closer inspection we are bound to admit that this is not really what he has said but merely the complexion we have put on it. In fact, what the narrator has said, if he has said anything at all, is that Tartaglio was 'an artistic glass-blower as mature as a citizen and patriot', which yields no reliable and coherent meaning. The comparison between Tartaglio's not forgetting his artistic secret and his not forgetting his patriotic duties is skewed. Normally we talk about someone doing his patriotic duty in the sense of defending his country in time of war ('koná svou vlasteneckou povinnost'). The unexpected plural in 'vlastenecké povinnosti' leaves us disorientated and struggling to work out what sort of duties these might be. It also serves to accentuate the rather strained singular in 'umělecké tajemství', emphasizing that Tartaglio, like his fellows, has only one artistic secret. Even 'nezapomínající' allows untoward associations. Not forgetting a secret does not necessarily entail not divulging it, just as not forgetting one's duties does not necessarily entail fulfilling them.

> Samy Benátky, jež byly jeho neklidnou kolébkou, jako slibovaly býti bezpečnou rakví, zdály se mu Boží mocí vytvořené jakoby ze skla: každý ze sta jejich průplavů svým záludným zelenavým třpytem utvrzoval ho v této představivosti.

By telling us that, to Tartaglio, Venice itself seemed to be made of glass, the narrator is trying to create a sympathetic background for his account of the development of his hero's creative talent. The author meanwhile is making sure that he does not quite succeed. His first attempt at subversion lies in the comparison of Tartaglio's native Venice to an uneasy cradle and a safe coffin. At first, we take 'neklidná kolébka' to be a reflection of turbulent times at the time of his birth and 'bezpečná rakev' to be a reflection of the security offered by the enduring homage paid to past masters like Titian. However, by leaving both terms unexplained, the author is consciously allowing for the compromising possibility both 'neklidná kolébka' and 'bezpečná rakev' are motivated by nothing more than the narrator's deap-seated fear of life that has also given rise to the religiosity expressed in 'Boží mocí'. That the relativization of reality in '[Benátky] zdály se' is unnecessarily compounded by '[vytvořené] jakoby [ze skla]' suggests that the narrator's case may be weaker than he would like us believe. This implication is followed up in the description of the water in the canals and Tartaglio's reaction to it. That a greenish shimmer should be a reliable sign of resemblance to glass strikes us as far-fetched. Of course, there was a kind of primitive glass, made from wood ash and sand in furnaces set up in forest areas, called 'forest glass' (> Ger. *Waldglas*), which did have a greenish hue due to impurities in the material.[263] However, remembering this hardly restores our faith in the narrator's comparison, because the glass concerned was of such poor quality that its production was in fact outlawed by the Venetian state. That the narrator's argument is not just strained, but fundamentally flawed is hinted at in 'záludný', which can suggest that the visual impression created by the water was a delusion. Matters are not helped by 'každý ze sta jejich průplavů [...] utvrzoval ho v této představivosti'. The deft substitution of 'představivost' for the expected 'představa' allows the author to imply that Tartaglio's impression was due more to the workings of an over-active imagination that

---

263 Forest glass was produced mainly in Germany and Bohemia. There were centres of production in the Black Forest (Schwarzwald), the Upper Palatinate (Oberpfalz), the Taunus, Mecklenburg, and the Ore Mountains (Erzgebirge/Krušné hory). There is a museum devoted to forest glass in Langen Brütz, near Schwerin, Mecklenburg, and historical replicas are produced in Bohemia by companies like Tureček in Cvikov and Lesní sklo in Maršovice. See also Ralf Wendt, *Waldglas* (Schwerin, 1977) and Philip Hopper, *Forest Green Glass* (Atglen PA, 2000).

to sound observation. If we have understood this, we can see that 'každý ze sta jejich průplavů', which at first seems to support the argument by force of number, actually undermines it, by suggesting that Tartaglio keeps having to look at every single canal in order to keep his imagination on the boil and to maintain his delusion.

> Vznosné budovy s loggiemi, do nichž pralo jižní slunce, křehce se nadnášely na hluché trachytové dláždění, a div že jemně a hudebně nezazvonily; mosty, jichž byl bezpočet, snažily se spoutati vodu do sklenné bezživotnosti, a nebe po celou většinu roku bylo tak bezmračné, jako by se bylo Tartagliovi podařilo v jeho peci roztaviti modrý korund.

At first there seems to be nothing wrong with the narrator's description of majestic buildings glistening in the southern sun. His reference to loggias and trachyte paving seems appropriate to the historical and geographical context: loggias are a typical feature of Italian Renaissance architecture and paving stones made of volcanic trachyte are typical of Venetian calles and piazzas. To understand the irony here, we need to remember that the narrator did not set out to provide a colourful description of Venice but to illustrate his contention that Tartaglio was inspired by the glass-like quality of his environment. For a moment, it seems as if the narrator has lost the thread of his unconvincing argument or has chosen to abandon it. It is only on closer inspection that we realize that the narrator is still perservering with his argument but is clearly having a hard time convincing us or even himself. Struggling hard to bring reality into line with his preconceived idea, he ends up telling us more about himself than he does about Venice. Initially the narrator's compromising failure is hard to spot. Our imagination may strain to accommodate the idea that the monumental palazzos to which 'vznosné budovy s loggiemi' presumably refers might appear fragile in the fierce sunlight, but we cannot it dismiss out of hand. We are more inclined to draw the line at '[budovy] div že jemně a hudebně nezazvonily'. That massive stone buildings should be thought to be on the verge of resonating with gentle musicality is hardly convincing even as a poetic metaphor, especially since it is unclear what, in terms of the metaphor, should cause the buildings to resonate. The author is banking on our resistance to accept what the narrator is saying at face value, and is hoping that we will be able to see that 'div že jemně a hudebně nezazvonily', like 'křehce' before it, owes less to the narrator's bold poetic imagination than it does to his reckless determination to make Venice appear as glass-like as possible in spite of appearances to the contrary. For the author, the source of the metaphor in 'div že jemně a hudebně nezazvonily' is the action of someone tapping a wine glass to test its quality by listening to the ring, and the motivation behind 'křehce' is the fragility of glass that the narrator tellingly emphasized earlier on. That the

narrator is working against his own perception of reality in trying to make
Venice seem glass-like is also brought out by 'hluché trachytové dláždění'. By
allowing this only seemingly gratuitous reference to the sound of the paving stones to immediately precede 'div že jemně a hudebně nezazvonily', the
author is trying to getting us to see that the narrator, irritated by the dullness
of sound produced by the paving stones and painfully aware of the fact that
it compromises his argument, has then, in a valiant attempt to save the day,
suddenly come up with the fantastic claim that the buildings almost emitted a
glass-like ring. This still does not exhaust the irony in the first half of the sentence. In 'vznosné budovy s loggiemi, do nichž pralo jižní slunce', we initially
take the mention of the loggias to be a piece of local colour and the mention
of the southern sun to be motivated by the need to create an impression of
bright sunlight illuminating the facades. What the author would like us to
understand though is that the narrator mentions the southern sun because
he hates the heat of the sun relentlessly beating down and mentions the loggias because he yearns for the shady respite they afford. This irony is heightened by a second irony concealed behind it. Since the antecedent of 'do nichž'
does not have to be 'budovy', as we initially suppose it to be, but may equally
well be 'loggie', we are left with the subversive possibility that the narrator is
so sensitive to heat that for him even the shady loggias do not offer adequate
protection from the scorching sun. We should also take note of the covert
semantic correspondence between 'vznosný' and 'nadnášet se', both used
of the buildings. Taken on its own, 'vznosný' means 'majestic, lofty', while
'nadnášet se' means 'to float, to drift across the surface'. However, taken together, the common element of upward motion (/-vz-/, /-nad-/ + allomorphs
/-nos-/ and /-náš-/) suddenly comes to the fore and makes us think of the
buildings as somehow suspended in thin air. When we come to 'mosty, jichž
byl bezpočet, snažily se spoutati vodu do sklenné bezživotnosti', we find our
inference that the narrator has not lost sight of his argument about Venice's
glassiness confirmed. However, in spite of the clear and explicit reference to
glass, this renewed attempt to convince us is set to fail. What brings the narrator down is not just the improbable nature of his image, which has bridges
like rings tying up water, but the tell-tale 'snažily se'. Trying is no guarantee
of success, and the narrator's desperate emphasis on the sheer number of
bridges engaged in the task cannot change that. What is more, the narrator's
failure has come at a price. If we think back, there can be little doubt that the
narrator was trying to paint a positive picture of Venice's alleged glassiness,
one worthy of its inspirational role, but now suddenly we find this glassiness
associated with lifelessness. The reference to the sky does not help matters.
One problem is that the allegation of glassiness, which was explicit, is now
again at best implicit. The reference to a cloudless sky can create a vague impression of glassiness and the mention of blue corundum may be thought

to reinforce it. However, while corundum may be shiny and vitreous in its solid state, it is hardly likely to be shiny and vitreous when molten. What is more, the clash between the comprehensiveness of 'celý' and the partiality of 'většina' in 'po celou většinu roku' prompts us to suspect that the narrator is exaggerating the level of cloudlessness. Another problem is posed by the provenance of the elaborate image involving Tartaglio's hypothetical attempt to melt blue corundum. This image may be the product of pure conjecture but we cannot help suspecting that it is motivated by a likelihood that the narrator regards as genuine. But this leaves us wondering why Tartaglio should think of melting corundum, the second hardest substance known to man.[264]

> Nebylo dne ani hodiny, aby nemyslel celou duší na své povolání a netoužil dáti sklu tolik barev a odstínění, do kolika je ošacena příroda ve své plesné oslnivosti [...].

We do not have to wonder for long because the narrator is quick to elaborate. However, the explanation he provides hardly inspires confidence. That Tartaglio might think of trying to colour glass by melting virtually unmeltable precious stones suggests naivety and desperation rather than artistic originality. His incompetence is ironically underscored in 'myslel celou duší', which, by confounding the sense of intellectual sobriety in 'myslet' with the notion of spiritual commitment in 'celou duší' and trading wanted and unwanted associations off against each other, is able to imply that Tartaglio's creative imagination is cerebral where it might have been impassioned, pallidly abstract where it might have been down-to-earth. It is worth adding that the narrator's use of 'celou duší', a phrase used several dozen times in the Old Testament alone, also hints at his religiosity.[265] That Tartaglio is said to think of his profession day and night may be seen as proof of artistic determination or as evidence of a nagging conscience in the face of failure. The description of the colours Tartaglio would like to create also fails to impress. In 'barev a odstínění', the impression of vibrant colour we might gain from 'barvy' is implicitly weakened by the sense of finest tinging and shade that attaches to 'odstínění'. This implication is followed up in 'je ošacena příroda', which suggests that the tones involved are not vivid natural colours but hues an immature picture-book imagination has shrouded nature in. Even 've své plesné oslnivosti' cannot save the narrator's argument. On the surface, 'plesná oslnivost' may create an impression of joyous radiant colour but the author

---

264 To melt corundum (melting-point 2044°C) you would need a modern ultra-high-temperature furnace.

265 The phrase 'celou (svou) duší' occurs in Genesis 34:3, 34:8, 44:30; Deuteronomy 4:29, 6:5, 10:12, 11:13, 13:4, 26:16, 30:2, 30:6, 30:10; Joshua 23:14; 1 Samuel 23:10; 1 King's 2:4, 8:48; 2 Kings 23:25; 2 Chronicles 6:38, 15:12; Jeremiah 44:14; Tobias 1:12, 13:16; Ecclesiasticus 6:28, 6:32, 7:20, 9:2, 51:20; Matthew 22:37 and Luke 10:27.

is eager for us to realize that the mere assertion of dancing dazzlingness provides scant guarantee of real colour. The main irony in this passage, however, lies in the way the need to explain the metaphor of the melted korund has provided the narrator with a pretext to abandon his embarrassingly deficient argument about the alleged glass-like quality of Venice.

> Dnem i nocí se mučil touhou, aby vybarvil sklo tak, aby věrně tlumočilo jeho barevný sen, sloučený ze všech nuancí nebes a květinových zahrad, jež jsou ve srozumění s promenujícími signorami.

That the narrator now launches into a new paragraph on his newly-found subject confirms our suspicion that he is glad to capitalize on the opportunity to change the subject that his explanatory digression provided. However, the picture he is now painting continues to suffer from the colour deficiency we have just described. In 'vybarvil sklo tak, aby věrně tlumočilo jeho barevný sen', the sense of colour is compromised by the use of 'vybarvit', which can refer to the childishly inept colouring in of picture-book outlines ('vybarvit omalovánky') and to the ultimate stage in a dyeing process where a final nuance of colour is imparted ('vybarvit do správného odstínu'), and by the mention of 'barevný sen', which can suggest that the colours in question are chimerical rather than life-like. These implications receive immediate support from '[sen] sloučený ze všech nuancí nebes', which insinuates that the colours are little more than ethereal nuances. The reference to the gardens of flowers seems to gainsay this, but only until we realize that the colour of flowers perceived to be in accord with sedate ladies, possibly even elderly widows, taking a gentle stroll in each other's company would hardly be overflowing with vibrancy and dynamism.

> Třebaže měl svoji uměleckou proslulost, nebyl bohat a úrodný deštíček mecenášského zlata se zdál snášeti se pouze na pečlivě obdělávaná role malířů, sochařů a stavitelů, zatím co cizí velmožové žádostivě hleděli na umělost benátských sklářů přes Alpy a Pyreneje.

In 'měl svoji uměleckou proslulost', Tartaglio's claim to fame is diminished by the use of 'proslulost' which leaves it open whether he is celebrated or merely notorious, and by the addition of 'svoji', which has a trivialising effect by suggesting that what is possessed is not of great value but at least one's own ('měl svůj dům a svoje auto'). If we have understood this, we are less inclined to accept the sense of being hard done by that the narrator goes on to argue for. The author is with us on this and is asking us to understand that the diminutive in 'deštíček [mecenášského zlata]' is not the expression of genteel reticence we initially take it to be but simply a reflection of the small amount of money that is at stake. He would also like us to see '[deštíček] se zdál [snášeti se]' as implicit confirmation of the fact that the unfair distribution of money is more a matter of subjective impression than objective reality. That Tartaglio is in any case not as hard done by as he thinks is also brought out by the metaphor of the carefully cultivated fields. What the author would like us to understand is that, even if the painters, sculptors and architects do indeed receive a greater share of patronage, this may well be because they at least have their house in order. The idea that this patronage is sufficient to bear fruit is neatly subverted by the terms of the same metaphor, because even 'úrodný [deštíček]' is insufficient to persuade us that the carefully cultivated fields actually produced a harvest. The narrator's assertion that there was considerable foreign interest in Venetian glass-making is undermined by the metaphor of the dignitaries looking across the Alps and the Pyrenees, because if we stop to consider what their line of vision would have been we are bound to admit that their sight would have been massively hindered by the inordinately long distances and the great height of the obstacles, not to mention the fact that looking across the Pyrenees, a mountain range between France and Spain, they would have been looking in the wrong direction. In other words, it is not only likely that they could not see what they were looking for but that they had no real idea of where it might be. That Venetian glass-making was in any case hardly worth the attention is brought out by the use of 'umělost', which suggests that it may have been more a matter of artificiality than high art.

> Usmíval se naň na jedné straně bezstarostný život, vychutnávající ovoce uměleckého tvoření, na druhé straně se šklebila smrtící samota v olovných komorách státního vězení, kterou by tajná justice mohla připraviti. A přece byla touha po hmotném blahobytu a tvorbě jím zabezpečené tak mocná, že ho nemohla od skrytých zrádných myšlenek odvésti ani surově trestající moc prokuratury.

In his attempt to construct a thriller scenario, which sees Tartaglio torn between the loyalty he owes to Venice and the temptations offered by foreign lands, between the prospect of a quiet life at home and the risk of long-term imprisonment, the narrator gets himself into even deeper water. The first problem lies in the narrator's admission that Tartaglio can look forward to a carefree life enjoying the fruits of his creativity. This effectively contradicts the narrator's previous claim that Tartaglio was financially disadvantaged and suggests that Tartaglio's feeling of being hard done by owes more to greed than a sense of justice. That the punishment Tartaglio fears is a period of imprisonment in the Leads (*Piombi*), the famous dungeon in the Doge's Palace reserved for traitors, rings seductively true but the narrator's description of its deterrent force as ' šklebila [se] smrtící samota', not only fails to give us any indication of the length of term involved but suggests that what Tartaglio fears most is being left alone for any period of time.[266] That we should not take this fear of loneliness too seriously is brought home to us by the manifestly exaggerated 'smrtící' and the harmlessly theatrical 'šklebit se'. A further problem is created by the conspicuous contrast between '[komory] státního [vězení]' and 'tajná [justice]'. Though it is not inconceivable that a secret judiciary might avail itself of state prisons, the unexplained contrast is so much to the fore that it is mildly irritating. Combined with the mere potentiality of 'by [tajná justice] mohla připravit' and the ambiguity of 'připravit komu co' ('to cause sb. sthg' but also simply 'to prepare sthg for sb.'), this contrast can make us wonder how real the imaginary danger is. When the narrator goes on to speak of Tartaglio's motivation, he lets himself down even further. On reading 'byla touha po hmotném blahobytu a tvorbě jím zabezpečené tak mocná', we cannot help noticing how the narrator's admission of a strong material motive ('touha po hmotném blahobytu') is immediately relativized by the subordination of this motive to an artistic one ('a tvorbě jím zabezpečené'). What the author would like us to understand from this is that the narrator, acutely aware of the fact that Tartaglio is driven by greed, has let slip more than he feels he should have, and has then hastened to cover things up as best he can. Our unease about the contrast between the state prison and secret judiciary is intensified by 'surově trestající moc prokuratury', which inadvertently admits that in the Venetian state the narrator is talking about prosecution and imprisonment are public acts that have nothing to do with a secret judiciary. Our impression that Tartaglio's imagination is over-active is thereby implicitly confirmed. That it is not only Tartaglio's imagination that is over-active is hinted at in '[odvésti] od skrytých zrádných myšlenek'. On the surface, it seems as if the reason why the thoughts are said to be concealed lies in their traitorous nature and the severity of the punishment imposed on any traitor. What the author is suggesting, however, is that they are said to be concealed because the narrator has no objective evidence that there are any truly traitorous thoughts and is merely imputing such thoughts to his hero.

Byli to zejména Švábové, jejich tolary solidní váhy i ražby stále se mu blyštěly před očima, ti nadbíhali jeho umělecké a občanské počestnosti a síle. Saský kurfiřt nemálo

---

266 This is not to say that the Leads were not a fearsome place. Windowless and situated directly below the lead-clad roof of the palace (hence the name), the main problem, according to famous inmate Giacomo Casanova, was the heat and lack of ventilation in summer. Socially the conditions seem to have been less harsh. Casanova notes that the guards were friendly and even ran errands for him. See Giacomo Casanova, *Histoire de ma fuite des prisons de la République de Venise qu'on appelle les Plombs* (Leipzig, 1787), written in Bohemia.

o to dbal, aby si němečtí skláři mohli osvojiti nejdokonalejší pročištění křišťálového skla po benátském způsobu.

That the narrator refers not only to the solid weight of the silver talers but also mentions their solid mintage and gleaming appearance is part of a last-ditch attempt to deceive us as to Tartaglio's real motives by making it seem as if what seduces him is not so much their monetary value but the craftsmanlike way they have been fashioned. There is similar verbal subterfuge in '[Švábové] nadbíhali jeho umělecké a občanské počestnosti a síle', because the narrator's invocation of his hero's alleged decency and strength and the claim that it is these qualities that the Schwabians are courting or pandering to is simply an inept attempt to obscure the fact that it is Tartaglio's greed that they are appealing to. When we come to 'Saský kurfiřt' another irony becomes retrospectively evident. We cannot help feeling that the forceful beginning of the previous sentence with its reference to Schwabians set the topic for this paragraph. But now we suddenly find ourselves confronted with the Elector of Saxony. A moment's thought is sufficient for us to make it clear to ourselves that Saxons (Sachsen) are not Schwabians (Schwaben). The perplexity that results is soon resolved as soon as we realize that the narrator did not mean 'Švábové' in the primary sense of 'Schwabians' but in the secondary invective sense of 'krauts'. That the narrator is secretly inveighing against the behaviour of these 'Švábové' also comes through in the markedly colloquial structure of the first sentence ('Byli to [..] Švábové, [...] ti...) with its emphatic, implicitly disparaging 'ti'. The narrator's allegation that the Elector of Saxony is interested in having German glassmakers learning from Venice is significantly weakened by the insertion of 'nemálo', which cannot convince us that the interest is both substantial and sincere; and 'mohlo', which ultimately fails to indicate commitment to a definite outcome. That it is Venetian crystal that the Elector of Saxony is interested in is ironic because we have no indication that Tartaglio had any special ability or interest in making crystal.

Augsburští pak, jejichž umělecký smysl byl znám po celém světě, žádali, aby jim zaprodal tajemství přípravy skla zeleného, tak zvaného lesního, jehož plání bylo tak živoucí, jako by si ranní slunce hrálo v korunách mladého kaštanového lesa.

The narrator's claim that the artistic sense of the citizens of Augsburg was known throughout the world fails to make it clear whether it was famous or notorious. That Augsburg wanted Tartaglio to sell them the secret of coloured forest glass seems more convincing and appropriate to his alleged interests than the previous reference to crystal but it conceals an important irony. This irony can be accessed in two different ways, depending on how much the reader knows about forest glass. One path is a purely logical one and rests on the insight that the only thing that follows from the fact that someone wants to buy a secret from someone else is that the prospective purchaser believes that person to possess that secret but not that the person actually does possess that secret. The other path presupposes our knowing that the greenish colour of forest glass is not due to the application of secret knowledge but to accidental impurities in the glass. Because forest glass was produced in makeshift furnaces set up in forest locations (hence the name), the glass-makers chose to use sand that was easy to melt. However, this sand contained iron oxides that lent the crudely made products their characteristic greenish tinge. That the narrator speaks of forest glass as if its name reflected the play of light in trees suggest that he does not know what he is talking about. What is more, the narrator's claim that the play of light was lively ('živoucí') is undermined by the terms of the comparison. We are right to assume that the early morning sun, the tips of the trees and the youth of the forest do not argue for any great vibrancy of colour. The narrator's failure on this point also brings out his alienation from vitality.

> A sám císař Rudolf toužil míti pražské skláře poučeny o tom, jak se mají lahodným způsobem točiti objímky vinných pohárů a konvicím dáti tolik ozdob z emailu a zlata, aby se mezi stolním náčiním vyjímaly jako urozené mezi robotnicemi. Mimo to se snažil zvýšiti svoje pokušení příslibem, že vystaví vzorné pece a kalící koupele, takže bylo srdce Tartagliovo už napolo přemoženo. Pak ještě uvědomělá připomínka na vlastní otčinu, denně bohatnoucí ze svých cest do Východní Indie, jež umění jeho po zásluze necenila, na druhé straně pohrůžkou ho přidržujíc k dodržení těžce získaných chemických tajemství, a v zásadě bylo rozhodnuto.

By letting the narrator say '[císař] toužil míti [...] skláře poučeny', the author is implying that the emperor's motive is less a desire for artistic innovation and development than impatience with the incompetence of present craftsman. That the emperor's concern is with the metal holders ('objímky') of the goblets and the enamel and gold ornamentation of the jugs strongly suggests that he has no interest whatsoever in the quality of the glass that he is keen to see well covered. The division of glassware into gentlefolk ('urozené') and villeins ('robotnice') not only brings out the narrator's social snobbery but also implies that the ordinary wine glasses were subjected to hard labour. That the narrator is not impressed by the emperor's current tableware comes through in his use of the word 'náčiní', which is more appropriate to describing kitchen utensils, fishing gear and farming tools. In 'snažil [se] zvýšiti svoje pokušení', the picture of the emperor adding temptation to temptation reminds us of the Devil's attempts to tempt Jesus in the wilderness and so brings out the narrator's importunate religiosity. That the additional temptation is said to reside in the emperor's offer to build what the narrator describes as 'vzorné pece a kalící koupele' is the author's way of letting us know that the narrator does not really know what he is talking about. Already 'vzorné pece' is suspicious because furnaces can be better or worse but it is not immediately clear how they could be exemplary. However, this is nothing compared to the oddity of 'kalící koupele'. The cooling bath into which freshly-blown glass is placed is standardly referred to as a 'chladící lázeň'. The use of 'kalit', which normally refers only to the tempering of steel, and 'koupel', which is more appropriate to a physiotherapy application ('léčivá, bahenní, rašelinná, hydromasážní koupel') than to a technical manufacturing process, strongly implies that the narrator does not really know what he is talking about. Because 'koupel' can also be used of an act of spiritual cleansing ('očistná koupel'), we may even suspect that the narrator's religiosity is again asserting itself inappropriately. Compromising for the narrator is also 'srdce Tartagliovo [bylo] už napolo přemoženo'. If we have paid attention to the author's hints that Tartaglio is driven by greed, we should not be unduly surprised to learn that the emperor's offer of ideal working conditions was not sufficient to sway him. In 'ještě uvědomělá připomínka na vlastní otčinu', the use of 'připomínka' ('remark, comment') for the expected cognate 'vzpominka' ('thought, memory') subversively reveals the hero's tendency to mutter to himself in indignation. That this particular remark is described as conscious even implies that the hero is not always conscious of doing this. The narrator's observation that the Venice did not value Tartaglio art by its merits ('umění jeho po zásluze necenila') leaves it tellingly open whether his art was under- or over-valued. The reference to the threat Tartaglio was allegedly under did not convince us earlier and it fails to impress us now, since 'pohrůžkou' alone is not enough to make it clear just what exactly this threat consisted in. In 'dodržení těžce získaných chemických tajemství', there is a double irony. The first thing we might notice is that 'dodržovat tajemství' is not the same as 'chránit tajemství', because it does not presuppose the keeping of secret only its correct implementation in practice. In other words, what Tartaglio is being expected to do is at most to continue working in his own established manner, which is surely comparatively harmless. The second thing that the author is hoping we will notice is that there is no connection between the degree of effort that has gone into discovering something and its value to society at large.

> Volil Augsburg, křižovatku uměleckých i duchových cest, jak tam z celého světa směřovaly.

If we have been paying attention to what the narrator has just told us, we should be shocked by his revelation that Tartaglio chose Augsburg. After all, everything seemed to be arguing for Prague. All the Schwabians and the rulers of Augsburg had to offer was money, while Rudolf of Prague could tempt Tartaglio with ideal working conditions, so that he was already half won over ('srdce Tartagliovo [bylo] už napolo přemoženo'). What doubts remained seemed to have been overcome the very next moment when his thoughts turned to the continual lack of freedom and recognition he was subject to, so that matters were basically settled ('v zásadě bylo rozhodnuto'). Our expectation that Tartaglio would chose Prague is now suddenly overturned and with it comes the ironic insight that Tartaglio has gone for the money. The characterization of Augsburg as a crossroads of culture, which the narrator has added in a vain attempt to draw our attention away from Tartaglio's greed, fails on a number of points. That all the roads are described as leading to Augsburg and none of them are described as leading from Augsburg anywhere else suggests that Tartaglio's new domicile is not so much a place of cultural interchange but a magnet for greedy profiteers. This irony is, however, qualified by two others. That the paths are said to be heading there from all over the world ('[cesty] tam z celého světa směřovaly') does not guarantee that they actually arrive. What is more, the connection of the relative clause to the head word 'cesty' by means of 'jak' rather than 'které / jež', leaves us free to conclude that the artistic and spiritual paths the narrator is invoking are not the same as, merely similar to, the paths from all over the world that he goes on to mention.

> Tartaglio byl bezdětek, jeho movité statky byly takového rázu, že se s nimi mohl rozloučiti bez obtíží; provázela ho jenom žena Hieronyma, jež byla vzorem bezpodmínečné příchylnosti. Neměla výhrad, neměla skrupulí, nestavěla ani na odiv nechutnou blátivou trpnost, s jakou ženy snášejí svá osudová spojení. Tartaglio byl přestrojen za mezkaře a ještě si hluboce do čela stáhl své soukenné capuccio [sic].

The narrator mentions that Tartaglio is childless to help explain why it is easy for him to move away from home. The author, however, hopes that we may see the hidden significance behind this unexpected revelation. If we remember what we were told about the ritual in which a dying glass-maker passes his secret on to his son, we cannot help feeling that Tartaglio's childlessness ultimately devalues his secret and so helps to explain why Tartaglio has no interest in keeping it. The reference to his property engineers a different irony. Normally it is real estate ('nemovité statky') that ties us to a particular place not our personal chattels, which are by definition moveable ('movité'). The surreptitious substitution of 'movité' for the expected 'nemovité' comically reveals the narrator's supercilious disdain for Tartaglio's material possessions. Similarly, the description of Tartaglio's wife Hieronyma tells us more about the narrator than it does about herself. In '[žena] byla vzorem bezpodmínečné příchylnosti', we have an expression of whole-hearted approval that suggests unalloyed appreciation of female submissiveness. However, when we come to 'neměla výhrad, neměla skrupulí', we can see the narrator slowly revising his judgment, realizing that female submissiveness, however desirable in itself, may have unwanted consequences when a wife fails to prevent her husband from making a moral mistake. What the author would then like us to see is how the narrator, perturbed by the negativity of 'neměla skrupulí', hastens to redress the balance and reestablish the positive picture he initially to convey. That all the narrator can now come up with is 'nestavěla ani na odiv nechutnou blátivou trpnost, s jakou ženy snášejí svá osudová spojení', in which he tries to construct a favourable contrast between Hieronyma's laudable submissiveness and other women's repugnant passivity, reveals the full extent of his misogynist prejudice and the extraordinary intellectual lengths to which he will go to defend it. His misogynist perspective also comes through in 'bezpodmínečná příchylnost', which substitutes affection into a context normally reserved for love, and the reference to marriage as a fateful bond to be endured. The irony continues with Tartaglio's disguise. The idea of a nobleman disguised as a muleteer is a stereotype of medieval chivalrous romance that has been heavily satirized from Cervantes onwards.[267] Not only can no modern reader takes this stereotype seriously but it is a necessary condition of the stereotype, which derives its rationale from extremes of social status, that the person disguised is a nobleman. Since Tartaglio is a mere craftsman, this disguise suggests that he and those who so disguised him have a ridiculously inflated idea of his, and possibly their own, importance. That Tartaglio is said to pull his hood down over his forehead fails to convince us that his costume is meant to be a serious disguise because anyone trying to cover up their features with a hood would surely try to pull it down over their eyes. That the narrator feels bound to point out the hood

---

267 In Cervantes' *Don Quijote* (Book 1, chapter 44), four horseman, arriving at an inn where the deranged hero is creating an almightly uproar, ask the innkeeper if he has seen a young gentlemen they believe to be the lover of their master's daughter disguised as a muleteer, only to find him lying next to a muleteer but not disguised as one and quite unconcerned about being found. In Jean de la Fontaine's 'Muletier' (*Contes: seconde partie*) (1666), Cupid causes a real muleteer to become enamoured of Tendelingua, Queen of Lombardy. The good-looking young man gains access to the Queen's chamber and spends the night with her, leaving her thinking that the man she shared her bed with is in fact her husband, King Agiluf, disguised as a muleteer. When Agiluf gets wind of this, he lies in wait for the muleteer. In order to be able to identify the culprit in daytime, Agiluf marks him by cutting off a lock of his hair. To escape detection, the muleteer then does the same to his fellows. Next morning the king is confronted with a large number of muleteers all effectively disguised by the missing lock of hair. In Balfe's famous comic opera *The Rose of Castile* (1857), Elvira, Rose of Castile, learns that her princely admirer Don Sebastian, brother to the King of Castile, intends to enter her chambers disguised as a muleteer. In order to meet him half-way, she decides to disguise herself as a peasant girl and in this disguise meets Manuel, a real muleteer. Thinking the muleteer is Don Sebastian in disguise, she falls in love with the muleteer.

was made of cloth may be taken to suggest that he would normally expect something finer.

> Rozpjal se soumrak a v jeho moci a vůli bylo utajiti slzy Tartagliovy. Byla to dlouhá a ostražitá cesta na sever k úpatím Alp, jež se dívaly svými tmavými jezery tiše a nepřátelsky. A odtud pak už dál a dál až do Bavorska, ale za této dlouhé pěší pouti nabývaly v něm převahy pocity psance nad volným vědomím světlonoše.

Here the narrator is trying to construct a dramatic scenario in which in a tearful Tartaglio sets off into the night on a long, arduous and dangerous journey across the Alps. The author, meanwhile, is making sure that this scenario does not quite come off. The narrator's first stumbling block lies in the opening phrase 'rozpjal se soumrak'. Normally we say 'rozpjala se noc', based on an image of the night as a large black cloak that spreads out and finally envelops all. The same image simply will not work with 'soumrak'. However, it is not just linguistic logic that requires 'noc'. When someone tries to steal away unnoticed, they normally do so under the cover of night, not under the cover of twilight. What the author is trying to do by undercutting linguistic and narrative logic in the way is to suggest that Tartaglio, setting off in the twilight, has no need of the cover of night, because nobody is really interested in his departure. Alongside this, we also have a comic weakening of the metaphorical 'rozpjal se', that makes us wonder whether the narrator is not so afraid of the night that even twilight is scary enough for him. However, behind these implication lurks an even more devastating irony. Since 'soumrak' can refer not only to dusk but also to dawn ('ranní soumrak'), we are left wondering whether Tartaglio is not simply trying to get an early start as any traveller would. That he should be able to set off at the break of day brings the idea that nobody in interested in Tartaglio's departure to a head. The idea that Tartaglio is overcome with emotion and tears are running down his cheeks is just as questionable. It is a pragmatic feature of the phrase 'bylo v čí moci' that it is normally used in the negative to comment on something that could not be prevented (e.g. 'nebylo v jeho moci tomu zabránit'). When used in a positive sense, it normally retains the same basic sense of inaction, signifying that something could have been prevented but was not ('bylo v jeho moci tomu zabránit, ale nic neučinil'). The implication of 'bylo v jeho moci' here is therefore that the twilight did not hide Tartaglio's tears, presumably because there were no tears to hide. The hypertrophic addition of 'vůle' can do nothing to change this. All it does is to reveal a sense of desperation in creating an impression of activity the narrator ultimately knows to be false. This brings us to journey itself. When we hear the narrator speak of the long and hazardous journey northwards, our first inclination is to be sympathetic since we can easily appreciate how challenging a journey across the Alps to

Bavaria must have seemed to someone at the time. However, when the narrator suddenly adds 'k úpatím Alp' our expectations are comically undercut, since this leg of the journey would normally be considered the easiest part. The narrator's case is not helped by 'ostražitá cesta', which implicitly replaces objective danger with a purely subjective sense of caution. Secretly aware of his failure to overwhelm us with his description of hardship and peril, the narrator tries to up his game with '[Alpy], jež se dívaly svými tmavými jezery tiše a nepřátelsky', playing on our knowledge that the calm, unruffled surfaces of Alpine lakes usually conceal cold, menacing depths. If he does not succeed, it is partly because the picture-book personification of 'nepřátelsky' is too innocuous to move us, but partly also because the reference to the lakes may be largely gratuitous. The narrator has told us that Tartaglio reached the foothills of the Alps, but there is no evidence that he actually crossed the Alps. The narrator would like us to think he did, but all we have by way of proof is the description of the lakes in a parenthetic dependent clause combined with an account of Tartaglio's continuing journey and arrival. Our suspicion that the narrator is deceiving us is reinforced by 'odtud pak už dál a dál až do Bavorska', where 'odtud' is naturally taken to refer back to '[k] úpatím [Alp]' and 'dál a dál' makes us wonder whether Tartaglio has not undertaken a lengthy detour around the Alps to the east. The characterization of Tartaglio's state of mind adds to the irony. Already 'pěší pouť' suggests that the narrator is putting his own religious slant on things, and this perspective is sustained in his appeal to terms like 'psanec' and 'světlonoš'. Given this implicit narrative bias, we begin to wonder whether Tartaglio's thoughts are exactly as the narrator has described them or whether his thoughts are not being misrepresented by a narrator who is afraid to tell us that Tartaglio was simply fed up. The most important irony, however, lies in the narrator's admission that Tartaglio travelled on foot, because this prompts the comic realization that he was effectively a muleteer without mules, something that would normally be considered something of a give-away. Just in case we should try to rationalize this contradiction away by assuming that Tartaglio was walking alongside mules loaded with the couple's possessions, the author has made it sufficiently clear in advance that Tartaglio did not take any possessions with him ('jeho movité statky byly takového rázu, že se s nimi mohl rozloučiti bez obtíží').

Došel k cíli. Nebylo to však jako doma nad záhadně zelenavými, třpytnými kanály, jež se bezpočetné prsteny mostů snažily ve sklennou nehybnost opoutati, ale cínové vlny Lechu a Vertachu posupně hlučely a hromobily.

The narrator's emphatic, and conspicuously singular, 'Došel k cíli' makes us wonder what has happened to Tartaglio's wife. Has our misogynistic narrator simply failed to mention her? Has Tartaglio managed to lose her on his long journey? Or did she in fact never come with him in the first place? Initially, we had confidently assumed that her submissiveness and unconditional devotion to her husband meant that she was happy to accompany him. However, when we think about it more carefully, we suddenly realize that we have no reason to believe that she actually did accompany him. Her submissiveness is as consistent with uncomplainingly accompanying him as it is with quietly letting him go, and the devotion supposedly expressed in 'bezpodmínečná příchylnost' does not have to be affection for her husband but may be some kind of indiscriminate friendliness. Then, to make matters worse, we have the narrator's unexplained failure to mention the disguise the wife would surely also have needed if she was to accompany her husband. In the description contrasting Augsburg with Venice, our attention is immediately drawn to the depiction of Augsburg since the portrayal of Venice seems to be mere poetic reiteration. That waves of the rivers Lech and Wertach, on which Augsburg stands, are described as 'cínové' at first seems like a bold metaphor for the silver-grey colour of the spume that fast-flowing rivers throw up. It is only when we take a closer look at '[vlny] hlučely a hromobily' that we begin to feel uneasy. It is difficult to ignore the way the metallic quality of 'cínové' carries over into the clattering of the waves, as if the waves were not merely pewter-coloured but somehow made of pewter. The author is hoping that we will pick up on this because he would like us to realize that the narrator's depiction of Augsburg is based on those pewter pictures and plates with their crudely engraved urban panoramas that were ubiquitous in late nineteenth- and early twentieth-century Germany, Austria and Switzerland.[268] If we recognize this, we may now cast our eyes back over the first half of the second sentence and ask ourselves whether the narrator's portrayal of Venice has not been culled from the watercolours of Turner and Monet in a similarly derivative manner. In fact, thinking back just a little further, we may wonder whether the description of the Alpine lakes is not based on Turner's famous panoramas of Swiss lakes and their mountainous surroundings.[269] This is precisely the response the author is hoping for, be-

268 My Swiss grandparents possessed quantities of these, some of which they displayed in the living-room of their Basel flat. Despite their immense popularity, I have not been able to find a full-length study dedicated to them. Some information can be found in Ludwig Mory, *Schönes Zinn*, revised and expanded edition (Munich, 1972); and in Ludwig Mory, *Bruckmann's Zinn-Lexikon* (Munich, 1977). The German pewter industry was set up in Krefeld in 1850 by Cologne businessman Engelbert Kayser. Kayserzinn, as the company was called, received many prominent international awards and was instrumental in making pewter a staple material of the German *Kunsthandwerk*. On Kayserzinn, see Gerhard Dietrich and Eckard Wagner, *Kayserzinn* (Stuttgart, 2011).

269 Turner's views of Swiss lakes include Lake Thun (1838), A Swiss Lake (1840), Lake Lucerne (1842), Lake Constance (1842), Blue Rigi (1842). Lake of Zug (1843), Lake of Geneva (1843), Oberhofen on Lake Thun (1848) and Lake in the Swiss Alps (1848). For an introductory account of Turner's paintings of Venice and Alpine lakes, see Monika Wagner, *William Turner* (Munich, 2011),

cause he would like us to realize that the narrator is so divorced from life that his perception of the world owes less to first-hand knowledge and to creative imagination than to sterile contemplation and a slavish rehashing of familiar works of art. There is another reason why we should look back over the first half of the second sentence. Though this part of the sentence at first appears to be nothing more than a poetic refrain – an artful summing up of the more extensive description of Venice that preceded it – it harbours ironies of its own. There ironies rely on subtle differences between the present and the previous description. Notice the discrepancy between '[nad] záhadně zelenavými, třpytnými kanály' and the earlier '[průplavy] svým záludným zelenavým třpytem [utvrzoval ho v té představivosti]. In the first instance, the narrator calls the greenish shimmer of the water insidious, which seems to reflect the elusive quality of its constantly changing hue. Now, he suddenly calls it mysterious, which is harder to explain away and ultimately prompts the amusing realization that the narrator does not quite understand why the water is this strange colour instead of being blue as he thinks water should be. There is a similar dislocation in 'kanály, jež se bezpočetné prsteny mostů snažily ve sklennou nehybnost opoutati', which harks back to 'mosty, jichž byl bezpočet, snažily se spoutati vodu do sklenné bezživotnosti'. In the first case, it is clearly the water that is meant to be frozen into immobility, but in the second case it is the canals themselves, which opens up the subversive possibility that the narrator is not only thinking about water that is flowing but canals that somehow seem to change position. This is, in all likelihood, a sly dig at the *changeant* quality of impressionist painting.[270] Quite apart from its telling appropriateness to 'cínové', the phrase '[vlny] posupně hlučely a hromobily' creates a subversively comic impression. It makes the narrator sound suspiciously like a disgruntled master moaning about disaffected servants rattling and banging pots and pans around in the kitchen, his exasperation at the clatter being underscored by his forcible transformation of the standard noun 'hromobití' into the notional verb 'hromobíti'.[271] This hint at the narrator's fastidious aristocratic perspective is combined with the impli-

---

pp. 39–47; and Evelyn Joll et al. (eds.), *The Oxford Companion to J. M. W. Turner* (Oxford, 2001). On artists' impressions of Venice, see Georges Duby et al., *A History of Venice in Painting* (New York, 2007); *Martin Schwander, Venedig: Von Canaletto und Turner bis Monet* (Ostfildern, 2008); Mark Evans, *Impressions of Venice from Turner to Monet* (Cardiff, 1992). On Turner and the Swiss Alps, see Andrew Wilton, *Turner in der Schweiz* (Zurich, 1976).

270   Venice was a favourite motif of impressionist painters from Eugène Boudin onwards. James Whistler's nocturnal lagoons, Auguste Renoir's views of San Marco and the Doge's Palace, Claude Monet's Venetian sunsets and his views of the Grand Canal and palaces have become legendary. See Alastair Grieve, *Whistler's Venice* (New Haven CT, 2000), Mary MacDonald, *Palaces in the Night: Whistler in Venice* (Berkeley CA, 2001), Philippe Piguet, *Monet et Venise* (Paris, 1986).

271   The verb *hromobíti* is not standardly accepted in Czech. It is not included in the *Slovník spisovného jazyka českého*, edited by the Československá akademie věd, 4 vols (Prague, 1971), but it is given as an incorrect form in the *Příruční slovník jazyka českého*, edited by the Československá akade-

cation of a sombre religiosity obsessed with divine retribution: 'vlny hlučely' sounds rather like the description of the waters of Babylon in Jeremiah while 'hromobití' reminds us of the seventh plague of Egypt in Exodus.[272]

Augsburští byli žáci učeliví a naučili se brzo barviti sklo zářící slunečně za lučební pomoci chloru, sklo tmavé rubínové jako ještěří krev příměsí ryzího zlata, modré jako letní obloha přítomností kobaltu, a takové, jak vybarvuje příroda krystaly ametystů, neberouc na potaz mistra Tartaglia. Německé sklo křišťálové nabylo takové čirosti ve své podstatě až klamné, jako by představovalo pojem nicoty absolutní.

This passage conceals the most important ironic twist in the whole narrative. When the narrator says that the craftsmen of Augsburg were good students and quick to learn ('žáci učeliví') and then lets us know that they were able to colour glass without asking Tartaglio's advice ('neberouc na potaz mistra Tartaglia'), he would like us to believe that they had learnt their skills from their master so thoroughly that they became independent of him. The author, however, would like us to remember that, while Tartaglio was eager to work out how to colour glass, he had little idea how to go about it, which is why the narrator imagined him trying to melt precious stones. Everything suggests that Tartaglio had nothing to teach the craftmen of Augsburg and that they worked everything out for themselves using the principles of chemistry. For the author, 'naučili se' means quite literally that they taught themselves. Though the Augsburgers come out on top here, the author does not allow them, or their creations, to shine. In 'sklo zářící slunečně', the brilliance of colour the narrator is arguing for is called into question by the way 'slunečně' is tagged on to 'zářící' as a modifier, leaving us wonder what to make of glass that is said to be 'shining sunnily'. That the ruby-coloured glass is described as 'sklo tmavé rubínové', with 'rubínový' being added to 'tmavý' to make it more specific, suggests that the glass was above all dark, and ruby-cloured perhaps only on closer inspection. The comparison of the colour to the lizard blood does not suggest the warmth of colour we might have hoped for, since lizards are known to be cold-blooded. The addition of pure gold also fails to impress since the purity of the gold would in any case be lost in the resulting mixture. That the sky-blue glass is said to have been coloured not simply by cobalt ('kobaltem') but by the presence of cobalt ('přítomností kobaltu') is an ironic reflection on the rarity of this element and the very im-

---

mie věd, 9 vols (Prague, 1935-57): ![nesprávné] *hromobíti* - ned. [nedokonavé] buráceti, bouřiti jako hrom. *Lid hromobil na náměstích a mostech, ohavným zpěvem tupě diadémy* (Opol.) [Opolský] As this entry shows, the only source quoted is another prose text by Opolský, where the word is almost certainly a similar ironic dislocation of normal usage.

272   Jeremiah 51:55; Exodus 9:23, 28, 29, 33, 34. 'Hromobití' is also found in 1 Samuel 12:17, 18, Job 36:29, Psalms 77:19, Revelations 4:5 and the deuterocanonical Book of Wisdom 19:13.

pure form in which it is standardly used in glass-making.[273] The description of purple glass as 'takové, jak vybarvuje příroda krystaly ametystů' uses the right words to make a good impression (barva, příroda, ametyst), but spoils it by admitting that the colouring must be highly uneven, as it is in naturally occurring crystals.

> I Tartaglio, sdíleje s nimi své umělé znalosti, měl dojem jakéhosi existenčního ubývání a mizení, jemuž nebylo lze ani ochrannými modlitbami zameziti. Jsa bezdětek, vydal se ze všech svých tajemství a jednoho rána pověsil se na svém opasku v návalu výčitek a domovinného stesku. Nebyla to smrt důstojná ani benátského měšťana, ba ani ne člověka, jenž je od Boha opásán citem a umělostí.

If we have understood the ironic import of the previous passage, we can see that the narrator's claim that Tartaglio shared his artistic knowledge with the Augsburg craftsman does not mean that they derived any benefit from this sharing. The substitution of 'umělé [znalosti]' for 'umělecké [znalosti]' once again reminds us that Tartaglio artistry is in any case more a question of artificiality that art. The description of the drastic psychological effect that revealing his secrets has on Tartaglio implicitly tells us more about the narrator than it does about his hero. Given the narrator's alienation from life and his overweening religiosity, we can well imagine that it is he who sometimes feels as if he caught up in some process of existential waning and fading away ('existenčního ubývání a mizení') which he vainly tries to contain by offering up protective prayers. The narrator's belated admission that Tartaglio's willingness to part with all his secrets is related to his childlessness implicitly confirms our earlier suspicions on this count. That Tartaglio's suicide is said to have been motivated by a surge of remorse and homesickness fails to specify what he felt remorse about. The narrator would still like us to believe that Tartaglio could not live with himself because he had betrayed his country and its artistic traditions by revealing his professional secrets to outsiders. The author meanwhile, knowing that Tartaglio has done nothing traitorous because he never had anything of value to reveal, is happy for us to interpret 'výčitky' as meaning nothing more than regret at having left home, something which is close to the idea of homesickness that no amplification of 'výčitky' is needed. The narrator's final rhetorical summing up falls equally flat. Most of us would consider suicide out of despair to be a form of death unworthy of any human being, so the narrator's reference to Tartaglio's status as a Venetian citizen and artist comes across as unbearably pompous.

---

273 Cobalt blue is produced using a compound of cobalt oxide and aluminium oxide called cobalt aluminate ($CoAl_2O_4$). Cobalt is a rare element that does not occur naturally in Europe. Today it is almost exclusively mined in Africa.

The characterisation of Tartaglio as an artist is also suspect. By having the narrator refer to him as a '[člověk] opásán citem a uměl ostí', the author is not only repeating his ironic intimations of artificiality but suggesting that the attributes in question are merely external, being worn about the person like a girdle. That the first attribute mentioned is 'cit' also fails to impress since emotion is something we are all endowed with. Finally, the narrator's use of the Biblical terms 'opasek' and 'opásán' bring out his religiosity even more clearly that his specification 'od Boha'.[274]

If we have been attentive to the irony in this story, we will have seen that Giacomo Tartaglio is not an inspired artist but a feeble-minded craftsman obsessed with an abstruse idea he cannot implement. Driven by greed and a craving for social status that his native Venice cannot satisfy, he sells himself to the highest foreign bidder. Although he does not possess the secret for which his services were procured, nor any other secret worth divulging, his deceit has no repercussions because his foreign pupils are easily able to manage without him. Finding himself superfluous, he kills himself in a fit of homesickness. The narrator is revealed as a person alienated from life, haunted by an overweening religiosity and given to misogyny, social snobbery and a passive but indiscriminate contemplation of artefacts.

---

274 In the Bible, 'opasek' ('girdle') occurs in 1 Kings 2:5, Isiah 45: 1, Acts of the Apostles 21:11, Matthew 10:9 and Mark 6:8; and 'opásán' ('girdled') occurs in 1 Samuel 2:4, 2 Samuel 21:16, Psalms 65:7 and Letter to the Ephesians 6:14.

11. CONCLUSION

The prose pieces we have examined are suffused with a subtle and sophisticated narrative irony that fundamentally transforms their content. The irony
in question is a stable irony that requires the reader to penetrate the surface reading in search of the determinate ironic meaning that lies beneath.
This distinguishes it from unstable ironies like Romantic irony, which fail
to establish a clear hierarchy of meanings. However, even if Opolský's irony
is not a Romantic irony, it may to some extent be what Roman Jakobson has
called an 'ironiia romantiky'.[275]

In this irony, the narrator is stylized as a figure alienated from the reality of life, estranged from a hypothetical norm of physical vitality and sober
realism. He is shown to be obsessively religious, concerned with superstition
and magic, and generally given to matters metaphysical. He is hostile to the
sensual and partial to the benumbing effect of narcotics. He has no adequate
sense of dynamism, tends to confuse abstract and concrete, figurative and
literal, personal and impersonal, and inclines also to vagueness. He is endowed with an oversensitive but shallow emotionality, with an exaggerated
but superficial aestheticism, and a liking for the artificial and coldly formalistic. He is sentimentally romantic, ingenuously idealistic, childishly naive
and extremely timid and squeamish. We also find him to be affected and often
staunchly bourgeois in attitude.

In deploying his ironic register, Opolský pulls out all the stops. His texts
draw on an astoundingly broad repertoire of verbal strategies. Sometimes
the irony derives from assertions that run contrary to our normal assumptions about reality or to expectations raised by previous assertions in the text.
This forms the mainstay of the irony in 'Rubensova Zahrada lásky', in which
initial expectations of godly nakedness are undermined by successive references to increasingly many items of clothing and jewelry; and it forms an
important structural principle in 'Čínská povídka', where the compromising
diminutiveness of the lacquer cabinet is only gradually revealed. Sometimes
the irony makes use of wide range of lexical, syntactic or referential polyse-
mia. This includes exploiting adverse connotations and associations of words
and phrases, extending or combining standard metaphors in such a way as

---

275 Roman Jakobson, 'Zametki na poliach *Evgeniia Onegina*', *Raboty po poetike* (Moscow, 1987), p. 220.

to create a comically literal image, and employing terms which are semantically redundant on one level of understanding but independently meaningful on another. It also includes the appeal to ambiguities afforded by negative comparatives and unreal comparisons, and the use of genitives which can be understood either as possessive genitives or as genitives of definition. Sometimes the irony derives mainly from various forms of incongruity. Here the range of devices ranges from the use of oxymora and the substitution of incongruous terms for accepted ones to the exploitation of deviant punctuation and syntax.

The irony in each of the texts is so similar and so consistently sustained in its makeup, so concentrated in its application and so intricate and sophisticated in its conception, that it is virtually impossible to believe that it is not the very *raison d'être* of Opolský's prose oeuvre.

Its presumably central role goes a long way towards explaining the characteristic brevity of his texts. Not only is sophisticated irony of this kind hugely difficult to sustain, there would also be little point in trying to sustain it over long stretches of narrative. Since it is the irony that provides the focus of interest and the principal source of tension, elaborate story-lines or sustained arguments are largely superfluous. The prose pieces need to be long enough for the reader reliably to identify the ironic message but at the same time they must avoid flogging it to death. The irony can also help explain the remarkable dearth of dialogue in Opolský prose pieces. Since the irony is vitally dependent on the narrator's idiosyncratic perspective, the author has no interest in providing a forum for alternative voices, except of course for his own.

It is perhaps because of its subtlety and sophistication that Opolský's irony has been consistently misunderstood. Irony of this complexity presents major challenges to the reader, and if the reader fails to spot this heavily veiled ironic intent, the ironist cannot step in to help. Writers like the eighteenth-century Russian poet Antioch Kantemir, who explains his irony in footnotes, are an embarrassing but instructive example of how the ironist's game should not be played. Opolský's failure to intervene in his own critical reception is not evidence of an intention to create a private irony, merely testimony to the fact that he understood and respected the unwritten rules of his craft.

Several elements in the ironic stylization of the narrator correspond to characteristics of Romanticism and the Decadence, but it is not entirely clear to what extent Opolský is actively concerned with mocking either of these movements. The creative strategy that informs this prose was adopted at a time when the late Romanticism of Julius Zeyer had run its course and the Decadence was gradually waning. In this period, mockery of Romanticism and Decadence still made tolerable sense. However, Opolský's prose production clearly does not peak until the twenties and thirties. By this time both movements had disappeared from the literary mainstream, though Jiří Karásek and Jaroslav Maria continued to write in the Decadent mode until the mid- or even late thirties. It therefore seems as if Opolský is ultimately more interested in exploring the potential of his ironic model for its own sake than he is in making a satirical point about contemporary attitudes. For the most part, the ironic stylization of the narrator is probably little more than a well-tried device that helps to make Opolský's peculiar brand of narrative irony possible. Those who have suggested that Opolský's pieces are characterized by 'samoúčelnost' (Josef Čapek) or are 'mnohdy jsou samy sobě účelem' (Jan Novotný) were therefore probably not far off the mark, though for reasons quite different to those they may have envisaged.

I think that it could easily be shown that Opolský's irony extends even to texts hitherto considered purely autobiographical ('Básník a jeho kraj', 'Z básnického testamentu'). However, I think that a qualification may need to be made for his occasional literary criticism, his children's stories, and his very earliest prose sketches ('Legenda o Gotliebovi [sic]', 'Srdce z vojny' and 'Žije, žije...'). Here I am not convinced that there is evidence of ironic intent and it is not difficult to see why this might be the case: literary reviews are normally commissioned and are expected to conform to standards of their own; children's stories are a wholly unsuitable medium for sophisticated narrative irony; and the earliest texts may be considered stylistically rudimentary.

An issue on which I do not wish to pronounce judgement is the status of Opolsky's verse in all this. Matters here are far from simple. On the one hand, we can hardly imagine that a writer who wrote both poetry and prose for most of his life would have changed his literary persona every time he changed genre. On the other hand, the sophisticated narrative irony that characterizes Opolský's prose would be difficult to replicate in narrative verse and almost impossible to replicate in shorter verse forms. I have recently discovered an example of a similar irony in a narrative poem but it happens to be the work of a poet of supreme genius whose exceptional mastery of his craft enabled him write without making the slightest concession to rhyme or metre.[276] But even allowing for this, there remains the issue of the shorter verse form. Resolving this issue for Opolský is a matter for further research. This research will need to bear in mind that the role of humour in Opolský's poetry has been underestimated, since the avowedly ironic and satirical poems collected in *Hrst ironie a satiry* represent only a fraction of what he produced for the satirical journals *Kopřivy*, *Nebojsa* and *Šibeničky*, with a second collection, *Satira válečná a popřevratová* never having been published.[277]

---

276 See my article 'Puškins *Mědnyj Vsadnik* Revisited: A Reading in Conventional Narrative Irony', *Russian literature* 72 (2012), pp. 45–108.

277 A persuasive argument for elements of satire in Opolský's early poetry has recently been put

Another subject for further research is the pedigree of Opolský's special brand of narrative irony. Again we confront a dilemma. On the one hand, it is difficult to believe that Opolský developed his ironic technique single-handed; on the other hand, there are no obvious literary forebears from which he could have learnt his artistic handiwork, especially within the confines of Czech literature. Irony has played a prominent role throughout the history of Czech literature, starting in the Middle Ages (*Podkoní a žák*, Smil Flaška's *z Pardubic's Nová rada zvířat*), continuing through the nineteenth century (Karel Hynek Mácha, Karel Havlíček-Borovský, Jan Neruda, Svatopluk Čech, J.S. Machar) and into the twentieth (Viktor Dyk, Jaroslav Hašek, Vítězslav Nezval, Jaromír John, Bohumil Hrabal, Milan Kundera, Václav Havel).[278] Indeed, it has often been said that ironic subversiveness is the mainstay of Czech literature, its default setting, so to speak. The only difficulty is that few Czech writers use irony in a similar way to Opolský. The sustained narrative irony in the anonymous medieval *Podkoní a žák* lacks the verbal sophistication of Opolský's irony. Mácha's *Máj* may be thought to offer a thoroughgoing and verbally sophisticated irony but the case for a interpreting it in this way has yet to be made.[279] In parts of the first story in *Malostranské povídky*, Neruda

---

forward by Lucie Kořínková. Speaking of his contributions to the journal *Nový kult* in 1900-1902, she comments: 'Náboženské hodnoty bylo [...] snadno možné skrze erotické hodnoty perziflovat – specialistou se v tomto ohledu v tom listu ukázal být básník Jan Opolský'. She instances his poem 'Svatá dějeprava', in which she sees him mocking Abraham's ultimately bigamistic fathering of Isaac by couching it in terms of sultry eroticism. See Lucie Kořínková, 'Nový kult jako tribuna sociálně vyloučených' in Zbyněk Hojda et al., *Útisk – charita – vyloučení. Sociální 19. století* (Prague, 2015) pp. 58-66, and Jan Opolský, 'Svatá dějeprava', *Nový kult*, 4 (1900-01), p. 74.

278 In the study of irony in Czech literature a disproportionate amount of attention has been accorded to Milan Kundera. See Bruce Donahue, 'Laughter and ironic humor in the fiction of Milan Kundera', *Critique: Studies in Contemporary Fiction*, 25 (1984), No. 2, pp. 67-76; Harry Hattingh, 'Being and the dialects of irony: a reading of some of Milan Kundera's novels', *Literator: tydskrif vir besondere en vergelykende taal- en literatuurstudie* 16 (1995), No. 2, pp. 95-121; Marek Nekula, 'Ironie v lásky hře osudné', *Linguistica brunensia: sborník prací filosofické fakulty brněnské university, A: Řada jazykovědná*, 44 (1995). No. 43, pp. 61-74; Peter Steiner, 'Ironies of history: *The Joke* of Milan Kundera', in Calin Mihailescu and Walid Hamarneh (eds), *Fiction updated: theories of fictionality, narratology and poetics* (Toronto 1996), pp. 197-212; Michal Bauer, 'L'ironie comme mode de la polémique et défi au vide dans les écrits de jeunesse de Kundera (1945-1970)', in Marie-Odile Thirouin and Martine Boyer-Weinmann (eds.), *Lire Milan Kundera* (Paris, 2009), pp. 101-130. On Vítězslav Nezval, Jaroslav Hašek and Václav Havel, see Wolfgang Schwarz, 'Paradigmenwechsel und Ironiestruktur in Vítězslav Nezvals Dramatik der zwanziger Jahre: Zum Problem des Übergangs vom Poetismus zum Surrealismus', in Hans-Bernd Harder et al.(eds), *Festschrift für Wolfgang Gesemann* (Neuried, 1986), pp. 355-364; Marie-Odile Thirouin, 'Chvêïk ironiste', *Cahiers de l'ILCEA*, 8 (2006), pp. 79-91; Kenneth Zagacki, 'Václav Havel and the rhetoric of folly', in Marketa Goetz-Stankiewicz and Phyllis Carey (eds), *Critical essays on Václav Havel* (New York, 1999), pp. 127-142.

279 Robert Pynsent has pointed to numerous types and functions of irony in *Máj*. Aside from the title itself, whose promise of vernal love is undercut by the reality of vernal death, and the 'well-nigh sarcastic' opening description of nature's vernal beauty, 'where a blossoming tree pretends to be love-struck', Pynsent points to the tragic irony of individual actions (e.g. Jarmila mistaking of the boatman for Vilém), the contrast between how actors/actants appear and how they act

occasionally strikes a kindred note, but what irony may have been intended is not adequately sustained. If Opolský's irony has literary forbears, they may well need to be sought elsewhere.

With Opolský's irony in mind, I have since come across a remarkably similar type of narrative irony in Nikolai Gogol's Ukrainian stories ('Old World Landowners', 'Terrible Vengeance', 'The Fair at Sorochintsy').[280] Here too the irony is dense, subtle and sophisticated, and here too the narrator is revealed as an eccentric, foppish, squeamish, overly sentimental and naively religious individual who is divorced from reality. The verbal devices employed are often remarkably similar (use of lexical ambiguity, semantic redundancy, oxymora, inappropriate terms, suggestive enumeration, over-extension of standard metaphors, syntactic incongruity etc.). Like Opolský's irony, this irony has been overlooked for generations and so it is unclear whether it could have acted as a source of inspiration here. Could Opolský, known to have been an ardent admirer of Gogol, have recognized the irony in these stories despite the unarguable challenges it provides to the Russian reader and the inordinate difficulty of rendering it adequately in translation? George Steiner has argued that a writer's creative understanding of another writer's work is often superior to the critic's response,[281] but can this explain how Opolský might have understood an irony others have failed to recognize with recourse to nothing more than an imperfect translation or an imperfectly understood original?[282] But can the evident parallels be entirely fortuitous, the result of an inadvertent process of artistic re-creation, the outcome of a

---

(e.g. the pale and slender Vilém as lord of the forests), the portrayal of the horrific in melodious language and the use of paradoxical verbal juxtapositions (e.g. amaranth na jaro svadlý) and rhymes (e.g vroucí/hasnoucí). See Robert B. Pynsent, 'Mácha, the Czech National Poet', in Marcel Cornis-Pope and John Neubauer (eds), *History of The Literary Cultures of East-Central Europe*, 4 vols (Amsterdam, 2004–2010), vol. 4, pp. 56–85 (pp. 66, 76, 77). He does not make the case for a sustained narrative irony, although I believe such a case could be made.

280 See my articles, 'How Gogol's *Old World Landowners* Is Made: The Ironic Weave Unravelled', *Russian Literature* (forthcoming) and 'Up The Dnepr: Discarding Icons and Debunking Ukrainian Cossack Myths in Gogol's *Strašnaja Mest'*', *Russian Literature* (forthcoming).

281 George Steiner, *Real Presences* (Chicago, 1991).

282 We have no indication as to how well Opolský may have known Russian. Gogol's works had become known in Bohemia from 1840 onwards, when Karel Sabina commended his Ukrainian stories in *Květy*. 'Old World Landowners' ('Starosvetskie pomeshchiki') was first translated into Czech as 'Starosvětští statkáři' by Karel Havlíček Borovský in 1845, 'Terrible Revenge' ('Strashnaia mest") as 'Strašná pomsta' by František Kořínek in 1852, and 'The Fair at Sorochintsy' ('Sorochinskaia jarmarka') as 'Soročinský trh' by Josef Podlipský in 1855. The first translations of Gogol's collected works were *Zábavné spisy M. Gogola* (Prague, 1846–1847), 4 vols, translated by Karel Vladislav Zap, Kristian Stefan and Karel Havlíček Borovský; and *Spisy N. V. Gogola* (Prague, 1891–1893), 4 vols, edited by Jiří Hrubý and translated by Ignác Hošek and Quido Hodura. In the intervening years a host of translations appeared in newspapers, magazines and periodicals such as the Prague-based *Národní noviny, Pražské noviny, Květy, Lumír, Světozor* and *Zlatá Praha*, and regional publications like *Moravská orlice, Česko-moravská pokladnice, Krakonoš* (Jičín), *Lužničan* (Tábor), *Velehrad* (Kroměříž) and *Zora* (Brno), from the pens of such translators as

chance meeting of like minds across time? For the moment, these questions too must be left open.

What I believe I have been able to establish is that Opolský, at least in his guise as a prose writer, is not in any sense a late Decadent or Decadent epigon but an original and gifted ironist who is out to entertain rather than shock the bourgeois. In this prose there is nothing of the Decadent sublimation of tragedy into aestheticism we find in Karel Hlaváček, the lightening of gloom through resigned laughter ('tristesse qui rit') we can see in Octave Mirbeau or Jean Lorrain or the sardonic twist in the tail typical of Jules Laforgue. It would also be inappropriate to characterize Opolský's narrative stance as Decadent self-irony or self-parody; for that, it is too central to his creative project and too readily explicable in terms of his biography: Opolský is not a self-styled Decadent aesthete mocking himself, but a skilled craftsman whom decades of painstaking labour have grounded in the routines and practicalities of artistic production (see pp. 13, 14) and who can therefore easily see through the unwordly pretentions of Decadent aestheticism. The studied complexity of his prose bears testimony to a creative impulse driven more by a pleasure in expert workmanship rather than by flights of eccentric fantasy.

Given the technical mastery of his art, Opolsky proves to be a far greater writer than anyone has ever supposed. When Hanuš Jelínek said of Opolský 'ses pages compteront parmi les plus parfaites de la prose tchèque', he was not far wrong, though for reasons he did not anticipate. Opolský has produced a formidable collection of miniature prose masterpieces that show him to be one of the finest ironists in Czech literature. At his best he may even be one of the most inventive and most skilful ironists to be found in any literature.

J. B. Kořínek, H. Libišanský, R. J. Rykava, L. Škorpil, J. Vincenc, to name just a few. See also Miroslav Zahrádka et al., *Slovník rusko-českých liternárních vztahů* (Ústí nad Orlicí, 2008), pp. 86–90.

APPENDIX

The following classification of Opolský's prose themes may be useful for reference. It shows the main topic areas and their relative weighting. In the case of the visual arts, which forms the largest subject category, it identifies the periods of European and Czechoslovak art Opolský dealt with, from the Middle Ages through to the twentieth century, while also indicating his interest in a range of artistic genres, styles and techniques.

We have assigned each title to only one thematic category, in the hope that the lack of overlaps will make the relative frequency of individual themes clearer than would otherwise have been the case. To the same effect, the categories have been arranged in order of size.

The letter and numbers in brackets following each title are cross-references to the appropriate subdivisions of section one of the bibliography. The titles without an 'A'-reference were never published in book form.

In the category 'Visual Arts', the artists have been assigned to centuries according to what is generally acknowledged to be their main creative period and not simply according to biographical dates.

VISUAL ARTS

1. History of art
(a) Individual artists and works of art
  (i) *European art outside Czechoslovakia*
  - Ninth century:
    Umění sv. Lazara (A 11)
  - Fourteenth century:
    Giotto (A 14, B 95)
  - Fifteenth century:
    Anno domini (A 16, B 78)
    Fra Angelico (D 3)
    Fra Filippo Lippi (B 143)
    List učitele žáku (D 3)
    Nadlidský úkol (B 194)
    Náhrobky (A 25, B 129)
    Rozhovor L.P. 1465 (A 15)
    Zrození Venuše (A 15, B 102)
  - Sixteenth century:
    Cesta slávy Domenica Theotokopuli –
    El Greca (B 164)
    Holbeinovy 'Tance smrti' (D 3)
    Lukáš Cranach (A 18, B 112)
    Malíř apokalypsy (B 140)
    Malíř mystické bolesti, Matyáš
    Grünewald (B 161)
    Mona Lisa Gioconda (A 16, B 96)

Ulehčená smrt (A 37, B 183)
Životní úskalí Albrechta Dürera (A 32)
  - Seventeenth century:
    Čaloun (A 25, B 117)
    Gian Lorenzo Bernini (A 18)
    Jan Steen (D 7)
    Nehynoucí láska (A 37, B 172)
    Rubensova 'Zahrada lásky' (A 15)
    V úsvitu baroka (A 35, B 142)
  - Eighteenth century:
    Honoré Fragonard (B 160)
    Wiliam [sic] Hogarth (D 3)
  - Nineteenth century:
    Félicien Rops (B 137)
    Gustave Courbet (A 34)
    James McWhistler [sic], umělec
    v dandym (B 166)
    O Paulu Cézannovi (B 153)
    Životní úděl malíře Délacroix (B 191)
  (ii) *Czechoslovak art*
  - Fifteenth century:
    Matěj Rejsek, stavitel (B 199)
  - Seventeenth and eighteenth centuries:
    Neustálený profil (B 157)
    O Václavu Hollarovi (B 181)
    Slavný portrétista (B 171)
    Škretův úděl (B 206)

Koszciusko (A 16, B 53)
Medium (D 12)
Milostná soška (A 22)
Moselské víno (A 22, B 114)
Odměna komponistova (A 14, B 36)
O loutnařce a kyrysarovi (A 14)
Paruka (A 31, B 107)
Pohár (B 85)
Prastará historie (B 186)
Představení v soumraku (A 4, B 11)
Ruce (A 11, B 31)
Síla zvyku (B 202)
Snář (A 4, B 13)
Staré prsteny (B 192)
Studna krásy (A 28)
Upír (A 16, B 61)
Vodomety trianonské (B 59)
Zázrak v basilice sv. Jiří (A 31)
Zrcadlo Kateřiny Medicejské (A 14, B 97)

ISOLATION, ASCETICISM

Anachoret (A 11, B 41)
Drama samoty (A 37, B 57)
Flagelanti (A 4, B 9)
Jaro (A 16, B 40)
Kartusián (A 15, B 103)
Klášter (A 7, B 21)
Mimo život (A 11, B 30)
Novicka (A 22, B 110)
Poustevník z Thebaidy (A 31, B 123)
Poušť (A 14, B 87)
Pustina (A 7, B 20)
Samota (B 163)
Snící země (B 120)
Věžný chrámu (A 37, B 261)
Visuté zahrady (A 31, B 113)
Zámek (A 16, B 83)

LOVE, EROTICISM, WOMAN

Apotheosa (B 45)
Dcera Zedechiova (A 14, B 101)
Háj (D 13)
Harém (A 35)
Judith (A 14, B 91)
Laura (A 14, B 88)
Lesní láska (A 11, B 35)
Monstrum (A 31, B 127)
Nevěstka Rahab (A 35, B 148)
Ohnivá cesta (A 14, B 94)
Podletí (A 16, B 74)

Pověst o královně Erině (A 16, B 52)
V pozdních hodinách (A 4, B 10)
Za starých časů (A 16, B 73)

HISTORY

Autodafé (A 35, B 145)
Belveder (A 26)
Dvůr Polykratův (A 14, B 92)
Gojím (A 16, B 98)
Jeanne d'Arc (A 7)
Karlštejn (A 35, B 121)
Krumlov (A 37)
Lázně v Bajích (A 16)
Malostranské paláce (A 16, B 71)
Na hradě Pecce (A 37)
Po cestě historie (B 39)
Ruská historie (A 16)
Sardanapal (A 16, B 64)

ANIMALS

Drobná rozkoš (B 169)
Hraboši (B 67)
Kapr (B 90)
Kohout (A 11)
O ježkovi (A 16, B 68)
Páv (A 16, B 81)
Sbohem, Lori (B 150)
Smrt myší (A 4)
Sojka (A 15, B 100)
Tři pěvci (A 7, B 27)
Zajíc (A 16)
Zastřený hlas (A 7, B 24)

CLASSICAL MYTHOLOGY

Aesculap (B 201)
Endymion (A 16, B 77)
Falešná historie (A 14, B 84)
Heracles (A 35, B 152)
Narcis (B 200)
O lyru (B 168)
Orfeus (A 16, B 58)
Pláč Nioby (A 15)
Selene (A 31, B 133)
Souhvězdí medvěda (B 184)
Sudba (A 16, B 86)
Tantalos (A 22)

AGING, DEATH

Den smrti (A 15)

Hluboká voda (A 14, B 104)
Hroby hrdin (A 11)
Konec (B 8)
Loučení (A 7, B 23)
Podzimní (A 11)
Smrt (Bylo jí vtáhnouti se mezi veřeje-
mi...) (A 14, B 39)
Smrt (Umíral chaboučký...) (B 60)
Staroch (A 37, B 162)
Stáří a smrt umělců (B 158)
U hrobu J.K. Šlejhara (A 14, B 128)

CHRISTIAN RELIGION

A pietoso (B 1)
Jitro v Týně (B 105)
Kostel 'V nejsvětější tichosti' (A 31, B 134)
Legenda (A 16, B 76)
Legenda o Gotliebovi [sic] (D 9)
Misie (A 37, B 174)
Starý obrázek (A 7, B 25)
Symfonie (A 7, B 29)
Vnitřek chrámu (A 4, B 6)

MUSIC

Cikáni (B 109)
Dílo (A 11)
Flétna (A 37)
Muzikant (A 37, B 180)
Na koncertě (A 37, B 111)
Opera s loutkami (A 11)
Stradivari (A 21)
Ztracený hlas (A 37, B 151)

THEATRE

Divadlo (Mnoho bylo řečeno lidmi povola-
nými...) (A11, B 38)
Divadlo (Stále a stále tane mi na mysli...)
(A 4)

Divadlo na venkově (A 16, B 70)
Herci jindy (A 16, B 62)
Pavla (A 11, B 34)
Truchlivá historka (A 4, B 3)
Večery v kabaretu (A 11, B 33)

LITERATURA

Básníci (A 16, B 75)
Básník a jeho kraj (A 37)
Matčiny modlitby (A 37)
Matteo Bandello (A 16, B 69)
Řecké idyly (A 16, B 80)
Z básnického testamentu (A 37)

NIGHT

Letní noc (A 16, B 55)
Měsíc (B 106)
Noc (A 4, B 8)
Noc chorého (B 14 4)
Noc v galerii (A 11, B 46)
Spánek (A 37, B 115)

CINEMA

Biograf (B 43)
Ještě k biografu I (B 48)
Ještě k biografu II (B 49)
Ještě k biografu III (B 66)
Konference (A 16, B 63)

DREAM, VISION

Císař mexický (A 22, B 108)
Ideál (A 11)
Konrad Pachta, stavitel (A 18, B 131)
Narkotikum (A 31, B 136)
Vasco da Gama (A 31, B 139)
Vzpomínka (B 138)

CLASSIFIED BIBLIOGRAPHY

1. WORKS BY JAN OPOLSKÝ

1.1 Publications in book form

1. *Svět smutných* (Prague, 1899) V
2. *Klekání* (Prague, 1900) V
3. *Jedy a léky* (Prague, 1901) V
4. *Kresby uhlem* (Prague, 1907) P
5. *Pod tíhou života* (Prague, 1909) V
6. *Hrst ironie a satiry* (Prague, 1911) V
7. *Demaskovaní* (Prague, 1916) P
8. *Nová země* (Pacov, 1918) P
9. *Verše o životě a smrti* (Prague, 1918) V
10. *Galerie zvířat* (Prague, 1921) V
11. *Muka a zdání* (Prague, 1921) P
12. *Dědictví* (Prague, 1923) V
13. *Hvězda mořská* (Prague, 1925)*V
14. *Z těžkého srdce*, first edition (Prague, 1925); second expanded edition (Prague, 1926) P
15. *Malé prosy* (Turnov, 1926) P
16. *Upír a jiné prosy* (Prague, 1926) P
17. *Ze tmy do tmy* (Prague, 1926)*P
18. *Medailony* (Prague, 1927)*V & P
19. *Pohádka o pěvci* (Prague, 1927)*V
20. *Vitrina* (Prague, 1927)*P
21. *Stradivari* (Prague, 1928) P
22. *Víry i tůně* (Prague, 1928) P
23. *Dětský hymnus* (Prague, 1929)*V
24. *Melusina* (Prague, 1929)*P
25. *Miniatury* (Prague, 1930) P
26. *Belveder* (Prague, 1931) P
27. *Hory a doly a lesy* (Prague, 1931)*V
28. *Studna krásy* (Prague, 1932) P
29. *Pražský hrad* (Prague, 1934) P
30. *Kameje* (Prague, 1935)*V
31. *Visuté zahrady* (Prague, 1935) P
32. *Životní úskalí Albrechta Dürera* (Prague, 1935) P
33. *Čtení z hvězd a obelisků* (Prague, 1936) V
34. *Gustave Courbet* (Prague, 1937) P
35. *Pod patinou věků* (Prague, 1937) P
36. *Nové Město pražské* (Prague, 1940) P
37. *Hranolem křišťálu* (Prague, 1944) P
38. *Růžena Jesenská* (Prague, 1944) P
39. *Představení v soumraku*, edited by Ivan Slavík (Prague, 1968) V & P
40. *Hadí král* (Prague, 1990) *V

41. *Sám všechen život býti: výbor z básnických sbírek 1899–1936*, edited by Petr Fabian (Prague, 2001) *V, online as *Zapomenuté světlo* at *www.petr-fabian.cz/zapomenute/opolsky/index.html* V
42. *Staré lesy*, edited by Václav Cílek and Pavel Kostiuk (Prague, 2011) V & P
43. *Povodeň* (Nová Paka, 2013), with a preface by Jaromír Typlt *P

* – Limited bibliophile edition; V – Verse; P – Prose

1.2 Prose publications in periodicals

1. 'A pietoso', *Rozhledy*, 7 (1897–8), p. 1048.
2. 'Svatba', *Kalendář revolucionářů na rok 1903*, 1 (1902), pp. 78–80.
3. 'Truchlivá historka', *Lumír*, 31 (1902–3), pp. 216–7.
4. 'Před pohřbem', *Rozhledy*, 13 (1902–3), pp. 150–2.
5. 'Hladový', *Rozhledy*, 13 (1902–3), pp. 758–61.
6. 'Vnitřek chrámu', *Rozhledy*, 13 (1902–3), pp. 1050–2.
7. 'Poledne', *Rozhledy*, 13 (1902–3), pp. 1232–4.
8. 'Dvě básně v prose', *Srdce*, 2 (1902–3), pp. 13–4.
9. 'Flagelanti', *Kalendář revolucionářů na rok 1904*, 2 (1903) pp. 57–9.
10. 'V pozdních hodinách', *Moderní život*, 2 (1903), pp. 14–5.
11. 'Představení v soumraku', *Lumír*, 32 (1903–4), pp. 109–11.
12. 'Lokální příběh', *Rozhledy*, 14 (1903–4), pp. 667–9.
13. 'Snář', *Rozhledy*, 14 (1903–4), pp. 1005–6.
14. 'Na pranýři', *Lumír*, 33 (1904–5), pp. 153–7.
15. 'Masky', *Rozhledy*, 15 (1904–5), pp. 629–30.
16. 'Jilemští', *Lumír*, 34 (1905–6), pp. 9–12.
17. 'Mlýn', *Rozhledy*, 16 (1905–6), pp. 226–9.
18. 'Manifestace', *Rozhledy*, 16 (1905–6), pp. 462–5.
19. 'Pocestní', *Rozhledy*, 17 (1907), pp. 360–2.
20. 'Pustina', *Lumír*, 36 (1907–8), pp. 145–8.
21. 'Klášter', *Lumír*, 36 (1907–8), pp. 337–8.
22. 'Povodeň', *Moravskoslezská revue*, 4 (1907–8), pp. 83–4.
23. 'Loučení', *Rozhledy*, 18 (1908), pp. 15–7.
24. 'Zastřený hlas', *Lumír*, 37 (1908–9), pp. 1–2.
25. 'Starý obrázek', *Národní obzor*, 3 (1908–9), p. 61.
26. 'Vývoj poslanectví', *Národní obzor*, 3 (1908–9), p. 93.
27. 'Tři pěvci', *Lumír*, 38 (1909–10), pp. 16–8.
28. 'Dobročinný ples', *Rudé květy*, 9 (1909–10), pp. 66–8.
29. 'Symfonie', *Lumír*, 39 (1910–11), pp. 2–4.
30. 'Mimo život', *Lumír*, 44 (1916), pp. 503–4.
31. 'Ruce', *Národní listy*, 6 August 1917, p. 1.
32. 'Lovy', *Národní listy*, 8 November 1917, p. 1.
33. 'Večery v kabaretu', *Venkov*, 28 October 1917, supplement p. 2.
34. 'Pavla', *Lumír*, 46 (1917–8), pp. 340–4.
35. 'Lesní láska', *Moderní revue*, 24 (1917–8), pp. 103–9.
36. 'Odměna komponistova', *Zlatá Praha*, 35 (1917–8), pp. 374–5.
37. 'Řeky a lidé', *Národní listy*, 8 January 1918, p. 1.
38. 'Divadlo' (Mnoho bylo řečeno lidmi povolanými...), *Národní listy*, 5 April 1918, p. 1.
39. 'Po cestě historie', *Cesta*, 1 (1918–9), pp. 61–2.
40. 'Jaro', *Moderní revue*, 25 (1918–9), pp. 253–6.
41. 'Anachoret', *Moderní revue*, 25 (1918–9), pp. 879–82.
42. 'Bez názvu', *Národní listy*, 20 February 1919, p. 1.
43. 'Biograf', *Národní listy*, 1 August 1919, p. 1.
44. 'Zázračná oslava', *Venkov*, 20 July 1919, supplement pp. 1–2.
45. 'Apotheosa', *Ženské noviny*, 1 May 1919, p. 2.

46. 'Noc v galerii', *Moderní revue*, 26 (1919–20), pp. 243–6.
47. 'Dvojí idol', *Zlatá Praha*, 37 (1919–20), p. 66.
48. 'Ještě k biografu', I, *Zlatá Praha*, 37 (1919–20), p. 194.
49. 'Ještě k biografu', II, *Zlatá Praha*, 37 (1919–20), p. 210.
50. 'Volná kapitola', *Československá republika*, 26 June 1920, p. 2.
51. 'Sedlák', *Země*, 2 (1920–1), pp. 85–7.
52. 'Pověst o královně Erině', *Země*, 2 (1920–1), pp. 119–20.
53. 'Kosciuszko', *Země*, 2 (1920–1), pp. 147–8.
54. 'Krčma', *Země*, 2 (1920–1), pp. 83–4.
55. 'Letní noc', *Země*, 2 (1920–1), pp. 285–6.
56. 'Orfeus', *Československá republika*, 6 February 1921, supplement p. 1.
57. 'Drama samoty', *Československá republika*, 17 April 1921, supplement p. 1; reprinted in *Národní listy*, 30 July 1933, pp. 1–2.
58. 'Malé město', *Československá republika*, 15 May 1921, supplement p. 1.
59. 'Vodomety trianonské', *Československá republika*, 4 December 1921, supplement p. 1.
60. 'Smrt' (Umíral chaboučký, klamně se domnívaje...), *Lidové noviny*, 12 May 1921, p. 2.
61. 'Upír', *Lidové noviny*, 27 August 1921, p. 2.
62. 'Herci jindy', *Národní listy*, 19 March 1921, p. 1.
63. 'Konference', *Národní listy*, 23 April 1921, p. 1.
64. 'Sardanapal', *Národní listy*, 21 May 1921, p. 1.
65. 'Zdravotní kolonie', *Národní listy*, 10 September 1921, p. 1.
66. 'Ještě k biografu', III, *Zlatá Praha*, 38 (1921), pp. 99–100.
67. 'Hraboši', *Zvířena*, 18 (1921), p. 20.
68. 'O ježkovi', *Zvířena*, 18 (1921), p. 28.
69. 'Matteo Bandello', *Země*, 3 (1921–2), pp. 217–8.
70. 'Divadlo na venkově, *Lidové noviny*, 7 April 1922, p. 2.
71. 'Malostranské paláce', *Lidové noviny*, 4 June 1922, p. 2.
72. 'Tartufferie', *Lidové noviny*, 25 June 1922, p. 2.
73. 'Za starých časů', *Lidové noviny*, 22 July 1922, p. 2.
74. 'Podletí', *Lumír*, 49 (1922), pp. 158–60.
75. 'Básníci', *Lumír*, 49 (1922), pp. 328–30.
76. 'Legenda', *Lumír*, 49 (1922), pp. 338–41.
77. 'Endymion', *Lumír*, 49 (1922), pp. 546–8.
78. 'Anno domini', *Právo lidu*, 28 January 1922, supplement p. 1.
79. 'Pracovníci různých národů', *Právo lidu*, 10 June 1922, supplement p. 1.
80. 'Řecké idyly', *Právo lidu*, 19 August 1922, supplement p. 1.
81. 'Páv', *Zvířena*, 19 (1921), p. 1.
82. 'Mědirytina', *Lumír*, 50 (1923), pp. 42–4.
83. 'Zámek', *Lumír*, 50 (1923), pp. 229–32.
84. 'Falešná histoire', *Lumír*, 50 (1923), pp. 427–9.
85. 'Pohár', *Právo lidu*, 7 March 1923, supplement p. 1.
86. 'Sudba', *Právo lidu*, 27 May 1923, supplement p. 1.
87. 'Poušť', *Moderní revue*, 30 (1923–4), pp. 188–91.
88. 'Laura', *Lumír*, 51 (1924), pp. 234–8.
89. 'Div', *Lumír*, 51 (1924), pp. 338–41.
90. 'Kapr', *Zvířena*, 21 (1924), pp. 25–6.
91. 'Judith', *Moderní revue*, 31 (1924–5), pp. 75–8.
92. 'Dvůr Polykratův', *Moderní revue*, 31 (1924–5), pp. 112–5.
93. 'Smrt' (Bylo jí vtáhnouti se mezi veřejemi...), *Moderní revue*, 31, No. 5 (March 1925), pp. 8–11; reprinted in *Lumír*, 58 (1931–2), pp. 84–5.
94. 'Ohnivá cesta', *Země*, 6 (1924–5), pp. 1–3.
95. 'Giotto', *Země*, 6 (1924–5), pp. 17–8.
96. 'Mona Lisa Gioconda', *Země*, 6 (1924–5), pp. 81–3.

97. 'Zrcadlo Kateřiny Medicejské', *Lumír*, 52 (1925), pp. 31-4.

98. 'Gojím', *Lumír*, 52 (1925), pp . 170-4.

99. 'Kreslíř', *Lumír*, 52 (1925), pp. 452-5.

100. 'Sojka', *Zvířena*, 22 (1925), p. 18.

101. 'Dcera Zedechiova', *Lumír*, 53 (1926), pp. 33-5.

102. 'Zrození Venuše', *Lumír*, 53 (1926), pp. 169-73.

103. 'Kartusián', *Země*, 7 (1925-6), pp. 17-9.

104. 'Hluboká voda', *Země*, 7 (1925-6), pp. 65-6.

105. 'Jitro v Týně', *Země*, 7 (1925-6), pp. 114-5.

106. 'Měsíc', *Národní listy*, 6 April 1927, p. 5.

107. 'Paruka', *Národní listy*, 31 May 1927, p. 5.

108. 'Císař mexický', *Národní listy*, 24 July 1927, p. 1.

109. 'Cikáni', *Národní listy*, 2 October 1927, p. 1.

110. 'Novicka', *Národní listy*, 18 October 1927, p. 5.

111. 'Na koncertě', *Národní listy*, 18 December 1927, p. 5.

112. 'Lukáš Cranach', *Lumír*, 54 (1927-8), pp. 9-12.

113. 'Visuté zahrady', *Lumír*, 54 (1927-8), pp. 284-8.

114. 'Moselské víno', *Národní listy*, 25 January 1928, p. 5.

115. 'Spánek', *Sever a východ*, 4 (1928), pp. 84-5.

116. 'Prostory světa', *Lumír*, 55 (1928-9), pp. 146-9.

117. 'Čaloun', *Lumír*, 55 (1928-9), pp. 338-40.

118. 'Lesy Julia Mařáka', *Lumír*, 55 (1928-9), pp. 433-5.

119. 'Miniatury', *Rozpravy Aventina*, 4 (1928-9), p. 211.

120. 'Snící země', *Národní listy*, 20 January 1929, p. 1.

121. 'Karlštejn', *Národní listy*, 16 June 1929, pp. 1-2.

122. 'Zbraslav', *Národní listy*, 14 July 1929, pp. 1-2

123. 'Poustevník z Thebaidy', *Národní listy*, 21 December 1929, supplement p. 4.

124. 'Biedermeier', *Národní listy*, 22 December 1929, p. 1; reprinted in *Lumír*, 59 (1932-3), pp. 5-7.

125. 'Lékárna "U jednorožce"', *Lumír*, 56 (1929-30), pp. 8-10.

126. 'J.V. Myslbek', *Lumír*, 56 (1929-30), pp. 73-5.

127. 'Monstrum', *Lumír*, 56 (1929-30), pp. 393-6.

128. 'O J.K. Šlejharovi', *Rozpravy Aventina*, 5 (1929-30), pp. 297-8.

129. 'Náhrobky', *Země*, 11 (1929-30), pp. 121-8.

130. 'Za Otokarem Březinou', *Almanach ČAVU na rok 1929*, (1930), pp. 7-15.

131. 'Konrad Pachta, stavitel', *Sever a východ*, 6 (1930), pp. 119-21.

132. 'Svátost umírajících', *Lumír*, 57 (1930-1), pp. 63-8.

133. 'Selene', *Lumír*, 57 (1930-1), pp. 225-6.

134. 'Kostel "V nejsvětější tichosti"', *Lumír*, 57 (1930-1), pp. 395-7.

135. 'Malíř podhoří', *Venkov*, 24 December 1931, p. 6.

136. 'Narkotikum', *Lumír*, 59 (1932-3), pp. 186-8.

137. 'Félicien Rops', *Lumír*, 59 (1932-3), pp. 268-70.

138. ‚Vzpomínka', *Sedmdesát let umělecké besedy 1863-1933*, pp. 200-201.

139. 'U kořenů umění dřevoryteckého', *Sborník grafické práce Hollar*, 9 (1933), pp. 25-31.

140. 'Vasco da Gama', *Lumír*, 60 (1933-4), pp. 187-9.

141. 'Malíř apokalypsy', *Lumír*, 60 (1933-4), pp. 419-22.

142. 'Okouzlení z grafiky', *Sborník grafické práce Hollar*, 10 (1934), pp. 99-110.

143. 'U úsvitu baroka', *Lumír*, 61 (1934-5), pp. 186-9.

144. 'Fra Filippo Lippi', *Salon*, 14, No. 12 (December 1935), pp. 12, 37.

145. 'Noc chorého', *Národní listy*, 8 September 1935, p. 1.

146. 'Autodafé', *Národní listy*, 10 November 1935, p. 10.

147. 'Závoj miniatury portrétní', *Dílo*, 27 (1935-6), pp. 116-8.

148. 'V závětří biedermaierů [sic]', *Dílo*, 27 (1935-6), pp. 146-8.

149. 'Nevěstka Rahab', *Lumír*, 62 (1935-6), pp. 1-4.

150. 'Dryáčník', *Národní listy*, 2 February 1936, pp. 1–2.
151. 'S bohem, Lori', *Národní listy*, 23 February 1936, p. 10.
152. 'Ztracený hlas', *Národní listy*, 12 april 1936, p. 10.
153. 'Heracles', *Národní listy*, 1 November 1936, p. 10.
154. 'O Paulu Cézannovi', *Salon*, 15, No. 12 (December 1936), pp. 20, 33.
155. 'Pod krovy kláštera', *Lumír*, 63 (1936–7), pp. 2–5.
156. 'Monumentalita', *Národní listy*, 12 March 1937, p. 5.
157. 'Dílo F. Koblihy', *Sborník grafické práce Hollar*, 13 (1937), pp. 153–170.
158. 'Neustálený profil', *Dílo*, 28 (1937–8), pp. 14–6.
159. 'Stáří a smrt umělců', *Dílo*, 28 (1937–8), pp. 66–8.
160. 'Umění silhouetní', *Dílo*, 28 (1937–8), p. 98.
161. 'Honoré Fragonard', *Dílo*, 28 (1937–8), pp. 128–9, 131.
162. 'Malíř mystické bolesti Matyáš Grünewald', *Dílo*, 28 (1937–8), p. 137.
163. 'Staroch', *Národní listy*, 6 February 1938, pp. 1–2.
164. 'Samota', *Národní listy*, 27 March 1938, pp. 1–2.
165. 'Cesta slávy Domenica Theotokopuli – El Greca', *Dílo*, 29 (1938–9), pp. 90–1.
166. 'Nad listy dřevorytu', *Sborník grafické práce Hollar*, 14 (1938–9), pp. 165–78.
167. 'James McWhistler [sic], umělec v dandym', *Sborník grafické práce Hollar*, 14 (1938–9), pp. 178–81.
168. 'Meditace o starých knihách', *Český bibliofil*, 11 (1939), pp. 2–4.
169. 'O lyru', *Lumír*, 65 (1939), pp. 173–5.
170. 'Drobná rozkoš', *Národní politika*, 27 October 1939, p. 2.
171. 'O Alfonsu Muchovi', *Národní politika*, 25 November 1939, p. 2.
172. 'Slavný portrétista', *Národní politika*, 17 December 1939, p. 2.
173. 'Nehynoucí láska', *Salon*, 18, No. 6 (June 1939), p. 10.
174. 'Únos Evropy', *Dílo*, 30 (1939–40), pp. 85–8.
175. 'Misie', *Národní obnova*, 6 April 1940, p. 6.
176. 'Malíři madon', *Národní obnova*, 11 May 1940, p. 7.
177. 'Pro památku Jaroslava Čermáka', *Národní politika*, 6 January 1940, p. 2.
178. 'Gabriel Max', *Národní politika*, 6 February 1940, p. 2.
179. 'Čínská povídka', *Národní politika*, 1 March 1940, p. 2.
180. 'O Václavu Brožíkovi', *Národní politika*, 4 April 1940, p. 2
181. 'Muzikant', *Národní politika*, 5 May 1940, p. 2
182. 'O Václavu Hollarovi', *Národní politika*, 24 May 1940, p. 2.
183. 'Zlatníci a zlatotepci', *Národní politika*, 3 July 1940, p. 2.
184. 'Ulehčená smrt', *Národní politika*, 24 July 1940, p. 2.
185. 'Souhvězdí medvěda', *Národní politika*, 10 September 1940, p. 2.
186. 'Baron Prášil', *Národní politika*, 20 October 1940, pp. 1–2.
187. 'Prastará historie', *Národní politika*, 26 November 1940, p. 1.
188. 'O Juliu Mařákovi', *Národní politika*, 13 December 1940, p. 1.
189. 'Dílo středověké samoty', *Polední list*, 24 March 1940, supplement pp. 1–2.
190. 'Mosaika', *Polední list*, 31 March 1940, pp. 1–3.
191. 'Sbratření mysli', *Polední list*, 7 April 1940, pp. 1–2.
192. 'Životní úděl malíře Délacroix', *Polední list*, 28 July 1940, p. 6.
193. 'Staré prsteny', *Polední list*, 20 October 1940, p. 6.
194. 'Tiskař, malíř a mědirytec', *Sborník grafické práce Hollar*, 16 (1940), pp. 2–10.
195. 'Nadlidský úkol', *Dílo*, 31 (1940–1), pp. 264–5.
196. 'Restaurátor', *Aukční katalog Zdeňka Jeřábka*, 17, No. 5 (June 1941), pp. 1–2.
197. 'Kuriósní sbírka', *Aukční katalog Zdeňka Jeřábka*, 17, No. 8 (November 1941), pp. 1–2.
198. 'O sochaři Stanislavu Suchardovi', *Národní politika*, 7 February 1941, p. 1.
199. 'Interviewy', *Národní politika*, 6 March 1941, p. 1.
200. 'Matěj Rejsek, stavitel', *Národní politika*, 17 April 1941, p. 1.
201. 'Narcis', *Národní politika*, 24 April 1941, p. 1.
202. 'Aesculap', *Národní politika*, 10 August 1942, p. 1.

203. 'Síla zvyku', *Národní politika*, 19 September 1941, p. 1.
204. 'O sochaři Václavu Levém', *Národní politika*, 19 November 1941, p. 1.
205. 'Malíř Fr. B. Zvěřina', *Národní politika*, 14 December 1941, p. 2.
206. 'Kursiva', *Polední list*, 2 March 1941, p. 8.
207. 'Škrétův úděl', *Polední list*, 23 March 1941, p. 8.
208. 'Vítězství barev', *Dílo*, 32 (1941–2), p. 122.
209. 'Kopista', *Aukční katalog Zdeňka Jeřábka*, 18, No. 3, (May 1942), pp. 1–2.
210. 'K litografiím Maxe Švabinského', *Sborník grafické práce Hollar*, 18 (1942), pp. 1–10.

Most of these writings were reprinted in the following books:

Kresby uhlem	– Nos. 3–17.
Demaskovaní	– Nos. 18–29.
Muka a zdání	– Nos. 30–5, 37, 38, 41, 42, 46.
Z těžkého srdce	– Nos. 36, 84, 87–9, 91–5, 101, 104.
Malé prosy	– Nos. 99, 100, 102, 103.
Upír a jiné prosy	– Nos. 40, 51–6, 61–4, 68–71, 73–83, 85, 86, 98.
Medailony	– Nos. 112, 131.
Víry i tůně	– Nos. 108, 110, 114.
Miniatury	– Nos. 116, 117, 119, 124, 129, 132.
Visuté zahrady	– Nos. 107, 113, 123, 127, 133, 134, 136, 139.
Pod patinou věků	– Nos. 142, 145, 148, 149, 152, 154.
Hranolem křišťálu	– Nos. 57, 111, 115, 122, 151, 162, 172, 174, 178, 180, 183, 188.
Představení v soumraku	– Nos. 11, 31, 54, 55, 56, 100, 106, 119, 131.
Staré lesy	– Nos. 77, 122.

Notes
1. The manuscripts 'Noc' and 'Konec' were published under the heading 'Dvě básně v prose' (8).
2. 'Jaro' (40) is reprinted as 'Poustevníkovo jaro'.
3. 'Dvůr Polykratův' (92) is reprinted as 'Polykratův dvůr'.
4. 'Sojka' (100) is reprinted as 'Imitátorka'.

1.3 Verse publications in periodicals

'Sám o sobě', *Lumír*, 60 (1934), pp. 217–9

Since Opolský's verse is extensive and of peripheral significance to the argument of this book, I append a skeleton bibliography of the remainder of his poetry in periodicals. I note the journals to which he contributed, the year of publication and (where appropriate) the number of the volume, but without reference to individual poems.

Aukční katalog Zdeňka Jeřábka, 16 (1940)
Československá republika, 1920–2
Kolo, 7 (1937), 8 (1938)
Kopřivy, 1 (1909) – 3 (1911)
Kramerius, 2 (1905–6)
Lidové noviny, 1921–2
Listy, 1 (1933)
Loutkář, 14 (1927–8)
Lumír, 27 (1899) – 66 (1942)
Moderní revue, 5 (1899) – 8 (1902), 22 (1916) – 31 (1925)
Moderní život, 1 (1902), 2 (1903)
Moravskoslezská revue, 4 (1907–8), 6 (1908–10)
Most, 2 (1923)
Národ, 1 (1917), 2 (1918)
Národní listy, 1918, 1926, 1928–30, 1933–8
Národní obzor, 1 (1906–7)
Nebojsa, 1 (1918) – 3 (1920)

Nový kult, 3 (1900) – 5 (1902)
Pokroková revue, 7 (1910–11)
Práce, 1 (1905), 2 (1906–7)
Pramen, 5 (1924–5) – 7 (1927–8)
Právo lidu, 1913, 1921–3
Rozhledy, 5 (1896) – 18 (1908)
Rudé květy, 1 (1901–2) – 6 (1906–7)
Salon, 11 (1932), 13 (1934) – 15 (1936)
Sever a východ, 1 (1925) – 6 (1930)
Srdce, 1 (1901–2) – 3 (1903–4)
Stopa, 1 (1910–1) – 2 (1911–2)
Světozor, 33 (1898–9)
Šibeničky (1), 4 (1916–7), 5 (1917–8), 12 (1924–5)
Šibeničky (2), 1 (1918) – 3 (1920)
Topičův sborník, 4 (1916–7), 5 (1917–8), 12 (1924–5)
Venkov, 1917–9, 1931, 1933, 1938–40
Volné směry, 1 (1897), 2 (1898)
Země, 2 (1920–1) – 7 (1925–6)
Zlatá Praha, 15 (1898) – 18 (1901), 22 (1905), 31 (1914), 38 (1921)
Zvířena, 16 (1919), 17 (1920)
Ženské noviny, 1 (1919), 2 (1920)

1.4 Publications in anthologies

Jan Opolský, (assorted poems) in Václav Jiřina (ed.), *Čestí spisovatelé vdovám a sirotkům našich vojínů* (Prague, 1916)
Jan Opolský, (assorted poems) in Ivan Slavík (ed.) *Zpívající labutě* (Prague, 1971)
Jan Opolský, 'O loutnářce a kyrysarovi' in Jan Robert [Jan Dvořák] (ed.), *Příběhy o citech* (Hradec Králové, 1975)
Jan Opolský, 'Starý obrázek' in Jan Ort [Pavel Eisner] (ed.) *Příběhy uplynulého času* (Hradec Krá-lové, 1977)
Jan Opolský, 'Imitátorka', 'Lovy', 'Vitrina', in Jan Ort [Pavel Eisner] (ed.) *Příběhy o lidech a zvířa-tech* (Hradec Králové, 1980), pp. 175–182, pp. 395–400, pp. 453–460.
Jan Opolský 'Letní noc', in Jiří Kudrnáč (ed.), *Vteřiny duše* (Prague, 1989), pp. 187–189

1.5 Translations

Jan Opolský, (assorted poems) in Jitka Utlerová (ed.), *Recueil de poèmes tchèques* (Pilsen, 1928)
Jan Opolský, (assorted poems) in Hanuš Jelínek (ed.), *Anthologie de la poésie tchèque* (Paris, 1930)
Jan Opolský, (assorted poems), *Vértice* 18 (1958)
Jan Opolský, (assorted pòems) in Jacek Baluch (ed.), *Czescy symboliści, dekadenci, anarchiści prze-lomu XIX i XX wieku* (Wrocław, 1983)
Jan Opolský, 'Predstawenie o zmierzchu' (translation of 'Představení v soumraku'), in Andrzej Sławomir Jagodziński (ed.), *Czas i smierć: Antologia czeskich opowiadań grozy z XIX i początków XX wieku* (Łódź, 1989)
Jan Opolský, 'Vorstellung in der Dämmerung' (translation of 'Představení v soumraku'), in Ivan Slavík (ed.), *Zum roten Drachen: Geheimnisvolle Geschichten* (Berlin, 1989); republished in pa-perback (Frankfurt, 1990)
Jan Opolský, 'Voorstelling in het schemerdonker' (translation of 'Představení v soumraku') in Wil Hansen and Kees Merckes (eds), *Praag en het fin-de-siècle* (Amsterdam, 1999)

1.6 Unpublished works

(unless otherwise stated contained in the Pozůstalost Jana Opolského, Literarní archív, Památ-nik národního písemnictví, Prague)
Works intended for publication in book form:

1. *Satira válečná a popřevratová* V
2. *Hlubina bezpečnosti* V
3. *Výtvarnické evokace* P
4. *V záři a v temnu* P
5. *U tůně* P
6. *Studna krásy*, edited by Bedřich Slavík (typescript in possession of editor) P

Prose works not intended for publication in book form:
7. 'Žije, žije...'
8. 'Ve svaté chvíli'
9. 'Legenda o Gotliebovi [sic]'
10. 'Srdce z vojny'
11. 'Barevné západy'
12. 'Medium'
13. 'Háj'

Manuscripts of published writings are also available, but are not listed here, since they do not differ from the first published version.

1.7 Published correspondence

To Jan Opolsky from:

Jakub Deml, 3 letters (12 October 1936, 20 October 1936, 26 October 1936) in Jakub Deml, *Zakázané světlo: Výbor z korespondence z let 1930-1939* (Prague and Litomyšl, 1999), edited by Jiří Olič, pp. 58-60 (first and third letters), and Jakub Deml, *Šlépěje XXII* (Tasov, 1937), pp. 84 and 112 (second letter).

1.8 Unpublished correspondence

(contained in the Literární archív, Památník národního písemnictví, Prague)

To Jan Opolský from:

Bass, Eduard, 1 letter (13 December 1918), Pozůstalost Jana Opolského (PJO)

Brunclík, Jan, 1 letter (7 January 1932), PJO.

Čapek-Chod, Karel, 1 letter (6 February 1919), PJO.

Čarek, Jan, 1 letter (19 March 1940), PJO.

Halas, František, 1 letter (6 September 1937), PJO.

Hampl, František, 2 letters (15 August 1937, 19 December, 1937), PJO.

Grund, Antonín, 1 letter (19 March 1930), PJO.

Jesenská, Růžena, 1 letter (4 March 1928), PJO.

Kafka, Bohumil, 1 letter (12 March 1937), PJO.

Kalista, Zdeněk, 1 letter (15 January 1936), PJO.

Kavan, František, 1 letter (13 July 1940), PJO.

Klášterský, Antonín, 1 letter (7 October 1940), PJO.

Kobliha, František, 1 letter (12 February 1941), PJO.

Kopta, Josef, 1 letter (4 May 1942), PJO.

Křelina, František, 5 letters (1 July 1940 3 October 1940, 2 January 1941, 7 March 1941, 27 May 1941), PJO.

Lifka, Bohumil, 3 letters (16 June 1937, 29 May 1939, 17 January 1940), PJO.

Majerová, Marie, 2 letters (13 September 1919, 30 January 1920), PJO.

Malý, Rudolf I., 1 letter (1942), PJO.

Novák, Arne, 1 letter (13 July 1935), PJO.

Novák, Arthur, 2 letters (25 September 1934, 12 November 1938), PJO.

Novotný, Jan O., 1 letter (23 February, 1937), PJO.

Palivec, Josef, 1 letter (2 February 1932), PJO.

Skácelík, František, 7 letters (23 August 1935, 30 September 1935, 26 February 1936, 11 November 1939, 20 January 1942, 23 March 1942, 3 April, 1942), PJO.

Svoboda, František X., 2 letters (12 November 1931, 31 July 1935), PJO.

Štika, Karel, 1 letter (10 August 1939), PJO.

Veselý, Antonín, 3 letters (14 May 1920, 2 February 1921, 6 March 1921), PJO.

Veselý, Jindřich, 1 letter (18 June 1928), PJO.

Vika, Karel, 1 letter (31 December 1930), PJO.

From Jan Opolský to:

Čech, Svatopluk, 1 letter (31 May 1896), Pozůstalost Svatopluka Čecha

Dyk, Viktor, 1 letter (undated), Pozůstalost Viktora Dyka

Dyková, Zdeňka, 2 letters (undated), Pozůstalost Zdeňky Dykové

Ehleman, Alois, 1 letter (31 December 1927), Pozůstalost Aloise Ehlemana

Endová, Františka, 12 letters (12 June 1898, 30 January 1899, 7 February 1899, 16 April 1899, 6 December 1899, 22 February 1901, 12 June 1901, 17 June 1901, 24 June 1901; otherwise undated), PJO.

Karásek, Jiří, 1 letter (13 November 1931), Pozůstalost Jiřího Karáska

Kolman-Cassius, Jaroslav, 5 letters (all undated), Pozůstalost Jaroslava Kolmana-Cassia

Majerová, Marie, 1 letter (undated), Pozůstalost Marie Majerové

Skácelík, František, 1 postcard (23 April 1928), Pozůstalost Františka Skácelíka

Vachek, Emil, 5 letters (21 April 1921, 12 May 1921, 23 May 1923; otherwise undated), Pozůstalost Emila Vachka

Veselý, Antonín, 2 letters (20 May 1920, 31 January 1921), Pozůstalost Antonína Veselého

2. CRITICAL AND BIOGRAPHICAL LITERATURE ON JAN OPOLSKÝ

Benčová, Yvona, *Osobnosti Novopacka* (Nová Paka, 2011)

Borecký, Jaromír, (Review of *Víry i tůně*) *Zvon*, 29 (1928–9), p. 166.

Brtník, Václav, (Review of *Muka a zdání*) *Zvon*, 22 (1921–2), p. 518.

Brtník, Václav, (Review of *Miniatury*) *Zvon*, 31 (1930–1), p. 307.

Čapek, Josef B., 'Nové prosy Jana Opolského', *Národní osvobození*', 25, August 1926, p. 4.

Čarek, Jan, *Jan Opolský* (Prague, 1949)

Dutšuková, Kateřina, 'Poetika secese v díle Jana Opolského a Růženy Svobodové', bachelors thesis, Masaryk University Brno, May 2013, available online at: *http://is.muni.cz/th/261748/ff_m/*

Dyk, Viktor, (Review of *Stradivari*) *Lumír*, 55 (1928–9), p. 136.

Fiala, Kamil, (Review of *Demaskování*) *Moderní revue*, 23 (1916–7), pp. 89–92.

Fraenkl, Pavel, (Review of *Z těžkého srdce*) *Rozpravy Aventina*, 2 (1926–7), pp. 47–8.

Fraenkl, Pavel, 'Opolského malé prosy', *Sever a východ*, 3 (1927), pp. 107–8.

Götz, František, (Review of *Z těžkého srdce*) *Národní osvobození*, 4 July 1926, p. 4.

Götz, František, (Review of *Víry i tůně*) *Národní osvobození*, 7 October 1928, p. 4.

Hampl, František, 'Básník života a smrti', *Nový večerník*, 13 March 1937, p. 3.

Hampl, František, 'Básník z nejskromnějších', *Lidová demokracie*, 5 June 1970, p. 5.

Hartl, Antonín, (Review of *Muka a zdání*) *Nové Čechy*, 5 (1922), p. 231.

Hikl, Karel, (Review of *Z těžkého srdce*) *Naše doba*, 34 (1926–7), p. 57.

Holub, Dalibor, 'Jan Opolský', in *Slovník českých spisovatelů*, edited by the Ústav Pro Českou Literaturu SAV Prague, 1964), p. 37.

Hudec, Marcel, 'Za Janem Opolským', *Polední list*, 26 May 1942, p. 4.

Jelínek, Hanuš, *Histoire de la littérature tchèque*, 3 vols, (Paris, 1930–5), III, pp. 106–7.

Juda, Karel, (Review of *Z těžkého srdce*) *Česká revue*, 19 (1926), pp. 309–11.

Kalista, Zdeněk, (Review of *Víry i tůně*) *Rozpravy Aventina*, 4 (1928–9), p. 174.

Kalista, Zdeněk, *Po proudu života*, 2 vols (Brno, 1996), vol. 2.

Karásek ze Lvovic, Jiří, 'První báseň Jana Opolského', *Lumír*, 61 (1934–5), pp. 445–7.

Karásek ze Lvovic, Jiří, 'Básník Jan Opolský mrtev', *Národní politika*, 21 May 1942, p. 1.

Karásek ze Lvovic, Jiří, 'Za básníkem Janem Opolským', *Národní politika*, 22 May 1942, p. 1.

Kolda, Emil (Konrad, Edmond), (Review of *Demaskování*) *Kmen*, 1 (1917–8), p. 9.

Kopal, Josef, (Review of *Z těžkého srdce*) *Nové Čechy*, 10 (1926–7) p. 284.

Kořínková, Lucie, 'Jan Opolský a jeho prozaické dílo v dobovém kontextu', M.A. thesis, Charles University Prague, January 2011, available online at https://is.cuni.cz/webapps/zzp/detail/93895

Krecar, Jarmil, 'Lyrické dílo malíře slov', *Polední list*, 26 May 1942, p. 4.

Krecar, Jarmil, 'Nad posledním rukopisem Opolského', *Aukční katalog Zdeňka Jeřábka*, 18 (1942), pp. 1–4.

Kropáč, František, 'Lyrika Jana Opolského', *Lumír*, 62 (1935–6), pp. 75–84.

Kunc, Jaroslav, 'Jan Opolský', in *Slovník soudobých českých spisovatelů*, edited by Jaroslav Kunc, 2 vols (Prague, 1945–6), I, pp. 616–20.

Novák, Arne, (Review of *Muka a zdání*), *Lidové noviny*, 19 January 1922, p. 4.

Novák, Arne, (Review of *Z těžkého srdce*, *Malé prosy*) *Lidové noviny*, 5 December 1926, p. 9.

Novák, Arne, 'Brusič drahokamů', *Lidové noviny*, 14 July 1935, pp. 1–2.

Novák, Arne, 'Malířské počátky Jana Opolského', *Lidové noviny*, 20 December 1935, p. 2.

Novák, Arne, *Stručné dějiny literatury české*, edited by R. Havel, A. Grund (Olomouc, 1946), p. 471.

Novák, Arne, and Josef Novák, *Přehledné dějiny literatury české od nejstarších dob až po naše dny*, fourth edition (Olomouc, 1936–9), p. 1006.

Novotný, Jan O., (Review of *Malé prosy*, *Z těžkého srdce*) *Cesta*, 9 (1926–7), pp. 208–9 (p. 208).

Novotný, Jan O., 'Vychutnávač krásy', *Národní listy*, 18 August 1935, p. 6.

Píša, Antonín A., (Review of *Miniatury*) *Právo lidu*, 11 April 1931, p. 6.

Pribić, Elisabeth, 'Jan Opolský', in *Lexikon der Weltliteratur*, edited by Gero von Wilpert, 2 vols (Stuttgart, 1975), I, p. 214.

Rydlo, Otakar, 'Básník a rodný kraj', *Pochodeň*, 11 September, p. 4.

Sezima, Karel, (Review of *Muka a zdání*) *Lumír*, 49 (1922), pp. 252–6.

Sezima, Karel, 'Malíř iniciál' in *Podobizny a reliefy*, second edition (Prague, 1927), pp. 175–96.

Sezima, Karel, (Review of *O studni krásy*) *Lumír*, 59 (1932–3), pp. 453–8.

Sezima, Karel, (Review of *Visuté zahrady*) *Lumír*, 62 (1935–6), pp. 112–6

Sezima, Karel, 'Brusič slovesných drahokamů', *Lidová demokracie*, 15 July 1945, p. 3.

Sezima, Karel, *Z mého života*, 4 vols (Prague, 1946–9), II, pp. 160–72.

Skácelík, František, (Review of *Víry i tůně*) *Lumír*, 55 (1928–9), pp. 188–9.

Skácelík, František, 'Enharmonie', *Lumír*, 61 (1934–5), pp. 447–9.

Skácelík, František, (Review of *Pod patinou věků*) *Samostatnost*, 14 July 1938, p. 3.

Skácelík, František, 'Básník Jan Opolský v zrcadle vzpomínek', *Národní politika*, 29 November 1942, p. 2.

Slavík, Bedřich, *Počátky básnické činnosti Jana Opolského* (Prague, 1935); reprinted from *Lumír*, 62 (1935–6), pp. 98–105.

Slavík, Bedřich, *U Suchardů* (Hradec Králové, 1973), p. 46.

Slavík, Ivan, 'Básník miniatur a devadesátá léta' in Jan Opolský, *Představení v soumraku*, edited by Ivan Slavík (Prague, 1968), pp. 7–23.

Šalda, František X., 'Svět smutných', *Lumír*, 27 (1899), pp. 299–300; reprinted in *Kritické projevy*, 13 vols (Prague, 1949–63), IV, pp. 256–8.

Šalda, František X., 'Hledá se umělecké zdraví a umělecká čestnost čili Slovo o takzvané moderní české lyrice náladové', *Novina*, 2 (1909), pp. 601–5; reprinted in *Kritické projevy*, 13 vols (Prague, 1949–63), vol. 7, pp. 333–40.

Štorch, Karel, (Review of *Malé prosy*) *Rozpravy Aventina*, 2 (1926–7), p. 34.

Theer, Otokar, (Review of *Kresby uhlem*) *Lumír*, 35 (1906–7), p. 451.

Václavek, Bedřich, *Česká literatura XX. století* (Prague, 1935), p. 51.

Vaněček, Arnošt, 'Portrét Jana Opolského', *Národní politika*, 19 September 1943, p. 2.

Vodák, Jindřich, (Review of *Demaskovaní*) *Lidové noviny*, 25 April 1917, p. 5.

Weiner, Richard, (Review of *Demaskovaní*) *Lidové noviny*, 3 January 1917, p. 4.

Zafouk, František, 'Básník Jan Opolský intimní', *Národní politika*, 20 May 1944, p. 2.

Zima, Vladislav, (Review of *Z těžkého srdce*) *Zvon*, 26 (1925–6), pp. 687–8.

Anon., 'Jan Opolský přijat do léčení', *Polední list*, 11 March 1932, p. 6.

Anon., 'Pozdní romantik českého symbolismu', *Národní politika*, 14 July 1940, p. 4.

Anon., 'Jan Opolský-100', *Nedělní Obrana lidu*, 12 July 1975, p. 7.

3. CZECH DECADENCE AND RELATED LITERATURE – PRIMARY SOURCES

3.1 Individual works

Auředníček, Otakar, *Verše* (Prague, 1889)

Auředníček, Otakar, *Zpívající labutě* (Prague, 1890)

Auředníček, Otakar, *Malířské novely* (Prague, 1892)

Auředníček, Otakar, *Pseudokontesy* (Prague, 1894)

Auredníček, Otakar, *Intimní dramata* (Prague, 1895)

Babánek, Karel, *Když slunce zapadá* (Prague, 1900)

Babánek, Karel, *Kniha písní* (Prague, 1908)

Babánek, Karel, *Vytržené listy* (Prague, no date)

Borecký, Jaromír, *Rosa mystica* (Prague, 1892)

Breiský, Arthur, *Triumpf zla* (Prague, 1910)

Breiský, Arthur, *Dvě novely* (Prague, 1927)

Breiský, Arthur, *Střepy zrcadel* (Prague, 1928)

Breiský, Arthur, *V království chimér. Korespondence a rukopisy z let 1902–1907* (Prague, 1997)

Březina, Otakar, *Svítáni na západě* (Prague, 1896)

Červínka, Karel, *Krajiny a nálady* (Prague, 1894)

Červínka, Karel, *Hledání samoty* (Prague, 1897)

Červínka, Karel, *Slunce v mlhách* (Prague, 1901)

Dyk, Viktor, *A porta inferi* (Prague, 1897)

Dyk, Viktor, *Síla života* (Prague, 1898)

Dyk, Viktor, *Marnosti* (Prague, 1900)

Geisslová, Irma, *Imortelly* (Prague, 1879)

Geisslová, Irma, *Zraněný pták: výbor z díla 1874–1914* (Prague, 1978), edited by Ivan Slavík (Hradec Králové, 1978)

Hlaváček, Karel, *Sokolské sonety* (Prague, 1895)

Hlaváček, Karel, *Pozdě k ránu* (Prague, 1896)

Hlaváček, Karel, *Mstivá kantiléna* (Prague, 1898)

Hlaváček, Karel, *Žalmy* (Prague, 1934), edited posthumously by Antonín Hartl

Houdek, Vladimír, *Vykvetly blíny* (Prague, 1899)

Houdek, Vladimír, *V pavučinách nervů* (Prague, 1901)

Jesenská, Růžena, *Konec idyly* (Prague, 1892)

Jesenská, Růžena, *Novely* (Prague, 1900)

Jesenská, Růžena, *Rudé západy* (Prague, 1904)

Jesenská, Růžena, *Estera* (Prague, 1909)

Jesenská, Růžena, *Mimo svět* (Prague, 1909)

Jesenská, Růžena, *Nocturno moře* (Prague, 1910)

Kamínek, Karel, *Dies irae* (Prague, 1911)

Kamínek, Karel, *Dissonance* (Prague, no date)

Karásek ze Lvovic, Jiří, *Bezcestí* (Valašské Meziříčí, 1893)

Karásek ze Lvovic, Jiří, *Zazděná okna* (Prague, 1894)

Karásek ze Lvovic, Jiří, *Kniha aristokratická* (Prague, 1896)

Karásek ze Lvovic, Jiří, *Legenda o melancholickém princi* (Prague, 1897)

Karásek ze Lvovic, Jiří, *Mimo život* (Prague, 1897)

Karásek ze Lvovic, Jiří, *Sexus necans* (Prague, 1897)

Karásek ze Lvovic, Jiří, *Ideje zítřku* (Prague, 1898)

Karásek ze Lvovic, Jiří, *Gothická duše* (Prague, 1900)

Karásek ze Lvovic, Jiří, *Renesanční touhy v umění: kritická studie* (Prague, 1902)

Karásek ze Lvovic, Jiří, *Sodoma* (Prague, 1895)

Karásek ze Lvovic, Jiří, *Stojaté vody* (Prague, 1895)

Karásek ze Lvovic, Jiří, *Chimaerické výpravy: kritické studie* (Prague, 1905)

Karásek ze Lvovic, Jiří, *Román Manfreda Macmillena* (Prague, 1907)

Karásek ze Lvovic, Jiří, *Sen o říši krásy. Čínská pohádka o dvou dějstvích* (Prague, 1907)

Karásek ze Lvovic, Jiří, *Scarabeus* (Prague, 1908)

Karásek ze Lvovic, Jiří, *Cesare Borgia* (Prague, 1908)

Karásek ze Lvovic, Jiří, *Endymion* (Prague, 1909)

Karásek ze Lvovic, Jiří, *Posvátné ohně* (Prague, 1911)

Karásek ze Lvovic, Jiří, *Ostrov vyhnanců* (Prague, 1912)

Karásek ze Lvovic, Jiří, *Král Rudolf* (Prague, 1916)

Karásek ze Lvovic, Jiří, *Obrácení Raymonda Lulla* (Prague, 1919)

Karásek ze Lvovic, Jiří, *Zlatý triptych* (Prague, 1919)

Karásek ze Lvovic, Jiří, *Legenda o Sodomovi* (Prague, 1920)

Karásek ze Lvovic, Jiří, *Barokové oltáře* (Prague, 1922)

Karásek ze Lvovic, Jiří, *Hovory se smrtí* (Prague, 1922)

Karásek ze Lvovic, Jiří, *Legenda o ctihodné Marii Elektě z Ježíše* (Prague, 1922)

Karásek ze Lvovic, Jiří, *Zastřený obraz* (Prague, 1923)

Karásek ze Lvovic, Jiří, *Ganymedes* (Prague, 1925)

Karásek ze Lvovic, Jiří, *Tvůrcové a epigoni* (Prague, 1927)

Karásek ze Lvovic, Jiří, *Umění jako kritika života* (Prague, 1927)

Karásek ze Lvovic, Jiří, *Genenda* (Prague, 1928)

Karásek ze Lvovic, Jiří, *Lásky absurdné* (Prague, 1929)

Karásek ze Lvovic, Jiří, *Pražské Jezulátko* (Prague, 1938)

Karásek ze Lvovic, Jiří, *Ztracený ráj* (Prague, 1938)

Klas, Eduard [Vladimíra Jedlíčková], *Povídky o ničem* (Prague, 1903)

Kles, Petr [Petr Klíč], *Petra Klesa pozůstalé spisy prózou i veršem*, ed. by Karel Sezima (Prague, 1931)

Kles, Petr [Petr Klíč], *Spisy veršem i prózou*, edited by Karel Sezima (Prague, 1932)

Knoesl, Bohuslav, *Martyrium touhy* (Prague, 1896)

Krecar, Jarmil, *Předčasné vinobrání* (Prague, 1903)

Krecar, Jarmil, *V mé duši věčný smutek dlí a věčně teskno....* (Prague, 1905)

Krecar, Jarmil, *Ilseino srdce* (Prague, 1917)

Krecar, Jarmil, *Sňaté masky* (Prague, 1917)

Krecar, Jarmil, *U zelené žáby* (Prague, 1925)

Křikava, Louis, *V nocích bezhvězdných* (Prague, 1899)

Křikava, Louis, *Pyrrhova vítězství* (Prague, 1901)

Křikava, Louis, *Blažej Jordán* (Prague, 1904)

Křikava, Louis, *Skrytá erotika a jiné povídky* (Prague, 1904)

Křikava, Louis, *Pavilón moru* (Prague, 1907)

Křikava, Louis, *Zločin na vsi a jiné povídky* (Prague, 1909)

Kvapil, Jaroslav, *Padající hvězdy* (Prague, 1889)

Kvapil, Jaroslav, *Trosky chrámu* (Prague, 1889)

Kvapil, Jaroslav, *Básníkův deník* (Prague, 1890)

Kvapil, Jaroslav, *Růžová keř* (Prague, 1890)

Kvapilová, Hana, *Literární pozůstalost* (Prague, 1907)

z Lešehradu, Emanuel, *Smutné kraje* (Prague, 1898)

z Lešehradu, Emanuel, *Květy samoty* (Prague, 1899)

z Lešehradu, Emanuel, *Ve dnech šerých* (Prague, 1901)

Lilia, Hermor [František Bíbl], *Řádky* (Prague, 1917)

Lilia, Hermor [František Bíbl], *Večery* (Prague, 1924)

Lilia, Hermor [František Bíbl], *Mysterion* (Prague, 1927)

Lilia, Hermor [František Bíbl], *Stíny* (Prague, 1931)

Lilia, Hermor [František Bíbl], *Verše tajného básníka*, edited by Ivan Slavík (Prague, 1982)

Lilia, Hermor [František Bíbl], *Osamělý chodec: výbor z díla*, ed. by Rudolf Matys (Prague, 2008)

Maria, Jaroslav [Jaroslav Mayer], *V podvečer věku* (Prague, 1898)

Maria, Jaroslav [Jaroslav Mayer], *Dobráci* (Prague, 1899)

Maria, Jaroslav [Jaroslav Mayer], *V exilu* (Prague, 1907)
Maria, Jaroslav [Jaroslav Mayer], *Werther* (Prague, 1907)
Maria, Jaroslav [Jaroslav Mayer], *Dramatická sonata* (Prague, 1907)
Maria, Jaroslav [Jaroslav Mayer], *Tristan* (Prague, 1908)
Maria, Jaroslav [Jaroslav Mayer], *Helénská kněžna* (Prague, 1911)
Maria, Jaroslav [Jaroslav Mayer], *Michelangelo Buonarotti* (Prague, 1912)
Maria, Jaroslav [Jaroslav Mayer], *Parisina* (Prague, 1918)
Maria, Jaroslav [Jaroslav Mayer], *Torquato Tasso* (Prague, 1918)
Maria, Jaroslav [Jaroslav Mayer], *Lucrezia Borgia* (Prague, 1920)
Maria, Jaroslav [Jaroslav Mayer], *Kyvadla věčnosti* (Prague, 1920)
Maria, Jaroslav [Jaroslav Mayer], *Tajnosnubní* (Prague, 1922)
Maria, Jaroslav [Jaroslav Mayer], *Sladký upír* (Prague, 1925)
Martén, Miloš, *Akkord: Mácha-Zeyer-Březina: Essaie* (Prague, 1916)
Martén, Miloš, *Básník illustrace* (Prague, 1927)
Martén, Miloš, *Otokar Březina* (Prague, 1903)
Martén, Miloš, *Edvard Munch* (Prague, 1905)
Martén, Miloš, *Styl a stylisace* (Prague, 1906)
Martén, Miloš, *Cyklus rozkoše a smrti* (Prague, 1907)
Martén, Miloš, *Kniha silných: umělci a básníci – eseje,* (Prague, 1909)
Martén, Miloš, *In memoriam Karla Hynka Máchy* (Prague, 1910)
Martén, Miloš, *Potrestaný faun* (Prague, 1910)
Martén, Miloš, *Cortigiana* (Prague, 1911)
Martén, Miloš, *Julius Zeyer* (Prague, 1910)
Martén, Miloš, *Karikatura věků* (Prague, 1912)
Martén, Miloš, *Dravci, tři novelly* (Prague, 1913)
Martén, Miloš, *Nad městem: dialog* (Prague, 1917)
Nejč, Karel, *Básně* (Prague, 1900)
Neumann, Stanislav Kostka, *Nemesis honorum custos* (Prague, 1895)
Neumann, Stanislav Kostka, *Satanova sláva mezi námi* (Prague, 1895)
Neumann, Stanislav Kostka, *Apostrofy hrdé a vášnivé* (Prague, 1896)
Neumann, Stanislav Kostka, *Jsem apoštol nového žití* (Prague, 1896)
Pammrová, Anna, *O mateřství a pamateřství* (Prague, 1919)
Procházka, Arnošt, *Prostibolo duše* (Prague, 1895)
Procházka, Arnošt, *Odilon Redon* (Prague, 1904)
Procházka, Arnošt, *Cesta krásy* (Prague, 1906)
Procházka, Arnošt, *České kritiky* (Prague, 1912)
Procházka, Arnošt, *Francouzští autoři a jiné studie* (Prague, 1912)
Procházka, Arnošt, *Literární siluety* (Prague, 1912)
Procházka, Arnošt, *Meditace* (Prague, 1912)
Procházka, Arnošt, *Na okraj doby* (Prague, 1913)
Procházka, Arnošt, *Polemiky* (Prague, 1913)
Procházka, Arnošt, *Tanec smrti* (Prague, 1917)
Procházka, Arnošt, *Diář literární a umělecký* (Prague, 1919)
Procházka, Arnošt, *Dnové života* (Prague, 1922)
Procházka, Arnošt, *Soumrak* (Prague, 1924)
Procházka, Arnošt, *Torza veršů, torza prózy* (Prague, 1925)
Procházka, Arnošt, *Relikviář* (Prague, 1928)
Rutte, Miroslav, *Smuteční slavnosti srdcí* (Prague, 1911)
Sezima, Karel, *Kouzlo rozchodu* (Prague, 1898)
Sezima, Karel, *Pasiflora* (Prague, 1903); revised edition (Prague, 1927)
Sezima, Karel, *V soumraku srdcí* (Prague, 1913)
Skarlandt, Julius, *Podzimní melodie* (Prague, 1900)
Skarlandt, Julius, *Kniha veršů* (Prague, 1903)

Skarlandt, Julius, *Smutní láska* (Prague, 1904)

Šarecká, Maryša, *Bettina* (Prague, 1921)

Šarlih, Karel, *Tvrdošíjní ilusionisté* (Prague, 1912)

Šarlih, Karel, *Erotické dobrodružství Nikity Ochalčuka* (Prague, 1914)

Šarlih, Karel, *Úšklebky sexu* (Prague, 1919)

Theer, Otakar, *Háje, kde se tančí* (Prague, 1897)

Theer, Otakar, *Výpravy k Já* (Prague, 1900)

Toman, Karel [Antonín Bernášek], *Pohádky krve* (Prague, 1898)

Toman, Karel [Antonín Bernášek], *Torso života* (Prague, 1902)

Toman, Karel [Antonín Bernášek], *Melancholická pouť* (Prague, 1906)

Vrchlický, Jaroslav, *Dědictví Tantalovo* (Prague, 1888)

Vrchlický, Jaroslav, *Hudba v duši* (Prague, 1886)

Vrchlický, Jaroslav, *Život a smrt* (Prague, 1892)

Vrchlický, Jaroslav, *Okna v bouři* (Prague, 1894)

Vrchlický, Jaroslav, *Nové zlomky epopeje* (Prague, 1895)

z Wojkowicz, Jan, *Mizení* (Prague, 1898)

z Wojkowicz, Jan, *Mysteria amorosa* (Prague, 1899)

z Wojkowicz, Jan, *O problemu individualizace* (Prague, 1900)

z Wojkowicz, Jan, *Poezie* (Prague, 1900)

z Wojkowicz, Jan, *Gerda* (Prague, 1901)

z Wojkowicz, Jan, *Meditace* (Prague, 1906)

z Wojkowicz, Jan, *Sny a touhy* (Prague, 1914)

z Wojkowicz, Jan, *Bolesti života* (Prague, 1915)

z Wojkowicz, Jan, *Tmy a světla* (Prague, 1918)

z Wojkowicz, Jan, *Básník a věčnost* (Prague, 1925)

z Wojkowicz, Jan, *Království snu* (Prague, 1932)

z Wojkowicz, Jan, *Noční milenec* (Prague, 1931)

Zeyer, Julius, 'Zrada v domě Han. Čínská legenda', *Lumír*, 9 (1881), pp. 289-292, 306-309, 323-326; reprinted in *Amparo a jiné povídky* (Prague, 1896) and *Obnovené obrazy*, 3 vols (Prague, 1906), vol. 2

Zeyer, Julius, 'Blaho v zahradě kvetoucích broskví. Podivná povídka', *Lumír*, 10 (1882), pp. 146-149, 161-165, 177-182, reprinted in *Novely*, 2 vols (Prague, 1879 and 1884), vol. 2.

Zeyer, Julius, 'Bratři. Čínská komedie ve dvou jednáních', *Lumír*, 10 (1882), pp. 513-516, 531-535, 550-552, 561-563; reprinted in *Tři komedie* (Prague, 1894)

Zeyer, Julius, *Gompači i Komurasaki. Žaponský román* (Prague, 1884)

Zeyer, Julius, 'Píseň za vlahé noci', *Lumír*, 13 (1885), pp. 5-10; reprinted in *Obnovené obrazy*, 3 vols (Prague, 1894), vol. 2

Zeyer, Julius, 'Lásky div. Žaponská komedie o jednom jednání', *Květy*, 10 (1888), pp. 505-520; reprinted in *Tři komedie* (Prague, 1894)

Zeyer, Julius, 'O velkém bolu bohu Izanagi', *Lumír*, 19 (1891), pp. 373-374; reprinted in *Obnovené obrazy*, 3 vols (Prague, 1906), vol. 2, and incorporated in 'Večer u Idalie'.

Zeyer, Julius, 'Večer u Idalie. Hrstka tradic, legend a pohádek z nejkrásnějšího východu', *Stratonika a jiné povídky* (Prague, 1892), pp. 1–66

Zeyer, Julius, *Tři legendy o krucifixu* (Prague, 1895)

Zeyer, Julius, *Dům u tonoucí hvězdy* (Prague, 1897)

Ziková, Louisa, *Spodní proudy* (Prague, 1896)

3.2 Anthologies

Kudrnáč, Jiří, *Vteřiny duše. Drobná próza české secese* (Prague, 1989)

Slavík, Ivan, *Zpívající labutě. Zapomenutí básníci devadesátých let* (Prague, 1971)

3.3 Journals

Moderní revue, edited by Arnošt Procházka, 1894-1925

4. CZECH DECADENCE AND RELATED LITERATURE – SECONDARY SOURCES

Bednaříková, Hana, *Česká dekadence* (Brno, 2000)

Blahová, Kateřina and Václav Petrbok (eds), *Cizí, jiné, exotické v české kultuře 19. století* (Prague, 2008)

Brabec, Jirí, *Poezie na předělu doby* (Prague, 1964)

Bugge, Peter, 'Naked Masks: Arthur Breisky or How To Be a Czech Decadent', *Slovo a smysl*, 2 (2005), No. 3, pp. 135–148

Chirico, David, 'Karel Hlaváček a Moderní revue', in Otto Urban and Luboš Merhaut (ed.), *Moderní revue 1894–1925* (Prague, 1995), pp. 145–160

Chlumská, Lucie, 'Pre-, post- a neodekadence', *Literární novinky*, 7 (2010), No. 1

Galik, Marian, 'Julius Zeyer's version of Ling Menchu's *Lady Xue Tao*: A Chinese story in Czech attire', *Archiv orientální* 72 (2004), pp. 298–313

Haeringová, Jarmila, 'Blaho v zahradě květoucích broskví', *Nový Orient*, 46 (1991), No. 2, pp. 44–45

Haman, Aleš and Dalibor Tureček (eds), *Český a slovenský parnasismus* (Brno, 2015)

Kořínková, Lucie, 'Nový kult jako tribuna sociálně vyloučených' in Zbyněk Hojda et al., *Útisk – charita – vyloučení. Sociální 19. století* (Prague, 2015)

Kudrnáč, Jiří, 'Česká dekadence. Příspěvek k hledání jejího typu', *Sborník prací filozofické fakulty brněnské university*, 29 (1982), series D, pp. 67–74

Kudrnáč, Jiří, 'K problematice české literatury devadesátých let. Kapitola o české dekadenci, *Universitas*, 11 (1978), no. 2, pp. 51–55

Kudrnáč, Jiří, 'Z typologie literárních let devadesátých', *Sborník prací filozofické fakulty brněnské university*, 34 (1987), series D, pp. 25–35

Kudrnáč, Jiří, 'Úvod do české secesní literatury', *Z časů Moderní revue*, (Prague, 1997), Literární archiv 28

Kuchař, Lumír, *Dialogy o kráse a smrti* (Brno, 1999)

Med, Jaroslav, 'Symbolismus – dekadence', *Česká literatura*, 33 (1985), pp. 119–126

Med, Jaroslav, 'Česká symbolistně-dekadentní literatura', in *Česká literatura na předělu století* (Prague, 2001), edited by Petr Čornej et al., pp. 43–92

Merhaut, Luboš, *Cesty stylizace* (Prague, 1994)

Merhaut, Luboš, and Otto Urban (eds), *Moderní revue 1894–1925* (Prague, 1995)

Moldanová, Dobrava, *Studie o české próze na přelomu století* (Ústí nad Labem, 1993)

Michalska, Halina, 'Dekadentzym Jerzego Karaska we świetle motywów jego poezji', *Modernizm w literaturach słowiańskich* (Wrocław, 1973), pp. 49–62

Leben, Andreas, *Aesthetizismus und Engagement: die Kurzprosa der tschechischen und slovakischen Moderne* (Vienna, 1997)

Pelán, Jiří, 'Dandyovská estetika Arthura Breiského', *Česká literatura*, 49 (2001), No. 3, pp. 243–253

Pynsent, Robert, 'Stirner und die tschechische Dekadenz', *Aeropag*, 6 (1971), no. 1, pp. 63–71

Pynsent, Robert, 'A Czech Dandy: An Introduction to Arthur Breiský', *Slavonic and East European Review*, 51 (1973), No. 4 (October), pp. 517–523

Pynsent, Robert, *Julius Zeyer: The Path to Decadence* (The Hague, 1973)

Pynsent, Robert, 'K morfologii české dekadence', *Česká literatura*, 36 (1988), pp. 168–191

Pynsent, Robert, *Decadence and Innovation: Austro-Hungarian Life and Art at the Turn of the Century* (London, 1989)

Pynsent, Robert, 'Desire, frustration and some fulfilment: A Commentary to Karel Hlaváček's *Mstivá kantilena*, *Slavonic and East European Review*, 72 (1994), No. 1, 1–37

Pynsent, Robert, 'Intertextuality, interstatualita, intersexualita: Osudová žena a Martenova Cortigiana', in *Symbolizmus v kontextoch a súvislostiach* (Bratislava, 1999), pp. 199–209

Pynsent, Robert, 'Dekadentní sliznice. Krafft-Ebbing, dekadence a Sezimova Pasiflora', in *Česká literatura na konci století* (Prague, 2001), edited by the Ústav pro českou literaturu AV

Pynsent, Robert, 'Czech Decadence', in Marcel Cornis-Pope and John Neubauer (eds), *History of the Literary Cultures of East-Central Europe*, 3 vols (Amsterdam, 2004), vol. 1, pp. 348–363

Slavík, Ivan, *Viděno jinak* (Brno, 1995)
Soldan, Fedor, *Karel Hlaváček – typ české dekadence* (Prague, 1930)
Staněk, Jan, 'Spor o dilentantismus a jeho podoba v literatuře české decadence', *Estetika*, 44 (2007), pp. 85–106
Stewart, Neil, 'The Cosmopolitanism of *Moderní revue* (1894–1925), in Marcel Cornis-Pope and John Neubauer (eds), *History of the Literary Cultures of East-Central Europe*, 3 vols (Amsterdam, 2004), vol. 3, pp. 63–70
Šalda, František X., 'K otázce dekadence', *Rozhledy*, 4 (1986), pp. 385–389; reprinted in *Kritické projevy 2* (Prague, 1950), pp. 206–222
Taxová, Eva, *Český literární esej z přelomu století* (Prague, 1985)
Urban, Otto, *Karel Hlaváček: výtvarné a kritické dílo* (Prague, 2002)
Urban, Otto, Le *Lupanar* du poète Arnošt Procházka er l'âme de l'artiste Karel Hlaváček, *Revue des études slaves*, 74 (2002–2003), No. 1, pp. 19–35
Urban, Otto, (ed.), *V barvách chorobných: idea dekadence a umění v českých zemích 1880–1914* (Prague, 2006), pp. 302–303
Vlček, Tomáš, 'Počátky dějin moderního umění', *Kapitoly z českého dějepisu umění* (Prague, 1987), vol. 2
Vlček, Tomáš, 'Ornament a styl. K problematice českého umění na přelomu století', *Umění*, 28 (1900), pp. 425–429
Vlček, Tomáš, 'České moderní umění', *Sen o říši krásy. Dream of the Empire of Beauty. Sbírka Jiřího Karáska ze Lvovic* (Prague, 2001)
Vojtěch, Daniel, *Vášeň a ideál: na křižovatkách moderny* (Prague, 2008)
Wittlich, Petr, *Česká secese* (Prague, 1982)
Wittlich, Petr, *Umění a život – doba secese* (Prague, 1987)
Wittlich, Petr, *Horizonty umění* (Prague, 2010)
Wittlich, Petr, *Malíři české secese* (Prague, 2012)
Zikmund-Lender, Ladislav, 'Nakřivo rostlý výhonek. Obrazy homosexuality v umění české dekadence', in Martin Putna et al. *Homosexualita v dějinách české kultury* (Prague, 2013)

5. EUROPEAN DECADENCE AND RELATED LITERATURE – PRIMARY SOURCES

5.1 Individual works
D'Annunzio, Gabriele, *Il piacere* (Milan, 1889)
D'Annunzio, Gabriele, *Il fuoco* (Milan, 1900)
D'Annunzio, Gabriele, *L'innocente* (Milan, 1892)
D'Annunzio, Gabriele, *Il trionfo della morte* (Milan, 1894)
Bang, Herman, *Stuk* (Copenhagen, 1887)
Bang, Herman, *Tine* (Copenhagen, 1889)
Barbey D'Aurevilly, Jules, *Du dandysme et de G. Brummell* (Paris, 1861)
Barbey D'Aurevilly, Jules, *Un prêtre marié* (Paris, 1865)
Barbey D'Aurevilly, Jules, *Une vielle maîtresse* (Paris, 1866)
Barbey D'Aurevilly, Jules, *Les diaboliques* (Paris, 1874)
Baudelaire, Charles, 'Dandyisme', *Journaux intimes* (Paris, 2001)
Baudelaire, Charles, *Les fleurs du mal* (Paris, 1857)
Bloy, Léon, *Le désespéré* (Paris, 1886)
Bourget, Paul, *Essais de psychologie contemporaine* (Paris, 1883)
Conti, Angelo, *La beata riva: trattato dell'oblio* (Milan, 1900)
Flaubert, Gustave, *Salammbô* (Paris, 1893)
Flaubert, Gustave, *La tentation de Saint-Antoine* (Paris, 1900)
Fogazzaro, Antonio, *Il Santo* (Milan, 1905)
Huysmans, Joris-Karl, *A rebours* (Paris, 1884)
Huysmans, Joris-Karl, *Là-bas* (Paris, 1891)
Huysmans, Joris-Karl, *La cathédrale* (Paris, 1898)

Gautier, Théophile, *Mademoiselle de Maupin* (Paris, 1835)
Laforgue, Jules, *Les complaintes* (Paris, 1885)
Laforgue, Jules, *Le concile féerique* (Paris, 1886)
Laforgue, Jules, *L'imitation de Notre-Dame de la Lune* (Paris, 1886)
Laforgue, Jules, *Les moralités légendaires* (Paris, 1887)
Leconte de l'Isle, Charles, *Poèmes antiques* (Paris, 1881)
Leconte de l'Isle, Charles, *Poèmes barbares* (Paris, 1881)
Leconte de l'Isle, Charles, *Poèmes tragiques* (Paris, n.d.)
Lorrain, Jean, *La fôret bleue* (Paris, 1883)
Lorrain, Jean, *Buveurs d'âme* (Paris, 1893)
Lorrain, Jean, *Monsieur de Bougrelon* (Paris, 1897)
Lorrain, Jean, *Monsieur de Phocas* (Paris, 1901)
Lorrain, Jean, *Princesses d'ivoires et d'ivresse* (Paris, 1901)
Lorrain, Jean, *Le vice errant* (Paris, 1902)
Lorrain, Jean, *Le crime des riches* (Paris, 1905)
Louÿs, Pierre, *Astarté* (Paris, 1891)
Louÿs, Pierre, *Les Chansons de Bilitis* (Paris, 1894)
Louÿs, Pierre, *Aphrodite* (Paris, 1896)
Louÿs, Pierre, *La femme et le pantin* (Paris, 1898)
Louÿs, Pierre, *Les aventures du roi Pausole* (Paris, 1901)
Mendès, Catulle, *L'homme tout nu* (Paris, 1887)
Mendès, Catulle, *La femme-enfant* (Paris, 1891)
Mendès, Catulle, *La messe rose* (Paris, 1892)
Mendès, Catulle, *Gog* (Paris, 1896)
Mendès, Catulle, *Arc-en-ciel et sourcil-rouge* (Paris, 1897)
Mendès, Catulle, *Le chercheur de tares* (Paris, 1898)
Mendès, Catulle, *Lesbia* (Paris, 1899)
Mendès, Catulle, *Le roi vierge* (Paris, 1900)
Mendès, Catulle, *Monstres parisiens* (Paris, 1902)
Mendès, Catulle, *Méphistophéla* (Paris, 1903)
Mendès, Catulle, *Les romans d'innocence* (Paris, 1904)
Mendès, Catulle, *La première maîtresse* (Paris, 1922)
Mendès, Catulle, *Zohar* (Paris, 1922)
Mirbeau, Octave, *Abbé Jules* (Paris, 1888)
Mirbeau, Octave, *Le jardin des supplices* (Paris, 1899)
Mirbeau, Octave, *Le journal d'une femme de chambre* (Paris, 1900)
Mirbeau, Octave, *Vingt et un jours d'un neurasthénique* (Paris, 1901)
Pascoli, Giovanni, *Myricae* (Milan, 1891)
Péladan, Joséphin, *Le Vice suprême* (Paris, 1884)
Przybyszewski, Stanisław, *Totenmesse* (Berlin, 1893)
Przybyszewski, Stanisław, *Vigilien* (Berlin, 1894)
Przybyszewski, Stanisław, *De Profundis* (Berlin, 1896)
Przybyszewski, Stanisław, *Im Malstrom* (Berlin, 1896)
Przybyszewski, Stanisław, *Satanskinder* (Berlin, 1897)
Przybyszewski, Stanisław, *Androgyne* (Berlin, 1900)
Rachilde, *Marquise de Sade* (Paris, 1887)
Rachilde, *Madame Adonis* (Paris, 1888)
Rachilde, *Monsieur Vénus* (Paris, 1889)
Rachilde, *L'heure sexuelle* (Paris, 1898)
Rachilde, *La tour d' amour* (Paris, 1899)
Rachilde, *L'imitation de la mort* (Paris, 1903)
Rachilde, *Le meneur de louves* (Paris, 1905)
Rimbaud, Arthur, *Poésies complètes* (Paris, 1895)

Schwob, Marcel, *Coeur double* (Paris, 1927)
Schwob, Marcel, *Le livre de Monelle* (Paris, 1927)
Swinburne, Algernon Charles, *Atalanta in Calydon* (London, 1865)
Swinburne, Algernon Charles, *The Masque of Queen Bersabe* (London, 1866)
Swinburne, Algernon Charles, *Poems and Ballads* (London, 1866)
Swinburne, Algernon Charles, *Poems and Ballads II* (London, 1878)
Symons, Arthur, *Silhouettes* (London, 1892)
Symons, Arthur, *London Nights* (London, 1895)
Symons, Arthur, *Amoris Victima* (London, 1897)
Symons, Arthur, *Aubrey Beardsley: An Essay with Preface* (London, 1898)
Symons, Arthur, *Days and Nights* (London, 1889)
Symons, Arthur, *Images of Good and Evil* (London, 1899)
Symons, Arthur, *The Symbolist Movement in Literature* (London, 1899)
Symons, Arthur, *Charles Baudelaire* (London, 1920)
Symons, Arthur, *Confessions: A Study in Pathology* (London, 1930)
Verlaine, Paul, *L'art poétique* (Paris, 1882)
Vicaire, Gabriel, and Henri Beauclair, *Les déliquescences d'Adoré Floupette, poète décadent* (Paris,
    1885)
Villiers de l'Isle Adam, Auguste, *Isis* (Paris, 1862)
Villiers de l'Isle Adam, Auguste, *Contes cruels* (Paris, 1883)
Villiers de l'Isle Adam, Auguste, *L'Ève future* (Paris, 1886)
Villiers de l'Isle Adam, Auguste, *Nouveaux contes cruels* (Paris, 1888)
Villiers de l'Isle Adam, Auguste, *Axël* (Paris, 1890)
Wilde, Oscar, 'The Decay of Lying', *The Nineteenth Century*, 13 (1889), January; republished in a
    revised version in *Intentions* (London, 1891)
Wilde, Oscar, 'The Picture of Dorian Gray', *Lippincott's Monthly Magazine* 23 (1890); republished
    in a revised version in *The Picture of Dorian Gray* (London, 1891)
Wilde, Oscar, *Lord Arthur Savile's Crime* (London, 1891)
Wilde, Oscar, 'The Truth of Masks', in *Intentions* (London, 1891)
Wilde, Oscar, *Lady Windermere's Fan* (London, 1892)
Wilde, Oscar, *A Woman of No Importance* (London, 1893)
Wilde, Oscar, *Salomé* (Paris, 1893) in French; (London, 1894) in English
Wilde, Oscar, *An Ideal Husband* (1895)
Wilde, Oscar, *The Importance of Being Ernest* (London, 1895)
Wilde, Oscar, *The Ballad of Reading Gaol* (London, 1898)

5.2 Journals
Le Décadent (1886–1889), edited by Anatole Baju
Yellow Book (1894–1897), edited by Henry Harland
Il Convito (1895–1907), edited by Adolfo de Bosis
Il Marzocco (1896–1932), edited by Enrico Corradini

6. EUROPEAN DECADENCE AND RELATED LITERATURE – SECONDARY SOURCES

Anderson, Mark, *Kafka's Clothes, Ornament and Aestheticism in the Habsburg Fin de Siècle* (New
    York, 1992)
Anvincola, Sandra, *Il decadentismo: la coscienza della crisi* (Rome, 1997)
Aslin, Elizabeth, *The Aesthetic Movement: Prelude to Art Nouveau* (London, 1981)
Barstad, Guri Ellen et al., *Dilettant, Dandy und Décadent* (Hanover, 2004)
Bauer, Roger, et al. (eds), *Fin de Siècle. Zur Literatur und Kunst der Jahrhundertwende* (Frankfurt,
    1977)
Bauer, Roger, *Die schöne Décadence: Geschichte eines literarischen Paradoxons* (Frankfurt, 2001)

Bernheimer, Charles, *Decadent subjects* (Baltimore MD, 2002)

Bernheimer, Charles, *Figures of Decadence: Subversive Paradigms in Fin-de-Siècle Art and Literature* (Baltimore MD, 2002)

Bourget, Paul, *Ernest Renan* (Paris, 1883)

Bruno, Francesco, *Il Decadentismo in Italia e in Europa* (Naples, 1998)

Carter, A. E: *The Idea of Decadence in French Literature* (Toronto, 1944)

De Palacio, Jean, *La Décadence. Le mot et la chose* (Paris, 2011)

Dowling, Linda, *Language and Decadence in the Victorian Fin de Siècle* (Princeton NJ, 1986)

Ellmann, Richard, *Oscar Wilde* (London, 1987)

Gilman, Richard, *Decadence: The Strange Life of an Epithet* (London, 1979)

Haupt, Sabine et al., *Handbuch Fin de Siècle* (Stuttgart, 2008)

Jackson, Holbrook, *The Eighteen Nineties* (Harmondsworth, 1950)

Lambourne, Lionel, *The Aesthetic Movement* (London, 1996)

Lemon, Robert, *Imperial Messages: Orientalism as Self-Critique in the Habsburg fin-de-siècle* (Rochester NY, 2011)

Lingua, Catherine, *Ces anges du bizarre: regard sur une aventure esthétique de la Décadence* (Paris, 1995)

Marshall, Gail (ed.), *The Cambridge Companion to the fin-de-siècle* (Cambridge, 2007)

Matich, Olga, *Erotic Utopia: The Decadent Imagination in Russia's Fin de Siècle* (Madison WI, 2005)

Moers, Ellen, *The Dandy* (Lincoln NE, 1960)

Noël, Richard, *Le mouvement décadent: dandys, esthètes et quintessents* (Paris, 1968)

Palacio, Jean de, *Figures et formes de la décadence* (Paris, 1994)

Pierrot, Jean, *The Decadent Imagination 1880-1900* (London and Chicago, 1981)

Pittock, Murray, *Spectrum of Decadence: The Literature of the 1890s* (London and New York, 1993)

Rasch, Wolfdietrich, *Die Décadence um 1900* (Munich, 1986)

Ridge, George Ross, *The Hero in French Decadent Literature* (Athens GA, 1961)

Schoolfield, George C., *A Baedeker of Decadence: Charting a Literary Fashion 1884-1927* (New Haven CT, 2003)

Spackmann, Barbara, *Decadent Genealogies: The Rhetoric of Sickness from Baudelaire to d'Annunzio* (Ithaca NY and London, 1989)

Spencer, Robin, *The Aesthetic Movement: Theory and Practice* (London, 1972)

Spivak, Gayatri, 'Decadent Style', *Language and Style*, 7 (1974), pp. 227–234

St. John, Michael (ed.), *Romancing Decay: Ideas of Decadence in European Culture* (Aldershot, 1999)

Thomalla, Ariane, *Die femme fragile: ein literarischer Frauentypus der Jahrhundertwende* (Düsseldorf, 1972)

von Sydow, Eckart, *Die Kultur der Dekadenz* (Dresden, 1922)

Whissen, Thomas Reid, *The Devil's Advocates: The Decadence in Modern Literature* (New York, 1989)

Zukowski, Karen, *Creating the Artful Home: the Aesthetic Movement* (London, 2006)

7. HISTORIES AND DICTIONARIES OF CZECH LITERATURE

Buriánek, František, *Česká literatura 20. století* (Prague, 1968)

Chaloupka, Otakar (ed.), *Příruční slovník české literatury*, (Prague, 2001)

Cornis-Pope, Marcel, and John Neubauer (eds), *History of The Literary Cultures of East-Central Europe*, 4 vols (Amsterdam, 2004–2010)

Forst, Vladimír, et al., *Lexikon české literatury*, 4 vols (Prague, 1985–2008)

Galík, Josef et al., *Panorama české literatury* (Olomouc, 1994)

Havel, Rudolf, and Jiří Opelík (eds), *Slovník českých spisovatelů* (Prag, 1968)

Hrabák, Josef, *Starší česká literatura* (Prague, 1964)

Janáčková, Jaroslava, *Česká literatura od romantismu do symbolismu* (Prague, 1997), vol. 3 of Jan Lehár et al., *Česká literatura od počátku až k dnešku*, 4 vols (Prague, 1997–98)

Jelínek, Hanuš, *Histoire de la littérature tchèque*, 3 vols (Paris, 1930–5)

Kunc, Jaroslav, *Slovník soudobých českých spisovatelů*, 2 vols (Prague, 1945–6)

Kunstmann, Heinrich, *Tschechische Erzählkunst im 20. Jahrhundert* (Cologne, 1974).
Magnuszewski, Józef, *Historia literatury czeskiej* (Wroclaw, Warsaw, Cracow, Danzig, 1973)
Meriggi, Bruno, *Storia della letteratura ceca e slovaca* (Milan, 1958)
Měšťan, Antonín, *Geschichte der tschechischen Literatur im 19. und 20. Jahrhundert* (Cologne, 1984)
Mukařovský, Jan, et al. (ed.) *Dějiny české literatury* (Prague 1959-1995), 4 vols, vol. 4 (*Literatura od konce 19. století do roku 1945*)
Mühlberger, Josef, *Tschechische Literaturgeschichte: von den Anfängen bis zur Gegenwart* (Munich, 1970)
Novák, Arne, *Stručné dějiny literatury české*, edited by R. Havel, A. Grund (Olomouc, 1946)
Novák, Arne, and Novák, Josef, *Přehledné dějiny literatury české od nejstarších dob až po naše dny*, fourth edition (Olomouc, 1936-9)
Papoušek et al., *Dějiny nové moderny: Česká literatura v letech 1905-1923* (Prague, 2010)
Papoušek et al., *Dějiny nové moderny: Česká literatura v letech 1924-1934* (Prague, 2014)
Pešat, Zdeněk, et al.(eds), *Čeští spisovatelé z přelomu 19. a 20. století* (Prague, 1972)
Schamschula, Walter, *Geschichte der tschechischen Literatur*, 3 vols (Cologne, 1990-2004), vol. 2 (*Von der Romantik bis zum zweiten Weltkrieg*) and vol. 3 (*Von der Gründung der Republik bis zur Gegenwart*)
Slovník českých spisovatelů, edited by the Ústav pro českou literaturu ČSAV (Prague, 1964)
Tarajło-Lipowska, Zofia, *Historia literatury czeskiej* (Wrocław, 2010)
Václavek, Bedřich, *Česká literatura XX. století* (Prague, 1935)
Voisine-Jechová, Hana, *Histoire de la littérature tchèque* (Paris, 2001)

8. IRONY AND RELATED TOPICS

Allemann, Beda, *Ironie und Dichtung* (Pfullingen, 1956)
Attardo, Salvatore, 'Humor, irony, and their communication: From mode adoption to failure of detection' in Luigi Anolli et al., *Say not to say* (Amsterdam, 2001), pp. 159-179)
Attardo, Salvatore, et al., 'Multimodal markers of irony and sarcasm', *International Journal of Humor Research*, 16 (2003). 243-260
Bal, Mieke, *Narratology: Introduction to the Theory of Narration* (Toronto, 1985)
Barbe, Katharina, *Irony in Context* (Amsterdam and Philadelphia PA, 1995), pp. 25, 26
Bednár, Alfonz, *Za hrsť drobných*, 3 vols (Bratislava, 1970, 1974 and 1981)
Behler, Ernst, 'Ironie/Humor', in Ulfert Ricklefs (ed.), *Fischer Lexikon Literatur* (Frankfurt, 1996), vol. 2
Booth, Wayne, *A Rhetoric of Irony* (Chicago, 1974)
Bond, Richmond, *English Burlesque Poetry 1700-1750* (Cambridge MA, 1932)
Bredin, Hugh, 'The Semantic Structure of Verbal Irony', *Journal of Literary Semantics*, 26 (1997), vol. 1, pp. 1-20
Brooks, Cleanth, 'Irony as a Principle of Structure', *Literary Opinion in America*, New York, 1937, edited by Morton Zabel, pp. 729-741
Butler, Peter, 'Puškins *Mědnyj Vsadnik* Revisited: A Reading in Conventional Narrative Irony', *Russian literature*, 72 (2012), pp. 45-108
Butler, Peter, 'How *Old Word Landowners* Is Made: The Ironic Weave Unravelled', *Russian Literature* (forthcoming)
Butler, Peter, 'Up the Dnepr: Discarding Icons and Debunking Ukrainian Cossack Myths in Gogol's *Strašnaja mest'*, *Russian Literarature* (forthcoming)
Cicero, *De oratore*, with an English translation by E.W. Sutton and an introduction by H. Rackham, 2 vols (London, 1942)
Chatman, Seymour, 'Defence of the implied author', *Coming to Terms* (London. 1990)
Clark, Herbert, and Richard Gerrig, 'On the pretense theory of irony', *Journal of Experimental Psychology. General*, 113 (1984), pp. 121-126
Cleese, John, 'Communication problems' in *The Complete Fawlty Towers* (London, 1998), pp. 159-186
Cohn, Dorrit, 'Discordant narration', *Style*, 34 (2000), No. 2, pp. 307-316

Colebrook, Clare, *Irony* (London, 2004)

Colston, Herbert, and Raymond Gibbs, 'A brief history of irony', in Herbert Colston and Raymond Gibbs (eds.), *Irony in Language and Thought* (Hillsdale NJ, 2007)

Cuddon, John Anthony, *A Dictionary of Literary Terms and Literary Theory* (Oxford, 1998), fourth edition

Currie, Gregory, 'Why irony is pretence', in Shaun Nichols (ed.) *The Archictecture of the Imagination* (Oxford, 2006)

Dalnekoff, Donna Isaacs, 'A familiar stranger: the outsider of eighteenth century satire', *Neophilologus*, 57 (1973), No. 2, pp. 121–134.

Déry, Tibor, *Niki. Egy kutya története* (Budapest, 1956), translated into German by Ivan Nagel as *Niki. Die Geschichte eines Hundes* (Frankfurt, 2001), and into English by Edward Hyams as *Niki. The Story of a Dog* (New York, 2009)

Draitser, Emil, *Techniques of Satire: The Case of Saltykov-Ščedrin* (Berlin and New York, 1994)

Enright, D.J., *The Alluring Problem* (Oxford, 1986)

Ernst, Fritz, *Die romantische Ironie* (Zurich, 1912)

Feinberg, Leonard, *The Satirist* (New York, 1965)

Fludernik, Monika, 'Defining (In)Sanity: The Narrator of *The Yellow Wallpaper* and the Question of Unreliability', in Walter Grünzweig und Andreas Solbach (eds), *Grenzüberschreitungen: Narratologie im Kontext /Transcending Boundaries: Narratology in Context* (Tübingen, 1999), pp. 75–95

Frye, Northrop, *Anatomy of Criticism: Four Essays* (New York, 1957)

Furst, Lilian, *Fictions of Romantic Irony in European Narrative* (London, 1984)

Genette, Gérard, *Nouveau discours du récit* (Paris, 1983)

Glucksberg, Sam and Roger Kreuz, 'How to be sarcastic: the echoic reminder theory of verbal irony', *Journal of Experimental Psychology. General*, 116 (1989), pp. 374–386

Goldsmith, Oliver, *Citizen of the World* (London, 2006)

Griffin, Dustin, *Satire: A Critical Reintroduction* (Lexington KY, 1994)

Gurewitsch, Morton, *The Ironic Temper and the Comic Imagination* (Detroit MI, 1994)

Haiman, John, *Talk Is Cheap: Sarcasm, Alienation and the Evolution of Language* (Oxford, 1998)

Hamon, Philippe, *L'ironie littéraire. Essais sur les formes de l'écriture oblique* (Paris,1996)

Hanan, Patrick, 'The Technique of Lu Hsün's Fiction', *Harvard Journal of Asiatic Studies*, 34 (1974), pp. 53–96

Handwerk, Gary, 'Romantic irony', *The Cambridge History of Literary Criticism* (Cambridge, 1993–2001), 9 vols, vol. 5, pp. 203–225

Heller, Erich, *The Ironic German: A Study of Thomas Mann* (London, 1958)

Hettner, Hermann, *Kleine Schriften* (Braunschweig, 1884), edited by Anna Hettner

Highet, Gilbert, *The Anatomy of Satire* (Princeton NJ, 1962)

Hodgart, Matthew, *Satire: Origins and Principles* (New York, 1969)

Hutcheon, Linda, *A Theory of Parody* (New York and London, 1985)

Hutchen, Eleanour, *Irony in 'Tom Jones'* (Alabama, 1965)

Jankélévitch, Vladimir, *L'ironie* (Paris, 1964)

Jump, John, *The Burlesque* (London, 1972)

Kaufer, David S., 'Irony, Interpretative Form, and the Theory of Meaning', *Poetics Today*, 4 (1983), pp. 451–464

Kermode, Frank, *The Art of Telling* (Cambridge, 1983)

Knight, Charles, *The Literature of Satire* (Cambridge, 2004)

Kreuz, Roger, and Sam Glucksberg, 'How to Be Sarcastic: The Echoic Reminder Theory of Verbal Irony', *Journal of Experimental Psychology: General*, 118 (1989), No. 4, pp. 374–386

Kumon-Nakamura, Sachi, et al., 'How about another piece of pie: the allusional pretense theory of discourse irony', *Journal of Experimental Psychology. General*, 124 (1995), pp. 3–21

Lee, Christopher, and Albert Katz, 'The Differential Role of Ridicule in Sarcasm and Irony', *Metaphor and Symbol*, 13 (1998), pp. 1–15

Lucian, *Selected Dialogues* (Oxford, 2006)

Lukavec, Jan, *Od českého Tokia k exotické Praze* (Prague, 2013)

Mai, Birgit, *Satire im Sowjetsozialismus* (Bern, 1993)

Martin, Robert, *Pour une logique du sens* (Paris, 1983), pp. 269–274

Martin, Robert, 'Irony and the Universe of Belief', *Lingua*, 87 (1992) pp. 77–90

Meyer-Sickendiek, Burkhard, 'Eine kleine Kulturgeschichte des Sarkasmus', in Konrad Ehlich (ed.), *Germanistik in und für Europa: Texte des Münchener Germanistentages 2004* (Bielefeld, 2006), pp. 277–292

Meyer-Sickendiek, Burkhard, *Was ist literarischer Sarkasmus? Ein Beitrag zur deutsch-jüdischen Moderne* (München, 2009)

de Montesquieu, Charles, *Défense de l'ésprit des lois* (1750)

de Montesquieu, Charles, *Lettres persanes*, edited by David Galand (Paris, 2003)

Muecke, D. C., *The Compass of Irony* (London, 1969)

Muecke, D. C., *Irony and the Ironic* (London, 1982)

Muecke, D. C., 'Images of Irony', *Poetics Today*, 4 (2003), no. 3, pp. 399–413.

Müller, Adam, *Vorlesungen über deutsche Wissenschaft und Literatur* (Dresden, 1807)

Myers Roy, Alice, 'Towards a definition of irony' in Ralph Fasold and Roger Shuy, *Studies in Language Variation* (Washington, 1977), pp. 171–183

Natsume, Sōseki, *Wagahai wa neko de aru* [I Am a Cat] (Tokyo, 1962), translated into German by Otto Putz as *Ich, der Kater* (Frankfurt, 2001) and into English by Aiko Ito and Graeme Wilson as *I Am a Cat* (Clarendon VT, 2002)

Nünning, Ansgar, 'Multiperspektivität aus narratologischer Sicht', in Vera Nünning et al. (ed.) *Multiperspektives Erzählen* (Trier, 2000)

Ophälders, Markus, *Romantische Ironie: Essay über Solgers* (Würzburg, 2004)

Pavlovski-Petit, Zoja, 'Irony and Satire', in Ruben Quintero (ed.), *Companion to Satire* (Oxford, 2007), pp. 510–524

Prang, Helmut, *Romantische Ironie* (Darmstadt, 1972)

Puttenham, George, *The Art of Poesie* (Amsterdam, 1971)

Pynsent, Robert B., 'Mácha, The Czech National Poet', in Marcel Cornis-Pope and John Neubauer (eds), *History of The Literary Cultures of East-Central Europe*, 4 vols (Amsterdam, 2004–2010), vol. 4, pp. 56–85

Quintero, Ruben (ed.), *Companion to Satire* (Oxford, 2007)

Quintilian, *Institutio oratoria*, 3 vols (Cambridge MA, 1980), with an English translation by H.E.Butler

Recanati, François, *Literal Meaning* (Cambridge, 2004)

Riffaterre, Michael, 'Paradoxes décadents', in Mary Shaw and François Cornilliat (eds), *Rhétoriques fin de siècle* (Paris, 1992)

Rimmon-Kennan, Shlomith, *Narrative fiction: contemporary poetics* (London, 1983)

Rockwell, Patricia Ann, *Sarcasm and Other Mixed Messages: The Ambiguous Ways People Use Language* (Lewiston NY, 2006)

Rose, Margaret, *Parody: ancient. modern and postmodern* (Cambridge, 1993)

van Rooy, C. A., *Studies in Classical Satire and Related Literary Theory* (Leiden, 1966)

Safranski, Rüdiger, *Romantik: eine deutsche Affäre* (Munich, 2007)

Schlegel, Friedrich, *Athenäums-Fragmente und andere Schriften* (Leipzig, 1986), edited by Andreas Huyssen

Schoentjes, Pierre, 'J.-K. Huysmans et l'ironie d'*A rebours*', in Perrine Galland-Hallyn (ed.), *Les Décadents à l'école des Alexandrins* (Valenciennes, 1996)

Schoentjes, Pierre, *Poétique de l'ironie* (Paris, 2001)

Simpson, Paul, *On the Discourse of Satire* (Amsterdam and Philadelphia PN, 2003)

Solger, Karl, *Erwin: Vier Gespäche über das Schöne und die Kunst* (Munich, 1971), edited by Wolfhart Henckmann

Solger, Karl, *Vorlesungen über Aesthetik* (Darmstadt, 1980), edited by Karl Heyse

Sperber, Dan, and Deirdre Wilson, 'Irony and the use-mention distinction', in Peter Cole (ed.), *Radical Pragmatics* (New York, 1981), pp. 295–318

Sperber, Dan, and Deirdre Wilson, *Relevance: Communication and Cognition* (Oxford, 1986)

Sperber, Dan, and Deirdre Wilson, *On Verbal Irony* (Los Angeles, 1989)

Sperber, Dan, and Deirdre Wilson, 'Rhetoric and relevance', in Bender and Wellbery (eds.), *The Ends of Rhetoric: History, Theory, Practice* (Stanford CA, 1990), pp. 140–156

Sperber, Dan, and Deirdre Wilson, 'On Verbal Irony', *Lingua*, 87 (1992) pp. 53–76

Steig, Michael, 'Defining the Grotesque: An Attempt at Synthesis', *Journal of Aesthetics and Art Criticism*, 29 (1970/1971), p. 260

Sterne, Laurence, *Tristam Shandy* (Oxford, 2008), edited by Tim Parnell and Ian Jack

Strohschneider-Kors, Ingrid, *Die romantische Ironie in Theorie und Gestaltung* (Tübingen, 1960)

Swift, Jonathan, *A Modest Proposal and Other Writings* (Harmondsworth, 2009)

Tanizaki, Jun'ichirō, 'Nikushimi' [Hatred] in *Iraka* [Tiled roof] (Tokyo, 1914); reprinted as 'Zōnen' [= *Zatsunen*, 'Idle/Stray Thoughts'] in *Tanizaki Jun'ichirō Zenshū*, 28 vols (Tokyo, 1966), vol. 2, pp. 287–300; translated into French as 'La haine' in Jun'ichirō Tanizaki, *Oeuvres*, 2 vols (Paris, 1998), vol. 1, pp. 91–100.

Thomson, Philip, *The Grotesque* (London, 1972)

Test, George, *Satire: Spirit and Art* (Tampa FL, 1991)

Tieck, Ludwig, *Werke*, 3 vols (Leipzig, Vienna, 1892), vol. 1 (Gedichte und Dramen)

Voltaire, François, *L'ingénu*, edited by Paule Andrau (Paris, 2002)

Walton, Kendall, *Mimesis as Make-Believe* (Cambridge MA, 1990)

Wilson, Deirdre, 'The Pragmatics of Verbal Irony: Echo or Pretence?', *Lingua*, 116 (2006), pp. 1722–1743

Wimsatt, William K., and Monroe C. Beardsley, 'The Intentional Fallacy', *Sewanee Review*, 54 (1946), pp. 468–488; revised and republished in *The Verbal Icon: Studies in the Meaning of Poetry* (Lexington KY, 1954), pp. 3–18.

Wittgenstein, Ludwig, *Philosophical Investigations* (Oxford, 1953)

Wood, James, *The Irresponsible Self: On Laughter and the Novel* (London, 2005)

Worcester, David, *The Art of Satire* (Cambridge MA, 1940)

9. OTHER LITERATURE

Adams, Douglas, *Hitchhikers Guide to the Galaxy* (London, 1985)

Allyn, John, *Forty-seven ronin* (Rutland VT, 1970)

Austen, Jane, *Pride and Prejudice* (London, 1993), edited by Donald Grey

Bauer, Michal, 'L'ironie comme mode de la polémique et défi au vide dans les écrits de jeunesse de Kundera (1945–1970)', in Marie-Odile Thirouin and Martine Boyer-Weinmann (eds.), *Lire Milan Kundera* (Paris, 2009), pp. 101–130

Beall, Joshua P., 'Prosaic Irony: Structure, Mode, and Subversion in The Good Soldier Švejk', *Follow The Comparatist*, 36 (2012), No. 1

Benč, Bohuslav (ed.), *Podkrkonošský spiritismus* (Nová Paka, 2014)

Berger, Klaus, *Japonismus in der westlichen Malerei* (Munich, 1980)

Blang-Süberkrub, Annegret, *Der Liebesgarten: eine Untersuchung über die Bedeutung der Konfiguration für das Bildthema im Spätwerk des Peter Paul Rubens* (Berne, Frankfurt, 1976)

Blecha, Jaroslav and Pavel Jirásek, *Česká loutka* (Prague, 2009)

Casanova, Giacomo, *Histoire de ma fuite des prisons de la République de Venise qu'on appelle les Plombs*, with an introduction and notes by Charles Samaran (Paris, 1922)

Cervantes Saavedra, Miguel de, *Don Quijote* (Madrid, 2010), edited by Francisco Rico Manrique

Chaucer, Geoffrey, *Canterbury Tales* (Harmondsworth, 2005), edited by Jill Mann

Christie, Agatha, *The Murder of Roger Ackroyd* (London, 1926)

Collins, Wilkie, *Moonstone* (Oxford, 2008), edited by John Sutherland

Collins, Wilkie, *The Woman in White* (Oxford, 1999), edited by Harvey Peter Sucksmith

Čech, Svatopluk, *Výlet pana Broučka do měsíce* (Prague, 1888)

Dietrich, Gerhard, and Eckard Wagner, *Kayserzinn* (Stuttgart, 2011)

Doležel, Lubomír, and Richard Bailey (eds), *Statistics of style* (New York, 1969).

Donahue, Bruce, 'Laughter and ironic humor in the fiction of Milan Kundera', *Critique: Studies in Contemporary Fiction*, 25 (1984), No. 2, pp. 67-76

Dostoevsky, Fedor, *Bednye Liudy* in *Polnoe sobranie sochinenii*, 30 vols (Moscow, 1942), vol. 1.

Dubská, Alice, *Dvě století českého loutkářství* (Prague, 2004)

Duby, Georges, et al., *A History of Venice in Painting* (New York, 2007)

Dvořák, Rudolf, *Čína. Popis říše, národa, jeho mravů a obyčejů* (Prague, 1900)

Dvořák, Rudolf, *Číňana Konfucia život a nauka*, 2 vols (Prague, 1887 and 1889)

Dvořák, Rudolf, *Dějiny mravouky v orientě*, 2 vols (Prague, 1904), vol. 1 (*Konfucius*)

Erasmus, Desiderius, *In Praise of Folly* (Mineola NY, 2003), translated by John Wilson

Evans, Mark, *Impressions of Venice from Turner to Monet* (Cardiff, 1992)

De la Fontaine, Jean, *Oeuvres complètes*, 2 vols (Paris, 2004-2005), vol. 1 (*Contes*)

Fletcher, Adam, *Wie man Deutscher wird / How to Be German* (Munich, 2013)

Freimannová, Marie, *Josef Tulka, malíř generace Národního divadla* (Prague, 1965)

Galdós, Bénito Pérez, *Doña Perfecta* (Madrid, 1876)

Gautier, Judith, *Livre de jade* (Paris, 1928)

Glück, Gustav, *Rubens Liebesgarten* (Vienna and Leipzig, 1920)

Gogol, Nikolaj, *Spisy N.V. Gogola* (Prague, 1891-1893), 4 vols, edited by Jiří Hrubý and translated by Ignác Hošek and Quido Hodura

Gogol, Nikolaj, *Zábavné spisy M. Gogola* (Prague, 1846-1847), 4 vols, translated by Karel Vladislav Zap, Kristian Stefan and Karel Havlíček Borovský

Goodman, Elise, *Rubens: the garden of love as conversatie à la mode* (Amsterdam, 1992)

Grieve, Alastair, *Whistler's Venice* (New Haven CT, 2000)

Grossman, Vassilii, *Žizn' i sudba* (Lausanne, 1980)

Guptil, M., *Niobe and the Niobids in Greek and Roman Art and Literature* (Chicago, 1928)

Vitěslav Hálek, *Srdce písněmi dotýkané* (Prague, 1974), edited by Ivan Slavík

Hanová, Markéta, *Japonismus v českém umění* (Prague, 2014).

Hattingh, Harry, 'Being and the dialects of irony: a reading of some of Milan Kundera's novels', *Literator: tydskrif vir besondere en vergelykende taal- en literatuurstudie*, 16 (1995), No. 2, pp. 95-121

Havlasa, Jan, *Okna do mlhy* (Prague, 1918)

Havlasa, Jan, *Japonská pohádka o dvou dědcích* (Prague, 1919)

Havlasa, Jan, *Japonským vnitrozemím* (Prague, 1924)

Havlasa, Jan, *Cesta Bohů. Japonské potulky* (Prague, 1926)

Havlasa, Jan, *Bloudění duše* (Prague, 1931)

Havlasa, Jan, *Japonské jaro* (Prague, 1932)

Havlasa, Jan, *Roztříštěná duha* (Prague, 1932)

Havlasa, Jan, *Přízraky a zázraky* (Prague, 1934)

Havlasa, Jan, *Schody do podvědomí* (Prague, 1939)

Heise, Richard, *Über Loyalität in Japan: 47 ronin* (Böhmisch Krumau, 1931)

Hirsch Jr., E. D., *Validity in Interpretation* (New Haven CN, 1967)

Hloucha, Joe, *Sakura ve vichřici* (Prague, 1905)

Hloucha, Joe, *Zátopa* (Prague, 1906)

Hloucha, Joe, *Vzpomínky na Japonsko* (Prague, 1906)

Hloucha, Joe, *Moje paní Chryzantéma* (Prague, 1910)

Hloucha, Joe, *Polibky smrti* (Prague, 1912)

Hloucha, Joe, *Pavilón hrůzy* (Prague, 1920)

Hloucha, Joe, *Dopisy neznámého* (Prague, 1923)

Hloucha, Joe, *Prodavačky úsměvu* (Prague, 1929)

Hloucha, Joe, *Mezi bohy a démony* (Prague, 1929)

Hloucha, Joe, *Japonečky* (Prague, 1931)

Höllmann, Thomas, *Das alte China* (Munich, 2008)

Höllman, Thomas, *Die chinesische Schrift* (Munich, 2015)

Hopper, Philip, *Forest Green Glass* (Atglen PA, 2000)

Horatius Flaccus, Quintus, *Satires, Epistles, and Ars poetica* (London, 1970), translated by H. Rushton Fairclough

de Huszar, George, 'Nietzsche's Theory of Decadence and Transvaluation of All Values', *Journal of the History of Ideas*, 6 (1945), pp. 259-

Jackson, Christine, *The Peacock* (London, 2006)

Jakobson, Roman, 'Zametki na poliach *Evgeniia Onegina*', *Raboty po poetike* (Moscow, 1987), p. 220

Jirásková, Marie, and Pavel Jirásek, *Loutka a moderna* (Brno, 2011)

Joll, Evelyn, et al. (eds.), *The Oxford Companion to J. M. W. Turner* (Oxford, 2001)

Kafka, Franz, *Die Verwandlung* (Leipzig, 1915)

Kaminský, Bohdan, 'Neštěstí v zahradě kvetoucích kaktusů', *Verše humoristické a satirické* (Prague, 1893)

Kantemir, Antioch, *Sobranie stikhotvorenii* (Leningrad, 1956)

Knížák, Milan, *Encyclopedie výtvarníků loutkového divadla v českých zemích a na Slovensku od vystopovatelné minulosti do roku 1950* (Hradec Králové, 2005)

Kořenský, Josef, *Žaponsko* (Prague, 1899)

Kotalík, Jiří, *Česká secese* (Prague, 1966).

Kurth, Julius, *Geschichte des japanischen Holzschnitts*, 3 vols (Leipzig, 1925-1929)

Lakoff, George, and Mark Johnson, *Metaphors We Live By* (Chicago, 1980)

Lakoff, George, and Mark Johnson, *Women, Fire, and Dangerous Things: What Categories Reveal about the Mind* (Chicago, 1990)

Lambourne, Lionel, *Japonisme* (London, 2005)

Lipton, Peter, *Inference to the Best Explanation* (London, 1991)

Littell, Jonathan, *Les Bienveillantes* (Paris, 2006)

Lodge, David, 'Fire and Eyre: Charlotte Brontë's War of Earthly Elements' in *The Language of Fiction* (London, 1966), pp. 114-143.

MacDonald, Mary, *Palaces in the Night: Whistler in Venice* (Berkeley CA, 2001)

Machar, Josef Svatopluk, 'Čína a Číňan', *Rozhledy*, 4 (1884/1885), pp. 25-28

Mathesius, Bohumil, *Černá věž a zelený džbán* (Prague, 1925)

Mathesius, Bohumil, *Zpěvy staré Číny* (Prague, 1939)

Mathesius, Bohumil, *Nové zpěvy staré Číny* (Prague, 1940)

Mathesius, Bohumil, *Třetí zpěvy staré Číny* (Prague, 1949)

Mitford, Algernon, *Geschichten des alten Japan* (Leipzig, 1875), translated by J.G. Kohl.

Mitford, Algernon, *Tales of Old Japan* (London, 1871)

Mory, Ludwig, *Bruckmann's Zinn-Lexikon* (Munich, 1977)

Mory, Ludwig, *Schönes Zinn*, revised and expanded edition (Munich, 1972)

Nabokov, Vladimir, *Lolita* (Paris, 1955)

Nekula, Marek, 'Ironie v lásky hře osudné', *Linguistica brunensia: sborník prací filosofické fakulty brněnské university, A: Řada jazykovědná*, 44 (1995). No. 43, pp. 61-74

Nietzsche, Friedrich, *Sämtliche Werke: Kritische Gesamtausgabe in 15 Bänden* (Berlin and New York, 1967), edited by Giorgio Colli and Mazzino Montinari

Ovid, *Metamorphoses*, 2 vols (London, 1928), with an English translation by Frank Justus Miller

Piguet, Philippe, *Monet et Venise* (Paris, 1986)

Pittrof, Kurt, *Böhmisches Glas im Panorama der Jahrhunderte* (Munich, 1987)

Plecháč, Miroslav, *Spiritismus v Podkrkonoší* (Prague, 1931)

Poche, Emanuel, et al. (ed.), *Encyklopedie českého výtvarného umění* (Prague, 1975)

Průšek, Jaroslav, *Sestra moje Čína* (Prague, 1938)

Průšek, Jaroslav, *Trojí učení o společnosti v Číně* (Prague, 1940)

Reynek, Bohuslav, *Rybí šupiny. Rty a zuby. Had na sněhu* (Prague, 1990), edited by Ivan Slavík

Richards, A., *The Philosophy of Rhetoric* (London, 1936)

Salinger, D. J., *The Catcher in the Rye* (New York, 1951)

Sand, Maurice, *Masques et bouffons* (Paris, 1860)

Schwander, Martin, *Venedig: Von Canaletto und Turner bis Monet* (Ostfildern, 2008)

Schwarz, Wolfgang, 'Paradigmenwechsel und Ironiestruktur in Vítězslav Nezvals Dramatik der zwanziger Jahre: Zum Problem des Übergangs vom Poetismus zum Surrealismus', in Hans-Bernd Harder et al.(eds), *Festschrift für Wolfgang Gesemann* (Neuried, 1986), pp. 355–364

Shcheglov, Jurii, *Antioch Kantemir i stikhotvornaia satira* (St. Petersburg, 2004)

Shakespeare, William, *Romeo and Juliet* (London, 1597)

Shimizu, Christine, *Les lacques du japon: urushi* (Paris, 1988)

Slavík, Bedřich, *U Suchardů* (Prague, 1973)

Slavik, Ivan, *Hory roků* (Prague, 1999)

Spengler, Oswald, *Untergang des Abendlandes: Umrisse einer Morphologie der Weltgeschichte* (Munich, 1991)

Stark, K., *Niobe und die Niobiden in ihrer literarischen, künstlerischen und mythologischen Bedeutung* (Leipzig, 1863)

Stašek, Antal [Antonín Zeman], *Blouznivci našich hor* (Prague, 1896)

Steiner, George, *Real Presences* (Chicago, 1991)

Steiner, Peter, 'Ironies of history: *The Joke* of Milan Kundera', in Calin Mihailescu and Walid Hamarneh (eds), *Fiction updated: theories of fictionality, narratology and poetics* (Toronto 1996), pp. 197–212

Steiner, Rudolf, 'Aus der Akasha-Chronik', *Rudolf Steiner Gesamtausgabe* (Dornach, 1955–1961), vol. 11, pp. 21–213

Stejskal, Jan, *Novopacko: portrét paměti a srdce* (Nová Paka and Harrachov, 2009)

Stewart, Basil, *Subjects Protrayed in Japanese Colour Prints* (London, 1922)

Stirner, Max, *Der Einzige und sein Eigentum* (Stuttgart, 1972)

Suchomel, Filip, and Oldřich Palata, *Japonská sbírka Severočeského muzea v Liberci* (Prague, 2000).

Svevo, Italo [Ettore Schmitz], *La coscienza di Zeno* (Milan, 1923)

Takeda, Izumo, *Kanadehon Chūshingura* [Kana Primer for the Treasury of Loyal Retainers], edited by Kenji Shuzui (Tokyo, 1937); translated by Donald Keane in *Treasury of Loyal Retainers* (New York, 1972)

Tamenaga, Shunsui, *Loyal Ronin* (New York, 1880), translated by Shuichiro Saito and Edward Greey

Thirouin, Marie-Odile, 'Chvéïk ironiste', *Cahiers de l'ILCEA*, 8 (2006), pp. 79–91

Tieck, Ludwig, *Werke*, 4 vols (Darmstadt, 1972), vol. 2 (Dramen)

Toman, Prokop, *Nový slovník československých výtvarných umělců* (Ostrava, 1993)

Twain, Mark [Samuel Clemens], *Huckleberry Finn* (New York, 1999), edited by Thomas Cooley

Veneziani Svevo, Livia, *Vita di mio marito* (Trieste, 1950)

Voltaire, François, *Candide ou l'optimisme*, edited by Frédéric Deloffre (Paris, 2003)

Wagner, Monika, *William Turner* (Munich, 2011)

Wendt, Ralf, *Waldglas* (Schwerin, 1977)

Wiemann, Elsbeth, *Der Mythos von Niobe und ihren Kindern: Studien zur Darstellung und Rezeption* (Worms, 1986)

Wilton, Andrew, *Turner in der Schweiz* (Zurich, 1976)

Yanagi, Yoshiyaki, *Urushi no bunkashi* [A cultural history of lacquer] (Tokyo, 2009)

Zagacki, Kenneth, 'Václav Havel and the rhetoric of folly', in Marketa Goetz-Stankiewicz and Phyllis Carey (eds), *Critical essays on Václav Havel* (New York, 1999), pp. 127–142

Zahrádka, Miroslav, et al., *Slovník rusko-českých liternárních vztahů* (Ústí nad Orlicí, 2008), pp. 86–90

Zdražil, Tomáš, *Počátky theosofie a anthroposofie v Čechach* (Příbram, 1997)

Zoshchenko, Mikhail, *Rasskazy i povesti* (Volgograd, 1983)

10. DICTIONARIES OF CZECH

Allgemeines Handwörterbuch der böhmischen und deutschen Sprache, edited by Josef Rank, ninth edition, 2 vols (Prague, Vienna, Leipzig, 1920)

Česko-anglický slovník, edited by H.T. Cheshire et al. (Prague, 1935)

Česko-německý slovník, edited by Hugo Siebenschein et al., 2 vols (Prague, 1971)

Příruční slovník jazyka českého, edited by the Československá akademie věd, 9 vols (Prague, 1935–57)
Slovník spisovného jazyka českého, edited by the Československá akademie věd, 4 vols (Prague, 1971)
Velký česko-anglický slovník, edited by Josef Fronek (Prague, 2000)

10. BIBLE CONCORDANCES

Biblická konkordance. K textu Kralické bible (Prague, 1993)
Konkordance k Bibli kralické, compiled by L.B. Kašpar (Prague, 1933)
Malá biblická konkordance, compiled by Josef Štifter (Prague, 1953)
www.biblenet.cz
www.biblegateway.com

PETER BUTLER

BEYOND DECADENCE: EXPOSING THE NARRATIVE IRONY IN JAN OPOLSKÝ'S PROSE

Published by Charles University in Prague,
Karolinum Press
Ovocný trh 3-5, 116 36 Prague 1, Czech Republic
Prague 2015
Edited by Martin Janeček
Cover and layout by Jan Šerých
Typeset by DTP Karolinum Press
Printed by Karolinum Press
First English edition

ISBN 978-80-246-2571-3
ISBN 978-80-246-2711-3 (pdf)